INTEGRATED PSYCHOTHERAPY

by Ferdinand Knobloch, M.D.
and Jirina Knobloch, M.D.

New York • Jason Aronson • London

To our coworkers

at the Charles University Policlinic in Prague, and its
affiliates in Lobec and Horní Palata, Czechoslovakia;
and at the Day House, University of British Columbia, Vancouver, British Columbia, Canada: For sharing with us the excitement, frustration and joy of
exploring new territories and for their creative contributions to Integrated Psychotherapy.

CONTENTS

Part II
The Clinical System of Integrated Psychotherapy

Contents

FOREWORD

Jerome D. Frank, Ph.D., M.D.

All forms of psychotherapy seek to help persons overcome psychologically caused suffering and disability. Since persons are psycho-socio-biological systems, perturbations in any area of their functioning affect all the others, including bodily functions, inner experiences, and interactions with other persons. Thus psychological distress and disability, though often manifested primarily in a few symptoms, actually pervade all aspects of the person's life. Most systems of psychotherapy, ignoring this obvious fact, use a limited number of procedures aimed at alleviating the patient's major complaints. They stress such techniques as provision of insights into origins, stimulation of emotional release, or modification of maladaptive behavior, while virtually ignoring the many other factors contributing to the patient's difficulties. Moreover, most of these techniques are applied at infrequent intervals and for relatively brief periods in the midst of the patient's ongoing interactions and activities.

For maximal effectiveness, a psychotherapeutic program should have the following characteristics. It should be pervasive, encompassing the patient's entire waking life and impinging on the patient-environment system at as many levels as possible. Interventions should include a wide variety of individual and group methods for influencing thoughts, fan-

tasies, dreams, emotional responses, and social behavior in such a way
as to enhance feelings of self-worth and competence and to encourage
their generalization into daily life. Thus the program, in addition to
psychotherapeutic maneuvers in a narrow sense, should include supervised work, play, and exercise. Selection of procedures should be firmly
guided by a conceptualization of human functioning and psychopathology, while relative emphases on different modalities should be determined by individual needs and vulnerabilities in the context of the total
program. Moreover, the program should be relatively brief and economical. Improbable as it may seem, the system of Integrated Psychotherapy presented in this book approaches such an ideal.

That this can be said attests to the unusual, if not unique, qualifications of Ferdinand and Jirina Knobloch. Widely familiar with the literature of European and American philosophy, psychology, psychiatry,
and psychotherapy, they were trained in psychoanalysis and various
forms of group therapy, and then accumulated extensive clinical experience in Czechoslovakia, England, the United States, and Canada.
By dint of their outstanding theoretical capacities, they have succeeded
in integrating all this into a theory that comfortably encompasses the
phenomena of small groups and therapeutic communities, as well as the
images, dreams, realistic perceptions, and overt behavior of individuals.
Leading concepts are group and role schemas and reward-cost balances.
This framework permits the use of any promising therapeutic technique, traditional or innovative, with criteria for evaluation of its limitations and advantages for different patients, all integrated and kept in
balance by the theory.

On this conceptual basis the authors have slowly developed a comprehensive program which reflects considerable clinical acumen and
therapeutic ingenuity, coupled with a willingness to experiment and to
entertain suggestions from patients and participating subprofessionals.
In its present form—and no doubt it will continue to be modified by
further experience—Integrated Psychotherapy is an impressive achievement.

Consistent with the authors' European background, the program places
a greater emphasis on discipline and control than many Americans, who
tend to place a high value on freedom, would readily accept. Control is
exerted primarily through the deliberate creation of powerful group
norms and mobilization of group pressures to help members change to
less maladaptive ways of thinking and behaving. This is in no sense
incompatible with giving patients considerable responsibility. In con-

junction these features may well do more to enhance a sense of autonomy and inner freedom than might a more permissive approach.

Also characteristically European is the considerable space devoted to theory. Readers impatient with this can rest assured that only what is necessary to understand the program has been incorporated in the text. The rest has been banished to appendices, which contain scholarly and illuminating expositions of the philosophy of science, learning theory, ethology, and action therapeutic techniques.

As the text illustrates, parts of the system can be incorporated into ongoing clinical programs; its full effectiveness, however, almost certainly depends on a day center in which the total program can be implemented. Since this requires complete administrative control, training of a staff, and close supervision of treatment, psychotherapists trained in other methods might be unwilling to make the necessary effort unless convinced of the clear superiority of Integrated Psychotherapy over their current practice. While the Knobloch's system has a high degree of validity, experience has shown that the therapeutic skills of the therapist probably contribute more to good results than the theory and method embraced; therefore, since the Knoblochs, in addition to their other qualities, are gifted therapists, it is important that their program undergo a controlled clinical trial. A footnote to one of the appendices describes a twenty-four-hour therapeutic community in a forest setting; the community proved both more effective and less costly than a day center, which in turn obtained better results more economically than a conventional inpatient service. This finding deserves replication with different therapists under different auspices. Comparison of the results of the day care program with those of customary outpatient psychotherapy would also be most worthwhile. Should such comparisons confirm the superiority of Integrated Psychotherapy, as I am reasonably confident they will, this would have a salutary impact on the entire field of psychotherapy.

Meanwhile the book provides a stimulating model for thinking about and conducting psychotherapy, as well as a rich source of ideas for expanding and improving whatever form of therapy the reader currently practices.

PREFACE

This book is a product of our experience in psychotherapy in two different worlds, two different economic systems and cultures —Czechoslovakia and North America. Whereas many psychotherapists moving from Europe to North America have been impressed by the differences between European and American patients, we were impressed by their similarities, by their accessibility to the same psychotherapeutic methods and their capacity for mutual help, which we have long regarded as the main potential of future psychotherapy. As we treated patients in Prague, Chicago, New York or Vancouver, or in workshops with professionals in Germany, Holland, Poland, Cuba or Japan, the words of Harry Stack Sullivan often came to mind: "We all are much more simply human than otherwise."

What is our orientation? Our American colleagues had some difficulty in classifying us. We were fortunate to have had first-hand contact with a variety of psychotherapeutic schools and their remarkable representatives. But before that, and before we both went through psychoanalytic training, we were inoculated by that philosophy of science begun in Prague by Albert Einstein and brilliantly developed by his successor Phillip Frank and his colleagues both in Prague and Vienna (Rudolf Carnap, Moritz Schlick, Otto Neurath, Herbert Feigl and others). Frank's book on causality (1932) inspired us to think about organisms and groups of organisms as systems. We learned that our common sense can lead us to erroneously believe that we understand a concept or statement when, in reality, we do not. We established the habit of asking about every statement, What difference would it make in the world if this statement was or was not true? What observations can contribute to its confirmation, either positively or negatively? We soon began to suspect that the field of psychotherapy in particular suffers from conceptual confusion and that it should be swept with the broom of logical analysis.

We felt that misunderstandings created by false dichotomies and diverse professional interests separate people working on the same problems. When one of us received a British Council Scholarship in 1948-49 and chose to study at the Psychology Section of the Maudsley Hospital in London lead by H. J. Eysenck, he was, at the same time, undergoing group-analytic experience with Henry Ezriel at the Tavistock Institute, attending the seminars of Anna Freud and Melanie Klein, and also studying the therapeutic community of Maxwell Jones. In the ten years which followed, 1949–1959, we were completely cut off from the West because of the Cold War. From our own resources, we built a system of integrated psychotherapy at the Charles University Policlinic in Prague. This was our answer to the challenge posed by the newly born socialized medicine: How can psychotherapy be rendered more efficient, less time-consuming, and less demanding of professionals, so that it can be available to all who could benefit from it?

In 1949, we still believed, being influenced by psychoanalysis, that the only proper place for intensive psychotherapy was an outpatient setting, with patients living and working under their usual conditions. This was strengthened by witnessing the poor results with psychiatric hospitalization of neurotic patients. However, experience compelled us to change our opinion. Experimenting with therapeutic communities of a special kind, at first in a residential setting and later a day center, we were persuaded that the mutual influence of patients can become the most powerful therapeutic factor known so far. Out of this knowledge, we developed, with the help of our coworkers, three interrelated settings: the outpatient clinic, the day center in Prague, and the Residential Neurosis Center in Lobec on a state farm in the countryside. From the very beginning, the significant persons—sexual partners, family, friends, and coworkers—were involved in the patients' treatment. We soon discovered that combining patients and significant persons in one group can enhance the efficiency of treatment, and we developed techniques of leading these combined groups. Whereas the North American psychotherapy and encounter movements to a large extent developed separately, we began with psychoanalytically oriented psychotherapy and changed gradually through an ongoing comparison of individual therapy with group and family therapy and with such nonverbal activities as the newly created psychomime, physical work, and sports. Only later, after we discovered that the best methods we could offer to our patients were also best for training purposes, did we introduce integrated psychotherapy for training and personality growth.

The persons who influenced us most through their writings and personal contacts were—chronologically—Jules H. Masserman, Norman Cameron, Charles Morris, philosopher, and Jerome Frank. We are grateful to them for their work and for the personal encouragement they gave us. We also gratefully remember those who made our transplantation to North America easier: Gerard Chrzanowski, Henry David, Elizabeth Davis, Jim Miles, Melvin Sabshin, Leon Salzman, John Schimmel, Jack Weinberg, Eric Witkower, and Israel Zwerling, as well as the late Nathan Ackerman, Asja Kadis and Emanuel Schwartz.

Jason Aronson encouraged us to write this book. Jim Miles, Judith Lazerson, and Chris Morrant gave freely of their time to read endless varieties of the manuscript and gave us valuable advice. Heather Fink, our secretary for six years, has given us her expert help during the period in which the text crystalized.

Our special thanks belong to Tony Marcus, Milt Miller and Don Watterson, former heads of the Department, and other colleagues of the Department of Psychiatry, University of British Columbia, Vancouver, without whose support neither the Day House nor this book would exist.

This book is dedicated to our dear coworkers both in Czechoslovakia and in North America, particularly to Mila Bendova, Hana Junova, and Judith Lazerson. Among our many associates, we wish to give special mention to Zdenek Mrazek, Vera Mrazkova, Marie Schanilcova, Slavka Patockova, Josef Nesvadba from Czechoslovakia; Angelo Guzzetti, Cynthia Quinn-Young, Fay Perry, and Judith Pound from the Day House, University of British Columbia, Vancouver; and C. Hunt (Sister Maria) from the Illinois State Psychiatric Institute.

INTRODUCTION

This book is written for mental health professionals to whom people turn for help because they are suffering or because they are dissatisfied with themselves. Whether the help is termed psychotherapy, personality growth, behavior modification, or marital counseling, it tries to offer a new experience designed to compensate for the ill effects of past experience or lack of experience.

There is no single name for all of these related activities, the basis of which is, at least in part, social relearning and new learning. We call our version of these diverse activities, derived from a unified conceptual framework, *integrated psychotherapy*.

We believe that integrated psychotherapy is broad enough to be of help to practitioners in all of the activities mentioned and in all types of socioeconomic systems and cultures. Our main aim is to share our practical experience of thirty years. But we cannot avoid theory; in fact, we believe, as does Kurt Lewin, that good theory is the most practical thing. Unfortunately, we do not possess this because the behavioral sciences, on which psychotherapy is based, are not yet sufficiently developed. Some compare the degree of development of the behavioral sciences to that of physics before Newton. However, even at our present stage, theoretical considerations can guide us in certain directions. Integrated psychotherapy, as presented in this book, could not have developed without inspiration from the different branches of the behavioral sciences. *Integrated*, in this context, does not mean that integration has been achieved, but refers rather to an approach and program for the future.

We would like to contrast integration efforts with superficial eclecticism. By eclecticism, we understand the piling up of ideas, techniques, and ploys without a serious attempt at their theoretical unification. Sciences such as physics are not called eclectic. Though they have grown from bits and pieces of the findings and theories of many people, they are distinguished by their unceasing effort towards integration.

Part I, *The Individual in the Group,* outlines the theoretical basis for integrated psychotherapy. It explains why human behavior can be understood only in the interpersonal context. Within the system approach, a small social group is chosen as the minimum system in which an individual's behavior can be understood by a psychotherapist. The full significance of the choice of the group as a system of reference, however, becomes apparent only after the fallacy of the intrapsychic-interpersonal dichotomy is analyzed and the concept of *group schema* introduced. A new paradigm emerges, based on a model of social group.

This is the most difficult portion of the book, since it demands revision of our dualistic thinking about "outer" and "inner" worlds—a thought pattern ingrained in our culture and language and augmented by such personality models as those put forth by Freud in his structural model. We believe the rewards are worth the reader's hardship. The conceptual framework of mental life is considerably simplified by the fusion of psychodynamics and sociodynamics. The way is open for the exploration of *phenomenal spatiality*—a concept useful for psychotherapy which has been obscured in the past. The intrapsychic processes are revealed as fantasies of interpersonal processes and become accessible for behavioral testing using psychodramatic and other techniques.

Part II, *The Clinical System,* explains the main practical guidelines derived from the theoretical framework. The *seven-step system* of integrated psychotherapy is then described. The system was gradually developed by us and our coworkers at the Charles University in Prague, in the therapeutic communities of its two affiliates, the day center and Lobec. Although designed as a model to be used throughout Czechoslovakia to make psychotherapy available to all who might benefit, the system is, we believe, not a second-class substitute for deep psychotherapy, but an efficient means of delivery for the maximum which can be offered in psychotherapy. The system, or its elements, can be transferred to other countries with different economic, social, and cultural conditions. This has been particularly confirmed by our building the Day House in Vancouver, Canada, described in chapters 18 and 19 of this part. The Day House represents the system of integrated psychotherapy in miniature. Finally, chapter 20 describes how the elements of integrated psychotherapy were gradually introduced into established settings, during our work in the United States.

The notes to individual chapters and the five appendices help to clarify some of the deeper philosophical, theoretical, and technical ramifications of integrated psychotherapy.

Appendix A, *Philosophical Background*, links integrated psychotherapy to that philosophy of science which strives for the unification of sciences, as represented by the Encyclopedia of the Unity of Science (Neurath et al., 1970, 1971). The authors explain reasons for their inclination to methodological behaviorism, as opposed to the radical behaviorism of Skinner.

Appendix B, *Psychotherapy as Learning Process*, outlines briefly the present conceptualizations of the learning processes. Learning, either as re-learning or new learning, is an essential part of the psychotherapeutic process and it is dealt with in common terms in the theoretical part and in the principles of treatment. However, at the present stage of knowledge, the authors do not commit themselves to any particular theory of learning and its jargon. Therefore, the different conceptualizations of the learning process are left to the appendix.

Appendix C, *Innate Basis of Behavior*, reviews briefly ethology as a tentative source of inspiration for psychotherapy. Human ethology is in its beginnings, yet some parallels between animals and human beings seem worth consideration. For example, "stimulus therapy" (Lorenz, Leyhausen 1973) of animals with dysfunctional fixed action patterns may have parallel in hyperstimulation in the treatment of dysfunctional female orgasm and in abreactions (anger, fear, grief, etc.).

Appendix D, *Action Techniques*, describes three techniques, namely, psychodrama, psychomime and abreaction, which are part of the armamentarium of techniques used in the system of integrated psychotherapy.

Appendix E, *Forms Used at the Day House*, illustrates the life in the Day House by giving instructions and forms used in that setting.

As the pages of this book piled up, we were surprised how much more there still is to say about the system. We hope, however, that enough has been said to stimulate the reader's curiosity and creative thinking both in theory and practice. Integrated psychotherapy is in a state of rapid development. By the time this book is read, our practice will likely be changed somewhat. It has developed and changed constantly in the past, and we are now working at our next task, a detailed comparison of group schema with other personality models.

Part I

CONCEPTUAL

FRAMEWORK:

THE INDIVIDUAL

IN THE

GROUP

Chapter 1

SYSTEMS

One of the earliest decisions a psychotherapist must make is whom he should include in the system of observation and treatment. Only the patient? His or her spouse? The mother? A friend? Or all of them? This decision may determine the success or failure of the treatment.

As the idea of a system is important to this book, let us clarify it. Our first example will be from astronomy, the solar system. For thousands of years, the astronomers were able to distinguish the planets from the fixed stars and noted that the planets behaved in much more complicated ways. A simple explanation of the complicated behavior of the planets, sun, and moon was constructed by Copernicus and his followers: the sun, seven planets, and the moon were recognized as being parts of one system. Later, the behavior of the whole system was explained in a simple way by Newtonian laws. Difficulties arose when measurements showed that Uranus behaved strangely, deviating from the Newtonian laws. Among the many attempts to explain this puzzle, one was especially attractive: there was a planet escaping attention which disturbed the orbit of Uranus. This prediction was confirmed; the unknown planet was spotted in 1846 and called Neptune. The solar system was redefined.

By a *system*, then, we mean *a set of interacting objects forming a closed causal network as seen from a certain point of view.* In the discovery of the solar system, the first step was the distinction between the objects belonging and not belonging to the system. Next came ideas about the spatial arrangement of the objects in the system—ideas which were modified many times. The essential step was explanation of how the system operates according to physical laws. Each step was tentative and conclusions were successively modified; for example, even when the system seemed to be fully understood, the discovery of Neptune and later of other bodies led to its redefinition. The greatest advantage of this heuristic process was the facility provided by regarding the system as a closed causal network: laws could be applied to explain the functioning of the system, by taking into consideration the interaction of the sun and planets alone, as if nothing else in the universe existed. In reality, nothing in the world is quite isolated; there are no completely closed systems. In the case of the solar system its environment later had to be considered. This not only led to a conception of the solar system as a subsystem of a larger one, but also led to the recognition that the Newtonian laws were only first approximations toward understanding how the solar system functions.

At the time Neptune was discovered, Europe was plagued by cholera, a deadly disease. Physicians tried to relate cholera to various factors, from bad air to volcanic activity, all without success. Finally, John Snow, a physician in London, succeeded in delimiting a system through which he not only could trace essential causal chains, but also could control the system itself. He found that five hundred people had died in ten days in a space of two hundred and fifty yards from the spot where the disease had begun. All these people had taken water from one public pump. None of the workers in a nearby brewery became ill and none had drunk water from the pump. After establishing his system through observation and formulating his hypothesis, Snow was able to intervene successfully. He persuaded the authorities to remove the pump handle, and the epidemic ceased.

It is perhaps clear by now that the choice of a system is not only dependent upon the nature of reality, but also upon the means we have to investigate it and the purpose of the inquiry. The larger the system we choose, the safer we can be in assuming that it will include the relevant causal relationships. However, such a system may not be manageable and therefore of no help at all. If Dr. Snow had chosen as his system of observation the whole of London, it would have included all the variables he needed, but he would have never made his discovery.

The right strategy is to seek a minimum system which nonetheless includes all the essential causal chains uninterrupted.

Our task as psychotherapists is somewhat similar to that of Dr. Snow. Although there are many details about our patients that we cannot know, nonetheless, our task is to delimit a system of observation in which we can trace the essential causal chains, and find accessible points, or handles, where interventions can be made.

Let us imagine a behavior problem in a little girl—bedwetting. She may have some anatomical and physiological abnormalities described as being associated with bedwetting. But unless it is taken into consideration that the girl wets her bed only when she is with her parents, but never when she is with her grandparents in the country, a sufficient system of observation has not been chosen and the possible target of intervention will be missed. Let us suppose that through family therapy, which includes the parents as well as the girl, an improvement is achieved. But after a while the girl starts to have nightmares, usually after she goes to her grandparents. Including the parents and grandparents in the system of observation does not help. Then, after some time it is discovered that an uncle occasionally visits the grandparents and spends some time with the girl and we find out later that he induces her to masturbate. As in the case of Neptune, he was originally invisible, he was missing in our system of observation as we tried to understand the causal structure of the system.

A patient with severe phobias was treated in a psychiatric ward by psychotherapy and anxiolytic drugs. There was no change for a few weeks, and then he started to improve rapidly. The improvement was ascribed to therapy. In actual fact, the improvement was due to a secret love affair with a female patient from another ward. ("Love treatments" are sometimes powerful, but unfortunately usually have only a transitory effect.) In this case, the staff did not know anything about the love affair and did not include the female patient in the observation system and so their explanation of the improvement was erroneous.

Living systems and their models

The understanding of living systems has always depended upon which physical models (particularly various advanced machines) each epoch could offer. Since the seventeenth century, there have been good models to aid the development of anatomy, and to a degree, physiology, but models of human behavior have been very deficient. As Norbert Wiener (1967) remarked, the automatons of the seventeenth and eighteenth centuries were dancing figures on music boxes worked by clockwork. These figures were blind, deaf and dumb, and unable to react to the environment.

Despite great progress in physics in the nineteenth century, there was not much progress in developing machines which could be models of human behavior.

Machines were still only able to respond to the environment in a very limited way, by a push button reaction. These were good models for reflex activity and in 1863 Sechenov (1965), the father of Russian physiology, as Pavlov called him, conceived all mental activity as brain reflexes. The nineteenth century machines provided large amounts of energy, and the concept of energy caught the imagination of philosopher, physician, and man in the street. Neurotic disorders were interpreted as nervous exhaustion, neurasthenia, and the problem seemed to be how to replenish the dwindling supplies of energy in the organism.

Are such facts about physical models necessary in a book on psychotherapy? We believe they are, since they have always played an important role, both positively and negatively. Psychoanalysis offers an instructive example. Although Freud gave up his attempt to describe mental life in terms of neurology and decided to formulate a purely psychological theory, he could not avoid physical analogies. In our view, the concept of psychic energy is particularly harmful, and a growing number of psychoanalysts agree. It is vague, based on a mixture of images connected with physical concepts of kinetic energy, force, and electric charge, and is sometimes colored by anthropomorphisms. Statements about psychic energy cannot be confirmed or refuted by observation. Norbert Wiener, the founder of cybernetics, argues the misuse of the energy concept with special clarity (note 1). John Bowlby, a psychoanalyst, rejects it in the context of psychoanalysis, from a similar point of view. Nevertheless, confusion about energy is still increasing among nonacademic psychotherapists. The concept appears to be a peculiar conglomeration of images of physical energy, supernatural *fluidum*, and principles of ancient Chinese philosophy. The influence of W. Reich (1949) is also apparent (note 2).

We want to stress that we criticize Freud's physical analogies, not because they are physical, but because they are inadequate and not useful. We differ in this from such psychoanalysts as Guntrip (1973) and Holt (1972), who criticize Freud's physical analogies from the point of view of their vitalistic position, that is, rejecting the analogies because they are physical (or, as they call them, mechanistic).

Present-day machines as models of behavioral systems

Present-day machines can serve as models for some aspects of human behavior. They may have receptors for messages coming from the environment, may recognize patterns such as written letters (although as yet imperfectly), can conduct computations and logical operations, solve problems, follow goals, check whether goals have been reached, and are able to learn from experience. Like organisms, they have a high energy storage which can be taken for granted. In studying them as systems, we are not interested in whether they are closed for the transfer of energy. We want to trace, as in behavioral systems, the causal chains of communication and control. In other words, we are interested in them as systems closed in relation to communication and control.

Homeostasis and goal-directed behavior. Two remarkable features of organisms which can be simulated in machines are *homeostatic mechanisms* and *goal-directed behavior*. Homeostasis, systematically described by physiologist Walter B. Cannon (1929), is the capacity of an organism to maintain certain variables within certain limits. For example, despite the changing temperature of the environment, the temperature of the body is maintained within a narrow range. The same holds for the concentration of salts, sugar, and other constituents in the blood and other body fluids. Organisms could not survive without numerous homeostatic mechanisms, which ensure that hundreds of variables do not deviate much from their standard values.

Since we can also regard a group of people, such as a family, as a system, we can ask what mechanisms maintain family homeostasis (Jackson 1959). Viewing a small group of people as a minimum system, even if interested in one of its members only, will be the basic approach of this book.

Another remarkable feature of organisms is *goal-directed behavior.* This is so remarkable that some biologists and philosophers claimed it to be a specific feature of organisms which needed supranatural explanation (note 3). On the other hand, although classical behaviorists had condemned such concepts as goal and purpose as unscientific, Tolman (1966) rehabilitated this concept in his purposive behaviorism and behaviorally redefined *purposiveness* as "persistence through trial-and-error, and docility, relative to some end." Boring, listing characteristics of a robot, noted that "there is little that will make a robot seem more human than his ability to choose one means after another until the goal is reached" (1946). Today, goal-directed behavior can be built into a machine.

Negative feedback. Both homeostasis and goal-directedness in machines are based on a mechanism called negative feedback. The term feedback is popular and overused, often wrongly. Feedback occurs when part of the effects of a given process are channeled back into input so as to affect the source of the process in question. An example of a homeostatic system with negative feedback is a room with a thermostat. The range of temperature of a room is the effect of the activity of a thermostat—which in turn is regulated by the temperature of the room. The causal chain is circular. If the temperature gets too high, the thermostat turns off the source of heat—that is, works in the opposite (negative) direction. When the temperature falls below the required value, more heat is produced until the temperature reaches the required value again.

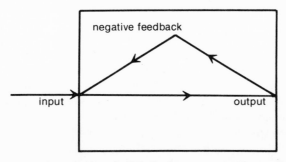

Homeostatic negative feedback: keeps some internal parameters of the system constant (example: room with a thermostat).

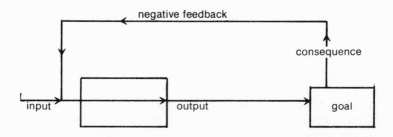

Goal-directed feedback device: The circuit passes through regions external to the system. (Example: a missile pointer and the goal, a jet.) If the goal object has a similar arrangement as the system on the left, this can be a picture of two human beings in interaction, forming a supra-system.

A room with a thermostat and an organism with a homeostatic regulation of body temperature are systems in which the feedback circuit runs *inside* the system. But a goal-directed behavior can be modeled by a system in which the negative feedback circuit passes through regions outside the system. For example, a missile guidance system has sensory organs which receive information through radar waves about a moving target, a jet, and point the missile at the target. Since the machine has to point at the target not where it presently is but where it will probably be when the missile reaches it, it makes analysis of past observations necessary; memory and learning have to be part of the machine.

Similarly, when I reach for a book, I do not know which muscles I am using. I turn into action various feedback mechanisms. My sensory receptors are not only exteroceptors, such as my eyes, but also proprioceptors in my tendons and muscles. They inform me continuously about each new position of my arm and the distance between my hand and the book determines a new command. Without thinking, I can reach the book from different initial positions, but again, memory and learning enter the process. A child has to learn how to coordinate the messages from exteroceptors and proprioceptors. These facts make possible what Brunswik (1937) called "psychology in terms of objects." I can study the relationships of the organisms with the *distal* objects in the environment, without being bothered by details of such *proximal* processes, such as pictures of an object on my retina, the distribution of muscles in performing the act of reading a book. The adaptive act and the object attained are the interests here. Such psychology is *functionalistic*, studying adaptation of the organism, but it is a *probabilistic* functionalism (Brunswik 1952). Organisms operate in a highly complex and variable environment, and the best they can do is to venture hypotheses as does the gun pointer which must cope with the direction of the wind changes, the jet trying to escape, and so on.

Positive feedback. Negative feedback counters deviation. Positive feedback amplifies deviation. If a thermostat had a positive instead of negative feedback device, each increase in temperature would lead to a further increase. The machine would run out of control.

Positive feedback can have similar effects in the organism. Certain pathological conditions may lead to high blood pressure, and the high blood pressure may in turn aggravate those pathological conditions, further increasing the blood pressure, and so on. Positive feedback may not always be undesirable, for example, money in the bank. The money creates interest and the interest creates further interest.

Neurotic paradox, described later, can often be described in terms of positive feedback. But desirable changes also sometimes accumulate through positive feedback. A patient in psychotherapy becomes more self-confident. His work associates feel it and show him more respect, which increases his self-confidence further.

Internal versus external causes of behavior

Modern machines with feedback can serve as simple models for human behavior in its interaction with the environment. Psychological medicine of the last century, was organically oriented and based on a one-person model. Its triumph was the discovery of the causes of such organic mental disorders such as general paresis. However, it failed completely when trying to understand neuroses.

Although of quite a different kind, it can be argued that Freud's model is basically also a one-person model. The causes of human behavior are sought in the interaction of internal factors, such as instinctual forces (Eros and Thanotos) and internal structures (id, ego, superego). In Freud's structural model, it is difficult to describe systematically the influence of environmental factors. The radical behaviorists, on the other hand, concentrated their attention on the relationship between external stimuli and behavioral responses. Watson, the father of behaviorism, was so impressed by the influence of the environment that he claimed that he could take any child and make him (or her) a doctor, lawyer, beggarman, or thief. Skinner's position, though much more complex, preserves this environmental bias. "Our 'independent variables'—the causes of behavior—are the external conditions of which behavior is a function. Relations between the two—the 'cause and effect' in behavior—are the laws of science" (1953). The position of American behaviorists has been criticized for decades by European ethologists (see Tinbergen 1951 and Lorenz 1965), and more recently, the environmentalistic bias of Skinner has been criticized by such behavior theorists and therapists as Bandura (1971) and Mahoney (1974). The relationship of organism and environment is reciprocal: behavior is a function of the environment and environment is a function of the organism. Machines with feedback help us keep in mind that the causal chains between the organism (or machine) and its environment are circular. For example, to understand the functioning of a system, be it a missile guidance system or an organism, it is imperative to include parts of the environment in the observational system. We will not fully understand the function and potential of the guidance system, if we do not include in our observation, beside the guidance system itself, also the jet maneuvering to escape. Similarly, we cannot understand and predict the behavior of a tennis player, unless we include into the system his partner and the interaction between them. In psychotherapy, we have to include other people also.

The limitations of a one-person system and the advantages of a broader system of observation will be shown through an example—a central phenomenon of the neuroses, one which O. H. Mowrer called *neurotic paradox*.

Neurotic paradox

Clinicians have been puzzled for decades by neurotics who, seemingly against known principles of learning, repeat their self-destructive behavior, repeating and aggravating their misery. This behavior was described by Freud:

> There are people in whose lives the same reactions are perpetually being repeated uncorrected, to their own detriment, or others who seem to be pursued by a relentless fate, though closer investigation teaches us that they are unwittingly bringing this fate on themselves. . . . (Freud 1933)
>
> What psycho-analysis reveals in the transference phenomena of neurotics can also be observed in the lives of some normal people. The impression that they give is of being pursued by a malignant fate or possessed by some "demonic" power; but psychoanalysis has always taken the view that their fate is for the most part arranged by themselves and determined by early infantile influences. The compulsion which is here in evidence differs in no way from the compulsion to repeat which we have found in neurotics, even though the people we are now considering have never shown any signs of dealing with a neurotic conflict by producing symptoms. Thus we have come across people all of whose human relationships have the same outcome: such as the benefactor who is abandoned in anger after a time by each of his *protégés,* however much they may otherwise differ from one another, and who thus seems doomed to taste all the bitterness of ingratitude; or the man whose friendships all end in betrayal by his friends; or the man who time after time in the course of his life raises someone else into a position of great private or public authority and then, after a certain interval, himself upsets that authority and replaces him by a new one; or, again, the lover . . . each of whose love

affairs with a woman passes through the same phases and reaches
the same conclusion. . . . (Freud 1920)

Freud explains this strange behavior, in his one-person model, by an
inherent instinctive mechanism, repetition compulsion. There is, according to him, "a compulsion to repeat which overrides the pleasure
principle." This self-destructive compulsion he regards as an expression
of the death instinct. Since the death instinct is a purely speculative
concept, there is no way of testing Freud's assertion. Moreover, Freud's
explanation does not offer any guideline for therapeutic intervention.

The first psychoanalyst who rejected Freud's explanation was Schultz-
Hencke (1942). He explained the neurotic paradox—or, as he called it,
the vicious circle of neurosis or devil's circle—as an interpersonal phenomenon. For example, a disturbed child provokes its mother, and she
behaves toward it in such a way that the child becomes more disturbed.

A man complains that no woman can be trusted—all women he has
had relationships with deceived him and were unfaithful to him. However, he is mistrustful and suspicious in every relationship from the start
and accuses each girlfriend unjustly about having relationships with
other men. His girlfriends feel hurt and out of rebellion do what he
suspects them of. As in a system with positive feedback, each disappointment he experiences increases his suspiciousness until he is unable to
have any relationship at all. Another man loses one job after another,
because each boss is a "bastard"—unfriendly and unjust. In reality, he
transfers his ambivalent feelings toward his father to each boss as soon
as he meets him and makes even the most tolerant boss unfriendly and
rejecting.

The neurotic paradox is certainly a phenomenon with many different
mechanisms. Attempts have been made to explain some cases in terms
of reinforcement contingencies. For example, a man will never lose his
fear of women if he avoids them systematically. But why does he avoid
them if he longs for a relationship with one? Because he is always rewarded by decreased fear when he avoids a woman. Another mechanism
for repeating neurotic behavior is created by a situation in which reward
comes first and the punishment much later. For example, a self-destructive habit (alcoholism) is difficult to break because the pleasure is immediate and punishment comes much later (gradient of reinforcement,
Dollard and Miller 1950). Other cases can be explained in terms of
cognitive learning. A patient is like a bad experimenter; he has a wrong
hypothesis about people, and behaves toward them in such a way that

his hypothesis is seemingly confirmed. This can be applied to the case of the jealous man and the man seeing every boss as a bastard. The neurotic paradoxes of many patients we meet in clinical practice are much more complicated. In the case of marital couples, often both partners present neurotic paradoxes which complement each other. Generally, a one-person system is not sufficient for describing the neurotic paradox; it is produced by the interaction of two or more people. The subject, systematically, though unwittingly, provokes others to react to him in such a way that his maladaptive behavior is aggravated. A special therapeutic community, which will be described later, is exceptionally suited to recreate partially neurotic paradoxes so that they can be identified, and, if all goes well, resolved.

This chapter has shown the great importance of an appropriate choice of the system of observation in which uninterrupted causal chains can be traced. Human behavior can seldom be successfully studied in a one-person system. As will be expanded in the next chapter, for the purposes of psychotherapy, a small social group seems to be the minimum system for studying an individual. This has been misunderstood often by group, family, and individual therapists, creating illusory dilemma: *individual or group*? "A family therapist has to abandon psychodynamic theory" (Haley 1975); "Group therapy is multiple individual therapy" (Riess 1976); "Family therapy abandons the centrality of the individual and teaches different epistemology" (Bloch 1976). However, as we will see, if the apparent dichotomies are analysed, different approaches can be accommodated within one epistemology. Even if we are interested in one specific individual, we cannot avoid studying and influencing his group. However, this does not imply that we wish to keep the group together. For example, in dealing with a young man as part of his family system, we may expect that the successful outcome of the treatment will lead to his breaking family ties and moving away.

A warning

As indicated, concepts such as *feedback*, and *model* are important theoretical concepts and should be protected against corruption. It is these very terms which seem to be dearer to the hearts of people the less education they have and the more educated they want to appear. "Give him feedback" is said, where it would be sufficient to say "Give him your reaction," or simply "Tell him what you think." Whether it will be feedback will depend upon the subject, since to tell somebody something may have no influence whatever. Total confusion is achieved when we say "He gave him positive feedback" meaning "he praised him," since, as we know, *positive feedback* refers to amplifying deviation. Patients should be encouraged to use observational words; words like *feedback, model, communication,* and even *emotion* are often misleading, a waste of time, sometimes used as resistance to treatment, and almost always interfering with treatment. Therapists themselves should set a good example by using observational language as much as possible and asking patients to do the same.

Another warning is necessary. In viewing a group of people as a system and using analogies to nonliving systems, we regard such a systems approach as useful and promising; as a matter of fact, it was the leading idea in developing integrated psychotherapy. However, we must be certain to use only general analogies which are heuristic or didactic. It is easy to forget and be misled into thinking that, by talking about systems, homeostasis, feedback, and so forth, we are explaining something. An erroneous impression is created that something is explained by talking in terms of *general systems theory*; such a tendency has been rightly ridiculed (Buck 1956). Writing about systems and groups without including any empirical content has become fashionable lately (note 4).

The systems approach will fully show its usefulness only when we are able to put some of the characteristics of a family or group of patients into a machine and compute predictions which may later be confirmed by observation of the group. We have no doubt that this is possible in principle. We also believe that this will happen when we find out which characteristics of individuals and groups to measure and how. Our lack of knowledge in this respect is the main obstacle. The computers are ready and waiting.

NOTES

1. Misuse of the concept of "energy"
The criticism and warnings have never been better expressed than by Norbert Wiener, the founder of cybernetics:

In our present-day attempts to build a scientific bridge between the biological and psychological sciences on the one hand and the physical mathematical sciences on the other, one of our first difficulties rises in the confused work of amateurs who have introduced into biology and psychology the language of the physical sciences without a full understanding of the implications of this language. One of the most abused terms in biology and psychology is that of *energy*. In its Aristotelean connotation, it signifies the potential of action, and is not really a physical, but rather a metaphysical term. Under these conditions there is perhaps a defense for using it for the tendency of an animal to follow a certain tropism, or for the mind to seek a certain goal. However, it is impossible in this day and age to use the term without a strong suggestion of its physical use, and this suggestion seems to be actually intended by many of those who employ it in the sciences of life. In physics, energy is a quantity which represents one of the constants of integration of a certain system of ordinary differential equations. Of its properties, the most important is that it is an additive element in a total expression which is invariant under time. If a quantity represents the constant of integration of a certain specific sort of differential equation, or is an additive element in a certain specific invariant, there is no question but that it falls well within the notion of energy and should be so named.

If on the other hand, there is another differential equation of a somewhat similar character (at least similar in form), of which it is the constant of integration, or if it is an additive term in some other quantity which is invariant with respect to the time, the analogical use of the term *energy* is legitimate. In the employment of the word by Freud and by certain schools of physiologists, neither justification is present; or at the very most, if it is, no one has proved it so.

There was a plethora of materialistic biological writing at the end of the last century, in which the language of physics was bandied around in a very unphysical way. The same sort of quantity was now termed an *energy* and now a *force*, regardless of the fact that the laws of transformation of force are widely different from those of energy. Chief among these books was *The Riddle of the Universe* by Ernst Haeckel. It is in the line of this scientific journalese that one finds the words *force* and *energy* interchangeably applied to whatever it is that drives the moth into the light and the flatworm away from it.

However, the moth is not pulled by light, nor is the flatworm pushed by it. They are steered—the one toward the light, and the other away. In this steering process, all the energy which the animal possesses in any true physical sense is ultimately converted into heat. The behavior follows a pattern very closely analogous to that of certain easily constructible steering machines, which no physicist claims to have an energy of attraction or repulsion towards light. This analogy is so close that even the types of defective performance are the same in the machine and in the living organism. The machine too is a dissipative system, and whatever physical energy it possesses bears no simply stateable relation to its motion. Thus the proper language for end-seeking processes is not that of energy, but of steering and directing. Energy is the thirty-two dollar word of the pseudo-scientific psychologists; the sixty-four dollar word is *field theory*. (1950)

It is unfortunate that the concept of *energy* has such an important role in classical psychoanalysis and other psychotherapeutic orientations, as it leads only to confusion. Since it is undefined, it has very little to do with the physical concept of energy and yet is connected with it vaguely in the imagination. Brenner tries to defend its use in the following way:

> The attribute which drives possess of impelling the individual to activity impressed Freud as being analogous to the concept of physical energy, which it will be recalled is defined as the capacity to do work. Consequently Freud assumed that there is a psychic energy which is a part of the drives, or which somehow derives from them. This psychic energy is not to be conceived of as the same as physical energy in any

way. It is merely analogous to it in the respects we have already mentioned. The concept of psychic energy, like the concept of physical energy, is a hypothesis which is intended to serve the purpose of simplifying and facilitating our understanding of the facts of mental life which we can observe. (1973)

A comparison with physics is wrong. The concept of mental energy is not defined, as it is in physics, and does not occur in any laws. It does not contribute to understanding, but to confusion. The reasons against its use are summarized in an excellent way by N. Wiener above. Fortunately, many psychoanalysts discarded the concept of psychic energy from their models (Kardiner et al. 1959; Holt 1967; Schafer 1976; and many others).

We have dealt with the concept of energy since it is so often misused, both by psychotherapists and patients. The indoctrinated patients use it in their resistance as they use other vague concepts, derived from different explanatory systems, ranging from physics through medicine to astrology.

2. "Magnetism" and "energy": A. Mesmer and W. Reich

Some physical concepts catch the fantasy of psychotherapists, philosophers, and metaphysicists. For example, the new discoveries about magnetism, electricity, and gravitation in the eighteenth century led Mesmer to formulate his principles about a physical fluid which fills the universe; diseases originate from unequal distribution of the fluid in the human body and, with the help of treatment, this fluid can be channeled, stored, and conveyed to other persons (Ellenberger 1970).

In the second half of the nineteenth century, it was energy which caught the fantasy of natural philosophers. Energetists, especially followers of Ostwald, claimed that mental entities like beauty, enthusiasm, etc., are kinds of energy (P. Frank 1957).

W. Reich, a brilliant thinker in his early career, contributor to psychoanalysis and innovator in the field of nonverbal psychotherapeutic techniques, had beliefs (delusions, some think) similar to Mesmer; only he talked about "orgone energy" instead of magnetism. He writes (1949):

> This "something", the "id", is a physical reality: the cosmic orgone energy. The living "orgonotic system", the "bioapparatus", represents nothing but a special state of concentrated orgone energy.

This uncritical use of the concept of energy continues even today, as is apparent, from a book by a pupil of Reich and the founder of bioenergetics, A. Lowen (1975):

> Bioenergetics is . . . the study of the human personality in terms of the energetic processes of the body. . . . Reich postulated the basic cosmic energy he called orgone which was nonelectric in nature. Chinese philosophy postulates two energies in a polar relationship to each other, yin and yang. These energies form the basis of the Chinese medical practices called "acupuncture". . . . He [Reich] invented an apparatus that could accumulate this energy and charge the body of anyone sitting in it. I have built these "accumulators" myself and used them personally. For some conditions they have proved helpful, but they have no effect on personality problems.

This uncritical and unscientific attitude must not deter us from valuable observations and techniques which both Reich and his followers developed.

3. Causality versus finality?

It is best to get over, as quickly as possible, the false dichotomy of causal versus teleo-logical (finalistic or goal directed). Some philosophers and psychologists maintained that in causal relationships the effect follows the cause (*causa efficiens*), whereas in goal-directed, purposeful behavior the present act is determined by the future, that is, by its goal (*causa finalis*). For example, Alfred Adler said:

> Individual psychology insists absolutely on the indispensability of finalism for the un-derstanding of all psychological phenomena. Causes, powers, instincts, impulses, and the like cannot serve as explanatory principles. The final goal alone can explain man's behavior. (1930)

Similarly, Sir Dennis Hill said recently:

> The causal connections between the past sequences of psychic experiences are them-selves dependent upon their future significance. . . . If this is so then psychoanalysis should admit to being a causal theory in the teleological rather than the mechanistic sense, and the hypothetico-deductive method of physical science is not logically appli-cable, except in a very limited sense. (1970)

Fortunately, the confusion can be clarified easily. If I am shooting at a target, I may say that the future result of hitting the target determines my present action—but I can say this only because the present state of my organism, that is, my present goal to hit the target, triggers the causal chain which ends by my hitting the target. Teleological (finalistic, means-ends) description is a short description of the behavior of goal-directed systems, which in each case can, in principle, be replaced by causal description. Bergson and others believed that goal-directedness in organisms needs a supernatural principle, entelechy, but that was before goal-directed machines were constructed.

As for Adler, he was a practical man and was right in stressing the goal-directedness of behavior which academic psychology rejected at one time. However, he was not right when he contrasted finalism with causality.

Let us conclude with a rare praise of Freud by Skinner:

> As a determinist, he convinced many people that things formerly believed to be acci-dental were really lawful, and I think he was right on that point. (Evans 1968)

Indeed, it is fortunate that Freud in an era of confusion about causality and finality adhered firmly to determinism as the heuristic principle. This enabled him to overcome tremendous obstacles and discover the causal chains of mental events in dreams, para-praxes, and neurotic symptoms.

4. Some fallacies of the systems approach

In regard to organisms or social groups, we often hear that "the whole is more than the sum of its parts." That sounds profound and leads some to think that the more is some nonmaterial, holistic principle such as entelechy, *élan vital*, or group spirit. However, there is no deep hidden problem that cannot be clarified by thinking about a nonliving system. Certainly, it makes a difference whether you have a running watch in your pocket or a pile of watch parts. The running watch is not "more" or "less" than its parts but is a system in which all the parts are put together.

Models can be of great help but can also be misleading. Talking in terms of systems has become fashionable, and sometimes an illusion is created that problems are solved by using that language. For example, we have serious doubts about the usefulness of the following pronouncements where quasi-theoretical entities and real objects are mixed together:

> Within psychoanalytic object-relations theory, internalized object relations constitute the subsystem of the target system represented by the overall psychic structures (superego, ego, and id), and the total personality is the suprasystem of the series. All the systems mentioned, from internalized object relations to social organization, can be placed within one hierarchical continuum. If this continuum were to be represented graphically, one could place concentric circles representing, from the center to the periphery, internalized object relations, overall psychic structures, personality, group and social organization. (Kernberg 1975)

In the camp of communication psychotherapists, J. Haley derives from the system approach untenable conclusions:

> When the unit shifts to two or more persons, as it does with a family orientation, the "cause" of behavior no longer resides within the person but in the context of other people. A person does what he does because of what someone else did.
> Discarding the individual as the unit, the family therapist asks us to believe that a person's history is irrelevant as a way of explaining why he behaves as he does. When "cause" is in the interpersonal context, it cannot be a program built inside the person by his past. With a unit of two or more persons, past traumas or other experiences of an individual become pointless explanations, as does any causal theory based upon previous learning or past conditioning. (1975)

Although Haley's attitude has some merits in practical work, he arrives at theoretically erroneous conclusions. It is only partly true that a person "does what he does because of what someone else did": his behavior is the result of someone's stimulation *and* his own disposition. However, it is fallacious to reason that when "cause" is in the interpersonal context, it cannot be a program built inside the person by his past. Of course, the programs of *all* the participants of the interaction have to be taken into consideration. Why would the previous social learning of two or more persons be irrelevant to the outcome?

Imagine a model social system composed of two interacting computors. The program and memory of both have influence on the outcome of the interaction. We can even take one part of the machine and repair it. However, we cannot isolate a member of a family and repair him or her. We can put that person in another system, such as a group of patients, and change the person inside that system. The person then reacts differently in his family system and may change that system. As we will describe in Part IV, this is what we often do in our clinical work.

It is sometimes easier and more economical to achieve changes in patients in an artificial group of patients, rather than with their families. This makes the following work with their families easier. For example, in the therapeutic community of the Day House, a young female patient shows the same rebellious attitude toward the female therapist as toward her mother, and the same jealousy toward a female patient as toward her sister. This may change during therapy, and when her mother and sister arrive to attend a mixed group of patients and relatives, the other patients double for them and speed up the change in the family system.

Some family therapists refuse to see one member of a family and insist that the whole family be present all the time. This has merit sometimes, both from the practical and research points of view, but sometimes it is only a demonstration by the therapists of the adherence to the system principle. As is so often true, rigid dogmaticism is based on half-truths.

Chapter 2

INDIVIDUAL IN GROUP

One chimpanzee is no chimpanzee.

R. M. Yerkes

No man is an Iland, intire of it selfe; every man is a peece of the Continent, a part of the maine.

John Donne

We primates do not operate in isolation. In the process of evolution, different species, repeatedly and independently, discovered that cooperation with each other increased their chances for survival. Gradually, through natural selection, innate mechanisms developed which helped ensure survival not only of individuals, but of supraindividual units. The social organization of ants, termites, and bees attracted the early attention of sociobiologists, but study of the social life of other species was neglected for a long time. The complex and flexible bonds between primates have started to be systematically studied only recently (for summary, see Wilson 1975). Our knowledge is still very scanty. The study of human ethology, which is of utmost significance, has barely begun.

As with the study of animals, it took human psychologists a long time to realize that "one man is no man." Psychology in its development was repeatedly sidetracked by studying fragmentary processes, such as sensations or associations of ideas, and was not able to study the broad functional interrelations of human beings with environmental objects, particularly with other human beings. To use the previous example of a tennis player, his behavior does not make sense when his adversary and the ball are invisible. One can understand his behavior only as part of a *system* in which two individuals interact and pursue their goals.

We will argue that for the purposes of psychotherapy *a small social group is the minimal system for the study of an individual*. Each of the next chapters will support the significance of a small group as a system of observation. By a *small group*, then, we mean *a system of two or more individuals interacting with each other, in pursuit of goals, some of which are shared*.

People spend most of their lives in small groups: the family, kindergarten, class in school, neighborhood children playing together, lovers, married couples, a group of friends, social parties, groups of coworkers, and people tied together by common interests, hobbies, beliefs, or purposes. Even in large organizations like an industrial plant, individuals are usually members of only one small group, even if superficially they meet other coworkers during the day. Many people spend most of their lives in two groups only—family and work. A patient and his therapist also form a group (a dyadic group). So do, of course, the therapeutic and encounter groups. Most of the experimental work in social psychology has been done on small groups without histories, that is artificial groups formed from strangers meeting only for the purpose of the experiment.

For thousands of years, extended families have been the units in which an individual has lived out his life. They fulfill most of the necessary functions of life: sexual partnership; raising and educating children; providing and preparing food, shelter, entertainment, and defense against enemies. Typical subgroups are sexual partnerships, mother and child, hunters, playing children, and adolescent gangs of one or both sexes. In modern society, many of the basic functions of the extended family have been taken over by other specialized groups. In most cases, the family is no longer a unit of economic production or the main source of education for the children; the factory and the school have supplanted it. Even so there remain only a small number of groups, or subgroups, of which an individual is a stable member.

BASIC CONCEPTS

Before going into details, let us consider an example which will help introduce some concepts which apply to small groups: group goals, social exchange, rewards-costs, influence, norms, roles, attraction to the group, dependence, and cohesiveness.

Let us imagine that a small airplane with twenty people aboard makes an emergency landing in the wilderness. The travelers did not know each other before the flight and so during the flight they formed an *aggregate*, not a group. After landing they quickly become a group, more and more structured as times goes on. Initially, the goals of the individuals may consist mainly of the survival of themselves and their children, but faced with a common danger, the safety and welfare of all emerges as a *group goal*. There is a supply of food and everybody has access to it, but since the supply is limited and some members do not respect the limits, it becomes imperative to establish some *rules* regarding the distribution of food. In this way, *norms* of conduct, binding for all members, develop. Since some people show more concern about the group than others and some show special abilities, a system of *roles* gradually develops and a group structure gradually emerges. Whereas some roles are related to external goals, such as building a shelter for protection, or finding food and water, other roles are related to such internal goals as taking care of the children, smoothing conflicts which may arise, and keeping the morale of the group high or boosting it.

Some members are attracted to certain roles; for example, a man starts to build something, since he knows how to, and is rewarded by feeling useful to the group, by having their esteem and gratitude, and by exerting power over those others who are helping him. His personality may make the performance of his role easier or more difficult. He may have conflicts with those working for him which interfere with accomplishing his task. He may even be replaced by somebody less knowledgeable, but who can organize the work better and have better relationships with those working for him so that more work is accomplished. This is an example of how external and internal group goals are tied together.

Members of the group have differing degrees of *influence* on each other. Those who have the most influence participate in *leadership*. This develops naturally, but a moment may come when the two most powerful members disagree on how the group should act. When the group gets tired of their power struggle, one of them is formally established as a leader. The leader has to be respected for his or her capacity to lead toward achieving the group's goals but need not be the most popular person. The leader may criticize those who do not work well on the construction, and to maintain power, he or she must keep somewhat aloof. Sometimes in addition to the leader who is a *task specialist*, pursuing external goals, another specialist emerges, a *maintenance (or social-emotional) specialist*, who is the most liked person, and he helps to establish satisfactory relations within the group and to increase its cohesiveness (Bales 1970; Hollander 1971).

The survivors of the plane crash constitute an *involuntary* group: individuals could not survive if they were to leave the group. But most of the groups we shall deal with, such as partnerships, families, coworkers, or therapy groups, are relatively *voluntary* groups; the individuals can leave, though it is often not easy. In a therapeutic community, a fantasy such as a plane crash or a shipwreck and two deserted islands is played to quickly generate information about both individual and group dynamics. (See Psychomime).

We are going to describe some group characteristics in more detail. Numerous social-psychological studies were taken into consideration—particularly those of Thibaut and Kelley (1959), Homans (1961), Bales (1970), and Hollander (1971). The main purpose of our discussion is to introduce a way of thinking not usual in psychotherapy. Later we will expand it to cover private events (the group schema) in order to achieve a unified conception of mental life.

Goals

People entering a group voluntarily have *individual goals* which they hope to achieve. For example, a housewife takes a job in order to actualize her potential, to contribute financially to the household, and perhaps to be less dependent on her husband. On entering the job she may also find additional rewards: esteem for some aspects of her ability previously unrecognized and enjoying the company of coworkers. She participates in group goals which are external and internal. She contributes to the *external* goals by working efficiently, and to the *internal* goals by forming good relationships with her coworkers who, in turn, like and respect her. Contributing to the group goals may not only be instrumental in achieving her individual goals but they may become her individual goals; for example, she enjoys helping her working group to become cohesive or she is proud of the success of the working team.

Rewards and costs

A group member, on the way to his goal and on reaching it, has *rewards* and *costs*. Costs are hardships, boring activities, punishments, which the individual would like to avoid, if it was not for his desire to reach his goal. The *outcome* is that rewards are received and costs incurred. It is thus possible to observe the activity of the group in terms of a multiple social exchange of rewards and costs. Usually, we have to regard rewards and costs separately. But we can, for limited theoretical considerations, use an economical model: the value of *outcome* would be *rewards* minus *costs* (Thibaut and Kelley 1959; Homans 1961). Differing opinions about the social exchange theory need not interest us here (note 5).

It must be stressed that rewards have to be understood rather broadly to include altruistic rewards: for instance, the success of a friend which may mean a sacrifice for the subject can also be a reward for him. An anticipated reward is also a type of reward. It is of great importance to assess the rewards and costs of all group members, and this is regarded in this book as one of the basic tasks of the psychotherapist. For example, with a married patient the therapist has to explore the rewards and costs of both spouses. There may be some hidden rewards for one or both partners which promote the neurotic symptoms. It is also useful to find out whether both partners regard their relationship as a *fair exchange*. It is hardly surprising that in an unfair exchange the person who takes advantage is less sensitive to the situation, reacting, if at all, with feelings of guilt. The disadvantaged, or the victim of exchange, reacts with frustration and anger. Since there is no scale to measure outcome, the members may differ in evaluating the fairness of the exchange. Society's values are also a determining factor. For example, the working wife of a nineteenth century factory worker accepted it as fair to take full responsibility for the household in addition to her outside job. This would not be acceptable today to most working wives.

Attractiveness and dependence. The *attractiveness* of a group for its members will depend on the *outcome*. (that is, how the rewards compare with the costs) and whether they reach or exceed the level of fair exchange. Although a member may be attracted to the group, he is not *dependent* on it if there is another group of at least the same attractiveness. The person could then leave the group for another if the *costs of transition* were not too high. The costs might be real or imaginary; for example, the wife of an alcoholic is unhappy and has an opportunity to enter another, more satisfactory, relationship, but as a Catholic she regards divorce as a sin. Hence, the costs of transition for her would be too high.

Since, for the patient, psychotherapy means both rewards and such costs as anxiety, painful memories and the activation of conflict, the therapist must continually assess the reward-cost balance. The most difficult and important thing for the therapist to learn is when to give rewards and postpone costs—when to instill hope, for example. The psychoanalytic rule *analyze resistance before content* is a part of the cautious handling of rewards and costs. In group therapy and the therapeutic community, the therapist must learn to use strategies which, through minimal intervention, ensure that the group process supplies an optimum reward-cost balance for everybody. The therapist also has to calculate the rewards and costs of the patients' significant persons, even when they are not seen. A female patient may be becoming more independent so that her husband, losing his power over her too quickly, may try to stop her therapy. The therapist must anticipate this and counteract it by helping her find new rewards for him. A therapist of a child or adolescent who does not care about the rewards and costs of the parents may lose the patient without helping the patient be more independent. The therapist's strategy must be to help determine rewards for the significant persons, so that they find advantages in the therapeutic change of the patient.

Digression: Sociometry

J. L. Moreno (1934) introduced sociometric procedures which have wide application in groups of all sorts. They offer valuable information about the group structure in therapeutic communities, ambulatory groups, and families in treatment; they are also of theoretical value. The reason we introduce them at this point is because we believe, with Thibaut, Kelley (1959) and Homans (1961), that the sociometric status of group members can be understood in terms of rewards and costs; that is, it reflects what rewards various group members offer other members and what costs they inflict on them.

In a Lobec therapeutic community, we periodically asked the same thirty patients to select and write down the names of those within the group they would select and those they would reject in a certain situation. For example, "Imagine you have to spend two months of holiday with others from this group. Please write under *plus*, the names of two people you would definitely want to have with you and under *minus*, the names of two people you definitely would not want to have with you. Who would you choose to be your friend, leader, your husband, wife, your father and your mother. . . ."

The test takes only a few minutes and the results are quickly summarized in a form of a matrix or a sociogram.

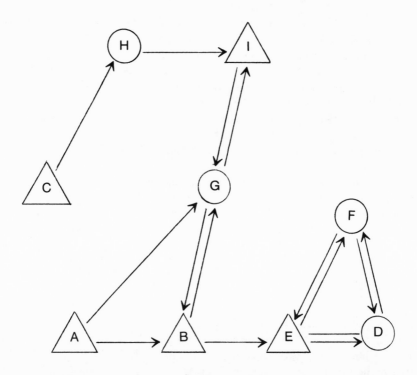

Sociogram of positive choices. Female G is the sociometric star, males A and C are isolates.

To clarify this procedure, let us give the results of an ambulatory group in our therapy, which has nine members: five men and four women. The results are answers to the first question asked above (the selection and rejection of others for an imagined two-month holiday). First we will show the results in the form of a sociogram, with only positive choices. Then we will show the same data in a matrix form, with negative choices (rejections) added. Men are represented by triangles and females by circles.

The female patient G is the *sociometric star*, with five positive choices. The two male patients, A and C are *isolates*, not chosen by anybody, but there is a difference between them in that A has only two negative choices whereas B seems to be disliked by most of the members. The patients D, E and F choose each other, which may suggest that they are

	A		B		C		D		E		F		G		H		I	
A	▨		+			-						-	+					
B			▨			-			+			-	+					
C					▨					-		-	+		+			
D						-	▨		+		+					-		
E		-				-	+		▨		+							
F		-				-	+		+		▨							
G			+					-				-	▨		+			
H								-				-	+		▨		+	
I						-		-	+				+				▨	
Σ	0	2	2	0	0	6	2	3	4	1	2	5	5	0	1	1	2	0

Sociometric matrix of the same data with the addition of the 'rejection' variable. The totals at the bottom show the scores of positive and negative choices each group member receives.

forming a subgroup and resisting the therapeutic process. A sociometric test may sometimes surprise the therapist, which, in turn, may lead to a useful reward-cost analysis.

Influence

The study of social influence is the central topic of social psychology. Human beings are so mutually interdependent for the satisfaction of all of their needs that influencing others and being influenced by them is an essential activity in their lives. If person A can change person B's outcomes, we call such influence the *power* of A over B. B, however, has *counter-power* over A if B can influence A's outcomes. A mother has power over her child by being able to punish it, but the child has counter-power over the mother by being able to cry loudly and incessantly, which can spoil the whole day.

Let us imagine the influence of a strict teacher on certain children. The children may tremble, have palpitations, and be unable to remember lessons which they know well. This influence may continue into later life and be seen in adult patients who become inhibited in the presence of authority, be it an employer or a policeman. At other times, influence from the past is more subtle, though nonetheless strong. Some patients may remember that they were afraid of their fathers or mothers and hence were unable to criticize them openly. The inhibition may be so strong that they are unable to criticize them even in their absence, as in a psychodrama when the roles of parents are played by other patients. They dread saying anything negative about their parents, as if their parents were actually present. (In a way, the parents' images are present as part of the group schema, which will be introduced shortly.)

Inhibitions of patients' feelings are sometimes so strong that the patients are not even aware that they have been angry with their parents; they are unconscious of their anger and resist becoming aware of it. The resistance is manifested by their denial, attempts to change the topic, and feelings of guilt, to give a few examples. All such phenomena were described by Freud, who was particularly impressed by the repression of sexual impulses and later by that of sexual and aggressive impulses. There seems, however, to be evidence that certain kinds of social pressure can make any mental content unconscious. For example, a person in hypnosis is asked not to perceive pain which is then inflicted. The person claims not to feel the pain, although when asked to write automatically, a dissociated knowledge of pain is revealed in the automatic writing (Hilgard 1973). Similarly, persons made aware of their anger toward their parents may say afterward that somehow this had been known to them all the time, though they could not express it.

Another example, not an unusual one, arises in marital therapy. The patient has many complaints about her husband but does not mention any of these in his presence. It is, of course, common that a patient does not want to criticize her husband in his presence. In this case, however, the patient is not even conscious of any complaints when he is present. The situation is somewhat similar to that of the person under the influence of hypnosis or that of the child who, out of fear of his teacher, forgets his lesson.

The social influence of a group can be stronger still. We all can remember, perhaps, the unpleasant feeling of getting up in a meeting and talking against an opinion shared by all the others. When the people in the meeting became angry, we may have experienced irrational feelings of panic and loneliness. Many children now and then experience a desperate feeling of being ostracized by other children. In adults, if this is connected with a threat to life, security, or status, it may lead to changes of conviction, attitude or even perception. For example, most Germans

studied in 1945, claimed they did not know anything about extermi-
nation camps for Jews. Their lack of knowledge was probably partly
due to selective inattention and repression.

The first to clearly understand how people can misinterpret social
reality or become unconscious of it because of social pressures, were
probably Marx and Engels. Their ideas in this respect were further
developed by Wilhelm Reich in the thirties and later by Erich Fromm.
Fromm's contribution can best be summarized in his own words:

> For man, inasmuch as he is a *man*, the sense of complete aloneness
> and separateness is close to insanity. . . . It is this fear of isolation and
> ostracism, rather than the "castration fear", that makes people repress
> the awareness of that which is taboo since much awareness would
> mean being different, separate, and hence, to be ostracized. For this
> reason the individual must blind himself from seeing that which his
> group claims does not exist, or accept as truth that which the majority
> says is true, even if his own eyes could convince him that it is false.
> The herd is so vitally important for the individual that their views,
> beliefs, feelings, constitute reality for him more so than what his sen-
> ses and his reason tell him. Just as in hypnotic state of dissociation
> the hypnotist's voice and words take the place of reality, so the social
> pattern constitutes reality for most people. There is almost nothing
> a man will not believe—or repress—when he is threatened with the
> explicit or implicit threat of ostracism. . . .

> Every society . . . develops a system, or categories, which determines
> the forms of awareness. This system works, as it were, like a socially
> *conditioned filter*: experience cannot enter awareness unless it can pen-
> etrate this filter.

> Freud was mainly concerned with the uncovering of the individual
> unconscious. While he assumed that society enforced repressions,
> these were the repressions of instinctual forces, and not the social
> repressions which really matter—the repressions of the awareness of
> social contradictions, socially produced suffering, of the failure of
> authority, of feelings of *malaise* and dissatisfaction, etc. . . . If uncov-
> ering the unconscious means arriving at the experience of one's own
> humanity, then, indeed, it cannot stop with the individual but must
> proceed to the uncovering of social dynamics and the critical ap-
> praisal of one's own society from the stand point of universal human
> values. (1962)

Fromm deals with important social factors of repression:

> Why do people repress the awareness of what they would otherwise
> be aware of? Undoubtedly the main reason is fear. But fear of what?
> Is it fear of castration, as Freud assumed? There does not seem to be
> sufficient evidence to believe this. Is it fear of being killed, impris-
> oned, or fear of starvation? That might sound like a satisfactory an-
> swer, provided repression occurred only in systems of terror and
> oppression. . . . Are there more subtle fears which a society such as
> our own, for instance, produces? Let us think of a young executive
> or engineer in a big corporation. If he has thoughts which are not
> "sound", he might be inclined to repress them lest he might not get
> the kind of promotion others get. This, in itself, would be no tragedy,
> were it not for the fact that he, his wife and his friends will consider
> him a "failure" if he falls behind in the competitive race. Thus the
> fear of being a failure can become a sufficient cause for repression.
>
> But there is still another and, as I believe, the most powerful motive
> for repression: *the fear of isolation and ostracism.* (1962)

We could give many examples of the phenomena mentioned from
Czechoslovakia in the fifties. For example, intellectuals in fields like
biology, psychology, and psychiatry were under social pressure to accept
Soviet teachings which they could have known were of dubious
value—teachings such as the theories of Lysenko and Lepeshinska, and
a simplified version of psychiatry in Pavlovian terms. Though it is true
that some only pretended to believe them, our observations persuaded
us that some accepted them sincerely. The influence resembled hypnosis
or brainwashing—the threat being directed not toward their life but
toward their social and financial status. Another example of behavior
changed under social pressure would be America during the McCarthy
era.

But social pressures can also open eyes to repressed cognitions and
feelings. For example, a trend toward equality for women in Czechoslovakia was supported by public encouragement and employment opportunities in the fifties and sixties. Here social pressure was positive and
was reflected in a new consciousness for women. Many neurotic women
who hesitated to join the general trend were helped by psychotherapy
to do so. The process was particularly efficient in the therapeutic community at Lobec. Usually, their self-confidence was raised, and they

obtained the courage to go to work. They were also able to reestablish their marital roles with their husbands on new and more equal bases.

Contracts, norms, roles

Contracts. When interacting with people, even casually, we make miniature contractual arrangements. They are usually not explicit and sometimes not verbal, but both participants agree to do or not do something, implicitly raising certain expectations and making certain promises. If you happen to talk in a friendly manner with a stranger in the street, you do not expect him to leave in the middle of the sentence or to hit you. If he does, you feel that he has deceived you with regard to some implicit rules, which for a time he indicated he would adhere to.

Our relations with people are based on both long-term and short-term contractual arrangements; these, however, may often be interpreted differently by the participants. For instance, a marital couple seeks help, and you find out that they interpret very differently the contract on which their marriage of eight years has been based. Is this new to them? Did the husband intentionally foster his wife's illusion that he agreed to the same contract? Clarification of all contractual arrangements, if properly timed, may be very helpful in marital and family therapy.

Some patients become frustrated in their relationships again and again, because they are unable to indicate what they want and let others dictate the conditions of the contract. Sometimes, they are inhibited in making any demands. They either suffer until the end of the contract or, when their frustration mounts, ask for a change—usually too late so that the other party is also hurt in some way.

Some contracts are deceptive and their goal is to hurt the other person. The following "game" can be played on many different levels of sophistication and subtlety, but its principle is simple. A girl indicates nonverbally to a man that she is available. Consequently he goes through all the steps of courtship, encouraged by her more and more, until she suddenly withdraws showing surprise that he had such an idea. In a therapeutic community we were able to study such cases in detail. Although the girls received their rewards by hurting the man, often taking revenge on him for somebody in their past, they were invariably unhappy and disturbed with their incapacity to love. Deceptive miniature contracts are described as one-upmanship by Potter (1951) and in an especially useful way for psychotherapists and patients as *games* by Berne (1964).

Often, the whole group is involved in a contractual arrangement with deception on all sides. For example, the whole group may encourage the neurotic symptoms of one member, if this results in positive outcomes for other members of the group. By an implicit contractual arrangement, a child may become the scapegoat of the family. Integrated psychotherapy tries to help the family to find better solutions, or if this cannot be done, to help those who suffer the most to find their independence.

Norms. Norms are rules prescribing what everybody is supposed to do and not do. Norms reflect power relations in the group, and they bring regularity into interaction while minimizing the direct use of personal power. To the degree the group members are involved in the norms' formulation, the norms are types of contractual arrangements. There are positive and negative sanctions for following or breaking the norms. Sometimes the negative sanctions, punishments, consist only of social disapproval.

We can distinguish *prescribed* norms, *accepted* norms, and *performed* norms. Patients coming for psychotherapy often have a decisional norm conflict, that is, they accept a certain prescribed norm and yet break it or want to, with strong feelings of guilt. For example, a patient was repeatedly admitted to emergency because of a phobia of dying. As it turned out in psychotherapy, his phobia was connected with his moral conflict: he had countless extramarital affairs, but at the same time felt extremely guilty and anxious about them. Because of his past experiences he was not able to find one of the two nonneurotic solutions: either to give up his extramarital affairs or to change his norms.

We will come back to norm conflict when dealing with group schema. Norm conflict is a topic of central importance in psychotherapy.

Roles. Rules which do not apply to all, but only to one or two persons, are called *roles*. The concept *role* has a broad spectrum of meanings, and is in need of revision. However, even at this stage it is useful for us. We will distinguish, as with norms, roles that are *prescribed, accepted* and *performed*. The role of the father has certain characteristics; if we were to observe ten fathers in our neighborhood, we would notice differences in *role performance*. These are due to differences in personality and in how they interlock with other roles in the family. Some roles are *assigned*, some are *chosen*. For example, the role of child in the family is assigned. If, on the other hand, one of two sisters functions as a go-between for fighting parents, whereas the other sister instigates the fights, their differing roles are probably determined by choice—choice which, however, may in turn have been determined by a long history of family dynamics. Similarly, in a therapeutic community or outpatient group, it is valuable to know both how the patients perform assigned roles and what roles they choose. Some strive to be members of the committee or work instructors, some avoid leadership roles. Some promote therapeutic goals while others work against them, openly or secretly. There may be a member, intelligent, creative, entertaining, very popular in the group, who is the focus of group resistance—a group seducer. The rewards the seducer dispenses may be of a different kind—entertainment, sympathy and support for those who resist. He or she may also be feared and therefore never criticized.

NOTE

5. Social exchange

We found that the systematic study of mutual rewards and costs for all participants in the psychotherapeutic process is essential, and we formulated it as the *rule of motivational balance* in marital therapy (F. Knobloch and Sefrnova, 1954). However, we do not commit ourselves to any theory like the social exchange theory, particularly when formulated in conditioning terms (Homans 1961). The exchange is complex and because of the unsolved problems of learning theory, with questions about the cognitive aspects of learning unsettled, it seems to us precocious to rely upon principles of operant conditioning.

On the other hand, we agree with Homans when he argues against common criticisms of social exchange theory:

> Let not a reader reject our argument out of hand because he does not care for its horrid profit-seeking implications. Let him ask himself instead whether he and mankind have ever been able to advance any explanation why men change or fail to change their behavior other than that, in their circumstances, they would be better off doing something else, or that they are doing well enough already. On reflection he will find that neither he nor mankind has ever been able to offer another—the thing is a truism. It may ease his conscience to remember that if hedonists believe men take profits only in materialistic values, we are not hedonists here. So long as man's values are altruistic, they can take a profit in altruism too. Some of the greatest profiteers we know are altruists. . . . Indeed we are out to rehabilitate the "economic man". The trouble with him was not that he was economic, that he used his resources to some advantage, but that he was antisocial and materialistic, interested only in money and material goods and ready to sacrifice even his old mother to get them. What was wrong with him, was his values: he was allowed a limited range of values; but the new economic man is not so limited. He may have any values whatever, from altruism to hedonism, but so long as he does not utterly squander his resources in achieving these values, his behavior is still economic. Indeed if he has learned to find reward in *not* husbanding his resources, if he values *not* taking any thought for the morrow, and acts accordingly, his behavior is still economic. In fact, the new economic man is plain man. (1961)

We may keep in mind the warning of Robert Bales pertinent to social exchange theories:

> One does not do well to found theories of behavior on statements about satisfaction, since he will never be able to measure his central variable. This is a problem with theories founded on the concept of "reward", "punishment", "self-interest", "pleasure", "gratification", "utility", "exchange of utilities", or the like. Such theories nearly always sound good—indeed one feels that they surely *must* be true, but on analysis, they are generally found to be true only by definition, and to be semantically and empirically almost empty. . . . To be of any practical use a theory has to *start* with something you can observe, and it must enable you to predict something else you can observe. (1970)

Nevertheless, we are not as pessimistic as Bales about the future of concepts such as *satisfaction*. Even today we are able to assess changes in the overall satisfaction of our patients or marital couples. The economic social exchange model has limited but definite usefulness, and it is certainly closer to observation than Freud's economic model. In chapter 9, we will argue for an extended social exchange model embracing imagined exchanges.

Chapter 3

PSYCHOLOGY IN TERMS
OF OBJECTS

In starting our discussion of human nature by describing a group, we are stressing the necessity of studying individuals in the context of objects.

Each transaction of living involves numerous capacities and aspects of man's nature which operate together. Each occasion of life can occur only through an environment, is imbued with some purpose, requires action of some kind, and the registration of the consequences of action. Every action is based upon some awareness or perception which in turn is determined by the assumptions brought to the occasion. These assumptions are in turn determined by past experience. All of these processes are interdependent. No one process would function without the others. (Cantril 1950)

The numerous aspects of man's nature Cantril talks about are described traditionally by many names— percept, image, emotion, attitude, thinking, intention, volition, conation. We often forget how imprecise and overlapping they are, so that pseudoproblems and false dichotomies easily arise. It is significant that there are about two dozen theories of emotion, from perceptual to motivational ones, but no generally accepted descriptive definition which would ascertain that the explanations deal with the same phenomena. Thus we will not take seriously questions like Is emotional change or insight more important in psychotherapy? unless they are formulated in more concrete terms. We sympathize with Kelly (1963) who "completely abandoned the classical threefold division of psychology into cognition, affection, and conation," but we will continue to use such terms, keeping in mind their limited usefulness.

We will only deal with *some* aspects of human behavior, either because we need them for developing the conceptual framework, or because they are often neglected in dealing with psychotherapy.

ASSUMPTIVE WORLD

There are similarities between building up an assumptive world in daily life and building a scientific theory. Cantril defines *assumptive world*.

The only world we know is created in terms of and by means of our assumptions. It is the world which provides what constancy there is in our environment; the world which gives our experience its consistency. And it *is* a world of assumptions—a world which we could not have at all except for our past experience in acting for the purpose of enhancing the quality of life. (1950)

Our senses are bombarded without interruption by millions of stimuli of all kinds. A baby cannot make sense out of the chaos at first; on rare occasions neither can we, for example, when we are slowly awaking in the morning or from general anesthesia. Some people, through certain brain damage, lose the capacity to make sense out of the chaos of stimuli; they cannot recognize objects, although they can see perfectly well (agnosias).

The baby gradually discovers regularities in the world and develops the capacity which is sometimes broadly called *object constancy*—the capacity to recognize objects again as the same even when they differ and to retain them as images even when they are not present. You see your friend as of the same size whether he is near or far; you do not take him for a midget when he is very far away, although in that case, his picture on your retina is much smaller than before. We recognize a sheet of paper as white whether it is illuminated or in shadow. We can read print of different sizes. This is a miraculous achievement of our nervous system—not really miraculous since the simulation of pattern, or Gestalt, recognition by a reading machine has been, at least in principle, solved. Object constancy developed in the evolution of animals, according to Konrad Lorenz (1973), because of selection pressure, since reliable recognition of objects under highly variable environmental conditions was of utmost importance. In primates, the development of space orientation and voluntary movements paved the way to the ever increasing capacity for abstraction and problem-solving.

In perceiving objects, we do not realize how much we add to the sensory input. With a glimpse, we recognize an object such as a table, but we can achieve it only because we use our former assumptions in the form of images of tables stored in our memory. We see much more than we really see. Already in perceiving, we have to venture hypotheses (Brunswik 1952), or assumptions, based on limited sensory input and complemented by images and concepts. There are, of course, as with all hypotheses, risks of mistakes, or misperception. I saw an animal in the garden and was sure it was a cat, and then looking again, I saw that it was a racoon. I made a mistake, because I had seen cats there every day but never a racoon. Or notice how difficult it is to discover printing errors, when you have to read proofs: we realize that we see much more in the direction of our assumptions than is really printed.

The perceptual process then is a dynamic fusion of cues from the environment, assumptions, and action.

> The process is one in which cues from the environment are related to assumptions, giving rise to perceptions which are "prognostic directives" for action. (Kilpatrick 1961)

But the assumptions are not isolated, they form more or less a coherent "assumptive world."

> Man strives to maintain his assumptive world intact. . . . It results from the fact that what we have built up as our assumptive world is the only universe within which our transactions of living can take place. It is necessary for us to maintain some degree of stability and continuity in our assumptive world if any of our value judgments are to make sense; if any of our actions are to be effective. Without an assumptive form world we would have no value attributes in experience. (Cantril 1950)

J. D. Frank (1973) expands the concept of the assumptive world further, and we recommend reading his excellent analysis. Here we will go further and utilize this graphic term for our analysis of the dualistic fallacy. Contrasting the assumptive world with the dualism of an inner and outer world shows that this dualism leads to unsolvable problems. It also makes exploration of such important areas as the spatiality of experience difficult.

WHAT DO "INTERNAL" AND "EXTERNAL" MEAN?

Let us analyze a simple episode. Al, a man, is certain he sees his friend Bill in a crowd of people. He calls him, goes to him, and puts a hand on his shoulder. The man turns around and it is not Bill, it is a stranger. Even without Al telling us, we as observers can guess what happened. For a while that man was for Al "assumptive Bill." Later Al modified his assumptive world, and "assumptive Bill" changed into "an assumptive stranger," which turned out to be more realistic. Obviously, the assumptive world at given points may be identical to or differ more and more from the real world. If Al continued to regard the stranger as his friend Bill, we would be concerned about him and perhaps regard him as schizophrenic.

You may not like talking about "assumptive Bill" and prefer to say that Al misperceived a person, that this was his inner experience and Bill was only in his head. However, talking about "*inner* experience" can be misleading. We would argue that Bill was not *in* Al's head but *outside* where the stranger was. To talk about "assumptive Bill" has the advantage of explaining Al's unusual behavior—going to a stranger and talking to him as if he were Bill. (For this purpose, the terms *behavioral world* and *phenomenal world* were also introduced; see note 6.)

If you disagree and want support for your position, you may go to Al and he will probably say, "Yes, Bill was only in my head." That is the language habit acquired through centuries. However, were we to ask him if he saw Bill in his head, he would certainly say, "No, I saw him in the crowd." That means that "assumptive Bill" was localized in Al's assumptive world *outside* himself, not *inside* his head or body. Of course, part of the assumptive world is also inside the person. You can imagine that you have a toothache, or imagine the taste of strawberries or visualize a cherry stone in your stomach which you have swallowed, and *that* part of your assumptive world is inside.

Now try an experiment. Have a look at a chair. Where is the chair?

"Over there, outside myself." Now close your eyes and imagine that chair. Where is it now? You may say, "Of course, in my head." That is, at least, what most people would answer without thinking. But is the answer correct? It depends on what you mean exactly. If you mean that your image of the chair is a process in your brain, you are right, but the same holds for the perception of the chair. If you mean that the immediate stimulus for the image came from inside your brain, as opposed to the outside stimulus for the percept of the chair, you are right again. But if you mean the location in your assumptive world, you are not right; your imagined chair is *outside* as is the perceived chair. You do not imagine it *inside* your head; you see it outside as Al saw "assumptive Bill" outside. In dreams, the persons you see clearly are assumptive persons outside yourself, (that is, not inside your head or body). In daydreams, you may have a conversation with somebody whom you do not see so clearly, but you still talk to the person *outside* you. Even if the image is vague, as it probably is when you imagine the chair with closed eyes, the location in your assumptive world is outside yourself.

Since most people have not thought about the spatiality of their assumptive world, we will add another example. Suppose you have to find your way through your house in complete darkness. You walk among assumptive objects from one room to another. As you walk you expect to touch an assumptive chair and immediately you touch it; it is a real chair. Did you have to shift from the image in your head to the perception of the chair outside? No. The location of the assumptive chair and that of the real chair are the same.

If you do not see yet where this discussion is leading and find it trifling, please wait. We believe that it may help to open new prospects for a spatial analysis of human experience, that it may lead us out of the blind alley of Freudian and similar models, and that it may contribute to establishing a common language with behavioral scientists who rightly complain about our dualistic, or homunculus, conception of human behavior.

But if we are right, why is it that it is so firmly fixed in our language that a perceived chair is *outside* and an imagined chair *inside* (our inner experience, part of our inner world), even though it is clearly imagined as outside ourselves? It is a conveniently short way to express that a percept is caused by an *outside* stimulus (outside our body) and an image by an *inside* stimulus (inside our body). To distinguish a percept from an image, reality from fantasy, has been extremely important to the development both of mankind and to that of every individual child. We are seriously concerned about those who hallucinate, that is, confuse images with percepts. By stressing the dichotomy outside/inside, we stress that we belong to that large community which *can* make the distinction. Another reason for the firmness of the concept is that the percept, being caused by an outside stimulus (or partially caused, since other partial causes lie in the organism), is independent of our will, whereas we can usually make the image come and go. It is partly dependent on our will and, therefore, *inner*.

Ranged against us is not only language usage but also traditional philosophy. According to Descartes and his followers, physical objects have extension in space (*res extensa*), whereas mental states have no spatial location (*res cogitans*). This has been regarded by dualists as a strong argument for dualism. Schlick (1974) and Feigl (1967), among others, showed the fallacy of this reasoning. As our examples show, our experiences have spatiality. A perceived or imagined chair is outside in my assumptive world, whereas a toothache, whether real or imagined, is inside. But if we are asking where in *physical space* the percept or image of the chair or person is located, the answer is: inside the brain.

Let us quote Feigl, a philosopher of science, rebutting the Cartesian argument that spatiality applies only to physical bodies, not to mental states. In the following, *phenomenal* has to be understood as approximately synonymous with *assumptive*. Feigl says,

> Using "mental" for the time being in the sense of "phenomenal", we had better—and without too much ado—introduce the indispensable distinction between phenomenal space(s) and physical space. I am perhaps not too acute in matters of phenomenological description but it does seem to me that my feelings and emotions pervade large parts of my body-as-I-experience it. William James has given us some striking illustrations of this. In the phenomenal field of the subject, specific feelings may be located at least vaguely or diffusely in some not very sharply delimited part of the organism. My feelings or sentiments of elation, depression, delight, disgust, enthusiasm, indignation, admiration, contempt, etc., seem to me to be spread roughly through the upper half or two-thirds of my body. Sounds and smells at least in the usual situations of "veridical" perceptions seem to be partly outside, partly inside the phenomenal head. (1967; see note 7)

Although our interest at this point is theoretical, the reader here should already be aware of the practical importance of exploring the assumptive space of a patient, both external and internal. The location of tensions and emotions in different parts of the body orients us to deal with that particular region, for example, by talking about it, by pressure on certain points, or with special exercises. A patient felt peculiar tension in his face. When certain points of his face were pressed, tics were elicited which he recalled having in childhood. Their release evoked memories of humiliating circumstances in childhood which were followed by the tics.

Besides *physical* and *assumptive or phenomenal* space, we have to pay attention to the *quasi-theoretical* space of models. For example, Freud's model of personality functioning reinforces the dualistic conception of external and internal world. According to it, one interacts with one's environment, but at the same time, *inside* the self, interactions go on between ego, id and superego. Freud's model is persuasive and even when not accepted in detail has had a broad influence on generations of psychiatrists and psychologists. It is in line with traditional dualistic thinking. Its deficiencies have had unfavorable effects on the conceptualization of the therapeutic process as we will show later.

We are now going to deal with the crucial objects of the assumptive world—self-schema and group schema.

NOTES

6. The assumptive/phenomenal and Nash's behavioral world

As we discovered during the time when we were analysing the pitfalls of internal-external dichotomy, H. Nash (1959) was moving in a similar direction. After consulting leading theoreticians such as Tolman, Leeper and Heider, Nash introduced the concept of a behavioral world. We will use the former example of Al, who confuses a stranger in a crowd for his friend, Bill. In Nash's terminology, Bill is part of Al's behavioral world, even though he is not present physically. We conclude this from observing Al's behavior. As Nash says: "In the hope of adding to the observer's understanding of S's behavior, the behavioral world-hypothetical structure conceived as being external to the boundaries of S- was introduced." The *phenomenal* world—that is, the way the subject consciously perceives reality—is for Nash one variety of the behavioral world, "since self-report is one of the varieties of behavior on which inferences relating to the behavioral world are based." S's behavioral world may correspond more or less closely to his phenomenal world, or to the real world. After the author's excellent exposition of the concepts of the behavioral and phenomenal worlds, he introduces the concept of *internal psychological structure*, which, however, he does not analyze with the same care and so confuses the discussion. He asks: How are psychological structure and the behavioral world related to each other? After discussing Freud and Lewin, who seem to him to use both kinds of constructs, he says:

It appears, on the basis of this brief summary, that internal psychological structure

and the behavioral world differ somewhat, both in regard to the events of the real
world which they represent, and in regard to the manner in which they represent
these events. A categorical statement of the precise differences between these two
concepts would be premature, since these terms referring to either concept are too
frequently obscure or else vary in meaning from observer to observer. (1959)

It seems to us that if Nash had fully analyzed the internal psychological structure, it
would dissolve and what would be left would be the behavioral and phenomenal world
with their internal and external space.

We have chosen Cantril's term *assumptive world*, which covers the whole spectrum from
a world close to reality to those misperceived, hallucinated or delusional. It is important
to distinguish clearly *physical space* (which is a construction based on many intersensual
and interindividual experiences) and *phenomenal* (perceptual, imaginary) *space*. As we argued with the support of the philosophers of science (Schlick, Feigl, etc.), if we avoid the
confusion between *physical* space, *phenomenal* space and the *quasi-space* of models, we can
simplify the description of mental life and, free from the burden of conceptual confusions,
turn our attention to the fascinating unexplored areas of phenomenal spatiality.

7. Feigl versus Descartes

Sounds and smells at least in the usual situations of "veridical" perceptions seem to be
partly outside, partly inside the phenomenal head. . . . The taste of an apple is clearly
experienced within the mouth. The stars as seen on a cloudless night are tiny bright
spots on a fairly distant dark background. These bright spots clearly have spatial
relations to one another. . . . There is no question then that we are "acquainted" with
the elements and relations in visual space.

We conclude then that *mental* data have their own (phenomenal) kinds of spatiality;
and that *physical* space is a theoretical construction introduced to explain the features
and regularities of phenomenally spatial relations. The exact and detailed derivation,
even only of the perspectival aspects of visual spatiality is a quite complex matter,
involving geometrical, physical, psychophysical, and psychophysiological laws. Our argument has so far disproved only the Cartesian contention that the mental is non-
spatial. To put it very strongly, mental events as directly experienced and phenomenally described *are* spatial. (Feigl 1967)

These issues are important to the theory of psychotherapy, but there is a lack of clarity
about them among psychotherapists. As an example, we will quote Schafer (1976), a
psychoanalyst who, as a member of the organized movement of classical psychoanalysis,
deserves great merit for his penetrating conceptual analysis of Freudian theory. We will
have an opportunity to deal with some of the results of his inquiry later. Here, however,
we want to criticize his Cartesian position.

What exactly is thinking inside of? Where is a thought? We can locate neural structures,
glands, muscles, and chemicals in space, but where is dream, a self-reproach, an in-
troject? If one answers, "In the mind", one can be making a meaningful statement in
only one sense of mind, namely, mind as an abstraction that includes thinking among
its referents. In this sense, there is no question of spatial localization. To argue otherwise about "in the mind" is to be guilty of reification, that is, to be mistaking abstrac-
tions for things. For mind itself is not anywhere; logically, it is like liberty, truth, justice,

and beauty in having no extension or habitation, requiring none and tolerating none. It is pure abstraction. The boundaries of mind are those of a concept, not of a place. (1976)

We assume that Schafer is talking about the mind (or mental activity) of *one* person, as seems indicated by his questions Where is a thought, a dream, a self-reproach? The answers to these questions are that they are processes inside that person, in the person's brain. The sentence "The boundaries of mind are those of a concept, not of a place" is puzzling. The mind or mental activity of a certain person is a part of reality, distinct from the concept designating it. To put the "mind of a certain person" in the same category as liberty, truth, justice, and beauty is, from a logical point of view, a category mistake.

We will conclude this discussion of Feigl's views with his presentation of one last example.

Concepts which are constituents of singular (specific descriptive) statements are applied to individuals. We say "Anthony Eden felt depressed after the failure of the Egyptian campaign." In this case there is quite clearly a location for the feeling of depression. It is in the person concerned! The question of location becomes then more sensible, but logically also more delicate, if we ask it of individual mental states. (1967)

Chapter 4

SELF-SCHEMA

What we are in our eyes is largely determined by our assumptive
world.

H. Cantril

As the baby starts to develop its assumptive world, it learns to distinguish objects and among them an object with unique qualities, his or
her own organism. Hand in hand with the development of object constancies we talked about goes parallel development of *self-constancy* (Kilpatrick and Cantril 1961).

The child's assessment of reciprocal relationships between object-con-
stancies and self-constancy provides the basis both for goal directed
activities and for constructing an assumptive world.

People react to themselves as physical and social beings. Sometimes
the reactions are simple, as when I am observing my hand. But often
self-reactions are complex and the whole next chapter on the group
schema will deal with self-reactions which make a circuit through assumptive objects—role schemas.

It is easy to become entangled in such terms as *self, I, me*, or terms
with a theoretical flavor such as *ego* and *identity*. We will avoid all of
them, using self-schema (and occasionally the partial term Body Schema)
when we want to stress the spatial distribution of self-reactions. It is
instructive to study the growing confusion caused in psychoanalysis when

identity (Erikson) and *self* (Kohut) are added to *ego* as quasi-theoretical terms (see Schafer 1968, 1976). *Identity* has become a fashionable term used by North American patients, but when they complain about their identity or lack of identity, the informative value is minimal. When asked, there are dozens of different meanings that can be dug out: self-dissatisfaction, not knowing what to do, being depressed, feeling depersonalized or fed-up, not belonging to any group, etc. Logically, *identity* is a term of relation which should not be used unless it is stated what is identical with what. Schafer recognizes the term's vagueness and ambiguity as used by Erickson and thinks it contributes to conceptual confusion in psychoanalysis:

> Perhaps one comes close to the spirit of Erikson's conception by regarding identity formation as the subject's relatively successful struggle for integrated functional and experiential continuity in a changing biological, familial, cultural, and experiential past, present and future. The term best serves a large and highly impressionistic view of man. (1968)

Here, we will deal with self-reactions which form the basis of self-awareness using some of the ideas of Karl Jaspers (1963).
1. *Space identity*: I am approximately identical with the spatial region occupied by my body.
2. *Time identity*: I am the same person as yesterday or ten years ago.
3. *Unity*: I am one, not two or three.
4. *Activity*: When perceiving, thinking, feeling, moving, I am active.

To be sure that what we say has empirical meaning (and we have to be very cautious when talking about *self, me*, etc.), let us ask whether we can imagine that these qualities can be absent or distorted. This is really so in some disorders, such as brain damage, epilepsy, schizophrenia, or intoxication (LSD, mescalin, psilocybin, hashish, for example). In psychotherapy, we usually meet less conspicuous disturbances, such as depersonalization, which is not usually noticed by other people as a disturbance but which contributes to the impression made on them.

Subtle changes in self-awareness are important leads for psychotherapists and, as psychotherapy progresses, can become dramatic changes. Let us look at the patient's self-perception in space first.

Identity in space
Self-awareness starts as an awareness of one's body as opposed to the nonself. When a baby touches an object, it has one sensation; if it touches

its own body, it has two sensations. Gradually, it discovers that different movements of the body have different outcomes and that they can be chosen.

In time, the child learns to integrate sensations coming from different parts of the body into a unity or *body schema*. We prefer this term, originally used by Sir H. Head and Paul Schilder, to the usual term used in English—*body image*. As Schilder says, we are not dealing with mere sensation or image; there are also mental pictures and representations involved. The body schema—beside images and concepts formed during previous experience—is based on the influx of sensations from the surface of the body (exteroceptors), from organs of movement and posture (proprioceptors, vestibular apparatus), and from inner organs (interoceptors). Striking disturbances of body schema appear in fever (the head grows, the body shape is deformed), in a high-speed elevator, in dreams (one can participate in two persons, as an observer and as a participant), in falling or in awakening from general anesthesia, and in different intoxications (alcohol, and particularly LSD, mescalin, hashish, and psilocybin). Fleeting changes of body schema appear normally and are overlooked; they occur more often in neurotics and are then sometimes presented as complaints. Occasionally, dramatic changes of body schema take place during psychotherapy, which correlate with important improvements. Patients who feel that their bodies are chained and shrunken, grow, feel their bodies expand, and become free. This is often reflected in their overt behavior. Friends and relations usually comment about it spontaneously.

In schizophrenia there are more serious disturbances of body schema. Schilder reports on a woman who complained, "When the street cleaner used to sweep the street, I felt as if he was sweeping over my genitals. It felt as if he was tearing me. It was terrible pain. It made me shiver." Body schema is often disturbed in psychogenic malnutrition (anorexia nervosa). A patient, usually a young adult woman, looks like a skeleton and yet may feel herself to be obese—a condition which may have been true in her past.

To give an idea of the massive changes of body schema which can occur during hypnosis, autohypnosis, meditation, or psychoimaginative exercise, we shall quote the experience of a person hypnotized by J. H. Schultz.

I am lying in water, in deep water, but I can look out. Above me lies a lean body. I know how I am lying but my body is turned around at a right angle. There is a deep hole in my chest. Out of it comes a long neck like a goose-neck with a very small head. The trunk with the head turns itself out of the body. (Schilder 1950)

Although we do not pay much attention to it in daily life, body schema continuously changes. Body schema may not be confined exactly to the boundaries of the body. Sometimes one's clothes are included, a suit or dress. If one explores a surface with a long stick, especially in the dark, the boundaries of body schema shift to the end of the stick. A driver may include the car in the body schema and feel the boundaries of the car as his own. On the other hand, a pregnant woman may not assimilate the changed form of her body into her body schema and thus may bump into a half-opened door.

According to Schilder, every emotion changes body schema.

The body contracts when we hate, it becomes firmer, and its outlines towards the world are more strongly marked. . . . We expand the body when we feel friendly and loving. . . . The body image is surrounded by a sphere of particular sensitiveness. . . . We feel these zones especially when somebody else tries to come near us. We feel if somebody comes near us he is intruding in our body-image even when he is far from touching us. This emphasizes again that the body-image is a social phenomenon. (1950)

In the following observation, Schilder considers the way in which body schema can be used in empathy.

I press my fingers tightly against the pipe and have a clear-cut feeling of pressure in my fingers. When I look intently at the picture of my hand in the mirror I now feel clearly that the sensation of pressure is not only in my fingers in my own hand, but also in the hand which is twenty feet distant in the mirror.
There is a community between my picture, my image in the mirror, and myself. But are not my fellow human beings outside myself also a picture of myself? (1950)

This community of different people's body schemata is according to Schilder an important, if not basic, mechanism in empathy and identification. Transitory changes in body schema can take place after watching a movie when one takes over the playful freedom of an uninhibited hero. A similar change may happen after watching an expressive dancer or mime, or after listening to music (see note 8). We have had opportunities to observe in detail, both in the business and academic worlds, how a person in a leading position about to retire began to be unwittingly imitated in posture and voice by those who aspired to succeed him.

Social status even determines the behavior of animals: a high-ranking chimpanzee walks and behaves differently than a low-ranking one. The same phenomenon can be seen in people, and is reflected in their body schema. "When he talks to me, I feel small." Some patients describe vividly how they shrink in the presence of authorities, in fear or guilt. Some people may feel this way all the time, even when no authority is present—at least, no authority in the form of a real person, since what we shall call *authority schema* may be present all the time in imagination. That such feelings exist is apparent from their posture and movement and is confirmed by their dreams and fantasies and by such techniques as psychodrama, psychogymnastics, psychomime, and free painting. (Free painting, asking patients to make pictures of their world, can sometimes give good information about body schema.)

One female patient had had since puberty a habitual stoop, which she had originally developed to hide her breasts and femininity. In her body schema she did not feel her feminine attributes, and her psychomotility corresponded to that of the prepubertal child of indefinite sex. Although she was an occupational therapist, her movements were poorly coordinated, and when she danced, she jumped around like an eight-year-old child. This changed radically after her conflicting attitudes toward her parents—compliance and protest—were ventilated.

If we disregard the traditional dualistic mind/body language, there is little difference between the concepts of body schema and self-schema. When running in cold air, I can perceive pain in my chest, but I can also feel an impatient expectation of important news in my chest, though usually the location is less clear in the second case. The spatial location of feelings can be misinterpreted as a *physical* disease, for example, anxiety being a heart disease. Close study of the location of feelings and impulses and then dealing with them through guided imagery and physical exercises has great theoretical and practical importance in psychotherapy.

Identity in time

I know that I am the same person I was in the past, despite the changes which have occurred during my life.

Typically, many of us experience deep changes of feelings and attitudes during puberty, yet we have no doubts that our childhood memories belong to us. Even in most cases when patients complain that they have completely changed and that they no longer recognize themselves, it is clear to them that they are the same persons as before.

Since the reliving of traumatic experiences which the patient was unable to handle in the past is regarded as important by many psychotherapists, the conditions under which such reliving takes place are of great interest. Reliving of past traumata sometimes happens in the process of psychoanalysis, although usually only after long preparation. It can happen more dramatically in hypnosis or through the use of abreactive techniques (described later) in the wakeful patient. Past events are elicited with particular clarity in therapeutic LSD intoxication. S. Grof describes how a complex of memories with one theme and a strong emotional charge is often elicited in LSD. He calls such a complex a COEX system, that is, a system of condensed experience. The memories unfold one after another during several treatments. Grof's description is interesting, since similar complexes are elicited under different conditions, particularly with abreaction techniques.

Various layers of a particular system can, for example, constrain all memories of the past exposures of an individual to humiliating and degrading situations that have damaged his self-esteem. In other instances, the common element can be anxiety experience in regard to shocking and frightening events, claustrophobic and suffocating feelings evoked by various oppressive and restricting circumstances where there was no possibility of fighting back and defending oneself or escaping, as well as an intense sense of guilt and moral failure triggered by a number of specific situations. The experience of emotional deprivation and rejection of various periods of one's development is another common motif of many COEX constellations. Equally frequent are basic themes that depict sex as dangerous or disgusting, and those that involve aggression and violence. Particularly important are COEX systems that epitomize and condense the individual's encounters with situations endangering survival, health, and integrity of the body. The excessive emotional charge which is attached to COEX systems (as indicated by the often powerful abreaction accompanying the unfolding of these systems in LSD sessions) seems to be a summation of the emotions belonging to all the constituent memories of a particular kind.

In each individual case, similar traumatic events from various life periods seem to be recorded in the memory banks in close connection with the oldest experience of such a series, which thus constitutes the primary trauma. (1975)

In such travelling back in time, sometimes called regression, the body schema from the past is revived along with memories about the situation. Again, the examples from LSD are most straightforward.

One of the most important aspects of this regression is the body image always corresponds with the age into which the subject has regressed. Thus, the reliving of memories from early infancy typically involves feelings of disproportion between the size of the head and the rest of the body. Reliving memories from childhood with sexual undertone, subjects state with surprise that their penis appears to be ridiculously small, or they might experience themselves without pubic hair and with undeveloped breasts. (Grof 1975)

Perhaps the observations of Penfield and Jasper (1954) form an experimental parallel to the phenomena of regression mentioned. During a brain operation they electrically stimulated the right temporal cortex and elicited detailed memories which had a vividness approaching that of perceptions.

Awareness of Unity
I know that I am one, not two or three. Even if I am divided about some decision, that is, in a state of decisional conflict, I still know that I am single. Even a patient who has obsessive thoughts which shock him, knows that they are his ideas and blames himself for them.

The extent of self-awareness fluctuates all the time. When I am thinking I do not realize that I have arms or legs, or certain unrelated knowledge, but I can quickly become aware of them if the context demands it. Sometimes important information about oneself is not accessible to a subject. Patients may actively resist being aware of a conflict; all they complain about is tension or some neurotic symptom. Traditionally, we talk about *unconscious* contents. Patients claim to be unaware of them, are surprised when finding them out, and yet often later say that in a way they knew it all the time. We agree with Schafer (1976) that *unconscious* describes not a state but a mode of action.

A narrowing of the field of self-awareness can be wrought in a person by social pressure, as described in the chapter on influence, but the social pressure may come not only from real persons, but also from assumptive persons (see chapter 5).

We prefer to talk about changing the extent of self-awareness, instead of talking about different selves or subselves. This is mainly, however, a question of terminology and it is perhaps wise to postpone decision in a field where there are so many uncertainties. The observation of George Herbert Mead started an important trend of thinking:

> We carry on a whole series of different relationships to different people. We are one thing to one man and another thing to another. There are parts of the self which exist only for the self in relationship to itself. We divide ourselves up in all sorts of different selves with reference to our acquaintances. . . . A multiple personality is in a certain sense normal. . . . There is usually an organization of the whole self with reference to the community to which we belong and the situation in which we find ourselves. What the society is, whether we are living with people of the present, people of our imaginations, or people of the past, varies of course, with different individuals. (1964)

Mead was the most important predecessor of present attempts to understand individual behavior in a social context.

Awareness of activity

All experiencing—be it perceiving, thinking, or feeling—is to a different degree accompanied by awareness of one's own activity. But interaction with the environment—that is, causing changes in the environment which reflect back on the organism—is particularly important for self-awareness. The child could not even learn the distinction between self and nonself, without acting upon and causing changes in the environment which are relevant (rewarding or punishing) or irrelevant to that child. The child's self-awareness develops with making choices and decisions and by learning to what degree the environment can be influenced. The child learns that he or she is part of the causal network of the world and that he or she can cause things to happen. Gradually, it develops a personal view about the self as a causal agent. Patients coming for psychotherapy see themselves often unrealistically, having a distorted view about themselves as causal agents; they may exaggerate their capacities, but more often they exaggerate the causal importance of the environment. As mentioned earlier, some blame their social environment, not being aware of how they have contributed to their own adversities.

We are going to deal now with more complex self-reactions, such as self-esteem, self-criticism, self-reproach. They are more complex because they are closely connected with interaction with the social assumptive world, mainly with the *group schema*, as we will call it.

NOTE

8. Musical experience as interpersonal process

Sounds in their rhythmic, melodic, and dynamic aspects have considerable influence upon animals and human beings. For example, caged squirrels synchronize their stereotyped jumping with metronome frequencies (Kneutgen 1964). Different frequencies influence the rhythm of breathing in many species from fish to man. The human heartbeat and those of other species studied can be altered by changing rhythms. The singing of birds has multiple functions in social communication and is innate in some species and partly innate, partly learned in others.

Before the relatively late emergence of language, the musical qualities of sounds probably played a prominent role in the communication of our ancestors. In primitive cultures, songs have important group-integrative functions (battle songs, hunting songs, laments) or coordinate dyadic interpersonal processes (love songs or lullabies). The sound qualities of language play an important role in influencing people, as is well known by actors, politicians, teachers, and clergymen. Improvement of interpersonal relationships in psychotherapy is often accompanied by a changed sound quality in patient language.

Several studies on musical semantics found highly significant agreement among listeners as to the interpersonal meaning of music (Knobloch, Postolka et al. 1964; Knobloch, Juna et al. 1968). The interpersonal categories used were: affiliation, detachment, fight, flight, dominance, submission, exhibition, and sympathy (care, pity) soliciting. Our underlying hypothesis was that music is capable of inducing a state which, as does a dream, activates interpersonal processes in one's group schema and satisfies some interpersonal needs in fantasy. This conception forms the tentative basis for our use of music as part of integrated psychotherapy.

Chapter 5

GROUP SCHEMA

Even the emotion of the lonely person is an emotion directed to an
imaginary onlooker. . . . Similarly, thinking is a social function even
in the lonely person.

                                                                    Paul Schilder

In fact no individual, however isolated in time and space, should be
regarded as outside a group or lacking in active manifestation of
group psychology.

                                                                    Wilfred R. Bion

   The assumptive world of a patient is too large for us to be able to
explicate in full theoretically. Its essential part for the purposes of psychotherapy, we call *group schema*. Although the concept may be new, it
is based on the findings of psychoanalysis, of both classical and cultural
orientation, and is a link to the social psychology and social learning
orientations. Its advantages over other models will, we hope, become
gradually clear.

   The *group schema* is a general group model a person has developed
on the basis of assumptions about groups from past experience. The
assumptive objects forming the group schema are *role schemas*. If we
enter a new group, role schemas influence our social perception. We
see people in different roles through the semitransparent masks of our

role schemas, so that what results are compounds of assumption and reality. For example, if an employee's male authority schema is rigid, he quickly interprets a new boss as malevolent and cruel, and unwittingly behaves in such a way that he drags out from the boss reactions which falsely confirm his assumptions about authorities.

The group schema is not just a cognitive map. It accompanies us wherever we go. We interact with role schemas in fantasy where they become vivid in dreams, daydreams, and hallucinations. They are around us, in external assumptive (phenomenal) space.

ROLE SCHEMAS

Social psychologists have noticed that roles in different groups are similar. Thibaut and Kelley state:

> Similar roles occur in quite different groups. For example, the role of a disciplinarian associated with the father in the family is also related to the company commander in the army or the foreman in a factory. Indeed, there may be a finite list of different roles by which we could characterize most or all roles in all groups. (1959)

Our psychotherapeutic experience is in agreement with Thibaut and Kelley. The following role schemas seem to be sufficient for a description of group schema: *Self-schema, male and female authority schema* (father schema, mother schema), *male and female peer schema* (brother schema, sister schema), *male and female subordinate schema, sexual partner schema*. We use the following schematic picture and try to fill it in for each patient:

Group schema is composed of typical role schemas

Let us enumerate the persons usually found in a particular group schema.

Male Authority Schema (Father Schema): Father; teacher; boss; army commander; physician; and, for some people, any man in an official role (policeman, customs official, etc.); God, in the Judeo-Christian religion

Female Authority Schema (Mother Schema): Mother; teacher; physician; nurse; supraordinate in a job; and other functions corresponding to those of the male authority schema; also, religious

Male Authority Schema	Female Authority Schema

Male Peer Schema		Male Sex Partner Schema
Female Peer Schema		Female Sex Partner Schema

Male Subordinate Schema	Female Subordinate Schema

figures, such as the Virgin Mary and other female saints for Catholics and goddesses in other religions

Peer Schema (Brother Schema, Sister Schema): Siblings; schoolmates; colleagues; other patients of both sexes in group therapy; and the imaginary companions of children

Subordinate Schema: For an adult, children and professional subordinates; for a child, younger siblings, pets, and dolls

Sex Partner Schema: Persons of the opposite sex for the majority; of the same sex, or of both sexes, for a minority; and persons of the same sex potentially for perhaps most people

The role schemas are heavily biased by our childhood experiences.

A male patient had a violent alcoholic father whom he never talked about in group psychotherapy. However, he often discussed his boss, toward whom he was unusually submissive. Although he felt he was unjustly treated and stewed about this, he was not able to protest. The fear he had about his boss was not realistic, but the patient had a very real fear of his father, who, during the patient's childhood, had killed a neighbor when drunk. The boss sensed that the patient disliked him and, accordingly, came to dislike the patient, and was probably as unjust to him as the patient anticipated he would be (self-fulfilling prophecy). The patient was just as submissive toward his therapist as he was toward his boss.

Finally, he started to talk about his father and his childhood and to feel an irrational rage toward the therapist, which he hid. On his way to the next group session, he ran into a policeman at a Prague crossing with his motorcycle and excused himself by stating: "Excuse me, Doctor!"

Additional material showed clearly that his male authority schema was heavily biased by his father and that his boss, therapist, and the policeman all belonged to that role schema. (For this substitution of one person for another, if maladaptive, we will use the psychoanalytic term *transference*.)

A new female patient reacted with alarm to every gesture of a male therapist. It became clear that her father had misused her sexually in puberty and that consequently she did not expect anything good from a man. She hung the mask of the father schema not only on every male authority, but on *all men*.

The role schemas of our assumptive world appear especially vividly in our dreams. In dreams, we see people, talk to them, and they talk to us. Haven't you ever been astonished by what resources we have, that we can stage in our dreams so clearly and vividly people who talk and act so naturally? As we will see later, psychodrama is another way to show, in a waking state, what vast resources we have for knowing people and being able to take their roles. Our daydreams and fragments of fantasy also deal with people, and although we see them less clearly than in dreams or hallucinations and our conversations with them are more fragmentary, they are lively enough to influence our thinking, emotions, and sometimes even such body processes as heartbeat, blood pressure, or tumescence.

We must remember that the people we imagine are in external assumptive (phenomenal) space. We imagine them as being outside ourselves, not in our heads, although our language leads us sometimes to suggest the opposite.

Let us now enumerate three main functions of the group schema: It functions as a cognitive map, as a model for social training, and as a system of substitute rewards and costs.

GROUP SCHEMA

A cognitive map

Group Schema is a *cognitive map* of groups, and it organizes the expectations of a person when he enters a new group or meets new individuals. This is a great help to the subject if the group schema supports a fairly good perception of reality. But if the group schema is biased and inflexible, the expectations often become self-fulfilling prophecies, as in the example or our male patient who sees his boss in a distorted way. Let us suppose that there is another man who had a similar father, but who partly managed to modify his male authority schema. He still may have a dream where he confuses his boss with his father, but this confusion is barely apparent in his manifest behavior toward his boss. His father schema is more flexible and does not lead to a serious misperception of his boss.

A model for social training

Group Schema is a model for rehearsing, training, and problem-solving. As a child uses dolls and real or stuffed animals for training in social skills (talking to them, reprimanding them, and role-playing with them), so we use our group schema, going through sequences of interactions with imagined persons. We interact with them and receive imaginary feedback from them. Many of our self-reactions—that is, when we react to ourselves as social objects—make a circuit through a role schema in external phenomenal space, before they boomerang back. This is also how we see moral deliberations and moral conflicts, as we will soon explain.

A reward-cost system

The third function of Group Schema is to provide us with a system of substitute rewards and costs. Imagined and anticipated rewards are also real rewards, though of a special kind. We all need them to compensate for a lack of rewards in hard times, when a difficult task is not rewarding at present, when we do not get the approval we think we deserve, and so forth. These rewards give stability to behavior. We even tend to believe, from our own observations in a German concentration camp, that in situations of extreme deprivation, the resources in the

group schema make the difference in whether people can survive or
not. Under difficult conditions, some people manage to add the rewards
coming from the group schema with real rewards to keep their mental
balance and optimism.

A Group Schema can also, however, be a serious obstacle to adaptation
in life. It may supply rewards which a person should receive from real
groups, and the person may thus miss important life opportunities. Or
a group schema may represent anachronistic norms, for example, sexual
prohibitions formulated by parents in childhood, but which are still
enforced by the parent schemas. It may involve a person in chronic
moral conflicts, for example, the father schema may duplicate the de-
vious moral tactics of the father not in agreement with the morality of
the mother schema.

We introduced earlier the notion of group activity as a multiple exchange of rewards and costs. However, this would leave gaps if limited
to the rewards and costs exchanged with real people in the present, to
the exclusion of the rewards and costs exchanged with role schemas.
The role schema can reward or punish, creating a feeling of self-satisfaction or guilt. For example, a child might do something which it would
enjoy tremendously, if it were not for the idea that its father would
disapprove. On the other hand, people may make great sacrifices in
order to help others, but they are rewarded by their group schema.
Hans Selye (1956) has suggested that nothing so powerfully contributes
to human happiness and health as one's habitual tendency to generate
satisfaction and gratitude in others. But the reward is not only the gratitude of real people but also approval from the group schema.

Tension between the patient and his parent schema usually leads to
unpleasant feelings, depression, or fear, even if the parent in question
is not alive. Improvement in the relationship to the parent schema is
usually a by-product of successful psychotherapy.

MORAL STANDARDS AND NORM CONFLICTS

When children gradually establish their group schemas, their behavior and even their thoughts are watched, even when no one else is
present. The three functions of the group schema—as cognitive map,
as rehearsal of behavior, and as distributor of imagined and anticipated
rewards and costs—are apparent in moral behavior. Children often try
out a forbidden act in fantasy and then scold themselves loudly as their
parents would do. Trial acting can be seen particularly clearly in some

pairs of dreams, described by psychoanalysts, where the first dream satisfies a forbidden wish and the second dream punishes it. Moral development in children can be understood as the development and stabilization of the group schema, which becomes gradually less dependent upon the presence of real persons.

The functioning of conscience and guilt feelings can be understood as relations with different role schemas. There is conscience related to authority roles, and conscience related to peer roles. Parents know well how children can react with fear and guilt feelings if the parents ask them to do something against the norms of their peer group. School-age children often find it easier to bear the anger and rejection of a teacher than to experience rejection and ostracism by their peer group for breaking solidarity. The group-schema model makes it possible to understand these different kinds of self-dependencies on different Role Schemas, resulting in different and sometimes conflicting kinds of morality. There may be conflict between morality as related to the father schema and mother schema. And there are considerable differences in moral pressures from authority, peer, and sex partner schemas. Some people like to seek the company of people who would alleviate these pressures. For example, some married men and women, from time to time, like to meet exclusively with peers of the same sex, in order to alleviate the moral pressure of the sex partner schema—a kind of vacation from marital morals, if not in deeds, then at least in talk and jokes.

As is apparent, different kinds of conscience can be described in terms of social pressures from different role schemas. This factor provides the group-schema model with an important advantage over Freud's psychoanalytic model in which the superego is mainly patriarchal (see Schafer 1976). In fact there are many unsolved problems arising from the study of moral development which can be better conceptualized by the group-schema model than by Freud's.

Problems in the theory of moral development are well-summarized in M. Hoffman (1970). The guiding concept of the research in this field has been that of *internalization*. In this regard, Bandura has criticized the concept of the "internalization of socially sanctioned prohibitions and mandates":

It is appropriate to question what, if anything, is internalized in the organism. It is perhaps misleading to talk of behavior being internalized since, after response patterns have been acquired, it is doubtful that they can undergo any further interiorization. The major issues, however, are less concerned with the locus of behavior than with the nature of its controlling conditions. (1969)

Bandura and Walters, among others quoted by Hoffman (1970), criticize the internalization concept and note that moral standards may merely reflect the norms of an absent referent group or individual. These are similar ideas to the group-schema concept which is primarily based on the study of adult neurotics and their conflicts. We do not deny that processes described later—such as identification—may play an important role in moral development and conflict. It is hoped that the group-schema model will help to create conditions for detailed phenomenological studies, which have been obstructed by a confusion of physical, phenomenal, and quasi-theoretical space.

NEUROTIC CONFLICTS AND DEFENSE TECHNIQUES

The symptoms of psychiatric patients, particularly neurotics, can often be traced back to chronic, unresolved predecisional and postdecisional moral (norm) conflicts in the group schema. Predecisional conflicts are discussions in the Group Schema of whether or not to take a certain kind of action. Postdecisional conflicts are discussions of how to justify actions which have already occurred or which have been omitted.

The defense mechanisms described by psychoanalysis will be understood here as interpersonal group-schema techniques, which, of course, are closely connected with interpersonal techniques in real groups. For example, the massive repressions of hysterical patients will be understood as interpersonal group-schema techniques which are often associated with lying in real groups.

The defensive techniques are security operations; they help to protect self-esteem and avoid conflict and guilt by decreasing the pressure in the group schema. They are often designed to deceive the role schemas; in other words, they are self-deceptive techniques. The self-deception is often skillfully combined with the deception of others. The group-schema model points out the similarity of interpersonal techniques one uses in fantasy (in one's group schema) and with real people.

In his important work, Mowrer (1964) stressed the function of neurosis as a strategy to avoid guilt feelings. His explanation is probably correct in many cases; in psychotherapy, the acknowledgment of guilt to a group of people and the harmonizing of one's acts with one's conscience—that is, with group schema—is a powerful and unavoidable part of treatment. However, Mowrer does not seem to deal with cases where the norms are anachronistic, as in those of sexual inhibitions in adulthood based on norms of childhood. We agree with many psychotherapists who see other factors, particularly fear, as mobilizing defensive techniques. For example, Guntrip (1969) takes issue with Mowrer that guilt is "the core of psychological distress," pointing out the importance of fear and the complex motivation of pathological guilt.

TRAVELING IN ONE'S GROUP SCHEMA

Complementarity and identification

A real group is a system of complementary roles. A little boy learns his *complementary* role to that of his father. But to learn it well, it helps to be partly able to take the role of the other, that is, of his father (G. H. Mead 1964). The usefulness of being able to take the role of another can be appreciated by considering tennis or chess players who anticipate what the opponent will do.

A little boy plays a complementary role to his father and to a degree *identifies* with him. Usually he identifies more with his father than with his mother and is supported in this identification, to a degree, by society. Society prepares its members for their future roles by offering models for identification and training in play and games. We are sometimes struck by how the phrases or questions we use with our children are similar to those of our parents when we were children. And perhaps we sometimes discover that as psychotherapists, we imitate our training psychotherapists, even after years of practical experience.

We are in a complementary relationship to our role schemas, but we can also identify with each of them, though with varying ease. Psychodrama shows how surprisingly extensive the capacity to identify with different roles is.

Transference

In complementary relationships to real persons, we use our group schema as the resource for our social skills. If this leads to serious misperceptions, it is what Freud called *transference*. Here let us use a simple definition of the term *transference* by the psychoanalyst R. Schafer:

> Transference involves the inappropriate repetition in a current relationship of previous, actual or fantasied interpersonal experience. (1967)

The clearest development of transference can be studied in classical psychoanalytic treatment. With minimal social feedback, with the therapist being out of sight and rarely reacting, the patient uses a role schema—most often the mother or father schema—and receives imagined feedback. After some time, the patient has a distorted picture of the therapist in terms of his group schema, and this discrepancy from reality can be demonstrated to him. If a patient feels in one session that the therapist is angry and in the next session that the therapist is friendly, without the therapist having said a word, it can be demonstrated that the patient misperceives the situation, especially if it can be shown that it fits into the content of his associations.

Although the peculiarities can best be studied in psychoanalytic treatment, the study of transference is important in any treatment and, in group psychotherapy, can be traced in relation to patients. Transferences—that is, inappropriate hanging of role schemas on the persons in one's environment—are a part of daily life, which usually escape our attention. If, however, we have an opportunity to analyze, for example, the dreams and fantasies of a male patient, we may discover that his relationship to his daughter is influenced by his sister schema and mother schema. Or if a mother is jealous of her daughter, we may discover that her jealousy is partly the result of the transference from her sister. As documented by H. E. Richter (1971), to the parent, a child may be the substitute for

1. one of the parents
2. a sibling
3. the spouse
4. a combination

The social-psychological concept of *prescribed role* becomes complex if we try to specify by whom it is prescribed and expected. The parents may have expectations about their children which they do not admit even to themselves. For example, there may be a general consensus about the role of the daughter, which is accepted by both her parents. But the father may have transference fantasies about his daughter—seeing her partly as his sister, mother, and lover—which he does not acknowledge. Nonetheless, the daughter may react to his fantasies as communicated by nonverbal cues, and this may influence not only her role as a daughter, but her role as a woman. Richter gives a grotesque example of a mother's transference attitude. She was accusing her one-year-old daughter of frustrating her out of spite, just as her mother had. Apparently, her mother schema was ever-present.

Self-projection

Another kind of activity of the group schema is attributing some characteristics of self-schema to somebody else. We will call it *Self-projection*; it is also called *narcissistic projection* or *projective identification* by different groups of psychoanalysts. According to Freud's distinction (without necessarily accepting his framework about narcissism), one is disposed to see in the other person

1. What oneself is
2. What oneself was
3. What oneself would like to be

As Richter (1971) shows, this can be demonstrated particularly easily in parents' relationships to their children. What oneself would like to be is often an ideal of self. The parents press the child to be a continuation of themselves and what they wish to be, for example, to study what they were unable, or too lazy, to study. But "to be what oneself would like to be" can also be a realization of something forbidden, what one has not dared to do. This is sometimes a factor in children's delinquency; the parent unwittingly supports prohibited acts in the child which he or she would not dare to do.

A female patient of ours was conspicuous by her seemingly very seductive behavior, yet she had not had any sexual life with her husband or anyone else for sixteen years. She was closely supervising her growing daughter, giving away, in her colorful suspicions, her own sexual fantasies. Growing up in this atmosphere, the daughter became pregnant when she was fifteen. The patient was shocked, but immediately reacted with an extramarital relationship: "If she can have it, although so young, then I can have it too."

Sometimes the child is a *scapegoat*, a projected negative self. That one's sins can be compensated for by punishing somebody else, is part of many old religions. *Scapegoat* is a concept from the Old Testament of the Bible (Leviticus 16:15 and 22): "He shall then slaughter the people's goat as a sin-offering, [and] The goat shall carry all their iniquities upon itself into some barren waste. . . ." The idea plays a basic role also in the Christian religion.

It is useful to distinguish between the function of scapegoat as self-projection (a shifting of one's own guilt to somebody else, just as our patient who, in suspecting her daughter, was realizing her own fantasies) and the function of *whipping boy*—the recipient of a displaced or redirected reaction from one object to another. For example, a female patient is jealous of her daughter, just as she was of her sister. (In this particular case it is also a transference reaction.)

GROUP SCHEMA VERSUS OTHER MODELS

H. S. Sullivan

We will now elucidate the group schema model by comparing it to some other models. We find ourselves in agreement with H. Stack Sullivan, one of the few thinkers who overcame the visual dualistic model of mental life. For example:

> Personality is . . . a function of the kinds of interpersonal situations a person integrates with others, whether real persons or fantastic personifications. (1953)

> Psychiatry is the study of phenomena that occur in interpersonal situations, in configurations made up of two or more people all but one of whom may be more or less completely illusory. (1964)

Apparently in his visual model he saw the "fantastic personifications" in the same external phenomenal space where real persons are. However, he did not explain his concept clearly, and misunderstandings ensued. Let us deal with the misunderstandings of Sullivan's position, since it will help to better understand group schema. Arieti criticizes Sullivan in the following way:

> The fundamental weakness of Sullivan's theoretical position is in his basic premise that psychiatry is the science of interpersonal relations. Although adding the gigantic dimension of the interpersonal is an enormous contribution, it should not entail the neglect of other dimensions. To try to explain everything psychological from an exclusively interpersonal point of view is a reductionistic approach. . . . Every interpersonal phenomenon is coupled with an intrapsychic one. The intrapsychic counterpart is at least as important as the interpersonal. . . . The areas that Sullivan has clarified must be

integrated with the study of the intrapsychic. . . . We must now integrate the inner self with what originates from the interpersonal—the subjective with the objective. (1967)

Mullahy defends Sullivan in the following way:

Like so many others, Arieti makes the mistake of thinking that intrapsychic process can be divorced from overt interpersonal relations. Sullivan did include "intrapsychic" in his theory of interpersonal relations. He thought that the subjective and objective are closely intertwined in various subtle ways. (1968)

Mullahy, however, does not give a full explanation either in his reply to Arieti, or in his book (1970). Discussions such as these usually reach an impasse—unnecessarily so, as we will show. Since the concepts *interpersonal, intrapsychic, inner self, objective,* and *subjective* are not explained, we have no way of knowing whether Arieti and Mullahy express different opinions about facts, that is, whether mental life would be different if either one were correct or whether they are only revealing their preference for different linguistic frameworks. We will show that the latter case is the more likely, that controversy results from different understandings of the same terms because Arieti and Mullahy refer to different visual models.

Arieti is apparently concerned that in concentrating on interpersonal relations, something is omitted—the intrapsychic world. His visual model is dualistic; the activities are going both between the person and environment and inside the person's intrapsychic self. But what is the referent of the *intrapsychic processes?* Thinking, imagination, and fantasy are, to a large degree, interactions with objects in fantasy. In the assumptive (phenomenal) space of the person, these objects of fantasy are *outside.* The actual duality is between acting in reality (perception, overt behavior) and acting in fantasy. However, the dichotomy is not sharp, since imaginary elements enter into perception and the choice of action. If we accept *intrapsychic process* as a way of speaking, meaning *interpersonal process in fantasy,* the difference between the views of Arieti and Mullahy disappears.

The imagined persons are localized *outside* in the assumptive (phenomenal) world of a person, but the process of imagination is, of course, inside the head of the person (note 9).

The psychoanalytic model

It is obvious that group schema is suggested here as an alternative to Freud's structural model of mental life. The differences have been explained and three will be expanded.

Assumptive space. The disadvantage of the group-schema model is that we are not used to thinking theoretically in terms of a person's internal and external assumptive space, particularly to visualizing the imagined persons *outside* the subject, although we do it all the time in daily life. This is especially hard on psychoanalysts who are used to visualizing the interaction of id, ego and superego *inside* the person. However, by rejecting Freud's quasi-theoretical spatial model, we can start to explore the internal and external assumptive space of the patient for important cues about self-schema and role schemas. The persuasiveness of the psychoanalytic model has severely inhibited such studies, since assumptive (phenomenal) space became confused with the quasi-theoretical space of Freud's structural model. We further found that many psychotherapists and even behavior therapists, although not psychoanalytically oriented, use visually dualistic models, probably because of the soul-body tradition anchored in language and the indirect influence of psychoanalysis.

In our attempts at conceptual clarification, unexpected support comes from a psychoanalyst, publishing in most respected publications of orthodox psychoanalysis, R. Schafer. Schafer's (1968, 1976) concern has been conceptual confusion in psychoanalysis, particularly in spatial characteristics. He distinguishes carefully the location in subjective (or what we call assumptive or phenomenal) space:

> As boundary between inside and outside develops, objects may be located primarily inside, outside, inside and outside, or their location may be unspecified or indeterminate.

He complains about psychoanalysts who talk about introjection, without documenting that the patient feels the fantasied person inside his body (which may, of course, happen, particularly with schizophrenics). According to his definition of internalization,

> . . . "inner" indicates that the subject locates the previously external regulatory agent within some self boundary. (1968)

Schafer rejects Loewald's additional criterion that interpersonal relationships become *inner* only after they lose ties with their original external object and evolve into truly *inner* impersonalized structures. Schafer rightly says,

> It would be hard to prove analytically the complete disappearance of the fantasy of continued interpersonal relationship. (1968)

We agree and regard this—without prejudging detailed phenomenal studies—as support for the group-schema concept, placing role schemas *outside*, around the subject.

Although Schafer wrote a book on internalization (1968), in continuing his iconoclastic development (1976) he has rejected the concepts of *internalization, introjection, instinctual drives, psychic energy, force*, and even *psychodynamics*. Our similar development in the past was one of the sources leading to the conceptual framework of this book.

It would lead us too far to go into all the difficulties from which the structural model of Freud suffers, even when modified by Hartmann and others. Schafer's book (1976) draws attention to some of them. Schafer also expresses reservations about the concepts of *identity* (Erikson) and *self* (Kohut). These terms cut across psychoanalytic terms such as *ego*, and introduce "a second kind of theory without discarding the first." We agree with Schafer's criticism and see this as symptomatic of the insoluble difficulties of the psychoanalytic structural model (note 10).

The group-schema model does not have similar difficulties. However, like all other models, it has not been studied as thoroughly as the psychoanalytic model.

Real persons and corresponding role schemas influence each other. Role schemas are images and expectancies; they contribute to perceptions and interpersonal actions. The real persons potentially help to confirm or disconfirm these images and expectations. For a psychotherapist it is of the utmost importance to understand the interconnection and two-way traffic between the group schema and real persons. A psychoanalyst visualizing the intrapsychic interactions of the id, ego and superego as separate from, and going on in a place other than, the patient's interaction with real people easily overlooks the social stimuli which keep the role schemas in existence. This is the "autonomous man" inside us, which B. F. Skinner rightly criticizes, though he goes to the other extreme of overestimating environmental stimuli. It is true, however, that psychoanalysts in practice often neglect to follow causal circuits between the patient and the environment—a practice which must lead to limited therapeutic efficiency.

In our model, self-schema is part of the group schema. Self-reactions such as self-esteem, self-deception, and Horney's self-idealization and related self-hate are complex processes in the group schema. But the processes in group schema are fused constantly with present processes in the patient's *real* groups. Although the real relationships are the starting point, psychotherapy often leads to exploring the past group schema of the person which contains traumatic memories of fear, humiliation, and rejection.

Testing Hypotheses. Whereas it is difficult to think of how to test hypotheses about a patient's id, ego, and superego, it is possible to test the qualities and relations of role schemas. For example, a comparison in psychodrama can show the degree of complementation and identification with certain persons, such as with a mother. For example, a female patient, a highly unarticulate and unexpressive girl who would not talk above a whisper and whose breathing was disturbed when talking, immediately started to shout angrily when asked to play the role of her mother. Psychodrama, nonverbal exercises, and guided imagery showed the degree of her identification with her mother—an identification which was, however, blocked by her fear of expressing anger toward her mother. If it is true that the change of group schema is important in psychotherapy, confirmation and testing of our hypotheses about the patient's group schema is of the utmost importance both for the analysis of an individual case, and for theoretical progress.

The dualistic model of social psychologists

The advantage of the group-schema model is that there is one model instead of two. Since dealing with people in fantasy imitates the interpersonal processes in reality, though sometimes in a distorted manner, just *one* model describing the structure and dynamics of a social group is sufficient. People are in imagined social exchanges with their role schemas and are rewarded or punished for following or breaking the norms. All concepts describing social groups can be applied to group schema.

It is interesting to note that dualistic thinking is an obstacle to a unified model not only for psychoanalysts but also for social psychologists. Peter Blau, one of the main representatives of social exchange theory, warns,

> Not all human behavior is guided by consideration of exchange. ... Excluded from consideration ... is behavior resulting from the irrational push of emotional forces without being goal oriented, for instance a girl's irrational conduct on dates that is motivated by her unconscious conflicts with her father. (1964)

The reader who by now understands the concept of group schema will likely object that the girl's irrational behavior is guided by a fantasy exchange with her father. If she wants to rebel against her father (and we know from clinical experience that sometimes it does not even matter whether or not the father is alive), she *is* guided by consideration of exchange, her reward is her punishing her father in fantasy. Her conduct on dates is guided by the *combined* rewards and costs in both her real group and group schema. If we do not include the exchange with the father in fantasy, there are gaps in the explanation of her behavior; it seems irrational. Social psychologists will find such gaps all the time, unless they are willing to take into account the social exchange with group schema figures (note 11). Their objection may be that they want to keep to what is strictly observable in behavior. Social psychology, however, retreated from that position, deeming it untenable, when the concept of *reference group* was introduced. Contrast Hollander's discussion of this concept with Shibutoni's:

> While it was common in the past to consider individuals to be directly affected by groups to which they belonged, it was found that this did not account for many variations of effect. (Hollander 1971)

> Any group known to a person that he takes as a standard of comparison or judgment—whether it is a membership group for him or not—influences his psychological field. (Shibutani 1955)

Obviously, *group schema* and *reference group* are related concepts, though derived from different experience. Patients may sometimes not be aware at all about the influence their group schema has upon them; they may even deny it. When asked, a patient may say he does not have *any* relationship with his father, and yet a significant amount of his behavior is determined by his exchange in fantasy with his father schema.

Berne's transactional model
Berne's useful description of *games* as fraudulent transactions was mentioned earlier. The term *game* should be, however, kept for a much broader field; the theory of games promises to be an important part of psychology. Berne's model is so simple that it would be convenient to use it. It also has the advantage that relationships (transactions) can be easily described in the model. Holland (1973) regards ego states as phenomenological realities, amenable to direct observation, whereas id, ego, and superego are theoretical constructs, inferred entities. R. Carson (1969) says the opposite; too frequently Berne's concepts have merely metaphorical relationship to observable behavioral events. Unfortu-

nately, he is right; we agree with Carson. We are asked to accept simplifications (for example, an Adult functions as a computer, or adult
sexual play is an activity of the Child) which, as with the psychoanalytic
model, close the door to further unbiased phenomenal explorations.
Such simplifications often become part of the patient's resistances, which
enable him to easily escape with ready-made formulas and avoid unpleasant confrontations. The richness of Berne's observations, however,
and some previously mentioned advantages of his model make us believe that the models of the future will contain some features of his
model.

Behaviorism

The behavioral sciences decried explanations of behavior in terms of
inner factors. At the beginning of this century, each piece of animal
behavior was explained by introducing a new instinct: Why is the animal
digging? Because of the digging instinct. Skinner particularly warns
against this tendency of explanation by duplication or hypostasis, or as
he calls it, explanation by means of *inner man, autonomous man, homunculus*, or the *possessing demon*. Arguing against the charge that he abol-
ishes man, Skinner states:

> What is being abolished is autonomous man—inner man, the ho-
> munculus, the possessing demon. . . . His abolition has long been
> overdue. Autonomous man is a device used to explain what we cannot
> explain in any other way. He has been constructed from our igno-
> rance. . . . Science does not dehumanize man, it de-homunculizes him.
> (1971)

Skinner (Evans 1968) also regards the psychoanalytic id, ego, superego, and their violent conflicts, as "versions of some sort of primitive
animism." This is partly recognized by psychoanalysts when they criticize
opponent schools; so Freudians talk about "Kleinian demonology." Psychoanalyst Schafer (1968) admits it is even a common problem in psychoanalysis. Indeed, inner structures such as id, ego, and superego, even
self and identity, offer themselves to homunculus interpretation in the
visually persuasive psychoanalytic model.

Skinner's warnings against duplications are important, as we all tend
to lean naturally toward this kind of pseudoexplanation. But Skinner's
fear goes too far when he rejects even a computer model and sees duplication there also:

[The] computer is a bad model. . . . The assumption of a parallel inner record-keeping process adds nothing to our understanding of
this kind of thinking. (1974)

Mahoney (1974) criticizes Skinner and defends the use of a computer
as a model of mental functioning, denying that an homunculus interpretation would necessarily be involved. He also takes issue with Skinner's equating mediational models, cognitive psychology, and information
theory with mentalistic perspectives. But Mahoney is well aware, as we
are, of how easily the homunculus metaphors creep into our models.
What about the group schema? It seems to us that a psychology in
terms of objects, describing carefully the observations about location of
real and imagined objects in assumptive space, can help in avoiding
homunculus explanations. We are avoiding the hopeless confusion which
stems from visualizing things happening in the inner world and after
a while mixing it with the neurophysiological ideas and pseudospatial
relations of intrapsychic models. Our starting points are observational
statements, both behavioral and self-reported. For example, nobody can
doubt that you are able, with closed eyes, to imagine pieces of furniture
in your room, that is, in your external phenomenal space, and that you
can even solve, in imagination, the problem of how to rearrange them.
Although more elaborate, group schema is a similar system of images
portraying people, including yourself, in certain roles. To explain the
model function of the group schema more clearly, let us suppose that
our task is to predict the location of a traveler in the country. We know
his destination, we have a good map of the country, and we know his
partly distorted map, his group schema. Our task is to predict how he
will deal with the discrepancies between his group-schema map and
reality. We are still in the realm of observable interactions between individual and environment, not in the realm of speculative intrapsychic
processes. The group schema is the result of social learning and it can
be changed by social relearning and new learning, which is the focus of
psychotherapy. You may have noticed how carefully we dealt with the
concept of self-schema—you and your self-reactions to yourself as a
physical and social object. We had no need to introduce such further
concepts as *I*, *me*, or *ego*. It is inconvenient that the group-schema model
necessitates changing traditional ways of thinking, but in return we
achieve a considerable parsimony of concepts and descriptions and avoid
homunculus pitfalls.
Franks and Wilson (1974) said that there can never be philosophical

unity between behavioral and psychodynamic schools. It seems to us that the concept of group schema points in the direction of philosophical unification. If this is surprising, let us remember that statements about group schema can be tested by the observation of behavior, both in artificial (psychodramatic and psychomimic) and in real situations (note 15).

NOTES

9. Guntrip versus H. S. Sullivan

To show how difficult it is for psychoanalysts, because of their visual models, to understand Sullivan's position, we will quote Guntrip, who reacts to Sullivan's ideas in the following way:

> We are almost on the verge of object-relations here. If Sullivan's "fantastic personifications" were recognized more fundamentally as Melanie Klein's "internal psychic objects"; and if the theory of impulses as cohering in "dynamisms" or "relatively enduring configurations of energy" were seen to imply Fairbairn's theory of impulses as reactions of dynamic ego-structures to objects, internal as well as external; then Sullivan would have transcended the purely "cultural pattern" type of theory. . . .

> But it is inadequate to speak of these inner figures simply as "fantasies" or as "nonexistent products of imagination". It is only from an outer and rationalistic point of view that they can be so described. Psychologically considered they have psychic reality, they have actual and continuing existence as persisting structural aspects of the total psyche. . . . They are the internal psychic objects which have become so important in British psychoanalytical developments, but which American analysts both of orthodox and the cultural schools have so far shown little evidence of understanding. (1961)

We are not concerned here with the question of whether there is some empirical material not well-covered in Sullivan's framework. We want only to show what importance Guntrip ascribes to *internal* location because of his dualistic predilection. He says further:

> The figures with whom we have relations in phantasies are called, appropriately by Melanie Klein, 'internal objects' because we behave with respect to them, emotionally and impulsively, in the same ways as we do towards externally real persons. (1961)

It is amazing that Guntrip insists in calling these objects *inner* because we behave toward them as toward *external* objects. Why not call them external, since they are probably most of the time in *external* assumptive (phenomenal) space? Here, a review of the observational material of Klein, Fairbairn and Guntrip would be interesting, since they seemed to be influenced in their localization by their intrapsychic spatial model. No doubt, in Guntrip's visual model, to localize the fantastic personifications as inner figure gives them more psychic reality.

10. Schafer's study of spatial concepts in psychoanalysis

Schafer's development as a psychoanalyst deeply loyal to Freud's central ideas is highly interesting. His uncompromising conceptual analysis has led him, as it did the present authors many years ago, to give up concepts blurring the empirical content of psycho-analysis. In 1968, he could still say: "Psychoanalytic theory being dynamic, it requires the concept of psychological force," and "Psychoanalysis being a dynamic psychology, it re-quires a concept of psychic energy." In 1975, however, he says,

> In discarding the term psychodynamics, we also disallow such closely related terms as instinctual drive, impulse, psychic energy, discharge, and resultant. And so we seem to be emptying the concept of the id of all its content. However . . . we can retain the important adverbial sense of id. . . . Specifically we can understand id to refer to a way of acting.

Schafer further tries to eliminate the quasi-theoretical spatiality of the psychoanalytic model when he says,

> Despite this spatialization of mind, when pressed for a strict metapsychological defi-nition of psychic structure, we do not resort to spatial metaphors. We refer instead to stability of modes of function, slow rates of change, resistiveness to regressive trans-formations, and the like . . . This is how we customarily speak of id, ego, and super-ego—as functions grouped together by the observer or theoretician. (1975)

In the same way, Schafer deals with the concept of *identification*. He says:

> Traditionally, however, psychoanalysts have assumed that identification goes on "in the inner world", gets established "there", and may transform its "internal" setting (e.g., in the case of superego identification). Once we dispense with the theoretical vocabulary of internality, however, we are able to speak about identification as a change in the way one conceives of oneself and perhaps a corresponding change in the way one behaves publicly; as before, the change would be modeled on personal and un-consciously elaborated versions of significant figures in real life or imaginative life (e.g., fictional or historical characters). (1975)

We see the merits of Schafer's criticism in showing how the pseudospatiality of common language and Freud's model interfere with empirical investigation of the patient's expe-rience. It is, however, not quite clear whether Schafer does not also discard phenomenal spatiality. It would be in line with his Cartesian notion that "mind itself is not anywhere" (see note 7). For example, he talks about "pseudospatial metaphors" in connection with "early notions of self strongly influenced by these archaic, concretistic factors. Self, too, is then thought of as being a place." It may, under appropriate conditions, be legitimate to talk about self as being a place, in terms of *phenomenal* space. For example, Schafer says:

> Additionally, dispensing with the idea of the inside, enables us to recognize that a woman, let us say, is not keeping ideas or feelings within her when she keeps them to herself, that is, remains silent about them. . . . "Private" is the key word. . . . "Private" is not just another word for "inner": it expresses an entirely different way of thinking about mental and other actions. (1975)

We have to be cautious to distinguish between linguistic and quasi-theoretical metaphor on the one side, and phenomenal description of experience on the other. For example, the woman mentioned by Schafer may describe a movement of an object from inside to outside in her phenomenal space when describing her experience of revealing a long-held secret. We stress here again the necessity of distinguishing between physical, phenomenal, and quasi-theoretical space. We fully agree with Schafer that the quasi-theoretical spatial models of psychoanalysis inhibit the progress of psychological understanding.

11. Is psychodynamics out of the realm of social exchange?

That the dualistic view prevents social psychologists from seeing the full extent of social exchange is documented by another prominent social psychologist, A. Zalesnik. He describes a group of workers in a machine shop, where a black machinist named Ron is often asked for help. For offering help to his colleagues, he has both considerable rewards (they speak admiringly of him, include him in their activities) and costs (helping them informally decreases his chances of receiving recognition from the management). Zalesnik says:

> The process of determining where the equilibrium point is in any transaction such as helping, is described adequately in the terms of exchange theory with one major exception. The elements of reward, cost and profit will not readily explain why an individual establishes the particular behavior that expresses the equilibrium. In other words, to understand the helping relationship means at some point to inquire into why an individual like Ron is willing to forego management rewards for rewards provided by co-workers. Such an inquiry would soon take us into the psychodynamics of behavior, which is out of the realm of exchange theory. We would see, for example, that Ron had certain strong passive-masochistic tendencies that were a function of his being a Negro, and of the closeness to his mother who had separated from his father and raised him alone. His helping behavior could be understood as an expression of maternal tendencies in looking after others and as a dampening of his aggressive tendencies in competing with others, seeking advancement, and seeking approval of superiors. (1965)

What we are interested in here exclusively is Zalesnik's dualism of social dynamics and psychodynamics. As the reader can probably see now, Ron's psychodynamics is his group-schema dynamics intertwined with the dynamics of his real group. In this model, psychodynamics is *not* out of the realm of social exchange, but part of it. Without including the subject's operations in his group schema, there must be gaps in his social exchange.

Our interest in Zalesnik's example is only his statement that psychodynamics is out of the realm of exchange theory. Leaving aside whether or not his comment about Ron's psychodynamics is correct, we stress only that the example does not indicate that Ron's psychodynamics is a separate field from his social relations and that it is not governed by social rewards and costs. It indicates only that, as with Blau's, and that of many psychoanalysts and psychotherapists, Zalesnik's model is dualistic. According to it, the external social relations are largely independent from intrapsychic processes. If, however, they both are processes in the assumptive world of a person, the exchange comprises combined rewards and costs from interactions with real persons and role schemas. Without such a comprehensive conception of social exchange there must be gaps in the reward-cost balance.

Part II

THE CLINICAL SYSTEM

OF INTEGRATED

PSYCHOTHERAPY

Chapter 6

THERAPEUTIC PRINCIPLES

PROBLEMS AND GOALS

The following five principles are, we believe, valid in all forms of psychotherapy. These broad categories of tasks in which therapist and patient must cooperate deal with (1) problems and goals, (2) the contract, (3) rewards and costs, (4) exposure and corrective experience, and (5) generalization to daily life.

Identifying the patient's problems and setting the goals of treatment is a process of successive approximation in which therapist and patient must closely cooperate. Although in the beginning patients are usually unable to see and formulate their goals adequately, their initial formulation is important. As they later understand their problems better, they reset their goals, and this process continues throughout the treatment. There are several important issues the therapist should assess carefully from the start.

Is psychotherapy indicated? Some people ask for psychotherapy from boredom or out of curiosity but do not seriously intend to change anything in their life. They may finally profit from psychotherapy but do not need it so much as other patients the therapist might treat instead. Others try to use psychotherapy as a substitute for real life. Becoming addicted to psychotherapy, they go from one therapist to another.

Social problems may be wrongly defined as mental health problems. This generally occurs when problems in a certain social area are not adequately solved. People may be referred to treatment in mental health centers because they are depressed even though depression is a normal reaction to social conditions such as unemployment or race or sex discrimination. The therapist should not misinterpret social problems as psychological ones. Psychotherapy should in no way divert or inhibit the patient from any action as a member of his community.

Maladaptive and incompatible goals. The therapist may find that some patients set maladaptive goals. A young woman dissatisfied with her marriage may want to become strong enough to live alone without further need of any close relationship.

Some goals may be clearly incompatible although the patient does not realize it at the beginning. For example, a young, single man who does not intend to marry in the near future wants to get rid of his fear of impotence but is a strict adherent of a religion that forbids sex outside marriage.

What does the patient really want? Patients may not want to reveal their real reasons for coming, or they may not be fully aware of what the reasons are. Some patients come to please a partner who wants them to undergo treatment. Sometimes patients start treatment mainly to postpone a difficult decision such as whether to get married. Some people assume that having undergone psychiatric treatment may help them as defendants in court. The therapist must also assess, as in some insurance cases, the rewards patients draw from their illness that would prevent them from making progress in therapy.

Sometimes the important motive in entering psychotherapy is to avoid a difficult decision. As the psychotherapy goes on and on, the situation is decided without the patient's active participation, often to his disadvantage. Psychotherapy, particularly long-term therapy, may result in the patient missing opportunities of his life. A middle-aged woman enters therapy because she is lonely and is unable to start a relationship with a man due to her neurotic inhibitions. Psychotherapy with a male therapist may become the surrogate of a relationship with another man and thus diminish her chances to overcome her neurotic inhibitions.

In these cases, the therapist has responsibility toward the patient. In other cases, he or she has responsibilities to other people also. For example, a man wants to leave his sick wife, but it is against his conscience. He comes to therapy with a hidden goal, although he may not be aware of it, to make the therapist approve his intent and alleviate his conscience. He gives the therapist a onesided picture of his wife, so that the therapist, perhaps unwittingly, approves his intent. However, the therapist should not allow himself to be misused in this way. He or she should express moral judgment only when planned, and that will be rarely; defending basic human values, but avoiding personal opinions. The therapist's main task is to clarify the patient's moral conflict. This is usually more easily done in group therapy than in individual therapy, since the group members express different opinions which often reflect the different views within the larger society. A group of patients can also be more helpful than an individual therapist in awakening the patient's conscience related to socially irrelevant values and norms as a result of rigid upbringing.

Setting subgoals

Subgoals are intermediary goals instrumental in achieving final therapeutic goals. In fact, the whole of psychotherapy consists of intermediary goals. We mentioned that the patients change their goals during psychotherapy. Subgoals may change more frequently. It is the role of the therapist and, particularly, of the patient group to help patients formulate and change their subgoals.

One such subgoal usually is agreement between therapist and patient about the explanatory framework in which treatment takes place. If the patient believes his nerves are depleted and needs substances which drugs can provide, how can he get well by just talking? Treatment, however, can start before such agreement is reached. If the therapist finds ways to alleviate the patient's symptoms, the patient is then more open to accept the therapist's explanatory framework—that the symptoms are psychogenic in origin. A long discussion about explanatory framework at the beginning of treatment is almost never helpful and can even make further treatment impossible. For example, starting to treat a patient with hysterical paresis with the explanation that the paresis is psychogenic may be sufficient to make the treatment fail. It is precisely what the patient does not want to know. The therapist first has to undermine the motivational structure of the disorder by controlling the rewards and costs—that is, achieve improvement—before any discussion about the nature of the disorder can take place. The explanatory framework may not be discussed at all if symptomatic improvement alone is the goal of treatment; the patient might lose face by admitting any psychogenic origin, for example in combat neuroses.

When the patient accepts the explanatory schema of the therapist, this often has a positive therapeutic effect; such an effect, however, does not say anything about the correctness of the explanation. In fact, the most fantastic explanations accepted by the patient may bring relief. The price, however, is high. It is likely that findings during the therapy will not fit into such schema and that this will limit or jeopardize the treatment.

PROBLEM AND GOAL AREAS

Even if patients come for help with one single problem, a responsible psychotherapist should be interested in having a full picture of their life problems and goals. During psychotherapy, patients may discover that their problems lie in areas other than originally thought.

Having experimented for two decades, we have developed a unified schema for the examination of a patient consisting of the patient's self-report, the charting of progress, and the evaluation of outcome.

The Vancouver Problem-Goal List (VPGL) (used in the Day House at the University of British Columbia) with fifteen problem-goal areas attempts to combine the advantages of standard ratings with those of individualized descriptions. The order of problem-goal areas is arbitrary, but as a whole it is in line with our program to explore thoroughly the patient's present life problems first and to refer to the past only as it is reflected in the present. We expect that integrated psychotherapy will help the patient to improve in most of the enumerated areas. In the therapeutic community with such problems as undesirable behavior in group, being overweight, and dread of physical or other stress, the patient's behavior can be more broadly observed than in individual psychotherapy where certain behavior escapes the therapist's attention or is difficult for the therapist to bring up.

The VPGL has three parts: *description of problems, ratings of problem areas* by the patients themselves and others, (therapists, other patients, significant persons), and detailed *goals and self-directives*.

Description of Problems	Problem Areas (Ratings)	Goals and Self-Directives
	1. Mood, happiness	
	2. Symptoms	
	3. Self-dissatisfaction	
	4. Accepting one's physical illness or disability	

5. Appearance, expression, speech
6. Work/Study/Money
7. Sex partner (and sex)
8. Children
9. Father (Male Authority)
10. Mother (Female Authority)
11. Siblings (peers)
12. Friends, people in general
13, Daily routine
14. Free time
15. Philosophy of life

Shown below is the middle ratings section of the VPGL of a thirty-year-old male patient who went through Day House and had the three usual aftercare visits. It also shows how he rated himself three months later. The ratings by the group were almost identical in this case and are not shown here. For the detailed rating scales, see Appendix E. Each area is rated on a scale from 0 (no problem) to 5 (extremely serious problem).

Weeks in the Day House	Problem Categories	Three Weeks of Aftercare	Follow-up after three months
4 3 2 2 1 1 1 1	1 MOOD, HAPPINESS	2 1 1	2
4 3 2 1 1 1 1 1	2. SYMPTOMS	1 1 1	2
4 4 3 2 1 1 1 1	3. SELF-DISSATISFACTION	1 1 1	2
0 0 0 0 0 0 0 0	4. ACCEPTING ONE'S PHYSICAL ILLNESS OR DISABILITY	0 0 0	0
3 3 2 2 1 1 1 1	5. APPEARANCE, EXPRESSION, SPEECH	1 1 1	1
4 3 3 3 3 2 2 2	6. WORK/STUDY/MONEY	3 2 2	3

2 4 3 3 2 2 1 1		7. SEX PARTNER (AND SEX)	3 1 1½ 2
2 4 3 3 2 1 1 1		8. CHILDREN	2 1 1 1
4 4 3 3 2 2 1 1		9. FATHER (MALE AUTHORITY)	2 1 1 2
		10. MOTHER (FEMALE	
5 5 4 4 3 2 3 2		AUTHORITY)	2 1 1 1
3 4 4 3 2 2 1 1		11. SIBLINGS (PEERS)	2 1 1 1
		12. FRIENDS, PEOPLE IN	
2 3 2 2 2 2 1 1		GENERAL	1 1 1 2
4 2 1 1 1 1 1 1		13. DAILY ROUTINE	0 1 1 2
5 4 3 2 2 1 1 1		14. FREE TIME	1 1 1 2
4 4 4 4 3 2 1 1		15. PHILOSOPHY OF LIFE	2 2 2 2
50 50 39 35 26 21 17 16		TOTALS	23 16 16 25

At the beginning of treatment, patients estimate the first two ratings—happiness and neurotic symptoms—throughout their lives. When they read their life history to the group, their *life curve* is on the blackboard. The turning points usually represent important episodes in the patient's life. The aforementioned patient saw his life curve and those for happiness and neurotic symptoms during and after treatment in the following way.

When discharged, the patients write a summary in terms of the fifteen problem goal areas. Here is the previously mentioned patient's summary (areas where there were no problems omitted):

Patient's Summary

Problems

1. I was generally depressed, unhappy, discouraged, hopeless, immobilized.

2. Generally tired, migraines in the past, often "acid" stomach, poor concentration, flashes of anger, then withdrawal.

3. Very dissatisfied with self, doubt of talents, severe indecision, goalless, concerned about weight and attractive-

Changes Achieved

1. I am rarely depressed, occasionally happy, somewhat encouraged, and often optimistic.

2. I have considerable energy, rare headaches, rare upset stomach; concentration improved in depth and length; much less anger.

3. High self-satisfaction in many areas, secure in some leadership talents, creatively decisive in the situation, clearer

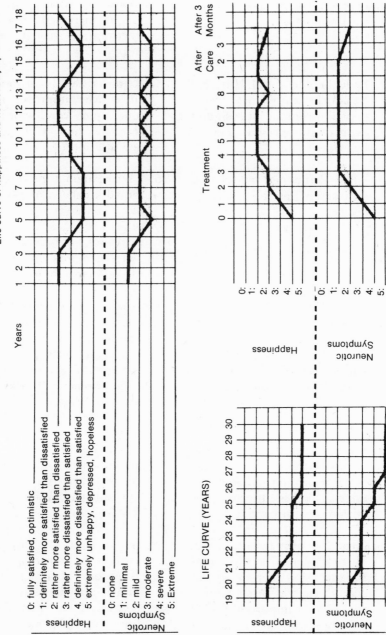

LIFE CURVE (YEARS)
Life curve of happiness and neurotic symptoms

Years

0: fully satisfied, optimistic
1: definitely more satisfied than dissatisfied
2: rather more satisfied than dissatisfied
3: rather more dissatisfied than satisfied
4: definitely more dissatisfied than satisfied
5: extremely unhappy, depressed, hopeless

Happiness

0: none
1: minimal
2: mild
3: moderate
4: severe
5: Extreme

Neurotic Symptoms

After Care   After 3 Months

Treatment

Happiness

Neurotic Symptoms

LIFE CURVE (YEARS)

Happiness

Neurotic Symptoms

ness sometimes, poor effort, weak will.

about emotional goals, stable weight, increased sense of attractiveness, stronger effort/ will.

4. Hide behind facial hair, cut at cuticles until they bleed, poor muscle tone, speech and expression present 'false' front.

4. Removed facial hair, does not cut cuticles, improved muscle tone and condition, more able to show true feelings and attitudes.

5. I had abandoned my six year old career as a university teacher.

5. I see resuming my career (after additional study) as feasible, considering study in other areas (still a significant problem). Less money-concerned, less cheap regarding self and family.

6. Masturbating daily, almost always in sexual fantasy at slightest stimulus (flagging attraction to, involvement with, and satisfaction for, self and wife). Wife discouraged and angry, almost given up.

6. I haven't masturbated since I entered the program. Sexual fantasy decreased rapidly but again on incline, but more realistic: *re* positive reaction from women at Dayhouse, more interested in and successful with wife.

7. Overly critical and insufficiently affectionate with daughter, often irritated and angry. She is insecure and 'afraid'—nightmares.

7. I am less demanding, more affectionate and physical, spend more time with her. She still has problems but is less explosive.

8. Abandoned by father, unsure about feelings toward him, distant with step-father although he was often kind to me, several important 'failed' relations with strong men in authority.

8. I am aware of my anger, sadness and sense of loss and suspicion about my 'real' father and father-figures in general. I see how this continues to affect me but I am much closer to my step-father

and . in regular communication with him.

9. I couldn't stand contact or communication with my mother. Made me nervous and angry, constant crisis. Refuse her affection or approval, she drains me/ constant expectations.

9. I am aware of great anger and resentment toward her, still unsure of other feelings, in regular communication expressing some feelings and demands on my part, setting limits on expectations I will meet.

10. Out of touch with brother John, immobilized by his crisis, guilty, not sure of what he expects from me.

10. Wrote several times, he is visiting me now, I am confident, setting my limits.

11. Few close friends, distant and false with people, attract but intimidate them.

11. Resumed contact with old friends, can be closer and softer with people. Still intimidating though, when insecure.

12. Many household tasks done but overly ritualized, over eating problem in past. Habituated to marijuana and hashish for ten years (stoned almost all the time in last few years). Cigarettes increasing over pack a day, coffee increasing. T.V. ten to twelve hours a day. Fall asleep in front of T.V. early each morning. Late too often.

12. Still do a lot of household tasks but different pace, not over eating, no drugs for seven weeks, T.V. a few hours a day or none at all, cigarettes and coffee cut in half. Sleep in bed with wife. Never late.

13, Free time weighed on me, fill it with self-stimulating drugs. T.V., reading. No hobbies, have to be dragged out of

13. Don't have enough free time, want to do more recreational and serious reading, go out every weekend, more sports,

house. Always procrastinated, then vigorous, last ditch effort but can not mobilize when I need to now.

guitar. Don't hardly procrastinate, can mobilize when I want to.

14. Confused, a wealth of ideas, a paucity of conclusions, skeptical but relativistic. Very empathetic but very briefly. Liberal and conservative.

14. More self-concerned (self and family needs) but over all approach not clearly settled. Want fairness, and use talents to 'achieve' and 'help.'

15. I had very little hope for myself, just survive as best I can, be strong, deny, I can't go on like this but——

15. I have much hope in every area of my life. I have changed my personality, my mental health and my life situation. I still have a lot to do, but I can and will achieve the things I need and want.

In this section we have limited ourselves to discussing only those problem-goal areas which are either difficult to assess or are often neglected by therapists. We will stress here the changes patients make in life which are not just changes in feelings. People may become sometimes miraculously euphoric with heightened self-esteem after a weekend encounter group. However, euphoria evaporates rather quickly.

Self-dissatisfaction. Self-esteem is introduced in childhood through the esteem shown by others. Good as well as traumatic experiences are often carried over into adulthood by the group schema, but self-esteem is also dependent upon present real relationships and one's ability to control his environment.

Human beings want to have some amount of influence over other people and the inanimate environment; they want to be causal agents. Our patients sometimes want that without putting effort into learning skills. Others have low self-esteem and complain that they have not achieved anything in life. We may agree they have not, despite their potential. Psychotherapy which aims only at making people feel good without changing their behavior does not fulfill its task responsibly. It seems that for many neurotics the following words by Lorenz are relevant:

Our self-esteem is dependent, to a large degree, upon the success we have in overcoming obstacles. To confirm our capacities in this way is indispensable for all of us. (1973, our translation)

It is, however, important that the overcoming of obstacles be socially valuable and a part of the fair social exchange. As Alfred Adler says:

The only salvation from the continuously driving inferiority feelings is the knowledge and the feeling of being valuable, which originates from the contribution to the common welfare. Where this automatized social feeling is deficient, the individual's interest is too self-centered and he feels that he is impotent or a nobody. (Ansbacher 1956)

Work/study/money (6). It is our experience that psychotherapists often neglect exploration of economic conditions and dependencies, although these may play an important role in human relations, leading to and maintaining neuroses. For example, we could not understand some mysterious factors in the marital crisis of one of our male patients in the Day House. It turned out that the patient had avoided talking about economic dependence in his marriage. He was professionally unsuccessful, whereas his wife had a prosperous business. When he started to work for her, his income increased. Dissolving the marriage would have meant a radical change in his economic and social status. Most often it is the other way around with the husband as the breadwinner and his wife, at home, economically dependent upon him. In a way he is also her employer, and although none of them may be aware of it, her economic dependence may affect their relationship.

Often it is difficult to explore and evaluate the significance of economic dependencies between husband and wife or parents and children, and among relatives, because patients are reluctant to talk about them. They either regard them as unimportant for psychotherapy or are unaware of them and resist awareness. The dependencies may be part of their unconscious.

We realized the relevance of shifting economic family dependencies during the rapid change of economic structure in Czechoslovakia after 1948. There were social and economic pressures for housewives to go out to work, but regardless of this, many husbands discouraged their wives, stressing their incapability to work. As the men sensed that the power balance in the family would change in favor of their wives, their doubts about themselves as men were mobilized. Many women went to work and this affected their marriages in different ways.

When the husband accepted the redefinition of roles—for example, helping more with household chores—the marriage often improved. As his wife became a more interesting person, the husband also benefited from her happiness and self-confidence.

When domineering husbands did not want to accept a new distribution of roles, the marriage often broke down. Many of our patients, housewives who had had neurotic complaints for years and who dreaded seeking work because of their low self-confidence, almost invariably had husbands who were, wittingly or unwittingly, feeding their inferiority feelings. Psychotherapy, especially in a therapeutic community on the State Farm, led to their increased self-confidence and made it possible for them to get jobs. At this point, it was not unusual for the husbands to develop neurotic complaints which they had not recalled having before. Analysis showed that these husbands needed dependent (neurotic, childish, helpless) wives in order to maintain their own mental balance and self-esteem and to feel superior.

Work is of the utmost importance for mental health. We agree with Freud that to love and to work are the pillars of mental health; we would like to add to *play*, but hopefully both love and work have elements of play. We disagree with those many psychotherapists of affluent North America who minimize the importance of work. Work is an important part of fair social exchange and they both contribute to self-esteem. Psychotherapy with patients who claim they will start doing something when they gain self-esteem is usually futile. If patients come to us seeking help for feelings of worthlessness, futility, and boredom but at the same time avoid work or study, we can help them only, as a rule, if we can bring them to change their life style and make work or study an important part. These are often people who isolate themselves out of fear or resentment and who seek excuses whenever they have to overcome obstacles of any kind.

Sex partner (and sex) (7). A common obstacle to understanding marriage and similar sexual partnerships is that our attention is too exclusively directed to the sexual relationship. "We do not fit sexually" may be a reflection of a frustration of many other needs which are not being fulfilled in mutual exchange. Marriage has many of the features of a small group with a long history in which the members' goals are to live in security and stability, to cooperate in the technology of everyday life (preparation of meals, house cleaning), and to share, at least partially, free time. A variety of natural groups emerging today—for example two divorced women with children, homosexual couples, groups in communes—have problems and conflicts similar to those which appear in marriages and families. The conceptual framework of the small group helps us keep the distance necessary to see common features and not be biased by our own family history and views of how a family should be. Even marital and family therapists sometimes transmit these biases, and this is one of the reasons that, finding the framework of family therapy too narrow, we progressed to integrated psychotherapy.

Marital couples and families come for help usually in times of crisis. The crisis may be the birth of a child which changes the reward-cost balance between spouses; an attempt to redefine roles, as when the wife wants to take a job or get involved in an activity important to her; the stages at which a young child struggles to become an independent person, from its first independent steps to leaving home; or divorce or death in the family. It is a difficult task for psychotherapy not only to assist the individual or individuals to achieve new equilibrium inside or outside the family but also to use the crisis as an opportunity for personality growth.

The parents (9 and 10). Clinical experience confirms the importance of the parents, whether living or not, to the whole life of a person. They are the most important part of the authority role schema. So strong is their influence that an idealized parent schema is worshipped in many societies as a god, or gods. The divine figure reflects the structure of that society; in the Judeo-Christian religion, the god is patriarchal, as is Freud's superego. Most patients coming for psychotherapy indicate they have some problem in relation to parents. The parental influence from the past is sometimes so strong that it reminds one of posthypnotic suggestion.

Sexual experience and fantasies related to parents are sometimes important in a patient's disturbing memories and often can be traced to the subtle or not so subtle seductive behavior of a parent. But the most common topics in disturbing memories are fear of being deserted or left in pain in a desperate situation, not being loved, not being appreciated, not being taken seriously, or being ridiculed in front of others. These feelings and attitudes form the background of a present negative or ambivalent relationships toward parents or persons on which the mask of the parent schema is hung. They appear in the transference neurosis which slowly develops through psychoanalytic technique or in abreactions directed toward parents or other persons from early childhood.

Philosophy of life (15). Beside more or less clear beliefs and attitudes—such as belief in God or astrological destiny—there are vague general beliefs and attitudes which the patients are often unable to formulate clearly and yet which influence their life. It is often important to help patients become aware of their philosophies. Frequently patients have been introduced to such implicit philosophies by their parents. They are concerned with:

> Others: All people are bad. All people of the opposite sex are bad. Everybody is selfish and deceitful. Everybody is out to do me harm.
> Self: I am not good. I am inferior. I am doomed to suffer. I have no power over anything. People can do what they want with me. Others are responsible for my misery. I cannot help being as I am (the causal focus is in others, in destiny, or circumstances, but not in self). If something goes wrong, I am guilty (the causal focus is always in self if things go wrong). Nobody can love me. I am not worthy to be loved or esteemed. I cannot accept what happened in the past and, therefore, I will never be happy. I have bad luck. I want to be either perfect or nothing.

In connection with the philosophy of life, *self-actualization* has often been stressed. A Maslow, who popularized it more than anybody else, was unhappy about its misuse.

> This term has proven to have unforeseen shortcomings of appearing (a) to imply selfishness rather than altruism, (b) to slur the aspect of duty and of dedication to life tasks, (c) to neglect the ties to other people and to society, and the dependence of individual fulfillment upon a "good society", (d) to neglect the demand-character of non-human reality, and its intrinsic fascination and interest, (e) to neglect egolessness and self-transcendence, and (f) to stress, by implication, activity rather than passivity or receptivity. This has turned out to be so in spite of my careful efforts to describe the empirical *fact* that self-actualizing people are altruistic, dedicated, self-transcending, social, etc. (1968)

In brief, the concept of self-actualization became confused with "doing one's own thing," as glorified in Fritz Perls' prayer. Self-actualization as understood by Maslow is well in line with the philosophy of life expressed by Carnap.

The main task of an individual seems to me the development of his personality and the creation of fruitful and healthy relations among human beings. This aim implies the task of cooperation in the development of society and ultimately of the whole of mankind towards a community in which every individual has the possibility of leading a satisfying life and of participating in cultural goods. The fact that everybody knows that he will eventually die, need not make his life meaningless or aimless. He himself gives meaning to his life if he sets tasks for himself, struggles to fulfill them to the best of his ability, and regards all the specific tasks of all individuals as parts of the great task of humanity, whose aim goes far beyond the limited span of each individual life. (1963a)

THE CONTRACT

In the most general sense, a contract is an agreement between two or more persons to do or not do something. An explicit contract is important for successful psychotherapy and should be used whenever possible. The more the patient is capable of establishing a therapeutic contract which covers essential issues and the clearer such a contract is formulated, the better the conditions are for successful psychotherapy. In a therapeutic contract, participants (patient, significant persons, therapist, other patients) in a therapeutic undertaking formulate what they expect from each other and under what conditions they are willing to cooperate.

The bargaining about the contract at the beginning of treatment is of basic importance for therapy. For example, a phobic indicates in the first interview that he cannot guarantee whether he will keep the appointments, since sometimes his fears are so terrible that he is unable to go out. If the therapist accepts this, it is likely that the patient will frustrate the therapist so much that sooner or later the treatment will fail. There have to be costs for a patient who misses sessions. When the patient pays, this is taken care of automatically since it is part of the contract that the patient pays anyway. Even so, difficulties may arise as Langs (1973) describes very thoroughly. If the patient does not pay, the therapist has to give special consideration to creating costs equivalent to paying for missed sessions.

Unfortunately, this does not happen often in clinics, and tardiness or missed sessions are taken lightly. For example, a highly conscientious psychiatrist working in a clinic presented the case of a neurotic patient who was always late. We were struck by the answer of the psychiatrist when we asked him what he had done about it. He had done nothing and remarked, "If it were in private practice, I would, of course, be mad. But in the clinic it does not matter." But it does matter. Even if we leave aside the cost to the taxpayer, or the time that could be used for another patient who needs it, it seriously endangers the therapeutic process.

From our extensive experience with both paying and nonpaying patients, we are convinced that in most cases paying is not essential for intensive psychotherapy if an appropriate reward-cost system is constructed. For example, a phobic woman entered the treatment in the Day House. During the first days she was in panic; she left the group meeting several times and was once three hours late because of her fears. She was put on probation by the committee of patients and told that if it were to happen once more she would be discharged. She was hurt and protested, but she was not late any more during her six-week stay. It was not even an issue. As became apparent later, she had tested the contract as she had manipulated her parents and sister in the past. The contract was an important part of establishing her commitment to the treatment.

Even so, there are patients—fortunately a very small minority—who, using the advantages of National Health Insurance, make a contract, break it, and go from one therapist to another; they would not do so if they had to pay for it. This can be counteracted by organizational measures and close cooperation among different institutions, but such cooperation is often missing. With most patients, the system of rewards and costs to be described is broad enough to motivate the patient to keep the contract. Only exceptionally do we have to ask certain kinds of patients to pay for missed sessions.

Whether for individual, group, or family therapy, the essential parts of the contract are:

1. Commitment to be present during all meetings (not being late, being present in all parts of the program, for example, in a therapeutic community)
2. Complete openness
3. Discussing important decisions in life (including terminating of therapy) before acting upon them

4. Accepting group goals and norms in group treatment, including the therapeutic community (described in Part IV)

REWARDS AND COSTS

If patients' only goals were to rid themselves of maladaptive behavior patterns, this chapter would be simple. But to the degree that the disorder is based on conflict, opposing goals (to get rid of the disorder and to keep it) are pursued. This situation is not unique to psychotherapy. A patient with a toothache may do everything to reach a dentist to get rid of the aching tooth, yet when the dentist is in the process of extracting the tooth, the patient may try to interfere by holding his hand. This is a good analogy to what happens in the treatment of neuroses. As the patients go through different stages of treatment, they develop resistances of differing kinds and degrees. They find different kinds of satisfaction which make them less interested in seeking therapeutic goals, or they lose hope so there is no need to try anyway, or they lose trust or are so angry with the therapist that they think they cannot continue in therapy. They also may act out, resorting to actions which complicate therapy or make it impossible. Freud and his followers have systematically studied resistance primarily as defenses operating in treatment (see Greenson 1967).

Since psychotherapy aimed at personality changes is often painful and provokes or increases symptoms, anxiety, guilt, shame, or sadness, one of the most difficult tasks for the therapist is to determine at each point of treatment the dosage of rewards and costs which would optimally motivate the patient to move toward the therapeutic goals. A reward-cost rule for the therapist can be formulated: *Try to make the rewards and costs of treatment contingent upon the patient's behavior in such a way that they optimally support and speed up the patient's movement toward therapeutic goals.*

This is a useful rule, but with present knowledge we are still not very efficient in satisfying it. The trend of development indicates that more efficient methods will be found in the future. Progress has to start with a much more precise assessment system of problems and goals and available rewards and costs.

One of the first rewards patients deserve is realistic support of their expectations of positive outcome, based on a careful assessment by the therapist. Hope is a powerful factor in psychotherapy and has been rightly stressed by J. D. Frank (1971). Support of positive expectations has to be given conditionally; a lot of effort is needed from the patient and the therapist. In the Day House, new patients listen to the reports of discharged patients. This not only supports their hope but also usually shows them how the results of treatment are correlated with the effort the discharged patients have put into their treatment.

Generally, almost any kind of reward the patients receive in the therapeutic situation may become a source of resistance. Some ask permanently for reassurance, without wanting to move forward. Others seek dependence upon the therapist or the group, avoiding the risk of disappointment in relation to people in real life.

One aspect of the reward-cost rule is expressed by Freud in his abstinence rule—treatment should be carried through, as far as possible, under privation, in a state of abstinence. He concluded:

> Cruel though it may sound, we must see to it that the patient's suffering, to a degree that is in some way or other effective, does not come to an end prematurely.

> The patient looks for his substitutive gratification. . . . A certain amount must of course be permitted to him. (1919)

This rule has often been misunderstood, perhaps due to its formulation. Although it is true that no successful treatment can be carried through without costs, rewards are just as necessary. The social exchange model reminds the therapist to assess continuously the reward-cost balance. Continuous assessment of this balance and elimination of inappropriate rewards and costs preclude precocious termination of treatment as a result of flight into health, transference cure, or despair.

The extended social exchange model covers exchange both with real people and with one's group schema. Most interactions are combinations of both and can be particularly easily demonstrated in therapeutic transference development. Sometimes the therapist is seen by the patient through the filter of the mother schema and is loved (the patient receives imaginary rewards from the mother schema). Sometimes the therapist, without changing in any way, is seen through the filter of father schema and is hated. Imaginary rewards and costs make the difference. In natural groups—among spouses, parents, and children, or employees and boss, the same happens, except that the nature of the transference is not seen so easily and changes in relationships usually occur much slower.

To assess and predict the reward-cost balance of a patient, it is necessary to assess those of the patient's significant persons. This holds particularly for the patient's family. Whether the therapist sees the family or not, it is imperative to constantly assess the rewards and costs of other family members. Since they are in intensive social exchange with the patient, they cannot fail to be influenced by the therapy and vice versa. For example, when a female patient in the Day House improves, her husband may start to have neurotic symptoms which he does not recall having had before. It is understandable that the therapist would like to be in direct contact with other significant people, both to study the social exchange and to influence it.

Nowhere is the importance of the reward-cost rule more apparent than in work with natural groups. Therapists sitting with a marital couple or the whole family have to calculate each of their moves in view of the reward-cost value for all participants. Through rewards and costs, they can help the family go through a series of shifts toward a new equilibrium which all participants accept as a fair exchange or can emancipate from the group adult children or marital partners neither able to live together nor to separate.

Since each patient is divided in his motivation, it is not surprising that patients not only support each other in therapy but also form alliances of resistance. It is the task of the therapist as a specialist in group dynamics, to influence redistribution of rewards and costs in such a way that resistances do not take over but are identified and utilized for therapy. Only once in the twenty year history of Lobec were we unable to handle the resistance of the group and had to dissolve the community.

It is necessary to study the social exchange not only of patients, but also of the therapist. In individual therapy, therapists are thrown upon their own resources of self-assessment, unless they have supervision or an opportunity for case presentation. In the therapeutic community, mutual analysis of rewards and costs is an important function of staff meetings.

EXPOSURE AND CORRECTIVE EXPERIENCE

Corrective experience is part of everyday life. Students fail in their exams; it is a traumatic experience and may influence how they feel for several months. They may have different doubts and fears about themselves, but when they take the same exam again and pass, that works as a corrective experience for them. When a pilot has a minor accident while landing and reacts emotionally, he is encouraged to start again as soon as possible. If a corrective experience comes soon after a failure, it cancels a developing phobia.

Candidates for psychotherapy are people not able to arrange corrective experience for themselves. Either they avoid situations, through fear or losing hope, which they could not master in the past or they try and try again but fail each time. Sometimes they unwittingly choose or arrange circumstances in such a way that they must fail.

Alexander, French et al. (1946) introduced the concept of *emotional corrective experience*, understanding by it reexposure under favorable circumstances to an emotional situation that the patient could not handle in the past. We prefer to talk about *corrective experience*, since we think that both the emotional and cognitive aspects of such experience are important.

By corrective experience *we understand partial reexposure to situations which the person was not able to master in the past, but reexposure under more favorable circumstances, so that successful mastery is achieved.*

In ordinary life situations, talking is sometimes sufficient partial rexposure to achieve mastery of the situation. One day a child does not want to go to school. When questioned, it turns out that he was ridiculed by his friends. The child cries, the situation is talked over, perhaps some ways of coping are suggested, and the child goes to school with new hope and supported self-esteem and finds new ways to cope with the situation. In this case, talking is sufficient partial reexposure, and so it often is in psychotherapy. However, talking about the situation is often a very inefficient and time-consuming method of reexposure. Psychotherapy has introduced different methods of partial reexposure to the crucial situation, from simple to very complex ones.

If a person is fearful of a situation, the person has to be exposed to that situation sooner or later to overcome the fear. This method, which has been used by educators and animal trainers for centuries, must, in most cases, be done gradually. Mary Cover Jones working at Thorndike's laboratory described a systematic procedure in 1924. Jones eliminated a child's fear of furry objects by bringing furry objects closer and closer while the child was eating and in a relaxed state. Even though Freud (1919) saw the causes of phobic neuroses as very complex, he regarded exposure of the patient to the feared situation as a necessary condition of treatment.

The exposure discussed so far is to real situations, but exposure to imagined situations has been used for some time (for example, J. H. Schultz 1932, 1966). It was systematically elaborated into a therapeutic technique, systematic desensitization, by J. Wolpe (1954, 1969). The patient is trained to relax in the therapist's office and is encouraged to practice at home. The patient also constructs a graded hierarchy of situations where the particular fear appears. The patient is asked to relax and is told to signal whenever he feels anxious. He is then asked to imagine a neutral scene which does not evoke anxiety, and gradually items on the fear scale are presented, starting with the weakest. The conditions of systematic desensitization are then

1. Training in progressive muscular relaxation
2. The construction of individualized hierarchies of fear
3. Systematic desensitization

Although the efficiency of systematic desensitization has been confirmed in many studies, no basic condition seems crucial for its success. Parallel studies seemed to show that neither relaxation nor hierarchy is necessary (see Yates 1975). Even the opposite procedure of flooding, implosive therapy, in which the subject is asked to imagine frightening situations, claims to be successful.

It is interesting to note that Masserman (1943) developed experimental neuroses in cats and treated them by six different methods, one of them being similar to progressive desensitization. The most efficient method was providing the cat with partial control of the experimental situation and the second best method was forced solution: that is, the cat was pushed despite resistance towards the feared food until it started to eat and the phobia was broken. Methods similar to both of these are used in our therapeutic community described later.

Transference. Analysis of transference is a complex corrective experience. In classical analysis, the therapist sits behind the patient's head, creating an unreal social situation. When we talk to somebody, particularly when we talk without restraint as is required in free association, our behavior is constantly influenced by feedback from the other person. For the patient on the couch the social feedback loop is interrupted since the therapist cannot be seen and reacts minimally. The patient's behavior is influenced by imagined feedback coming from role schemas; with their help, the patient reconstructs the therapist's behavior. According to the state of the patient's group schema and although the therapist does not react, the patient may feel that the therapist is angry or bored, that he despises the patient or is attracted to him, and so forth. A role schema is superimposed upon the therapist. For example, the patient may see in the therapist his father's features, have similar expectations of him, and try to involve him in a similar relationship.

The analysis of transference was a great discovery. For centuries the patient pressed the healer—physician, priest or shaman—to take the lead, answer questions, or give advice, and it was difficult to withstand that pressure. Freud was the first able to systematically withstand that pressure and by minimizing the social feedback foster the development of transference. With minimal interference, the transference progresses and takes interesting turns, reflecting patients' group schema. In this way, patients become strongly motivated in their relationship to the therapist, who now represents for them different people in their childhood; they are reexposed to the traumatic interpersonal situations from their past which they were not able to master. The conflicts are actualized, old wounds are opened, and old neurotic symptoms reappear (the transference neurosis). The situation of reexposure provides an opportunity for corrective experience. Talking about transference, Freud stressed reexposure:

> It is on that field that the victory must be won—the victory whose expression is the permanent cure of the neurosis. It cannot be disputed that controlling the phenomena of transference presents the psycho-analyst with the greatest difficulties. But it should not be forgotten that it is precisely they that do us the inestimable service of making the patient's hidden and forgotten erotic impulses immediate and manifest, for when all is said and done, it is impossible to destroy anyone *in absentia* or *in effigie*. (1912)

There is scarcely another opportunity for a psychotherapist to powerfully experience psychological determinism as in witnessing transference development. The stages are often predictable, since they develop gradually. The patient usually resists developing transference; "I had a dream about a doctor, but it was not you." The next time the patient has another dream and after some inner struggle has to admit that "it was about you."

If the therapist transplants classical psychoanalytic technique to group therapy (minimum of reactions, evenly distributed observation of group members, and interpretation of patient-therapist relations), the transference to the therapist becomes the central phenomenon of the group process. Perhaps nowhere was this technique more extremely developed than at the Tavistock Institute in London by Wilfred Bion (1974) and Henry Ezriel (1950, 1952). One of the authors was a member of Ezriel's group and later experimented with this technique. As one of the choices of the therapist leading a group, it is interesting, but in our opinion, of very limited therapeutic value.

The transference relationships among patients which emerge if the therapist evenly pays attention to all events in group therapy, become an important therapeutic factor, if they are interpreted by the therapist. As a source of corrective experience, they are perhaps more important than transference relationships to the therapist.

In our therapeutic community described later, we discovered that therapists, as targets of transferences, can *shift* them to other patients. It is extremely taxing to be the target of the transferences of thirty patients and, at the same time, to function as an administrator responsible for the tasks of the community—that is, the amount of work being accomplished. We discovered that by shifting most administrative and disciplinarian functions to the patients' committee, the therapists become more objective observers, and can pay full attention to the process of corrective experience in individual patients. The patients, as committee members and work instructors, become targets of transference as authority figures.

The strategy of shifting transferences does not rely only on inviting patients to participate in leadership, it can be fostered in various ways—for example, if a therapist is represented in psychodrama by a patient.

As the target of transference, the therapist becomes a substitute for father, mother, sibling, or other persons of the patient's childhood and later years. When we learned that transferences could be shifted, we also learned that the transference to the therapist could be minimized and that direct interaction between patient and the imagined role schema could take place. The first realization of this strategy was developed in psychodrama. A patient may imagine he is five years old and interact with his father, who is represented by another patient, the therapist, or an imagined father sitting in an empty chair.

A psychodrama episode, if it elicits deep feelings, can become an important element of corrective experience. Psychodrama, or psychomime, is sometimes only the first step, to be followed by abreactive techniques which make the experience for the patient as real as possible. The abreactive state begins with a vivid memory of some event which was not mastered in the past and which is still disturbing. Usually, it is a memory of being hurt, deserted, or humiliated by a significant person, and it is revived with unusually painful strength. The abreaction usually ends with the relief of tension and a closer feeling to members of the

group who may represent significant persons of the patient's life. Though
sometimes very important or even necessary, psychodrama and abreaction are only *episodes* in the process of corrective experience. Abreaction,
especially, because of its dramatic flavor and instant effect, tends to be
overvalued by beginners and fame seeking psychotherapists. J. Frank
(1973) has shown the rise and fall of abreaction's popularity in the history of psychotherapy.

GENERALIZATION TO ORDINARY LIFE

The final test of psychotherapeutic progress is the capacity of patients
to function better in ordinary life after treatment. Many patients, however, believe that the treatment is a waiting period and that when they
finish it, their wishes will be miraculously fulfilled without much effort.
It is precisely this belief and the avoidance of action which often makes
psychotherapy fail. Their attitude is caused by resistance; the patients
want to get rid of the most distressing symptoms but do not want to
change their neurotic style of life.

Of course, action is a broad concept. Some action may be essential for
treatment and some may destroy it. We said before that Freud demanded action when asking phobic patients to cross bridges which they
dreaded. On the other hand, Freud asked patients not to make important decisions during treatment. There are good reasons for this rule,
since it reminds the patients that by certain actions (acting out) in their
lives, they can jeopardize the treatment. Unfortunately, this rule can be
misused. In fact, there are patients in psychoanalysis who for years have
used treatment to postpone decisions and maintain their neurotic life
style.

Our rule is that patients should not make decisions during the treatment without discussing it fully before acting. It is, however, made clear
that the purpose of discussion is not to get approval or disapproval since
they themselves must decide.

Therapists must be cautious not to unwittingly impress their hierarchy
of goals and values upon patients. For example, it is known that in the
past some psychoanalysts overtly discouraged the careers of female patients, interpreting them in terms of their values and theoretical views
as reluctance to accept the feminine role. We agree with Haley who says,

Many wives, for example, discontented with the narrow pattern of
suburban life, have been stabilized for years by intensive analysis.

Instead of encouraging them to take action that would lead to a richer and more complex life, the therapy prevents that change by imposing the idea that the problem is within their psyche rather than in their situation. (1973)

As this example shows, psychotherapy has political implications (see P. R. Bergin 1975) which we intend to deal with in a separate study. Here, we want to stress the advantages of treatment in groups. The group members faced with a patient's dilemma can freely express their views, advice, and moral indignation. They do not need to be as cautious as the therapist, for two reasons. First, the patient does not consider their comments as expert advice, and second, they often represent a spectrum of different and sometimes opposite opinions. Usually though, they correctly discern the acting out character of the patient's intentions.

Any generalization from psychotherapy to real life must be the concern of the therapist from the beginning of psychotherapy. There are two main channels for accomplishing this.

First, the patient has to be encouraged to accomplish certain acts during treatment—homework. Correct timing is a difficult issue and is dependent upon the stage of the treatment and upon the reward-cost assessment. The acts include commitments of undoubted value—such as the antiphobic acts recommended by Freud, meeting persons of the other sex, or taking steps to start work or study. A therapeutic community such as that in the Day House described later can give the kind of support and encouragement which rarely occurs in any other form of treatment. Rewards and costs exist in the form of social approval and disapproval, both informal and formal (ratings and positive and negative awards once a week).

Second, at some point of treatment, significant persons in the patient's life have to be directly included in the process of psychotherapy. Without this, generalization to real life is doubtful. Since we regard it as an integral part of efficient psychotherapy, this is one of the reasons why we avoid talking about family therapy.

It is amazing how the patients, although they come because they are unhappy with their present lives, seek ingenious excuses to avoid actions important for therapeutic progress. In a well-functioning therapeutic community, the avoidance of appropriate action is a much more frequent problem than acting out.

Chapter 7

SEVEN STEPS OF THE SYSTEM

Just show me some good, new methods of how to do efficient psychotherapy. I am not interested in organization and administration.

This may well be a wish of many psychotherapists and we understand
it only too well. When we started in psychotherapy, we just wanted to
be left in peace with our patients, doing good psychotherapy, investing
all of our effort and enthusiasm in helping our patients, trying new and
more efficient methods, and not having to bother about physical facilities, staff, policies, grants, and the whole network of outside services.

Of course, we soon realized that good and efficient psychotherapy
can be performed only to the extent that certain conditions in the structure, organization, and policy of service delivery have been met. Since
no one would realize these conditions for us if we did not contribute to
them, we built the system of integrated psychotherapy, later modifying
it further in the U.S.A. and Canada. We did this not out of a love of
organizing and building systems, but out of necessity, as we loved to do
good, efficient psychotherapy.

There was another major motive. We lived in a country which had
just started to develop a unified system of medical care. It became a
challenging task for us to build a system of psychotherapy in the newly
developed area of mental health care, which would serve as a model for
other parts of the country.

When medicine was socialized in Czechoslovakia after 1948, the social demand for coherent psychotherapeutic help for all who could benefit was felt. The possibilities of unified medicine were a challenge to us, and we designed and realized a unified system of psychotherapy which could be used as a model across the country in terms of efficiency and economy. We established at the Charles University Department of Psychiatry, in Prague, a system of integrated psychotherapy based on three interrelated units: the Psychiatric Clinic, the Day Center, and the Residential Neurosis Center at Lobec. The psychiatric clinic, which was part of the university policlinic, functioned as a regional center to which more complicated cases were referred by district psychiatrists. The city of Prague is a region of one million inhabitants divided into ten districts, each with a population of approximately a hundred thousand. The district psychiatrists referred the most complicated cases of neuroses not amenable to the treatment which they were able to offer.

The socialization of medicine created favorable conditions for building a unified system of integrated psychotherapy. Even we had to overcome the unspecific resistances and prejudices which typically inhibit realization of new ideas and methods in psychiatry anywhere in the world, as well as those specific for that developmental period of Czechoslovak society. When working in North America, we replicated parts of the system. It became clear to us that the system had transcultural validity.

A fully developed system consists of seven steps carried out by the same staff in three interrelated units: a clinic, a residential therapeutic community, and a day center. The Clinic should be located in a large metropolitan area. It is the administrative center of the system. Here initial assessments take place and patients return to see their therapists at various stages of the system. Open groups and groups of marital partners and family members meet at the clinic. The day center is a separate unit located in a house with a garden and some sports facilities. The residential therapeutic community is located in a rural area and offers an opportunity for patients to work in agriculture and forestry.

This system provides mental health practitioners, be they psychiatrists, social workers, or psychologists, with a rich variety of treatment modalities for their patients.

The steps
1. Individual interview (clinic)
    a. Identified patients

    b. Clients (people seeking help in partnership and marital
       problems)
2. Open group (clinic)
3. Therapeutic community (residential community or day center)
4. Group of significant persons (clinic or day center)
    a. Significant persons
    b. Significant persons, patients, and clients
5. After care (clinic or day center)
6. Ongoing therapy (clinic or day center)
    a. Individual therapy
    b. Small group
    c. Family therapy (oriented toward one family)
7. Club of patients and friends (day center)

The *first* step consists of one or two individual interviews. In the *second* step the new patients mix with improved patients coming from the therapeutic community in a large open group. The *third* step is treatment in a therapeutic community, either a residential community located outside the city or the day center. The patients' partners, family members, or other significant persons are invited into a group at the *fourth* step. Also at this step, the patients attend several group meetings together with their partners and family members. The *fifth* step consists of aftercare for patients from the therapeutic community. Only if patients have failed to achieve satisfactory results and are well motivated for further psychotherapy, may they then be accepted for any other type of ongoing treatment at the *sixth* step. This might take the form of individual psychotherapy, treatment in a small, closed group, or family therapy limited to one family unit. The *seventh* step is a club for patients who have completed their treatment. The systems requires that (1) no method is used before a less time-consuming method is fully utilized; (2) using one step does not preclude the use of the next step; (3) the order of steps represents a screening procedure which tests motivation for further psychotherapy; and (4) an improved patient can stop the treatment at any step, according to his motivation, which we cultivate only to the extent of the time we have available.

ADMISSION INTO THE SYSTEM

There are two main categories of people admitted into the system: (a) persons referred, or coming on their own, because of their symptoms (identified patients) and (b) persons who usually come on their own, seeking help in open partnership, marital, and family problems (clients).

We soon realized that there was a special advantage to bringing together both categories mentioned in such a setting as a group. Both categories, although they have come through different channels, have much in common. They may have a similar pattern in their group schema. For example, let us compare a male patient who complains of neurotic symptoms with a male client who comes seeking help with a marital problem. Each has a similar mother schema, but each has developed a different way of coping with the problem. Both means are ineffective in that both people had to seek professional help. The identified patient suffering from various neurotic symptoms is not aware of the significance of his special attitude toward women as partners. This attitude developed through a one-sided experience with an intelligent, authoritative, and highly supportive mother who loved her son and fostered his dependence on her. The patient still enjoys the mutual warm relationship but often feels depressed and has various psychosomatic problems. In his late thirties, he does not have a satisfactory sexual life.

The client, who came because of the impending collapse of his marriage, had a quite similar personal history and background with a similar type of mother. The client realizing (or being told) his dependency on his mother was inappropriate at his age sought a quick solution. He ran into a marriage with a highly efficient career woman and became dependent on her, expecting the same attention and devotion from her as from his mother. His wife loved him and enjoyed her supportive role at the beginning but later became dissatisfied with her husband who was jealous of her and asked her to give up her career for him. She finally suggested divorce.

The identified patient felt the victim of his symptoms, while the client felt the victim of his marriage, especially of his wife's alleged lack of understanding. In general, patients are often not aware of their interpersonal problems; clients are not aware of how unrealistic their expectations in their interpersonal relationships are and how neurotically they behave. Both categories, patients as well as clients, are experts at unwittingly developing vicious circles which lead to personal unhappiness though each uses different tactics. Mutual confrontation of such tactics stimulates those in each category to better define their therapeutic goals, to evaluate themselves, their partners, and other significant persons more realistically, and to experiment with new roles. The first individual interview is carried on separately for either category. The therapist may cover the same ground with both, but the tactics may differ.

When two clients come together, for instance a married couple, the therapist sees each partner separately at first and then together in a combined interview. Confrontation techniques are used when the couple is asked who will see the therapist first; the therapist can see each individual's various reactions.

The individual interview

In this interview with the prospective candidate, the therapist has first to assess the character of the candidate's complaints and his suitability and motivation for systematic psychotherapy. The methods of this interview do not differ generally from those described in many textbooks on psychotherapy.

Over the years we have experimented with various kinds of schemas and questionnaires in performing the first interview. The form we found most useful is the Problem-Goal List, which we described in chapter 6.

In this section, we will concentrate on factors we consider of special importance in the interview which are often not given sufficient consideration in the traditional psychiatric interview.

Starting with the actual complaints. The interview should begin with a discussion of the candidate's actual problems and complaints and not by exploring the history of the candidate's early infancy. The history has to be covered later, going as far into the past, and in such detail, as the therapist considers necessary.

Why has the candidate decided to undergo treatment? And why now? The reasons for the candidates' decision to seek professional help and for doing it now should be discussed. What contributed to their decision besides the symptoms? What happened recently in their lives? What has changed? What do other people close to them such as their partner, spouse, parents, other family members and significant persons think or do about their symptoms? Do they know about them at all? How did they react to the candidate's decision to undergo treatment? This may offer an interesting view on the candidate's marital or family situation. Asking about the reasons for coming, may be significant in assessing a candidate's motivation for therapy.

What do you think your friend (spouse, mother, son) would say about you if he or she was here alone? We have found it useful to ask candidates this question directly. There may be many different answers. The candidate may be wrong about the significant person's real feelings and probable reactions. The therapist must not become biased even though such answers are important in illuminating how the candidates see their marital and family situation. If the candidate does not seem confident in his reply, this may be useful information in exploring further the candidate's attitude toward authorities.

Do not just gather information, use it. The candidate's life situation, including its economic and financial aspects, his dependency on others, should not only be carefully explored but taken into consideration when assessing motivation for therapy.

If, for example, a woman candidate is being paid an exceptionally high allowance by her divorced husband mainly on the grounds that she is suffering from a neurosis, this fact will probably influence the forces working for or against her complete recovery, and the therapist should be aware of it. The therapist may not know all of the facts. Or he may have read them in the patient's file, but not have noted them as issues of significance.

What do you expect from the treatment? What will happen in practice? Will it change your life? In what way? Such questions have to be raised, and the therapist should not be satisfied with such vague answers as To get better or to feel freer, but should continue: What do you expect will happen when you get rid of your symptoms? From what do you want to be free? Is there anything you do now that you would like to do differently? Sometimes a candidate seems surprised. He cannot imagine life without symptoms. The answer may often clearly point to some conflict.

One candidate said: "I will be a new person. I will go to Australia to start a new life." He was asked if he planned to take his family (spouse and three children) with him: "Oh no, my wife would never leave home and her mother."

Here, in a short time, the whole area of conflicting wishes and forces working for and against the candidate's full recovery was exposed. In the candidate's mind were such thoughts as: "I would like to be free from my family—so much trouble and responsibility and my interfering mother-in-law. But it is not easy. I am afraid to start and be alone. It is so hard to decide. But I do not have to decide now because I am so ill."

Clear and simple language. No cliches. The language used should be simple and clear. The therapist should not accept, without further clarification, a candidate's vague answers and use of cliches and must not use them himself.

In some cases, we may listen for many hours to talk about lack of communication, ego-boosting, or people's wishing to get in touch with their feelings. Some want to get closer to people, to be free, to be themselves, or to get rid of all that social conditioning. Such language may seem significant to those speaking, though each may mean different things by the same phrase. Without further specification, all of this remains superficial talk, and such talk may avoid other more important but painful issues.

No real information emerges from an interview full of these well-worn phrases. We do not know whether the partners having poor communication ever talk to each other, whether they live together or apart, how they spend their free time, or if they have some common interests and mutual obligations. Who takes care of their children? Who supports them? We still may not know what a person really does when depressed. Does he cry, drink excessively, or think of commiting suicide? We may not know whether a woman complaining of not being close enough to people spends all her time sitting at home meditating, takes care of three small children in an isolated suburban home, or feels distant from people at work as a clerk in a big office. We would not know what a young man means by wanting to be free. Free from what? From the expectations and pressure of his parents? From his sexual problems? From the rigid moral principles he was raised with from birth in an isolated social group and has been carrying ever since? Or free from *any* moral principles?

What do you expect to happen to your relationship (marriage, family) in two years time? It is important to explore the partners' or family members' perspectives on their relationship, and see how they differ. We ask each partner first when seeing him or her separately. Answers may illustrate the difference in value the relationship has for each partner. One husband, when asked how he visualized his marriage in five years time, said, "This is funny to imagine, that after five years—"and stopped. As it became clear later, he wanted to say that it would be funny, after five years to still live with the same wife. The therapist does not interpret clients' answers, but merely records them. He may find them useful in assessing the reward-cost balance that the relationship represents to both partners.

Who would be most unhappy if something tragic happened to you? This is another question we use first with each partner separately. One male client answered promptly: "My mother, she is the one who loves me." A woman may talk about the probable reactions of her three small children and not mention her husband at all.

Various psychomimic techniques may be used in the first interview. We may ask the partners to step several feet apart and then ask one of them to slowly move toward the other, who stays immobile, and advance as far as the distance the partner estimates between both of them in their relationship. After one partner has performed the task, the roles are reversed. There may be a significant difference between the estimates of each partner. The task may elicit strong emotions and lead to more open confrontation between the partners.

If the candidates have been found suitable for psychotherapy, their therapeutic goals have to be clarified. The goals are often preliminary at first, such as symptomatic relief, although it may seem obvious to the therapist that significant personality change is needed. The therapist does not have to press this issue since the candidates will be able to identify their therapeutic goals further in later steps of the system. The majority of the candidates are referred into step 2, the open group. This represents the first part of their therapeutic contract, that they commit themselves to attend the open group three or four times and then return to share their experiences with the therapist and make plans for future treatment, if needed.

The therapist who first saw the candidates becomes their assigned therapist, and the patients return to their assigned therapist any time they have completed a step in the system. The assigned therapist then makes the first draft of the therapeutic plan for the next step. The plan is usually modified during the step as new developments occur and as knowledge of the patient's personality and problems grow. Assigned therapists do not see their patients while the patients are enrolled in another step except in exceptional cases in which the therapists in charge of the step refer the patient back. Assigned therapists function more or less as resource persons and do not develop a close relationship with their patients. Although there are always elements of transference involved, they are not especially stressed. If the patient, after having passed through several steps in the system, including the therapeutic community, still needs treatment and if the therapist assumes the patient would benefit from ongoing individual psychotherapy (step 6) and starts it, then the patient-therapist relationship becomes closer and additional elements of transference are deliberately fostered.

What happens to clients and patients after the first interview

Clients and patients may continue in the system, entering various steps according to their special circumstances. If the candidate comes

alone, usually after having dissolved one or more dissatisfactory relationships in the past, he may be referred directly to step 4 to meet in
group with other clients, patients, and significant persons. He or she
works there for several sessions and comes back to the therapist again
where further therapeutic plans are made, if necessary. Some, especially
those who complain of overt neurotic symptoms, may go into step 2, the
open group, and continue from there, progressing to further steps of
the system as their need and motivation for therapy continues.

If both partners, or several family members, seek treatment and are
therapeutically well-motivated, they may continue together through the
various steps of the system. In the past, we had frequently treated families and couples in a way which is now usually understood as family
therapy. After we developed the therapeutic community and step 4, we
found it far more efficient to enroll in the system those clients and
patients who would otherwise have been treated with traditional family
therapy. (We elaborate on our methods of family therapy in the section
on step 4.)

Our favored combination for couples, partners, or family members
is that they usually have another session with the therapist in which the
assessment of the relationship continues and psychodramatic and psychomimic techniques may be used. After that, several options are open.

1. Both partners of a couple, or several family members, are referred
to group b in the fourth step with the commitment to attend the group
several times, four or five sessions, and then return to the same therapist. This is often enough for a couple to start solving their problems
on their own in a more healthy way. The treatment may be terminated
with the option of future therapy left open.

2. One partner may be referred into the open group, the other into
the 4b group for the same length of time, and then both meet with the
therapist again.

3. The therapist may continue having sessions with both partners or
with the whole family for a while and then refer them to group 4b or
another step.

In general, policy is very flexible. Clients or patients may go as far in
the treatment as their motivation allows, and as far as the therapist
considers it useful. These steps may be combined in the same way with
identified patients. The therapist has a variety of treatment options
available.

THE SECOND STEP: OPEN GROUP

The optimal number of participants in the open group is eighteen to twenty; however, there may also be guests in attendance, bringing the number to twenty-five or twenty-eight. We have found the open group useful for training students and mental health professionals in psychotherapy. The group meets once weekly for approximately four hours.

Participants. The open group combines two categories of patients: those starting treatment who have just been assessed by the therapist, and those who have completed a major part of the treatment in the residential therapeutic community (ex-patients). Both categories (patients and clients) attend the group at least three times as part of their contract.

Leadership. The same therapist is responsible for leading the group for several months at a time. He may alternate with another therapist for a short while, but the basic methods and techniques have to remain constant. If possible, there is always another member of the staff present who is familiar with some of the patients, either ex-patients or new patients from the admission interview. The therapist from the therapeutic community sometimes visits the group. Even with other staff members present, the strategy of the group is directed by one person only, the therapist in charge.

Limitations in attendance. The attendance of the group is limited in time for every participant. For example, new patients are told by the admitting therapist to visit the group three times. Ex-patients have a commitment to visit the open group two or three times after returning from the therapeutic community. The number of visits required is flexible, depending upon other modalities and methods available in the system. We found limitation of attendance useful, since patients worked harder if they considered it a task to be accomplished in a certain time.

Physical Setting. The best place for the open group is a room in which all members can sit comfortably in a circle and see each other's faces. We have always preferred simple, light chairs which can easily be moved when the members need space for role-playing or psychodrama. The chairs should be comfortable enough to sit on for one or two hours, but not heavy easy-chairs in which the participants become so comfortable that they grow sleepy and have difficulty getting up from. Such details may seem obvious, but great differences in the activity and liveliness of the group result from space arrangement and equipment. In some therapeutic settings for example, one may find the group arranged in large, squarely-shaped halls with heavy, immovable easy-chairs that line the four walls. People sitting in corners hardly see or hear the people in the opposite corner, and the therapist does not have a proper overview.

The staff may spend long hours discussing how to increase the interaction and communication between the participants and fail to see that the setting itself is important for an active and communicative group.

What therapeutic goals can be achieved in just a few meetings? In the open group, the participants are exposed to the following therapeutic experience: The patients see that they are not alone in their difficulties and that there are others who have more serious problems. They realize that physical symptoms are not necessarily the result of a physical illness, that patients are accepted by others, and the others are ready to listen and give sympathy and emotional support. Some patients may abreact emotions which have been pent up in them for years. A rudimentary insight received is sometimes sufficient for the patient to lose symptoms and partly change his or her life.

Factors responsible for the group's therapeutic effectiveness

Several aspects of the large open group allow it to develop a therapeutic capacity in a relatively short time.

The referral. The patients invited into the group know that this group represents a regular part of the systematic treatment that a new patient goes through. They do not feel deprived of individual therapy. They also realize, from the beginning, that groups are a form of treatment highly regarded by the staff and by the other patients. This helps develop their positive attitude toward treatment from the start. In fact, patients often feel positive toward the group even before entering it.

The combination of new and ex-patients. This factor, correctly used as we will illustrate, represents a powerful tool that may be used with modification in many other therapeutic modalities.

Combination of methods and techniques. Flexible use of various verbal and nonverbal psychotherapeutic techniques often enables the therapist to create moments of significant therapeutic experience for a patient in a short time, during their first or second visit. In this regard ex-patients are eminently helpful as they take on role playing, psychodrama, or nonverbal tasks quite naturally.

Therapeutic strategy. One therapist is responsible for the leadership of the group. In a particularly large group, the leader must play a very active and skillful role. The leader need not be the psychotherapist highest in rank or skill; all the therapists should lead the group in turn under supervision. The leader may come with a plan based on the group situation as analyzed in the staff meeting preceding the group session. The plan, however, should be flexible so that as the situation in the group develops, the leader can change the focus.

The therapist actively structures the session by asking patients to cooperate in a certain way—for example, asking the new patients to introduce themselves or asking them to comment on what the other members of the group have just said or done. The therapist may insist upon a person going to the center of the group and performing a special task, such as a dialogue with a significant person in his life; the therapist may even gently push a person into role playing or any other activity in the group.

The therapist does not make any immediate interpretations or diagnostic conclusions, nor does he or she make any judgments or give any recommendations about the patient's personal life, interpersonal relations, or life philosophy. The therapist often confronts the patients in the group with the reactions of others or may ask others to show, in role-playing and psychodrama, how they would react in the patient's situation or how they would solve a particular problem. It should be clear, however, that final decisions are to be left to the patient.

Open group as the place of further assessment
In the open group, the assessment of the patient continues. The patient's problems, motivation for therapy, and whole life situation are further explored. Patients are exposed to intensive stimuli both through the catalytic influence of ex-patients or by listening to other participants reveal themselves in discussion, psychodrama, or psychomime. After one or two sessions, the participants of the open group know more about a certain person than a therapist would know after months of individual interviews.

A typical group session
Twenty-nine persons present, belonging to the following categories:

1. Four new patients coming for the first time
2. Six new patients on their second or third visit
3. Five patients who had already been in the group three times, had returned to their assigned therapist for one or two individual interviews, and then came back to continue in the group (Later some of them will go into the therapeutic community)

4. Four patients who returned from the therapeutic community the preceding week (ex-patients)
5. Five patients who returned from the therapeutic community two weeks previously, this being their second visit to the group after treatment in the therapeutic community
6. The therapist in charge of the group
7. Another therapist (social worker, psychologist, or nurse) who regularly attends the group, helps check in new patients, and acts as host before the group starts. It is helpful if this staff member is a person familiar with as many patients as possible, having interviewed them previously or knowing ex-patients from regular visits to the therapeutic community
8. Two junior mental health professionals who attend the group for a limited time as part of their training
9. One guest, a medical professional

Chairs have already been placed in a large circle; people who come take their places with visitors and staff members intermingling with the patients.

First half of the session. The therapist walks in and addresses the group with a simple greeting. He asks new patients to identify and introduce themselves. As each patient rises, the therapist, who at the beginning, was sitting in one of the chairs, stands up and moves around the circle, stopping in front of each speaker. The therapist walks around from one new patient to another. He is close to the patient, introduces himself, and acts in a supportive way, but the introduction is addressed to the whole group, not just to the patient, and has to be distinct and loud enough to be audible to all.

The introduction of new patients is kept short. The therapist does not go into any details and does not encourage other group members to participate in interviewing new members, although he may do this later.

The use of simple language is stressed from the start, especially when discussing symptoms. For example, although the term depression is commonly used, the therapist should request further explanation for several reasons: First, people often mean different things by depression. Second, and this may be the most important reason, if people use technical or psychological terms to describe their mood or symptom, it is easier for them to omit the interpersonal quality of the mood or symptom described. For example, it is easier to say or feel "I have depression" than to realize "I am sad, I am alone because I have no friends, my lover left me, my son is not interested in me anymore," and so forth. In other groups, we have found people to talk for many hours in psychological jargon about their depression, lack of communication, or difficulty in expressing their feelings. At the same time, they omitted all details about their interpersonal relationships and the reality of their lives.

The introduction of new patients helps them feel a part of the group as quickly as possible, but there are other techniques used for the same purpose. If the new patient describes some of his symptoms, the therapist may gently interrupt and ask if anyone else has experienced the same symptoms at some time in their life. The new patient may see several hands raised and realize that he is not alone in his suffering. If an ex-patient has had the same symptoms in the past but lost them during treatment, this may represent the first hope for the new patient.

After the new patients have been introduced, the therapist may suggest a short overview of all other persons present. He briefly asks the group to identify the people who had come for the second time, those who had visited the group more than twice, and the ex-patients. Other staff members and guests are also briefly introduced. This enables new members to become more familiar with the group as a whole and also makes them feel less anonymous and less exposed in front of the group.

After the new patients have been introduced and the others briefly identified, the therapist may suggest various ways in which to continue. Sometimes the discussion with the new members leads to a specific problem, for example, if someone expresses doubt concerning whether or not he belongs in the group, ex-patients will spontaneously step into the discussion.

After the introduction of the new patients, the therapist will often ask ex-patients to form a small circle in the center of the larger one and discuss their experiences. The ex-patients from the therapeutic community in Lobec, described in detail below, spoke about it using the name *Lobec*.

Therapist: Please imagine that you are here alone, a small group, discussing what has happened to each of you in the past few weeks. (*He repeats*) We are not here, you are alone. (*Four ex-patients, the last group that had returned from the therapeutic community, stand up and take their chairs into the middle of the large circle. Peter, a man in his early forties, who had been the chairman of the patients' committee in the therapeutic community during the last week of his stay, spontaneously takes over the leadership of the small group.*)

Peter: I think that Barbara made the biggest change of all of us.

Barbara (a twenty-seven-year-old single woman): Yes, I think so.

Alan: I think I am in the middle. I feel much better now, but maybe you don't notice it so much with me.

Barbara: And what about you Peter, won't you start first?

Peter: Sure. I remember sitting here for the first time in this group about three months ago. I felt rather annoyed when my doctor told me "you need something special, something more inten- sive——treatment in the therapeutic community." I did not expect much. I have seen many doctors and psychiatrists in the past two years. I had been in a hospital. . . . I still had my terrible chest pains, palpitations, and sometimes I was afraid I might die at any moment. I was repeatedly told that it was not my heart, it was psychological, but it did not help, it did not relieve me of the pain or the fear. Then, on top of all this, I had to pack and go somewhere in a small place in the country and live with strangers for several weeks. The first time I came here I felt "I do not belong here, this is completely irrelevant to me and my problems. These people seem healthier than I feel." They had various, serious problems in their lives; then had lost their spouses, they had difficulties with their children, they were in financial trouble, they had lost their jobs. This all seemed different from my trouble.

Barbara: And was it, in fact, so much different?

Peter: No. You must know Barbara; you role-played my wife and my daughter several times, and you were the first person I spoke really openly to about Claire. I never made a secret of the fact that I was not excitingly happy in my married and family life during the past few years. I could not say what had changed, but all of us, my wife, my daughter and myself, somehow went our separate ways. I have had several affairs with other women; the last and longest one with Claire. But I considered it quite common, and many of my friends and colleagues are in the same boat. I am a specialist in a technical field, working in business, and I teach part-time at the college, mostly night classes. I have the opportunity to meet many people younger then myself, especially women. In the past I had never felt that my personal life had any relevance to my illness. True it became a fa- vorite topic of conversation for my doctors and mental health people, but all of it left me cold. I let them talk, feeling that it had no connection with my heart troubles.

Alan: And what persuaded you it was relevant?

Peter: It was not direct persuading. I mean, nobody tried to persuade me about it since I started here, but at a certain time, the same things started to have a different meaning to me. I remember the breaking point, when Barbara asked me to play her boyfriend, a married man, practically a man of my age. I started, quite formally, dutifully trying to present the same features Barbara had described in her friend. I simply wanted to help Barbara, who is a nice girl. But later, in our dialogue, it became more and more personal and familiar to me. I suddenly realized that this was the same situation I had been in with Claire during the past few years. She loves me and she expects more from me than I am probably willing to give her. She probably has various ideas about the future of our relationship, and I would not like to lose her. I felt the dilemma in me, in my chest. I started to have intense pains which I had not had for several days previously. Another important moment was when I heard Maria talking about her husband and when she tried to tell him openly what she thought of him. She said something like, "You see, Robert, I realize that I do not have much to lose if I separate from you, and this is a relief to me. What was my life in the past ten years with you? I was your housekeeper. You did not treat me as a person close to you, and I was not able to become close to you either." Not that these words were unfamiliar to me. I have heard similar expressions from my wife in some of our rare arguments, but it did not impress me then. But it was like a blow to me when I heard Maria. I somehow felt close to her and understood how she felt, and I felt angry with her husband. I realized, with a funny feeling, it was me. I was similar to Maria's husband, probably not a bad guy in general, but someone who makes Maria so terribly unhappy.

Barbara: You know Peter, you remind me of Tom, my boyfriend. I told you already, when we were at Lobec, I idealized him so much and I was terribly disappointed when he started to skip our dates and finally to talk about "slowly dissolving our relationship." I invested all my thoughts and feelings in him. He appeared to me to be a lonely, unhappy man who needed me to love him and protect him, in spite of his having a wife and family. I felt so important to him, and confident in our relationship. Well, I am over it now, and I will not take any more pills. I think you helped me to see Tom as a real human being—partly good, partly bad—more or less an ordinary man, not just that fascinating man and lover I saw once a week. I gained a lot of confidence in Lobec; I can exist and survive no matter how the future with Tom will be.

Peter: And what about you Alan? By the way, you know how I resented you at first. You reminded me of some of my younger colleagues; bright, handsome, self-confident, ironical, and thoughtless.

Alan: Yes, and I resented your patronizing, your efficient-executive attitude, and I criticized you when you were foreman of our group. I always hated my bosses, feeling they pushed me unnecessarily into things I did not want. It started with my old man at home. He wanted me to be a lawyer like him, but I dropped out of college in the first year. But really, I got to like you later, and Michael too (*another patient, a man in his fifties who was still in the therapeutic community*). I have not figured it out fully yet, what to do with my rebelliousness. Somehow, I always liked to blow up, to clash with my boss, or with anyone in authority. It was a pleasant feeling, but now I know it is a dead end—it leads me nowhere. I feel great for a while. I quit the job or get fired, and I feel free. But later, I get miserable and this lasts a long time. I start drinking more than is good for me, and with girls everything goes wrong.

Peter: I see a change in Alan. I remember him reading his life history. He did not see anything wrong with himself then. He complained of an impossible boss and bad luck with girls. By the way, you realize how suspicious you are with girls, always expecting something to go wrong. Even the best one must get tired pretty soon.

Alan: Yes, that's another story, but we do not have time for it now.

Helen (a twenty-nine-year-old woman, office clerk, married with a 2-year-old boy): (*Laughing*) Well, everybody is looking at me now. All right, let's start. I'll try to make it short, so that I finish before the break. In one way I feel as though I am in a similar position to Alan. I also felt that I was always pushed, not appreciated enough, exploited in my job; and it's worse for a woman. Every man, no matter how stupid, gets the better position or gets a raise before a woman does. Sometimes I couldn't tolerate it any more. I became angry with my boss, was hypercritical to my colleagues and finally became sick, so that I could not work any more. And it was the same at home. I felt constantly overburdened; everything depended on me: the house, the child, the babysitter, the payments, and Ted, my husband, who was calm and cool studying for his exams.

Barbara: Helen, I know you a little bit from Lobec, and I agree with everything you said about how things are at work and a woman's situation. But if one listens to you, one would wonder: All right, you are a victim of circumstances, but why are you here? What use can psychotherapy be to you?

Helen: I know. This is the way I present myself, exaggerating some things and belittling others. I think I badly needed treatment. I appreciated that people at the therapeutic community, even men, took me seriously and I became friendly with most of them. The therapists never tried to interpret my social criticism and my political views as lack of femininity, or other similar garbage. But I realized that I had to find other ways of coping with the complex situation I was in. Partly, I created it myself, agreeing to be the main supporter of the family with Ted studying and working part-time until he finishes law school. We could easily have waited for a family, but it was me who insisted upon starting so early. Ted and I have had several talks about it recently, and I must say that it has helped us both.

Therapist: I think we have to take a break. Thank you very much, all of you.

The second half of the session. Besides its function as a relaxation for the patients as well as the staff, the break serves other important purposes. People are able to talk directly to each other; newcomers become acquainted with the others and are able to talk with the ex-patients, obtaining information about how the ex-patients felt when they began, what things are like in the therapeutic community. The ex-patients are very open in discussing their own experiences and feelings, but they do not give information about others or about others' problems. We realize that this type of coffee break is better than any type of booklet in supplying information about the treatment, and especially about the therapeutic community.

The therapist decides how to start the second half of the session. He has to make a plan, taking into account the general mood of the group, the outcome of the first half, specific problems which appeared during the first half, and the special tasks that the group has to accomplish at this particular session. For example, it may be important to work more intensively with a member of the group who has visited the group several times and who may be feeling depressed and hopeless, or asking for special attention.

This time, the therapist decided to suggest further discussion of the ex-patients and continue later with some of the new patients.

Therapist: Now, I think that we may stop pretending that we were not here during the discussion of the people who have returned from the therapeutic community. Some of you probably have comments and questions about it all. Please go ahead.

Diane (a new patient, a woman in her early thirties): I feel uneasy and confused hearing all this. It seems to me that all these people here are not really ill, not as ill as I feel. I have been having headaches and pains all over my spine for the last three years. I cannot work, I can't do anything. All their problems seem so remote to me. I would be happy if I could get rid of my pains for one day, or one week, and if I could get rid of them for good, I would not wish for anything else. Some of these people here, like this young man—excuse me, I forgot your name—didn't mention any illness. They talked about jobs, bosses, girlfriends, boyfriends and drinking. (*Alan raises his hand.*)

Therapist: Please go ahead.

Alan: I think you meant me, my name is Alan. First of all, I don't want to argue or dissuade you. You have a right to your own views about us. In a way, I felt something similar when I started here. I thought, "What's the sense in talking about my problems, or having some sort of treatment? I am alright, it is the boss, it is the girl, who makes me sick. They are wrong." I would not listen to anyone who tried to persuade me that it could be my fault. However, I did have symptoms. I had headaches, I could not sleep, and at one time, my sexual life became so bad that I was close to ending my life.

Therapist: (*To the new patient Diane*) Would you mind telling us something more about yourself?

Diane: No, but I already told you everything on admission, about my previous treatment and the last x-rays and medications.

Therapist: Yes, but I do not mean the admission interview and the physical examination. That remains in the file, and I do not reveal any information from the file to the group. This group is something different.

Diane: (Rather hesitantly) Well, what would you like to know?

Therapist: (To the whole group) Would you help me, and ask Diane?

Peter: I remember when you introduced yourself you said that you were

married and a housewife, and that you have been having your symptoms for quite a long time. How long was it?

Diane: About three years.

Peter: I would like to have a picture of your husband. What does he
look like, how old is he, and what does he do for a living?

Diane: He's an engineer in the mining industry. He's forty, looks pretty
good and is tall and blonde, with blue eyes.

Barbara: Is this the first marriage for both of you?

Diane: The first for me, the second for my husband. He divorced his
first wife.

Barbara: Does your husband support his first wife? Does he have any
children?

Diane: Yes, he supports his first wife and the two children by his first
marriage.

Helen: What did you do before you got married? Did you work?

Diane: I was trained as a secretary. The last job I had was as a secretary
to the director in the place where my husband worked. We met at
work. But this was when he was separated from his wife.

Helen: Did you continue working after you got married?

Diane: I worked for about a year after, but then I became ill and had
to stop working.

Alan: You stopped working because you became ill?

Diane: Right.

Helen: And did your husband appreciate your work?

Diane: I think he did. Yes, he did.

Helen: You do not seem quite sure about it.

Diane: You know how men are.

Helen: Is your husband jealous of you?

Diane: I do not give him any reason.

Helen: But you know that some men are jealous no matter what you do.

Diane: Yes. (*After a while*) I would say he is. But listen, I don't like to
blame my husband. I know that you will start to persuade me that it
is my marriage, that I am unhappy in my marriage, but it's not true.
I have so often heard this.

Therapist: Nobody will persuade you about anything here. We do not
have any preconceived ideas, and we don't know anything about your
marriage. I would like to suggest something else to you. I realize that
you are serious about your treatment and you would like to achieve
results. Why not start today? All these questions and discussions about
you are already a part of your treatment. (*The therapist purposefully*

does not take the cue and ask Diane why she is so afraid of anyone doubting the happiness of her marriage. First, because on the basis of the material available, any judgment of the quality of the marriage and its connection with the patient's symptoms would be premature and speculative. Second, even if there is a connection, to pursue such a line would make Diane too defensive at this particular time. Instead, the therapist adopts a different tactic.)

Diane: O.K., what shall I do?

Therapist: I would like to suggest something to you so that you may work more intensively with us today, but I cannot press you. It is completely up to you whether or not you continue. You may refuse, if you wish.

Diane: What is it?

Therapist: Would you try to do things in practice, as this is better than long explanations.

Diane: *(With a note of resignation)* O.K.

Therapist: Now, please do me a favor and step here in the middle of the circle.

Diane: *(Steps into the middle of the circle.)*

Therapist: Sit down on this chair and imagine that you have become healthy. All your pains and troubles have gone, cured by treatment, or a miracle. You are free of your symptoms and you know they will not return.

Diane: It's silly. It's impossible.

Therapist: I have not yet finished. Imagine further that you have just realized this and that you are healthy and cured. You would probably like to talk to someone about it. Under these circumstances, who is the person that you would like to talk to?

Diane: My husband.

Therapist: Suppose that your husband is on a business trip and you are unable to reach him. Who else would you call?

Diane: It is difficult. It is so unreal.

Therapist: Try to think, who else could it be?

Diane: Mmm—it might be Bernie. She worked with me in the past. Now she's married and lives close to us.

Therapist: Alright, arrange a meeting with Bernie. Who will volunteer to represent Bernie? *(Three women, Helen, Barbara and one other woman, a patient who had been visiting the group for a longer time, raise their hands.)*
(To Diane) Would you like to pick one of the volunteers, maybe someone who is similar in appearance to your friend?
(Diane picks Barbara.)
Good. Now tell us where the talk will take place. In your house?

Diane: Yes. In the sitting room.

Therapist: Can you describe your sitting room? The type of chairs or chesterfield, the shape of the room?

Diane: It's a big, square room, there is a chesterfield at this side, a big window here, some potted plants, a little table, and two big easy chairs here.

Therapist: What is the color scheme?

Diane: The furniture is light brown, the upholstery light beige, and the carpet is almost a white, or cream color.

Therapist: You may start. Bernie is just coming in.

Bernie (Represented by Barbara): Hi Diane, how are you today? Do you feel better?

Diane: Yes, I feel fine. In fact, I feel perfect. The last cure was successful, all the pains have gone, and the doctor told me it is definite. They will not come back. (Diane's voice is dropping down as she speaks these last words and she is looking rather sad.)

Bernie/Barbara: (*Walks closer to Diane and puts her hands on Diane's shoulders, looking into her eyes.*) That's marvellous, you must be delighted.

Diane: (*Without any enthusiasm*) Yes.

Bernie/Barbara: This is something you have wanted so deeply. Now you will start a new life, won't you?

Diane: I don't think so. What should I change?

Bernie/Barbara: I don't know, but I suppose that now you are healthy you will be more active. Maybe you don't want to stay at home any more.

Diane: Why not? There is so much to do around the house if you do it properly.

Bernie/Barbara: I know. I am home now, but that is mostly because of my children, otherwise I wouldn't be. I sometimes find it boring. It is pleasant not having to get up every morning and drive to the office, but on the other hand, we had a lot of fun there. Do you remember? I felt I was somebody, and it's not a bad idea to have your own money either.

Diane: My husband gives me all the money I need.

Bernie/Barbara: I see. Then you will probably do more sports now. You are pretty good on skis as far as I can remember. Please correct me if I'm wrong as I am improvising.

Diane: Ski. Yes, but I would not like to go alone, and my husband, Bob, has very little time. He quite often works on Saturday, and some of his weekends are reserved for his children.

Bernie/Barbara: Do you invite the children into your home for weekends?

Diane: At first we used to, but it did not work out. The boys are quite noisy and it made me nervous. I could not stand it when I had pains. Now he takes them out for a trip, or sailing, on Sundays most of the time.

Bernie/Barbara: I see. (*Cheerfully*) And what other plans do you have Diane now that you are finally healthy?

Diane: I don't know. I have to think about it first. It all came so suddenly. (*Diane looks uneasy and rather sad.*)

Therapist: Well, I think that will be enough for the present. No, do not leave (*to Diane and Barbara who were about to return to their places*). Stay there for a short while. (*Looking round the group*) Any comments?

Peter: I would like to ask Diane something. How old are the boys of your husband's first marriage?

Diane: Now let me see. They might be eight and ten years old. They are probably more reasonable now, but you can imagine how it was about four years ago.

Peter: And how do you get on with them?

Diane: I tried my best from the start, I am sure, always preparing their favorite dishes, as well as helping my husband to pick out gifts for them. They did not seem to appreciate it. Of course they stick to their mother, and I have not seen much of them for the past two years. Most of the time Bob takes care of them alone.

Helen: Do you think your husband helped you in relating to his children?

Diane: I believe so. It's funny you asking me that. You see, I always felt nervous when I was with the boys, but I remember that I felt more confident and could get along more easily with them when we were alone, rather than in Bob's presence.

Maggie (one of the new patients, on her third visit to the group): I had the same experience many years ago when my husband introduced his two daughters from his previous marriage to me. He was so anxious that I succeed in developing a good relationship with them that he made me uneasy and nervous.

Some comments about the techniques used

This last scene illustrates a technique we often use in the group before starting systematic psychotherapy with a new patient. It helps to explore the patient's present life. The therapist does not have to ask questions himself since the whole group, especially the ex-patients, are helpful in doing this. It serves as the first step in explaining and estimating the role that the illness plays in the patient's everyday life and in his motivation toward treatment.

For people who have had symptoms for a considerable length of time, the sole fact of being ill represents an important factor. Their lives change and they adapt to the existence of illness, thus changing the hierarchy of values and resources from which they draw satisfaction. Sometimes the illness brings new sources of satisfaction. For example, people may receive more attention and love from the people around them than they did before. A man who feels unhappy and insecure in his relationship with his wife may feel happier when he becomes ill because his wife begins to care of him more. The change may be genuine. The wife, realizing that her husband needs and appreciates her attention, may come to love him more.

The illness may save a person from many worries, such as making a difficult and unpleasant decision: for example, whether to continue in an ambivalent relationship with a partner; whether to get married; whether to start a family. A long term bachelor, living in a close relationship with his loving, overpowering, and overprotective mother, may be spared the decision of whether to stay with his mother indefinitely or leave her and start a new life with his girlfriend, a life that he views as full of unknown problems and dangers. The illness resolves the decision for him, as he is no longer fit for marriage. The illness may free a person from the remorse felt at not being as successful in life and career as he or she had wanted to be or was expected to be by others, such as parents. The illness may absolve a person of guilt feelings, and free him or her from responsibilities. A certain limitation of activity, caused by the illness, may bring peace of mind to an overambitious and restless person.

This is as true for a physical illness as for an emotional one. If we assume that the symptoms can be cured and expect them to be cured by the treatment, we then have to take into consideration that the patients are simultaneously facing the difficult task of rebuilding their reward-cost systems and hierarchy of values and experiencing changes in their personal relationships. If psychotherapy is to be effective, the process of rebuilding the reward-cost system must go hand in hand with treatment or be one of the treatment goals. This is not an easy matter. Sometimes, the rewards from their illness may be so great that patients are barely motivated for change toward health, and thus for any type of treatment. For example, in some cases, there are high financial compensations for neurotic symptoms.

The therapist has to be aware of all of this and to take into consideration the complex relations between the symptoms of illness, the patient's life situation, and the character of his or her interpersonal relations before starting on any systematic stragegy.

Rewards and costs in Diane's neurosis

In Diane's case, for example, it seemed probable that there was a significant relationship between her illness and her marriage, but most likely one more complex than indicated by some of her past therapist's interpretations. Diane was not simply ill because she was dissatisfied and unhappy in her relationship with her husband. She was relatively happy and satisfied in this relationship *because* she was ill. The price she paid was her illness. What she was mainly dissatisfied with was her social role in the marriage, not the relationship with her husband—a distinction often not taken enough into consideration in traditional family therapy.

How would one interpret Diane's performance in the aforementioned scene? Although no far-reaching conclusions should be made from one single role-playing, Diane nevertheless revealed important material about herself and her marriage. She would never have done this at the start of psychotherapy, in such a short time. She also showed clearly that the idea of becoming healthy was new and rather embarrassing to her.

Let us now jump two months ahead and summarize how we saw Diane's problems after she completed treatment in the therapeutic community.

Diane was an intelligent, capable career woman before marrying her husband; she was confident in her work and very popular with the other employees. The director of a big firm completely relied on her; she worked independently in many areas; and to a certain extent, she was one of the most important people in the management of the whole firm. Diane enjoyed her work and her popularity. She accepted other men's friendship and admiration, dated often, and had had several romances with men, none of them long lasting or serious. She decided not to commit herself to any serious relationship unless she met a man suitable for a good partnership and marriage. Diane planned to have a perfect marriage, to be an excellent wife and a perfect mother to her children.

All these plans went wrong. Diane started to date Bob after he was separated from his first wife, and became fond of him. She did not know that Bob's separation from his wife was, at first, meant by both to be a trial. Bob and his wife had hoped that this would help eliminate some of their mutual problems and find a happier life together. But Bob had also complained that he felt tired of the marriage routine and needed a break and a fresh outlook on his life and marriage. Bob had meant this seriously at first, but after becoming involved with Diane he had gradually changed his mind and given up any plans of restoring his marriage. Later, in some of their arguments, he suggested that Diane had contributed to the complete breakdown of his first marriage, which Diane resented as unjust. When Bob started divorce proceedings, his first wife made it difficult, for him and especially for Diane. She complained to Diane's boss and other company executives. All of this made the start of Diane's marriage less pleasant and perfect than she had planned.

Soon after Diane and Bob were married, the problem arose with the children of Bob's first marriage. After Bob was released from the marriage routine, as he called it, he began to enjoy his children's company more and more. Parenthood being limited to weekends and other times of leisure appealed to Bob. He could always turn the children back to their mother when he became tired of them, or when any problem arose with them. This happened, for example, when they became ill, had a little accident, or simply started to be too noisy and wild. Bob tried hard to make the childrens' visits exciting for them, and the children responded well.

The relationship they had with their father was, of course, different from that with Diane. The boys felt the atmosphere of tension between their mother and Diane and felt that Diane was an intruder into the life of the family. At first, Diane tried hard to please the children and become their friend. Although Bob was unhappy when she could not succeed, he was unable to help her. Diane became jealous of the children and resented being left out of their relationship with Bob.

Diane wanted to have children of her own but did not become pregnant for several months. Bob did not mind postponing the new family; in fact, he did not miss children since he had those of his first marriage. He would not have minded had they had no children, when he considered the cost of supporting two families. He did realize, however, and was fair enough to understand, that his younger wife had a right to experience her own motherhood. After several months of trying to conceive, Diane consulted a specialist, who suggested a lengthy form of treatment and an operation. She was still working at that time. Going through the treatment and being unhappy and frustrated, she felt more and more tired. She also started to have pains and other symptoms. Once, when she complained of her symptoms to the gynecologist, he suggested she stop working and have a complete rest.

At first, it seemed a reasonable solution. Bob was also happier, expecting his wife to become less nervous. It also removed some of his jealousy at seeing Diane popular and friendly with other men at work. He became jealous easily and felt more confident having his wife at home. Bob was willing to offer her more attention and took care of her when her symptoms were more and more unpleasant. He helped around the house and worked in the garden when Diane could not do it. The couple became closer and spent more time together than they had before. They found many mutual interests in planning and improving their home.

And so Diane's dream of a perfect marriage and a happy family, run by an efficient, loving wife and mother, shrank to the life of a sick, childless housewife, living in an empty house with her husband. She experienced it more and more as a kind of dead end.

Diane improved after treatment, lost her pains and was able to rearrange her life, making it more satisfying. She did not have children as far as we know from her two-year follow-up.

Alan

We present more information about Alan, one of the former patients who acted in the first part of the group session.

Alan was in his early thirties. He was referred to the clinic for systematic treatment by a psychiatrist who had been seeing him at irregular intervals over the past four years. Alan went to his doctor's office in times of crisis: when he became tired of his job, became depressed, started to drink, suffered from sleeplessness, or had sexual difficulties. Before his treatment, Alan considered himself unlucky—a victim of circumstances. He had come across an impossible boss, the atmosphere in his job had become intolerable, and he had met the wrong type of girl. Most of the time, Alan was correct in his criticism of circumstances and the people around him, but the way in which he tried to cope with it was ineffective and damaging to him.

During treatment in the therapeutic community, it became obvious that Alan was partly instrumental in creating the sort of life he led, and even more instrumental in creating difficulties for himself. Alan carried two characteristic attitudes in his group schema which, in simplified form, can be formulated as: (1) all males in authority are too strict, domineering, unjust or intolerable and (2) women, as love and sex partners, are unfaithful and ultimately frustrate and disappoint me. Without going into many details, we can only mention that both attitudes developed during Alan's early experience with significant persons in his life, mostly with his parents. Alan's father was a strict disciplinarian, a man of high principles who loved and cared for his family but remained distant to his wife and children. Alan's mother was much warmer and more tolerant than her husband and, in individual contact, was much closer to her children, especially to Alan. However, she was also very loyal to her husband and, for the sake of peace in the family, outwardly sided with him, often against Alan. Alan always felt frustrated by his mother. When Alan was ten years old, his parents separated and he was left to live with his father. The mother took the younger child, a girl, with her and later remarried. This contributed to Alan's disappointment with his mother.

Alan's behavior towards men in authority, and towards women, became a part of a complex vicious circle. In the therapeutic community, it quickly became obvious how Alan anticipated his teachers and employers being bossy and unjust to him and how he actively antagonized them into becoming so, regardless of how tolerant and kind they were originally. This further reinforced his unrealistic attitude toward them, as well as toward persons with similar authority.

An important factor in his more complex attitude toward women was his recurrent choice of a girl friend competed for by many other men. The girl was usually very pretty, and Alan tried to impress her as a hero, often boasting of qualities he did not have. At the same time he became anxious and anticipated the girl's leaving him for someone else—an event which would hurt and anger him. He was tense and unable to develop any warm and close relationship with his girlfriends, and he was ambivalent about the idea of a long relationship because he was afraid to involve himself too deeply. His relationships with girls went their usual way, deteriorating in a short time. Alan experienced this as proof of all women's lack of stability and faithfulness.

Observers or participants, students and visitors in the large open group?

Students and professional guests sit in the circle intermingled with the patients. They do not observe the group from outside. They are participants although they have to observe certain rules discussed with them previously or communicated to them during the session if necessary. The students and guests talk if they wish, act, take part in the session and are free to do this as long as they react genuinely as private persons and not as therapists. For example, a student social worker may be asked by a patient to play his girlfriend in a psychodrama. The student then acts the way she feels she would act in that situation. She may get emotionally involved, become angry or cry, but must not give her partner professional advice or discuss his treatment. If she starts to do so, the therapist will interrupt and ask her to talk about herself and her reactions to the situation played.

Medical students and residents coming to the session as part of their training may be asked to role-play in psychodrama or to form a small group in the middle of the circle and discuss among themselves their own reactions and feelings about what has just happened in the group. The group listens and later discusses it with them.

A middle-aged hospital administrator once came as a guest. After he witnessed a played argument between a young patient and his father, represented by another patient, the administrator started to talk very openly about his marriage and about tension between himself and his wife related to their teenage son. For a considerable time the whole group focused on him, showing interest and support. After the session, the administrator said he could not understand what made him talk so much, that it was unusual for him. He added that he felt quite happy about having done so in the group.

Problems and Pitfalls of a large open group

The open group may be effectively used in community mental health centers as well as in the psychiatrist's private office, provided that certain conditions are fulfilled. Before starting, or taking over a group, therapists should ask themselves the following questions:

What are the therapeutic goals of the group?

How are the patients selected?

What methods and tactics are appropriate?

What is the general attitude towards the group in that particular setting and what role does the group play in the system of treatment?

Goals. A large open group may have a wide range of goals, from support to offering corrective experience. The therapist must be fully aware of the range of goals in his group and use appropriate methods.

Patient selection. The capacity of members of a group to understand and follow what is going on, verbally or nonverbally, should not greatly differ. A person with a brain syndrome; a slow, chronically depressed person; a person hampered to a certain extent by disorders of perception and/or thinking—all may benefit from group if patients are properly selected and appropriate methods used. But to combine in the same group patients who greatly differ in their capacity to understand, follow, and concentrate on therapeutic tasks makes the group hard to manage even for an experienced therapist and often practically useless to the patients.

Being in the same group with a neurotic expert in verbalization or intellectualization may increase a feeling of inadequacy in deeply depressed or partly disordered group members. It may interfere with their active participation in the group which they otherwise might have been able to offer. On the other hand, the presence of severely disordered patients makes intensive psychotherapy for neurotic patients impossible.

Members of the same therapeutic group should be able to follow and adhere to the same set of norms. Although these may differ substantially in complexity and severity in various groups, there are basic rules such as punctuality, remaining to the end of the group, and not leaving the group without a proper explanation. Patients who cannot follow and obey the norms of a particular group, either because they do not understand them or because they cannot control their behavior appropriately, cannot be treated effectively in that group.

All groups should have basic norms appropriate to their goals and the settings in which they operate, as well as sanctions against transgressing the norms. Without norms and sanctions a group cannot develop the cohesiveness necessary to become a therapeutic group.

Group members should not differ substantially in their potential to respond positively to the same therapeutic methods and techniques. For example, exposing patients to the criticism and social pressures of the group may be beneficial for many patients with abnormal personality traits and neurotic symptoms; such experience may be a crucial point in their treatment. The same method may be inappropriate and potentially dangerous to a group member who has just recovered from a psychotic episode and needs great support.

In psychiatric wards in many North American hospitals, severely disturbed and psychotic patients are mixed with nonpsychotics. Such mixing benefits neither group. The nonpsychotic patients often gladly accept the relaxed norms geared to the most disturbed patients. In one psychiatric hospital, nonpsychotic patients rarely came to community meetings because they were busy begging for money at the entrance (a problem never discussed at community meetings). Such wards become social slums which demoralize patients and staff. We often witnessed talented and enthusaistic nurses become apathetic because of organizational deficiencies they could do nothing about. The community meetings in some American institutions—with a mixed population of acute psychotics, neurotics, and psychopaths—often seemed to us a grotesque ritual. A valuable hour or two is spent each day in a more-or-less leaderless group, with a depressing effect on patients and staff.

We have heard mental health professionals reason that it would be undemocratic to separate patients and that they dislike pigeon-holing patients or labeling them mentally ill. We are not interested in diagnostic labels per se, but in homogenizing groups to achieve a social structure that maximizes therapeutic results with a minimum of staff; it is not, after all, undemocratic to have special cardiac wards to facilitate efficient treatment. It also has to be remembered that the question of mixed wards applies, in the United States, primarily to poor patients; affluent neurotics seldom go to psychiatric hospitals and in private hospitals are not often placed with psychotics.

Methods and tactics. In many places we have come across a special type of philosophy shared by the staff and transferred to the patients. This philosophy, though unspecified in any rational system, is more or less experienced by the staff as a fear of interfering or indoctrinating the patient and a rather magical belief that bringing people together in a group is sufficient treatment. Any effort to structure the group process and to offer a specific therapeutic experience to the members of the group is wrongly identified with indoctrination and with the effort to press the patient into adopting certain rigid social norms, particularly the norms of the establishment. Therapists are inhibited to lead the group in any possible way.

In some places there are several therapists reasonably able to lead group, but the problem is that they all try to lead at the same time.

There is no clearly defined leadership in the group. One person may be formally responsible for the group, but other staff members come and feel it their duty to talk, question, interview, interpret behavior, and suggest lines for group discussion and thought. The contribution of one staff member, though well meant, may completely jeopardize the therapeutic tactic of the other, even when the staff members have similar theoretical backgrounds and the best intentions. This often happens, for example, in a large group in psychiatric inpatient units or mental health clinics. The situation is even more complicated if many therapists work only part time, do not know each other properly, and do not know the patients, yet still feel obligated to contribute to the group.

Sometimes therapists try to apply methods they are learning in individual training but which are inappropriate to the patients and setting. Most common, in this respect, are the efforts of some therapists to apply strategies and tactics appropriate to a small closed group of highly motivated nonpsychotic patients, to an outpatient group of different selection with a low level of motivation and different therapeutic goals.

The role of the group in the therapeutic setting. Groups should constitute an organic part of the system of treatment. Patients should be enrolled into a group to be exposed to the specific therapeutic factors available in that group. The range of therapeutic group goals should be defined. Patients, as well as the whole staff, should consider group as a treatment modality on its own merits and not just as compensation for inaccessible individual psychotherapy. The progress of patients in the group has to be regularly evaluated by the group itself, and by the staff.

We have seen many settings where group therapy is not an organic part of systematic treatment. Groups start, continue, and stop whenever someone feels that he would like to lead a group, when someone offers his time and energy, or when the institution obtains a special grant. Patients are sometimes selected to fit the group. A memo is sent asking for referrals who fit certain criteria—for example, being able to talk freely, being interested in the group, or having free time on Wednesday afternoons. Such selection often attracts good talkers in superficial and general matters, experts in rationalization and intellectualization, and people who use groups as a compensation for real life. Sometimes the referral serves to relieve the therapist of a patient who is not improving and makes trouble. In such cases there is little serious consideration of the specific usefulness of the group for the treatment of that particular patient.

In some places, there is hardly any control over other treatment patients receive while attending the group. No one there considers the group as the most significant treatment. We meet patients in such places who visit the group twice a week, meet regularly with the social worker for marital therapy, and have regular appointments with their individual therapists several times a month. At the group they speak about general matters, to the social worker they complain of their spouses, and with the individual therapist they discuss their symptoms. They show different attitudes in each situation and receive different therapeutic treatments, including tranquilizers and antidepressants. Their therapists are dissatisfied with them and with their progress, which leaves the patients feeling disappointed by the therapist and the whole treatment. There is no proper cooperation between various therapists handling the same patients, and, in some departments or clinics, one therapist does not know the others exist.

The group, in such circumstances, does not develop cohesion and cannot offer emotional support to its members; the therapist cannot use group pressure on individual members when necessary. There is a typical vicious circle. Since the therapeutic potential of such groups is low, patients are not inspired and motivated enough to go into their own problems—to see, for example, the connection between their symptoms and problems in their relationships to significant persons. When patients in such groups start working more seriously, their tensions, anxiety, or other symptoms commonly increase. In a group with higher therapeutic potential, in different circumstances, the increase of anxiety and tension is met with emotional support from the group; this balances the anxiety and discomfort which develops as therapy progresses. A group with low therapeutic potential, or practically none, cannot provide this balance. At the same time, since there are no norms and no sanctions, the patients seek easier outside ways to relieve the tension, such as skipping the group or leaving it for good. Patients can easily obtain symptomatic relief through medication or emotional support from another therapist. A social worker may be willing to listen for hours to patients' complaints without expecting them to do anything themselves. Such patients leave the group or return to superficial participation.

In many psychiatric departments and clinics, group leadership is a sign of social and professional status among the mental health workers and is often jealously guarded against competition. Leading small verbal groups in which the patient and the therapist sit and talk is considered more prestigious than leading groups which use nonverbal and action techniques. Little concern is given to whether verbal groups are appropriate for the group population. Paradoxical situations occur. On one university hospital ward, an occupational therapist, well trained in various nonverbal and action techniques, sat twice a week with a group of five to six patients who greatly differed in the character and severity of their symptoms. The patients hardly talked. Some used the session to show their resistance toward the treatment and their negative attitude toward the whole hospital. Others, not understanding what was going on, often interrupted the group and walked out. The therapist was dissatisfied but never used any other technique for fear of losing her status as leader of a verbal group. Ward patients benefit much more by having two large homogenized groups, each using social games, pantomime, and other techniques, with only short discussion breaks focused on the problems of daily living in the unit. Such a practice relieves part of the patients' negative feelings toward treatment.

Back to the first therapist again

After the patients have attended the open group, fulfilling the commitment set at the first interview, they return to their assigned therapist. The therapist usually asks the patients how they felt in the group, which impressions they had and whether anything had changed in the way they see themselves and their problems since the last visit. The patients may react in many different ways. Here we present the most typical reactions.

I feel fine and don't need any further treatment. The patients look much better than before, they report that such symptoms as anxiety, headache, and sleeplessness have significantly decreased or completely disappeared. They feel healthier, more active, and report that they are about to resolve a personal crises such in partnership, marriage or family. They feel confident that they are able to resolve it satisfactorily. If the therapist finds that their behavior is genuine and in accordance with the report, which he regularly receives, of their attendance in the open group, the therapist may interrupt the treatment at this point and part with the patients in a friendly manner, leaving the door open if need arises in the future.

The short, intense therapeutic experience has helped the patient view problems more realistically, acquire more efficient social techniques to cope with them, and finally, actively overcome various personal crisis. The patient no longer reacts with symptoms, as he did previously.

Is it genuine or a flight into health? The therapist should not mistake a system of resistance for genuine improvement. To avoid this, he must watch for inconsistencies in the patients' verbal and nonverbal behavior. He must also use information from other sources, such as reports from the open group.

The patient may report that she feels great but looks tired, sleepy, and sad. Another patient assures the therapist he is doing well; however has just left his job giving no reason, sits home all day alone, and does not seem to be enjoying his leisure. He does not have any future plans but seems rather uneasy when asked about them. A patient may state she has resolved all of her personal problems but be vague about what they are, and the group reports that she was the same with them.

The therapist usually has to continue assessing such patients' problems and their real motivation for further treatment in one or two more sessions. The therapist may find that the patient was not sufficiently motivated for the therapy from the start, receiving too much reward from his illness. In the open group this is usually discovered more easily and earlier than would have been possible in many individual interviews.

Feels slightly better but wants further treatment. Patients may report that they feel relieved of some of their anxiety or other symptoms, but they realize they need more treatment to get rid of their symptoms completely. Some patients may have complained solely of physical symptoms at the first interview, often openly denying any interpersonal problems. In the group they start to have the first glimmerings of insight that their symptoms may be related to difficulties with people, although they may still be vague about the nature of these difficulties. Some patients may be especially interested in the therapeutic community because they found some of their problems similar to those ex-patients reported about themselves. New patients are also often impressed by the changes that the ex-patients report resulted from treatment. If what the patients report about themselves is consistent with the report from the group and their therapeutic motivation seems appropriate, they are referred to step 3—the therapeutic community. The staff member responsible for admission into the therapeutic community approaches the new candidates, introduces them to the norms, and supplies further details about the treatment.

It is in my marriage or my family. Some patients return from open group with the idea that they have identified their problems as clearly being in partnership, marital, or family relationships and want to focus on them in further treatment. Often they already have their partners or other significant persons interested in cooperating in psychotherapy. The therapist may suggest a joint interview to assess the situation, with partners or whole families, and then continue in the way he considers most useful. Often both partners are referred directly to step 4. A group of significant persons meet with ex-patients from the therapeutic community and work there together for several sessions, about a month. They return again to the therapist. Or the identified patient may be encouraged to continue in the therapeutic community, while the partners are referred to step 4. Both work independently and meet together when the patient returns from the therapeutic community.

Both methods mentioned are favored by us over therapy focused on only one family.

THE THIRD STEP: THE THERAPEUTIC COMMUNITY AT LOBEC

In the development of integrated psychotherapy, Lobec—as a special kind of therapeutic community—held a pivotal position. In all aspects, it was a comprehensive model of real life—people working, living, and having fun together. In addition to providing a variety of everyday situations, the model therapeutic community gave us freedom to experiment with and develop techniques using *surplus reality* (Moreno 1959)—psychodrama, psychomime, fantasy games and rituals.

The therapeutic power of the peer group was most striking at Lobec. This was confirmed by its Canadian counterpart, the residential therapeutic community at the Haney Forestry Camp. Lobec showed us which elements were missing in other forms of therapy, and gradually the techniques developed there infiltrated all other forms of treatment, especially those at the Day Center in Prague and later at Day House in Vancouver.

In discussing step 3 of the system, we will not describe the Prague Day Center; its structure and program are basically the same as those of the Day House in Vancouver (described in chapter 8), except that the Prague center also organized an evening program and weekend workshop.

Patients and setting

To be referred to Lobec, patients have to meet the following criteria:

1. Age 20 to 60
2. Absence of somatic illness which would require medical and dietary treatment and prevent the patient from fully participating in the program, which includes work and sports

3. Motivation to get better and willingness to observe Lobec's rules, reflected in a formal commitment
4. Nonpsychotic disorder (neurotic symptoms, character disorder, psychosomatic illness)

Lobec was developed and designed for nonpsychotic patients. However, significant elements of the treatment and program are applicable for patient communities in other categories—for example, patients in remission from psychotic illness, or alcoholics.

The patients stay at Lobec from four to six weeks. Only occasionally is the stay prolonged. Staying longer than eight weeks does not seem to lead to any significant improvement; it may, in fact, hamper the patient's return to normal life.

The community of twenty-five to thirty patients and three therapists is located about sixty-five kilometers from Prague, in the small village of Lobec, (pronounced Lobetch). It is housed in an old building on a state farm in pleasant countryside. The living quarters are simple; the first patients had to manufacture their own beds. Even after many changes over the years, such as the building being remodeled and modernized, the patients, who are mostly city people, still live there less comfortably than in their own homes. Men and women are separated in two-to-four-person bedrooms on one floor. The therapists have their apartments in the same house. At the beginning the therapists, two at that time, lived there permanently. Now the therapists use the apartments when on duty (which consists of several days and nights) but leave for their homes, mostly in Prague, on their days off. There is always at least one therapist present, either with the group or in the house, after the program as well as on weekends. For several years the therapists, helped by the patients, coped with all house management and administrative tasks, but now the centre has a house manager, a janitor, and complete kitchen staff.

The house sits on a hill isolated from the village by a large garden and park. Originally the house was a small castle. The patients have only superficial contacts with the village people like shopping. Only the therapists and manager have direct contact with the farm employees. The travel connections to Prague and other places the patients came from are poor, and the patients do not keep their cars at Lobec.

Visits by professional guests are regulated and limited to certain days. Visits by patients' families, relatives and close friends are limited to Sunday and holiday afternoons. A new patient invites his visitors only after fourteen days at the center. Significant persons are expected to become part of the therapeutic process from the beginning and are invited to special groups of family members, partners and other significant persons in Prague. (These groups of significant persons will be described in step 4.)

The staff
For the first eight years, the Lobec staff consisted of two therapists—both women without any previous professional training in mental health but with a great deal of experience of life. They were both healthy, middle-aged women, capable of working with the patients in the fields and forests, intelligent and well aware of the limits of their knowledge, and experience in organizing groups of people. They were fond of people, trusting but not naive, with a high frustration tolerance and a gift of inoffensive humor which dissolved tense situations. They both possessed a natural mental health talent. It was after they took their positions that they were trained by us, more or less on the spot, although the training was always a mutual process. We also learned much from our therapists. In their special position, being with the group all the time, they invented their own subtle methods and tactics for handling group tension, tolerating frustration, and turning various stressful group situations and outside pressures into a therapeutic process that finally increased the group cohesiveness and its therapeutic capacity.

This was the first step. Later the staff increased to three—usually social workers, occupational therapists, or nurses. All of them received additional training, part of which was a stay in Lobec as a regular group member for a whole six-week treatment. The therapists as well as supervisors considered this the most important part of the training.

The visiting therapist
The Clinical supervisor or his alternate, visits Lobec once a week for about eight hours accompanied by another therapist (usually a psychologist or social worker) from the clinic or the Day Center in Prague. The clinical supervisor knows many of the patients from their previous presence at the open group in Prague, of which he is usually the leader. Other visiting therapists know many patients from their individual interviews in the clinic or from open group sessions. The visiting therapists are usually familiar with Lobec, as they visit it regularly and some of them have spent several weeks there previously as part of their training.

The clinical supervisor spends an hour or more with the Lobec therapists, discussing their experiences during the past week—situations they found difficult, problems they may have with the group and with individual patients, steps they made, and suggestions they may have for the therapeutic strategy at the next session of the whole group. The main objective of this meeting is to give support to the therapists.

After that, time is reserved for individual interviews. Although patients have an opportunity to see the clinical supervisor and other visiting staff, they only rarely use it. Sometimes, Lobec therapists ask the supervisor to see certain patients for reassessment. Most of the time of the clinical supervisor and other staff members is spent in a session with the whole group in which the committee presents its weekly reports and the progress of the group and individual members is evaluated.

The therapeutic program

Lobec attempts to model daily life through a broad range of group activities and work. All patients work six hours a day on the state farm or in the woods, starting early in the morning; this is not occupational therapy, but real work with specific goals. Patients usually work in one or two groups, led by one of the therapists and one elected patient who is the work coordinator. No absences are permitted. Patients are given work clothes, for which they are responsible during their stay.

During the first phase of the Lobec operation, when it was considered an outpatient facility, the patients received normal wages for their labors and had to pay for their meals, which were delivered from the farm kitchen. Since Lobec is now an inpatient center, the university hospital pays for the meals. The work is still paid for by the state farm, but the money goes into a special fund in the university hospital. Half of this fund can be used to purchase things for Lobec like television and carpets. Purchases are proposed by the patient committee, but must be approved by the clinical supervisor.

After lunch, there is a two-and-a-half-hour rest devoted to the writing of life histories, catching up with chores, or sports. Members of the patient committee may have separate meetings. The whole group then meets together with one of the therapists for the afternoon group session. Time is always reserved for discussion and role-playing related to the various immediate problems arising from recent events in work, in other activities, and in the free time. During the other part of the afternoon, either autobiographies are presented, or the attention of the group is concentrated upon evaluating the committee or on the adjustment of the new patients and parting with the old ones. On the days of the supervisor's visit, the afternoon group session continues, usually after dinner, in the night program. After dinner the group and the therapist meet for the night program which may be psychomime (described in chapter 22), social games, dancing, an improvised fancy dress ball, free painting and modeling, playing fairy tales, or competitions in improvising short dramatic scenes.

Norms

Since norms are part of all group living, a therapeutic community, as a model of real life, must have norms. It would fail both diagnostically and therapeutically, if it did not have appropriate norms. Some norms are *basic*: that is, they are part of the contract and cannot be changed by any further group decisions.

It is essential that all norms can be convincingly explained as means to therapeutic goals and that basic norms be kept to a minimum. All other forms are formed by community decisions and, in time, may be changed.

Candidates for treatment at Lobec are introduced to the norms—the Lobec rules—before they go there. When discussing the norms, we stress that observation of the norms is sometimes unpleasant and demands sacrifice; this could hardly be asked of someone who is not really deeply interested in improving. If the candidates agree with the norms they are asked to sign them as a part of the therapeutic contract.

Lobec rules

Do you want to achieve maximum improvement? Do you want the same for others? Then you have to follow these rules:

1. Speak openly and frankly about everything in the meetings of the whole community.
2. Take care not to do anything which would make it difficult either for yourself or others to speak openly.
3. Use every opportunity to be with the whole community. Do not isolate yourself.
4. Do not form subgroups. And do not form any sexual attachments. Meeting group members outside is almost always harmful to the therapy.
5. Help others to become members of the community as quickly as possible.
6. Listen to opinions and recommendations of others, but take the responsibility for your own decisions.
7. You may not leave the program unless you first discuss it with

the group. You are part of the program and your separation
affects everybody.

8. While in the program, all medical care and drugs are given by
the staff. Any other appointments and drug use should be first
discussed with the staff.

9. Keep your contract, which includes full participation in the program, inviting relatives, and attending at least three aftercare
meetings.

10. You do not have to believe in the therapy; just stick to the rules
and see.

Point four may need clarification; it has been sometimes misunderstood, especially by outside observers. Any relationship of the group
members outside the group, whether sexual or not, disrupts the closed
system of rewards and costs in the therapeutic community. The approval
and disapproval of the group as a whole then no longer represents the
main incentive promoting the patients' therapeutic efforts.

The situation is even more complicated in the case of sexual involvement, since the ties of mutual secrecy and loyalty, typical of such a
relationship, hamper the persons involved from being open in their
therapy.

Sexual attachment, however, rarely causes a problem at Lobec. We
assume that this is mainly because early verbalization and, in many cases,
clarifying the transference nature of the patients' mutual relationship
is an important part of therapy. People talk freely about their sexual
feelings and experiment with them in fantasy—in psychodrama or psychomime.

The therapists must ensure that all important norms are reinforced.
In most instances, this is done by social approval and criticism. In a well
functioning therapeutic community, the group as a whole should be the
main body generating social approval or disapproval, not the therapist.
The group accomplishes this task through elected members, the committee. If the whole group functions this way, as it has been realized at
Lobec and later at Haney and the Day House, then the social approval
of the group becomes a powerful motivating force in the continuing
treatment of the patient.

The role of the committee
Besides their therapeutic roles, the therapists function as administrative leaders as well. They are able to fulfil this complex role, and in

particular become the target of the patients' transferences, only if as much power as possible has been transferred to the patients themselves. This is the role of the committee. At Lobec, the term *cogovernment* is used; here we use the term *committee* in talking about all three settings, Lobec, Haney, and the Day House.

The committee usually consists of three members, headed by a chairperson elected for one week by the community (patients and staff). It is stressed that patients should be elected who have put special effort into treatment and have made progress.

The committee is responsible for the smooth running of the program. In practice this involves a wide range of tasks. For example, the committee ensures that everybody gets up in time in the morning and is ready for work, that people come on time to the various sessions, that people keep their bedrooms and personal effects in order. The committee shares the power with the therapists, reinforcing norms and suggesting measures if group members transgress the rules. In a well developed group, as at Lobec, the community also shares responsibility for the main group task—the improvement of the patients. It becomes the function of the committee to help new patients adjust to their new environment and to the whole Lobec system. The committee calls the group's attention to people who are passive, who do not speak openly about themselves, who try to avoid important issues, and who do not make a great enough effort. The committee members are the first who show interest in such patients, offer emotional support, or criticize them if necessary. The committee praises members who make progress and criticizes those who do not show enough effort.

The committee writes a weekly report on the group and on every patient. The report of the committee is discussed, sometimes opposed, with great vigor. Although patients criticized for poor effort are often hurt and defend themselves, they are finally mobilized to better efficiency. To be well accepted by the committee, as representatives of the patient's peer group, is highly valued, as is shown in patients' diaries.

The committee itself is closely watched and evaluated by the group during its time in office, especially at the end before the new elections. Committee members may be sharply criticized if they do not function well. At the same time, the group is interested in why a committee member functions poorly. Is she weak as chairperson, because she tries to avoid tension and conflicts and tries always to be a nice person? Is he afraid to make decisions? And why? Is he bossy, unnecessarily antagonistic toward others? Why? How is this related to his life and problems outside? How is it related to his experience with significant persons in his life?

The committee's written reports are also regularly brought to the session attended by the clinical supervisor.

Therapeutic potential of therapeutic community

If we think about the principal ingredients of the psychotherapy process—formulating problems and goals, the contract, the reward-cost system, exposure and corrective experience, and generalization—there are unique advantages to pursue each of them in the therapeutic community described. These advantages are connected with three features of the therapeutic community: (1) it is a *closed system*, (2) it is a *model of natural groups*, and (3) yet it possesses certain *differences from natural groups*.

Closed system. Since the community is isolated, almost every event can, without crossing the system boundaries, be traced in a causal chain to people and their interactions inside the community.

Let us imagine that a patient in the community suddenly becomes depressed, feels hopeless, anxious, angry, or gets a headache. There are four typical stages in a patient's recognition of the symptom's origin. In the first stage, the patient does not know how the symptom came about. In the second, he admits that it is a *reaction* to the behavior of some members of the group. In the third stage, it usually emerges that their behavior had been a *reaction to his behavior*; the patient has an opportunity to see just how he contributes to his own destiny. If everything goes well, the patient reaches the fourth stage. Through corrective experience and overcoming resistances, with the support and pressure of the group, he *changes* his self-defeating behavior. From the state where he felt a helpless victim of outside forces, he reaches the state where he understands that his behavior is a link in the causal network of the group system; he begins to understand what he does to others and why they react to him as they do. But more important than just understanding, he is able to act effectively on his environment so that he can be an important causative factor in reaching his goals.

What would happen if the community were *not* a closed system? The criticized patient might, for example, go out to have a beer with friends or meet his girlfriend, and thus compensate the criticisms by rewards outside the system. His vicious circles running outside the system would be difficult to trace. This would decrease the group pressure for change.

A patient may come believing that everyone hates him, and the group shows him how he manages to achieve this. A girl may break down

because of repeated disappointments in love affairs with unsuitable partners; in the group, it becomes apparent that she does everything possible
to become attached to another unsuitable partner. Another man explains that his symptoms are caused by overworking and attributes them
to tasks imposed on him by an inconsiderate boss. After ten days as a
member of the patient committee, he begins to invent new duties and
regulations which exhaust him, as well as other committee members,
even further. A patient cannot escape the consequences of his behavior
when, being dependent upon the group for his rewards and costs, he
is under group pressure to change. Instead of feeling that he is a helpless victim of outside forces, he becomes aware that he is the cocreator
of his own destiny.

A Model of natural groups. The therapeutic community embodies all
important types of normal activity except sexual relations. There are
serious tasks—not just therapeutic tasks but also group tasks—to be accomplished in working for the State Farm. Close living together under
rather primitive conditions must be accomplished twenty-four hours a
day. Play and entertainment arise mainly out of the patients' own resources. Such activities as viewing TV are discouraged. No other psychotherapy offers such a broad spectrum of situations to which patients
must react. In reacting, they show what is peculiar about their group
schemas and how their vicious circles work.

The patients, on the committee and as work instructors, participate
in leadership and this gives the group opportunities to observe their
leader-follower qualities. There are sports and competitive games, which
test achievement, motivation, and perseverance. Whatever cannot be
imitated is re-created in *surplus reality* (Moreno 1959)—that is in a group
fantasy (psychodrama, psychomime, psychoimagination) covering not
only present, but also past and future.

Our efforts have been to design such group fantasies in such a way
that interpersonal vicious circles are elicited soon after the patient arrives and in a form which can be easily identified by the community.
The multiplicity of situations usually works as a quick catalyzer and
reexposes the patient's maladative patterns of behavior.

Differences from natural groups. If the therapeutic community were the
same as a natural group in all respects, patients would merely repeat
their neurotic vicious circles. The group's most difficult task is to help
patients break these circles and find new adaptive solutions. This sounds
simple but is in reality a complex and sometimes dramatic process in
which more than one person—sometimes the whole community —par-

ticipate. The therapeutic community is certainly not a calm place, although a lot of fun compensates for a lot of tears. We used to joke that a well-functioning therapeutic community goes from one crisis to another. But crises can be productive, if creatively solved by the community.

The basic difference from natural groups is that this is a *transitional* group—the patient's behavior has no consequences other than therapeutic. The patient's stay is not endangered by quarreling with the committee or disliking the therapists unless the rules are severely broken. (The patient does not participate in the program, lies repeatedly, etc. The discharge of a patient is very rare, one patient in two hundred). In the therapeutic process, the relationships are very flexible; two patients may shout at each other and the next day be friends. The committee is elected for one week only so that most of the patients have an opportunity to be members of the committee or work instructors.

Feeling safe, the patients experiment freely with new behavior patterns. A man who has been so inhibited all his life and mumbles so that people do not take notice of his presence shouts at somebody for the first time. Another, who never dated a girl, shows in a free sketch how he would do it.

The main difference from real life lies in the peculiar combination of seriousness and playfulness. There would be no discussion in the morning whether somebody could work or not because of neurotic complaints; there would be no excuses, and the committee would apply negative sanctions. But in the afternoon, the breaking of norms would be discussed in group psychotherapy, perhaps with the aid of psychodrama or psychomime. Fantasy and creativity are encouraged—in painting, creative dance, and improvised dramatic sketches, as well as in psychodrama, psychomime, and psychoimagery.

Special advantages of the therapeutic community

A residential therapeutic community, such as Lobec, may become an important part of a treatment program for many types of human problems, in many areas of mental health. We see special advantages in introducing the therapeutic community in countries that are developing a new system of mental health care with only a few trained professionals. One professional, provided he or she has been trained in operating a therapeutic community elsewhere, may then start such a unit with staff without professional training selected on the basis of personal qualities. The staff can learn from experience on the spot, under proper supervision. Even at its inception, this may represent an efficient treatment modality. When we started the therapeutic community in Lobec, our methods and techniques were much less sophisticated than in the following years, but the results were still better than those of established settings.

Residential therapeutic community at Haney Forestry Camp

Lecturing on Lobec in North America, we invariably heard the objection that Lobec could not be established on this continent because the patients would not want to live in a primitive environment and would not want to work as part of the treatment. We do not believe it, and we have had the opportunity to confirm our belief.

One of us established a therapeutic community at the Haney Forestry Camp, twenty miles from Vancouver in British Columbia, Canada. The therapeutic community was planned to last four months and was part of a research project comparing its therapeutic outcome with two other treatment centers, a day care and an inpatient unit (note 12).

In the therapeutic community at the Haney Forestry Camp we tried, as much as possible, to approximate the conditions of treatment which existed at Lobec. It was a closed system, modeling important features of real life with a small group of patients and a minimum number of therapists. The closed system was realized by forming an isolated unit by a mountain lake deep in the forest. Due to the University of British Columbia's forestry regulations, private cars were not allowed at the camp and people had to park at the gates six miles away. Relatives and friends visiting the patients on Sunday afternoons were transported to the camp by the staff. At the time of the project only a small crew of maintenance people, such as kitchen staff and caretaker, lived on the grounds and their contact with the patients was rare and superficial.

As at Lobec, there were similarities to real life. The task of living and working together in the forest created stressful situations which the patients had to handle as a group. Different attitudes toward norms and tasks created conflicts and criticism. As a whole, the group morale was high and not different from Lobec, although some patients had not worked for quite a long time before coming to the Haney camp. (It is interesting that the majority of them started working after they were discharged.)

There were twenty-two patients and three camp therapists. The therapists worked in shifts so that there were two of them present at all times. The clinical supervisor and the resident in psychiatry visited the camp once or twice a week, and one would lead the group session with the significant persons who visited the camp on Sunday afternoons. The visiting therapist had to deal also with the most difficult problems at the group meeting. The advantage of such a setting was that very serious discussions would be followed by outdoor games which offered plenty of diagnostic material and could be used therapeutically.

There is no need to describe the Haney Forestry Camp in more detail since the norms of the community, tasks, roles, committee, daily program, etc., were similar to those at Lobec. We are convinced that a therapeutic community such as Lobec, with some modifications, can be used anywhere.

Anne at Lobec: her treatment history

Anne, a thirty-six-year-old law school graduate working in an administrative position, was married and lived with her husband and two children. She complained of depression and headaches and had been referred to the system by her district psychiatrist who had been seeing her individually for about two years. After attending two sessions of the open group, Anne was referred to the therapeutic community at Lobec. Anne's husband attended two sessions of the significant persons group (step 4a) and two others together with his wife (step 4b).

We present in this section several significant episodes from Anne's treatment.

Anne is introduced to the group. At the whole-group session, presided over by the chairperson of the patient committee, Anne introduced herself and started to talk about her problems:

Anne: What troubles me most is my headaches. Sometimes I cannot even sleep properly and wake up feeling pain. The doctor told me that they couldn't find anything physically wrong with me, but I don't know. Also I cry easily and sometimes feel depressed the whole day long. But I think I have a reason. I went through a lot of difficulties in my job. It's mostly my boss——he does not understand a thing, but likes to give orders.

Chairperson: And what about outside the job?

Anne: Oh, nothing extraordinary. I have been married for fifteen years. My husband graduated from the same school, but he joined the Army. I think we have the usual amount of problems that every marriage has.

Chairperson: Can you be more specific? What kind of problems? What kind of a man is your husband?

Anne: Well, quite a typical man, I would say. It's hard to make him do anything around the house. And he's also had some affairs with other women.

The next day at the group meeting Anne entered the discussion complaining about her boss and the circumstances in her job:

Anne: My boss is quite inconsiderate. He expects me to attend meetings after hours— With all my responsibilities at home and two children! I do a lot of work and carry a great deal of responsibility, but he takes all this for granted. He only remembers that last month I came to work ten minutes late.

Anne meets the clinical supervisor. On the day of the clinical supervisor's visit to Lobec, the group performed various psychomimic tasks. Afterwards, when the participants talked about their feelings, Anne said, "I had a strong feeling that this was silly, and you must be a charlatan." (*Authors' note: Anne showed her skill at antagonizing men in authority. It was the first time she had seen the clinical supervisor.*)

Anne in the work program. In the next few days, during the work program, Anne volunteered for the hardest and most strenuous work, such as cutting wood and digging in the garden. She did it well, but it was obvious that she was also trying to demonstrate her efficiency over her male coworkers.

Anne gets criticized. At one of the next group sessions the attention focused on Anne. Several group members told Anne that they found her irritating, and showed this in pantomime and psychodramatic episodes. Some of them, for instance, the male therapist and the chairperson, did this in quite a friendly manner. One group member, however, a young man, got very angry with her. (*Author's note: Although the group's reactions showed Anne how she antagonizes men, the group members were more kindly toward her and showed more understanding for her than had other men in her life, such as her boss and her husband.*)

Anne's nonverbal behavior comes into focus. When she first arrived at Lobec, Anne walked with a heavy step. Her whole posture seemed rigid. All this became even more visible when she performed such psychomimic tasks as *walking softly so as not to wake someone you love.* Anne walked clumsily and seemed a much heavier person than she really was.

Anne's husband in the significant persons group. In the meantime, Anne's husband was invited to the significant persons group (step 4a). Besides him, two other husbands, two wives, the mother of a married female patient, and the mother of a single male patient were present. When his turn came to speak, Anne's husband said that his wife had been depressed lately, that she complained of headaches, and that she often cried and got irritated because of the children. He complained about her boss, calling him inconsiderate. Anne's husband explained the situation at home: they had two schoolage children, and he was often away from home on army assignments. Mrs. R., whose husband was also in Lobec, began the following discussion:

Mrs. R.: You remind me of my husband. He keeps saying, "Please realize that I cannot help you at home at all. I have my work and studies." But I still have to work, take care of the children, and now take care of him. Is he really so ill that he must go to Lobec? Sometimes I think I am more ill than he is, but nobody seems to care about me.

Therapist: But we do, and that is why we have invited you here, not just because of your husband. Perhaps we can find out now what we can do for you.

Mrs. R.: Well, thank you, but it is not as bad as that. True, I used to have headaches, and I am not always very happy (*she turns to Anne's husband*), but if your wife has a difficult job with a lot of responsibility and two children, I am not surprised that she breaks down.

Anne's husband: I don't know. There are other women who have as much to do, and they don't become ill. She was always a very strong woman. Actually she is a sort of general at home.

Mrs. T. (mother of married female patient): And was she always like that?

Anne's husband: In fact, my wife was always an active and strong woman. That's what I liked about her. We married when we were university students. She became pregnant but continued her studies. She sat for an important examination shortly before our daughter was born. And she got excellent marks.

Mrs. T.: My daughter also married before finishing her studies. Oh, they had difficult times—lack of money, paying for furniture, the children were ill. And finally they had everything that they needed for a satisfactory life, but my son-in-law started to come home late at night. And then we heard that he had an affair with a young, stupid girl who worked in the laboratory of his institute. It was a terrible shock for my daughter. I do not know how it will go on——

Mrs. R.: One cannot rely upon men. Every one of them goes crazy as soon as he sees the first good-looking girl; his wife, family, are turned aside.

Anne's husband: Do you think that only men are unfaithful? How many wives are, and even mothers! I think that much depends on how the wife behaves and what sort of atmosphere she creates at home. Some wives are not able to show tenderness and be feminine with their husbands. Some do not care about their appearance at home.

Therapist: Does this hold for your wife, too?

Anne's husband: Yes.

Mrs. T.: And does she take care of her appearance if you go out together?

Anne's husband: We almost never go out together. She goes out alone.

Mrs. R.: And where does she go?

Anne's husband: I do not know, I never ask.

(*Authors' note: It was apparent that the marriage was in crisis. It seemed that the husband had been attracted to Anne partly because she was a strong and self-confident person and he needed support from her. Then something had changed in the mutual balance of the relationship. Anne's husband was still rather vague about the present situation and problems in the marriage.*)

The record of the session was sent to the therapists at Lobec as usual, and served as confidential material for them. (They do not reveal information obtained from the significant persons to the patients, but use it for their own orientation toward the patient's problems.)

Doing psychomime. The following occurred about two weeks later. The group started moving and dancing freely to a piece of music. Anne started to move with unusual freedom and grace. She looked happier than before. Then the group was asked to imagine they were on a voyage and were shipwrecked on a desert island (see Part 5). Anne was lively and playful. Finally, as part of the fantasy, she isolated herself with another group member, a young man, and showed such unbelievably seductive behavior toward him that everyone was surprised. It was an improvisation, a game that both actors enjoyed, and quite often it verged on caricature. Anne interjected her usual brisk movements into it once in a while, as if two different persons were alternating within her.

(*Authors' note: Anne had an opportunity to experiment with a variety of roles and different ways to deal with the opposite sex. Instead of being competitive and trying to dominate, she became relaxed, playful, and even experimented in a kind of courtship behavior.*)

Anne reveals more about her problems. In another session, the *forbidden fruit* task was performed. An object was placed on a chair, symbolizing something one longs for in one's life, but is forbidden (see Part 5). First Ivan, a male patient, came to the chair, took the forbidden object (in this case a ball) with much tenderness, kept it for a while, and then returned it to the chair quickly. Talking about it afterwards, he said, "I thought that I was ready to start having a love-affair with every good-looking girl I met."

Therapist: And how is it really?

Ivan: The same as I performed it here. I "borrow" the object for a short time. Nobody knows, and certainly not my wife.

Ivan suffered from heart pain and fears that he had coronary disease; before coming to Lobec, he feared that he would die on the street. He developed a street phobia. His wife had been accompanying him everywhere for several months.

Anne went to the chair, took the symbolic object, and went back with it, hiding it under her sweater. Then she sat quietly and looked around proudly. Nobody spoke; the tension in the group was rising. Then Anne made a movement as if to throw the object back, but did not do so. She repeated the gesture several times and the group, in great tension, watched her. Then she shook her head and quickly gave the ball to the social therapist.

Therapist: What did you imagine: (*No reply.*) Would you like somebody to make a guess? (*Anne nods her head.*)

Female patient: I think that it is Peter. Anne told us about a man who appreciates here more than her husband does but is well aware that she is married and has children, and she knows that some solution has to be found.

Anne: Yes. During the performance I was going through the motions of saying farewell to Peter. But I can't, I did not solve it. I gave the ball to the therapist.

Male patient: To let the therapist solve it for you?

Anne: Yes.

(*Authors' note: This activity showed more about Anne's problems and, at the same time, her attitude toward treatment. She had not been very open about her problems initially. Now the situation in her marriage and her husband's affairs appeared in a different light.*)

Anne becomes a committee member. In the third week of her treatment, Anne became a member of the patient committee, along with Harry, a man of forty, and Jane, a woman of twenty-three. At the group meeting where the work of the committee was evaluated, the following discussion took place:

Jane: (Joking) And you see there is no need for me to do anything. Anne does almost everything, decides everything, and still has time to direct Harry's every step.

Harry: It is not as bad as that. True, Anne tries to do everything herself. She would wake people up in the morning, or collect fines, although this is not her function——

Anne: (Interrupting him) Can you be relied upon?

Therapist: And what about Jane? You cannot rely upon her?

Anne: Oh well, she is young. Why should she bother so much——

Harry: I do not take Anne seriously in that matter, otherwise I would get mad. She is a very industrious and hard-working person, but at the same time rather unpleasant. And she can be so aggressive. She makes me feel like a little boy. I wanted to help her when she was chopping wood with that heavy axe; and this wasn't her job anyway. She said, "Go away, you will cut yourself."

Therapist: Does she remind you of somebody?

Harry: Oh yes, my first wife. With her I felt the same. You see, if Anne is the same at home, taking charge of everything, no wonder she feels so tired and overworked.

Female patient: How about your children, Anne, do they help you?

Anne: Not really, but they go to school, they have to study.

Male patient: Sometimes I feel I understand why your husband tries to keep away from home.

(*Authors' note: In the short time of her function on the committee Anne succeeded in producing a situation similar to that in her home, taking over a high degree of responsibility unnecessarily and overworking herself, and at the same time feeling exploited by others. She tried her best to discourage the cooperation of other group members in the same way that she inhibited her husband and children at home in doing household chores. She also sheltered the young Jane unnecessarily in the same way as she had her daughters. This episode shows in practice how the therapeutic community is a model of real life situations, providing an opportunity for patients to exhibit their maladaptive patterns. It also shows how the model differs from real life. Group members react to Anne differently from the way her own significant persons react to her at home. The committee members did not accept the roles Anne imposed on them; they criticized her, although always in a friendly and understanding manner.*)

Anne's autobiography. In the fourth week of her stay in the therapeutic

community, Anne read her life history to the group. The following is
a summary of her autobiography:

Anne lost her father when she was eleven. He left for army service
abroad and never came back. Anne's mother and grandmother did
not believe, however, that he died but thought that he stayed abroad
because he was not interested in his family. Anne's mother never
talked favorably about him and stressed that he was constantly unfaithful to her. There was a strong tradition of frustrated women in
the family; Anne's maternal aunt had committed suicide because her
boy friend had been unfaithful to her and made another girl pregnant.

Anne had one sister who was short, graceful, and delicate, "quite
different than I." She was often ill and the parents, according to
Anne, liked the sister better than Anne. Anne's father was strict and
made heavy demands on her school work. Anne did well at school
and was very ambitious. She dreamed about being a famous solicitor.
She became a lawyer but for reasons not clear even to herself, she
worked in administration, which she despised. After the father left,
the family had a hard time and Anne's mother had to work as an
unskilled factory worker.

While she attended school, Anne had few girl friends. She did not
mix with boys either. Her opinion was that the boys were interested
only in beautiful but stupid girls or girls who hide their cleverness,
but she could not do that. She met her husband while at the university. He was, according to her, extremely good-looking, attractive to
girls, and therefore she did not take his proposal of marriage seriously. "Why would he marry me?" she thought. She wanted a child
very soon. She had two children before finishing her studies, although this led to a chain of sacrifices.

She began to neglect her husband as she transferred all her interest
to the children. Her husband went abroad with a group of young
people and there he had, according to him, the extramarital affair.
During the last five years, she had suspected him several times. She
herself had two extramarital experiences. The first man was a for-
eigner, much older than she, who used to advise her to be more
tolerant of her husband. The other one, Peter, was ten years older

than she, without formal education, but with a lot of experience, and well-traveled. He did not have a high opinion of degrees and titles, but simply liked her as she was. Her conclusion was, "He is a primitive." He would marry her, but he did not suggest that she divorce her husband. She did not think she could do it, because of the children. Both children are attached to their father.

Psychodrama: Anne talks with her father. One of the psychodramatic performances suggested by the therapist for Anne was a meeting with her lost father. For the role of her father, Anne chose a middle-aged man, single, and very attractive to many of the women patients.

Anne: Hello, Dad, strange to see you after so many years. How are you getting on?

Father/Male 1: Not so well, you know. I was wounded and then ill for a long time. I could not come back to you.

Anne: Oh well, you were glad to get rid of us, I guess.

Father/Male 1: How can you say that?

Anne: Anyway, you returned because you are ill and you need us to take care of you, as you used to return to Mom, when another woman ruined you.

Father/Male 1: You were too young to understand what goes on between parents. It was not so easy with your mother.

Anne: Right, but why didn't you care about us children? Not even about Rose (the younger sister), whom you preferred to me!

Father/Male 1: That's not true; I liked you both the same. But she was weak and ill. You never showed any tenderness. But I liked you too. Can you remember how together we bought small trees for our garden? (*Anne had recalled this incident earlier.*3

Anne: And yet, you left us.

Father/Male 1: I had to—there was a war. And I thought you would not care. You did not show any feelings, you were like a boy and, like me, you did not always stay at home.

(*Anne is lost in silent thought.*)

Anne/Martha, doubling: But I loved you Dad, I did. When Mom said nasty things about you, I was angry. I wanted so much to have a real father, the best one in the village. Rose and I both thought about you very often, but Mom did not like that. And grandma kept saying that you were a monster.

(*Anne starts to cry.*)*Therapist*: Tell him what you are feeling now.

Anne: (*After a long pause*) Dad, why did you leave me?

(Anne continues to cry. Her "father" and the other group members come closer to Anne and comfort her.)

(Authors' note: Anne recalled her old conflict; her feeling that her father did not love her, had rejected her. She reexperienced that conflict intensively, including its emotional components. At the same time, the group supported her and helped her handle the situation better than in the past.) Once more Anne became the focus of the group's attention:

Martha (who shares a room with Anne): Once, before going to sleep, Anne said that she is too tall and stout, that no man could like her because of her figure. And yet many of us are as tall as she is. The truth is that she is pretty; she has regular features and naturally curly hair. With what she has, another woman would be able to do miracles and certainly would not regard herself as unpretty. But Anne is proud, she does not take care of herself and rather neglects herself.

Peter (patient): She was clumsy only at the beginning when she walked heavily and took long strides, and her voice was shrill. Now she is quite different.

Therapist: Can you show us how she used to walk when she came to the center?

(Authors' note: This is a usual mirror technique of psychomime in which all the patients, one after another, try to reflect some nonverbal aspect of another patient's behavior. Some of the patients dramatize the difference, how it was and how it is now.)

Henry (patient): Once, in psychomime she changed her way of walking and moved more freely to music.

Dan (patient): I have been here only a week and I do not see anything special about the way she walks. I only want to say that she dances lightly, and with grace. And she was tolerant with my dancing—you know I am no expert.

Maria (patient): I am not quite clear about her husband. Anne, you speak about him as though you were before a court of justice: he is unfaithful, failed to take care of the family. If he were such a terrible man, you would not have had his children, you would not have stayed with him for such a long time, and the children would not like him.

Martha: My impression is that Anne feels guilty because of the relationship with Peter and therefore tries to find as many faults in her husband as possible. It is as if she were trying to convince herself that he is bad. But here nobody will judge her. Here, there are many people who went through similar experiences. Me too. I fell in love with a man after being married ten years. I was mad about him. We met for one year, then we parted. I did not want to leave my children and, as a matter of fact, neither did I want to leave my husband. I thought it was all over, but here I found that it is still inside me.

(Martha came because of breathing difficulties when she is in a crowd of people. She had had to stop going to parties with her husband.)

Therapist: Has anybody an idea what Anne's husband feels? Can somebody show that?

Husband/Henry: (*Comes to the stage and sits down*) Well, Anne will return on Wednesday. I hope it will be better now, I couldn't bear it any longer. She came home and complained about everybody, especially about her boss. Everybody was stupid, impossible to her, no character. And she was eager to offer her opinion to everybody. When she wrote a letter to the director complaining about her boss, I advised her to write only what related to her problem. But she wrote everything that she thought about her boss. Naturally, he was furious. I think that I did what I could. We talked about it every evening, but it was a waste of time. She ignored what I said and she did what she wanted to. She can be so aggressive. I agree that she can be very efficient, but I am a sort of unskilled laborer for her at home. She says, "Bring this or that! Run there!" and my two daughters take over this attitude toward me from her.

Husband/Martha, double: And do I like her at all?

Husband/Henry: Certainly! Otherwise I wouldn't have stayed with her so long.

Husband/Martha, double: And did I tell it to her?

Husband/Henry: Why talk too much? We wanted children together.

Husband/Martha, double: Isn't it repellent when she does not take care of herself?

Husband/Henry: It does no good to talk about it, she does what she wants.

Final comments

Anne had several hypotheses about people and herself in her group schema that unfavorably influenced her life.

Anne's father schema Anne had a rather short experience of her real father and even that was influenced by her mother's and grandmother's negative judgment of him. Anne's father schema was a blend of an ideal loving father she was proud of—one who cared for her and her sister and protected them—and a bad father, irresponsible, who did not care, preferred her younger sister, left the family, and rejected Anne. Anne wanted to love and to be loved by her ideal father. She also identified

with him, protecting her younger sister, and later taking over the responsibility for her own children. At the same time Anne felt deeply
hurt by the bad father in her father schema, and wanted revenge on
him. She wanted to show him that she did not need him, that she was
better than he, that she was better than any man. This was also in accord
with her mother's attitude toward men. Anne applied her father schema
to other men in her life—such as her supervisors and colleagues; sooner
or later she stimulated them into unfriendly and rejecting behaviour
that confirmed her original hypothesis. She applied most of it to her
husband too, distrusting him, pushing him into a passive role in the
family, and trying to take all the responsibility. In Lobec, she applied
her father schema to the male therapist and to such male patients as the
chairman of the committee.

Anne's mother schema. Anne saw her mother as a hard working, strong,
dependable person who took good care of her family, but also as a
person deeply dissatisfied with her husband and proud that she could
stand alone not needing any men.

Anne incorporated her mother's personality features into her mother
schema and identified with her in many aspects, including her negative
and revenge seeking attitudes toward men.

Anne's sister schema. Anne had a younger sister, a girl of small build
and delicate health. Anne's sister schema had the features of a lovable
delicate girl that Anne loved and protected. But Anne also believed that
her father preferred her sister over her and felt she had to compete
with her for her father's attention. At the same time Anne was ambivalent toward such a competition. She was proud of her strength and
capability and did not want to attract attention by pretending weakness.
This conflict probably contributed to Anne's feeling of inadequacy in
regard to her physical appearance so that she overcompensated in stressing her physical strengths which resulted it in her rigid posture and
clumsy movements.

Anne applied her sister schema to her girlfriends, protecting them
usually so much that they resented it and considered her authoritative
and domineering. Anne tried her sister schema on her daughters, unnecessarily sacrificing herself for them. At Lobec she tried the same
with the young committee member Jane.

Male peer schema. Anne had no brother and no other representative
experience with men as peers. From the beginning, she confused her
male peer schema with her father schema. She also applied it to her
school mates and colleagues; from the beginning this made it difficult

for her to develop normal friendships with boys and young men—relationships that would correct her onesided hypotheses about men. Anne antagonized her schoolmates, her colleagues during her study at the university, and other men in her jobs, which contributed to the tension she experienced in her work.

Sexual partner schema. Anne's father schema and male peer schema influenced her relationship to men as potential sex partners. Her competitive attitude, her tendency to show she was better, more competent, usually stimulated her boyfriends to reactions that were incompatible with sexual attachment. In general her boyfriends gave up soon and switched to less complicated girls. That reinforced Anne's hypothesis that men prefer simple, stupid girls and decreased her self-esteem even more.

The relative success of the relationship with Peter can probably be explained by the fact that Peter may be mature and self-confident enough not to get trapped within her vicious circle and by the fact that she feels safe and superior intellectually (He is a primitive); she can be more relaxed and less competitive with him.

Treatment results

Anne lost the neurotic symptoms which led her into therapy. She also changed considerably, becoming more relaxed, more flexible in taking various social roles, more understanding and tolerant toward others, especially men in authority and her colleagues. She no longer felt the need to provoke them. She also changed in her physical appearance—taking better care of, and having more confidence in, her appearance. This above all helped her in the various areas of her life, particularly in her job. She was able to see her boss and colleagues more realistically. She developed friendly relationships with some of them. She finally decided to leave her job and found a better, more independent position in another area of her profession.

Anne was also able to change the situation at home, transferring some of the household responsibilities to her husband and children. Her marriage also changed. Both she and her husband became interested in rebuilding their relationship to promote greater closeness and mutual satisfaction. This was an on-going process, initiated by Anne's therapy at Lobec and by the involvement of both marital partners in therapy. Later on, they were able to continue without professional intervention.

The role of the treatment. In the model situation at Lobec, Anne was motivated to reveal her hypotheses and the mechanism of her vicious circles. The people at Lobec did not enter into her vicious circles (at least, not to a degree that would prevent their coming to light). Anne's noisy behavior was soon discovered to be a mask behind which she hid her fears and her uncertainty about herself. The reactions of male patients helped her learn how she determines the behavior of men around her. After a few weeks she changed, became less provocative with men and did not hide herself behind self-irony. She was able to become friendly with several men and to sympathize with them in their complaints about their wives. She also realized for the first time that men can suffer because of marital and familial problems.

Anne changed her opinion of her husband. At the beginning, she saw him as self-confident and extremely attractive to and successful with women; later she saw what others saw, that he was insecure in many areas, that he needed her support, and that he was deeply devoted to their relationship.

At the meeting of partners and relatives with the patients, Anne's husband said that she had changed a great deal, that she was milder and less stubborn, that she sought his opinion in matters which she earlier had decided dictatorially. At that meeting, Anne agreed that she had changed, but she saw it also as the result of her husband's change: he spent more time at home and took more interest in the home. The family as a whole functions better.

The change in Anne's behavior can be explained by the corrective experience (both cognitive and emotional) at all the therapeutic steps. The corrective experiences took place in relation to male and female figures in authority when the male therapist was not offended by her provocative behavior, or when in the psychodrama she was confronted with her father. They took place in transactions with male patients, as coworkers or possible erotic partners. In dance she found to her surprise that she was wanted as a partner, and during the psychomime, a man asked for her help and she responded to him with tenderness. She also went through a corrective experience in relation to her sibling schema, especially her younger sister, who was represented by several younger girls in the group.

Anne's situation. It was not considered unfeminine in Czechoslovakia in Anne's time if a woman graduated from the university and followed a career, and at the same time was married with children. Women did not have to face the dilemma of having to choose between a career or marriage. Nevertheless, such women, especially those with children, did not have an easy life. Usually, cooperation between the couple and the whole family regarding the division of labor at home was needed. Anne's criticism and dissatisfaction with certain aspects of her life situation was legitimate. She was still at a disadvantage compared with her male colleagues. However, prior to her treatment, her means of coping with the situation were mostly inappropriate and highly inefficient.

Final note on costs. Over the course of her treatment, thirteen weeks, the expenses were 36.7 percent (per diem) of those for hospital inpatient treatment. Anne spent

2 hours in individual interviews
1½ hours in conjoint interviews (therapist and couple)
26 hours in various group sessions
6 weeks in the therapeutic community

Her husband spent

1½ hours in conjoint interviews
12 hours in various group sessions

Anne attended

1 individual interview
2 open group sessions (28 and 30 patients, 1 therapist)
1 individual interview
6 weeks in the therapeutic community (30 patients, 3 social therapists; plus a clinical supervisor and a social worker 8 hours each a week)
2 open group sessions (28 to 30 patients, 1 therapist)
2 sessions with her husband (16 group members, 1 therapist)
2 after care sessions (8 group members, 1 therapist)

Her husband attended

2 group sessions (7 significant persons, 1 therapist)
2 group sessions with his wife (16 group members, 1 therapist)

THE FOURTH STEP (A & B): THE GROUP OF SIGNIFICANT PERSONS

From family therapy to integrated psychotherapy. We always regard a patient as a subsystem within some group system of significant persons. This may be the family, but a person may have other important group systems, especially today when alternatives exist to the traditional family. People live in many different groups in which many of the same regularities of group dynamics appear as in the family. Friends and coworkers may be significant persons in the patient's life. Integrated psychotherapy goes beyond the concept of family therapy, which sometimes involves the preconceived idea that only the family is a group worthy of consideration.

Contact with significant persons is an important part of assessment as well as treatment. The patient's relationship with significant persons represents a reward-cost source in the life of both. Psychotherapy which does not include this area in the field of observation can never fully understand the patient's behavior.

In integrated psychotherapy the therapist always watches the balance of rewards and costs of all persons involved and assesses it before and after every move. There are many rewards available to patients as well as significant persons—rewards such as emotional support from the therapist and from the group, and social approval or disapproval of the group.

How significant persons are involved in therapy. In integrated psychotherapy, patients deal with their significant persons in the following manners:

1. *In their absence,* the patients develop *substitute* (transference) *relationships* to other patients and to the therapists, or they deal *directly* with their significant persons in *fantasy*—as in psychodrama and abreaction.
2. *In their presence*, the patients deal *directly* with *real significant persons* in the various groups in which they meet together, such as in the group (4b) described in this section or in family night described in the chapter 7.

Significant persons also have the opportunity to deal with their partners (patients) first in fantasy, when significant persons attend the group before their partners join in. Later, they meet in that group with real partners and continue in therapy with them in the same group.

We have used various methods for treating partners, marital couples, or whole families and have concluded that the methods described in this book are the most efficient and least time consuming. Therefore we also use them for clients seeking help in overt family or other partnership problems.

Two kinds of groups will be described in this section. In the first group, the significant persons meet with the therapist. In the second group significant persons and patients in various stages of their treatment meet together with the therapist. These groups offer a more intensive involvement by significant persons in the whole therapeutic process.

Significant persons meet together with the therapist (step 4a)

The group meets the same day each week in the evening for about two hours. Attendance consists of the significant persons of patients who have been recently admitted into the residential therapeutic community or the day center (step 3). The patients themselves invite their significant persons to this group, explaining its meaning and importance to them. All of this is part of the patients' therapeutic commitment. The same therapist is in charge of the group for a considerable length of time; there may be another therapist-in-training present. The session is recorded and the summary is available as confidential material to the staff of both therapeutic communities.

The group starts by introducing the therapist and the participants, as well as clarifying the participants' relationship to the patients.

The therapist then briefly explains the purpose of the session. This may be done in many different ways, depending on the situation, but the following message has to be conveyed to the significant persons:

> We regularly see relatives, partners, spouses or friends of our patients. You all have been invited by your people, our patients, because you are close to them, you are part of their life. If they have suffered and have decided to undergo treatment, this must have influenced your life as well. It will help us in our work if you tell us what you think and feel about your people, their problems and yours, in your life together. Since we have offered our professional help to your people, we have already interfered in your life. Tell us more about it. We are here to face the consequences. And we really want to be of assistance to you if we can.

After the introduction, each participant has a turn to speak in front of the group. They should speak clearly and audibly so that other participants can easily follow and react. The therapist may ask questions, or cut out unnecessary details—for example the patient's previous treatment. The stress is on the present, on the actual character of the significant person's and patient's life together, including its financial aspects. The significant person should also discuss any dependencies and how he sees the future of the relationship. The therapist must constantly assess the reward-cost balance that the relationship supplies to each partner.

After all the participants have had their turn, a discussion follows. The therapist encourages the exchange of experiences among the participants and tries to stimulate mutual reactions between those who have had experiences in complementary relationships: the wife of a patient reacting to the husband of a woman patient; a son of a patient, reacting to the father of a patient. (This is illustrated in the case of Anne.)

Significant persons are expected to come at least once, but they are encouraged to continue in attendance for as long as they wish and many do so. They then function as a nucleus of more experienced participants that can help new ones and take a more active part in discussion. Some of the participants, mostly partners in marital and other relationships, are referred right away into group 4b.

The goals of this group

Exchange of information. This is always a mutual process. The therapist obtains and confirms certain information about the patient, and at the same time the significant person gains information about the setting and the therapist. This happens, even without the therapist's intention. The significant persons draw conclusions about the therapy, from the physical appearance of the setting and from the behavior of the staff, starting with the receptionist. All this time their conclusions may be wrong. Therefore, we consider it useful to encourage the significant persons to ask direct questions when they meet with the therapist, and for the therapist to answer them within certain limits.

We answer questions about the physical setting of the treatment and its program. The therapist in charge is free to answer various personal questions at his own discretion—such questions as his training, experience, and marital status (the female therapists are often asked this latter question); the therapist should not go into any details. We do not engage in general talk about psychotherapy or about the theoretical principles. We make it clear that we feel confident about the theoretical principles and clinical methods in our work but consider it irrelevant to talk about them during the treatment.

We do not inform the significant persons what the patients have said about them, and if the significant persons ask, we encourage them to discuss it with their partners or family members directly or, best of all, at the meeting with them and the therapist.

Clearing up misunderstanding. Quite often, information leading to misunderstanding about the treatment is furnished by the patients themselves. For example, a patient may stress certain aspects of the treatment and not mention others, thus giving a distorted impression to the significant persons. This may be connected with the patient's ambivalent feelings toward the significant persons, the treatment, or both.

Glenn's wife came to the significant persons meeting believing that the treatment Glenn had started was a kind of sex therapy in which patients were encouraged to experiment in mutual sex. She explained that she had come to that conclusion because of Glenn's enthusiastic talk about the open atmosphere of the therapeutic group, especially when discussing sexual matters, and because he strongly stressed that physical proximity and bodily closeness were important factors in treatment. Glenn, at the same time, forgot to mention that one of the rules of the program was that sexual relationships with other members during treatment were forbidden. Talking about this misunderstanding brought us to the core of their marriage problems. Both partners married when very young and after several years felt they had missed something important by not having had sexual experiences with any other partner but their spouse. Naturally, there were other problems in the marriage. The idea that extramarital sex might be prescribed as part of therapy seemed attractive to both partners and contributed to the misunderstanding Glenn's wife developed.

Peter's parents expressed a strong conviction at the significant persons meeting that their twenty-four-year-old son had chosen the wrong type of treatment. They argued that since he had enrolled in the psychiatric day center he had become even more depressed, tired, and withdrawn than he had been before. The parents were concerned with Peter's physical tiredness on one particular evening. Peter regularly complained of depression and tiredness when he went home from the day center and withdrew into his own room shortly after dinner. When complaining of physical tiredness on the night in question, Peter had not told his parents he had been on an all-day hiking trip in the mountains. Peter's father was ready to call the family doctor and ask him to intervene by going to the head of the psychiatric department. All of this was discussed with the parents and later with Peter at the patient group at the day center. It drew attention to some of Peter's typical attitudes in relation to his parents and other significant persons. Although Peter complained of his parents' overprotectiveness and interference, he was not aware how much he was signalling them that he was weak, depressed, and helpless and how readily he accepted their attention and support. Peter also revealed in the day center group that when he felt tense and had negative feelings toward therapy, he played with the idea of his parents interrupting the therapy.

Clearing up misunderstandings may become necessary for such practical reasons as preventing actions which may hamper the therapy or encourage the significant persons to irreversible actions. An experienced therapist not only clears up misunderstandings, but uses them to come closer to the root of some of the patient's important problems.

Creating a basically positive attitude. We do not ask significant persons to believe in our psychotherapeutic program or expect them to be enthusiastic about it. We just try to achieve the following goals:

That the significant persons are willing to meet with us, or the whole group if this can be done, whenever they are invited, and try as best they can to be active participants in it.

That the significant persons trust us, insofar aş we do not carry any preconceived ideas of what their relationship to our patients is, either in the present or in the future. That whatever course this relationship takes depends upon them and their partners.

That the significant persons honestly discuss with us the negative feelings they may have toward us and the whole setting, and all arguments they may have against the treatment, before they take any practical steps in the matter.

That the significant persons inform us, bringing it up at our mutual meetings, of any new events in their life and the partner's life and about all decisions and plans they may have in that regard—a decision to move, to change a job, to start going to school, to have a legal separation, etc.

Coping realistically with changes. People may react in different ways to changes in a person close to them. We try to help the significant persons understand and cope with the changes in the patients and, to some degree, to change themselves. Both partners in the relationship may then be able to rebuild it to a certain extent. There may be considerable changes in mutual dependency, and in the set of rewards that each partner has been receiving from it. The relationship may move either toward greater closeness or toward greater distance and separation.

One patient's mother, who until recently had been drawing much of her feeling of importance and self-confidence from the fact that her phobic daughter (our patient) was completely dependent on her special care, found it difficult adjusting at first to the changes that her daughter was going through in the treatment. (She was becoming more active and independent.) But, helped by the attention of the therapeutic group and being exposed there to various social cues, the mother developed other sources of reward—helping others in the group, increasing her capacity for social contact, and becoming interested in various activities and hobbies. She was able to tolerate it when her daughter moved into an apartment and was able to appreciate that her daughter was a far more pleasant person to her during her short visits than she had been before. If the mother had not been involved in the therapy, she would more likely have made it difficult for her daughter to stay in treatment. She might have argued and used her influence upon her daughter, or indirectly offered her easy outlets in times of resistance to the therapy, or developed severe neurotic symptoms herself.

Close involvement in the whole process. The process usually starts in this group and continues further in the groups described later in this section.

The group (4a) of significant persons meeting with the therapist is different from meetings with patients' relatives and partners common in the mental health area.

The significant persons meet in a group and function together *as a therapeutic group*. They not only supply information, but also go through therapeutic experiences in the group. They realize that other people have similar problems. They get support from other people who are interested in them. People having experience in different relationships—spouses, parents, adult sons or daughters of patients—meet there and exchange a wide range of social stimuli. Each participant of this group at the same time helps others to see their problems from a different point and broaden their often narrow views about how their partners feel and what they think.

We have described this group in detail because we consider it an element of the system of integrated psychotherapy that could easily be transferred into other settings as well. We have introduced such a group in the inpatient unit of a psychiatric hospital.

Significant persons meet with the patients and other clients in a group (step 4b)

This group of about twenty people meets for about three hours with one therapist, on the same evening each week.

The basic category of participants in this group are patients who have returned from the therapeutic community at Lobec and their significant persons. In addition, at each session there are some significant persons of patients who are still at Lobec. Other participants may be referred from various other steps of the system, such as open group, either coming alone or with their significant persons. *Clients*—persons who came to the system because of overt marital, family, or other problems—may be referred directly to this group.

In this setting, the artificial group (patient group) is combined with the natural group (family, couples, or partners).

Once the participants enter the group they are all treated as people with personal problems. There is no discrimination between the sick and the healthy, between the guilty party and the victim. This shows in the approach of the therapist and especially in that of the ex-patients. However each participant's category is identified in the group and they are so introduced at the beginning. This identification is necessary because each category—patients, significant persons, and other clients—have different needs and motivations, and differing tactics must be used to keep a proper balance between rewards and costs during their therapy. For example, the group must be more tolerant and supportive toward newcomers or significant persons, but can afford much more criticism and social pressure toward an ex-patient. All of this is well known to the more experienced patients, and they usually treat the others sensitively in this respect. It must be known who is who in the group.

The session. After the preliminary greeting and everyone is introduced, the session starts. One therapist, a full time member of the system staff, is in charge of the group. Usually, the same therapist is also in charge of group 4a. The therapist thus knows some of the significant persons from the 4a session and may have met other participants working in the other steps of the system.

At the beginning the patients from the therapeutic community and the ex-patients, usually have their turn. They summarize the development in their relationship with their significant persons in the recent past and especially during their treatment. Significant persons contribute what they think and feel about it, often describing what they experienced as their family members, partners, and other close persons underwent treatment. Problems may be viewed differently than at the beginning of treatment and new solutions sought. The confrontation may be in the form of a dialogue about future plans or a scene replaying a recent argument. Other patients get involved, doubling for both sides, often encouraging the significant persons to express themselves more openly. The stress is on the present and future perspectives of the relationship. (This technique is described in more detail in "Family Night" in chapter 18.) After each confrontation, a short discussion follows during which comments from other participants, especially other significant persons and newly arrived clients, are encouraged. Usually, there is a break; all participants not only relax but also have an opportunity to talk informally to each other and ask ex-patients various questions about their experiences in the therapeutic community.

In the second part of the session, the group may talk about new participants and ask them to introduce themselves. Or the question may be raised, whether anybody has an acute problem that they would like to present to the group.

For example, a woman who complains at the beginning that she can not get her husband to come may ask for attention. She may be asked at first by the ex-patients to say more about herself, the husband, and their marriage. Then the therapist would ask her to show the group how she invited her husband and how he reacted to it, playing in succession both herself and the husband. After replaying the episode the woman may realize that her invitation was not an encouraging one. She might then be asked to explore this in psychodrama—playing with another group member and with ex-patients doubling for both—what she really wants from her marriage, to be closer to her husband or to leave him. Later, the woman might play another episode talking with her girlfriend, a former schoolmate. After both episodes it would become apparent to other group members, and to the woman, that her main problem is not lack of attention from her husband, but that she is ambivalent toward her husband coming to the session and questions the whole marriage. A short therapeutic experience could help her explore her problems and better define her therapeutic goals.

The therapeutic goals. In addition to emotional support, universalization, and the instillation of hope, there are specific goals for each category of participants.

For ex-patients, the main goal is transferring the changes undergone during treatment to normal life—to their natural groups and to the relationship to significant persons. Some relationships become closer; other relationships develop greater independence and distance. A man whose unrealistic attitudes toward male authorities originated in childhood with his authoritative, rigid father may now see him as an aging man and either develop a new relationship based on friendship and equality between two adults or, finding him uninteresting, wish to withdraw from him. The patient, no longer afraid of him, does not enjoy making him feel guilty for his miserable life.

Partners, such as a married couple, may start rebuilding the balance of rewards and costs they had obtained from their relationship, and at the same time rearrange certain values in their scale. For example, a husband who previously enjoyed his wife's utmost closeness and devotion, badly needing it to maintain his self-esteem, may no longer need it after the treatment, since he feels more self-confident, less dependent on his wife, and more interested in an enlarged social life. If the wife were not prepared for this change, she might consider it due to his lack of love and find it threatening. If she had an opportunity to get involved in the treatment herself, attending the group during the husband's treatment in the therapeutic community, she might find new value in her husband being a more interesting and emotionally balanced partner. She might also enjoy having more time for herself and her interests.

Ex-patients may help significant persons define and express their own needs in discussion or by doubling for them in psychodrama. Significant persons often need encouragement in speaking for themselves, and may be inhibited for various reasons. (See the case of Mike and his parents in chapter 18.)

For the newcomer, either significant persons or other clients, the main task may be to define their own goals as they receive impulses from others. The mother of an adult son may find other people of her generation parting with their children and reorganizing their life and their set of values. The group may stimulate her to develop interest in others, enjoy helping others, and make plans for her future.

A wide range of social stimuli and life philosophies. This is a significant characteristic of this group. Time spent there is always part of the therapeutic experience whether the participant has a turn or not. Witnessing the action of others, sometimes also cooperating in others' psychodrama, stimulates the participants' thinking about their own life and problems, often releasing strong emotions at the same time.

In this group, people from different natural groups with different philosophies of life meet; homosexual partners may meet members of small communes or family groups. Group participants may broaden their narrow concepts of the family, men's and women's roles, and of various social values. The danger that the therapist's own social concepts could influence the group is minimized or completely excluded—a danger that may be significant in family therapy.

Benefit from a natural and artificial group. A combination of both the artificial patient group and the natural group (family members, couples) makes it possible for psychotherapy to benefit from both.

On one hand, there are elements of the patient group such as the friendly, supportive atmosphere of peers, the use of fantasy, the imaginative amplification of roles, and experimenting in new roles. On the other hand, in the same group there are elements of the natural group, such as reality testing, the training of new attitudes and social roles directly with family members and partners, and a direct therapeutic cooperation with significant persons.

A combination of the artificial and natural group in one setting also helps eliminate possible disadvantages each may have alone. People in an artificial group get "addicted" to it and substitute it for real life, avoiding reality or naively believing the whole world can be made one big therapeutic group. This is eliminated by the presence of members of the natural group. On the other hand the disadvantages of the natural group—strong ties maintaining the same family homeostasis, the mutual loyalty of partners preventing them from being open—are eliminated by the action of members of the patient group.

THE FIFTH STEP: AFTERCARE

All patients who have completed treatment in the residential therapeutic community attend two subsequent aftercare group sessions during the third and fourth week after their arrival from the therapeutic community. During the first two weeks they have been attending the open group, functioning there as ex-patients, and as the group in step 4b in which they work together with their partners, family members, and other significant persons.

The participants and physical setting. About twelve to fifteen ex-patients, who have returned from the therapeutic community in the past three or four weeks, meet together with the therapist in a group session for two to two and a half hours. One therapist, who knows most of the participants from previous encounters in the system, is in charge. The therapist's assigned patients may even be participants.

The group meets at a place and time convenient to those who have already begun outside employment. It may be at the clinic or the day center in the late afternoon, the same day each week.

Goals support but also set limits. The main goal of the aftercare is helping the patients to turn into practice what they have acquired during their previous intensive treatment. Not only what they have learned about themselves and about the reasons and origin of their symptoms, but also what they have changed in their attitudes toward other people and the world in general. They have to use it now when coping with daily stresses and problems. The results of their therapy should show in action, not just in words.

It is our opinion that professional help has to be offered to the patients during this difficult period, but for a limited time only, and that a special therapeutic technique has to be used which stresses present and future perspectives, not those of the past. Without aftercare, patients are more likely to slip into old patterns and symptoms. If, on the other hand, the opportunity to further treatment is unlimited, clients may easily become the subjects of endless therapies, going from one therapist and one group to another without seriously working in any of them. Undergoing therapy then becomes a goal in itself.

The group session usually starts with each participant reporting in turn what they have done during the last week or two. The whole group usually participates in each person's turn. Patients present at the group know each other from the last weeks at the therapeutic community and from the subsequent meetings in the past two weeks. They also know each other's significant persons that they met in group 4b. They still feel a part of the big group in the therapeutic community. Therefore, the aftercare group soon develops a considerable cohesiveness and therapeutic potential. The group supports the members who feel tired, depressed or afraid, facing a difficult task. If, for example, one of the participants starts complaining that he or she is afraid to apply for a better job, the attention of the whole group is temporarily focused on him or her. Various psychodramatic episodes may be played, representing various options in the effort to get the job wanted. Other group members play employment personnel, bosses, or double for the patient. An unexpected guest might ask if this were vocational counseling, assertiveness training, or psychotherapy. It is all these and still psychotherapy. In this special period of treatment, mobilizing the capacity of a person to find a suitable job is the proper therapeutic goal.

Another group member may become afraid of making the final move, leaving his parent's house and looking for a place of his own. He may have decided he would like to live an independent life, but fear of loneliness seems overwhelming to him.

The group, although generally friendly and supportive, may on the other hand strongly criticize a member who rationalizes and tries to avoid practical action. Others may say openly, "Alright, we all know that you felt neglected by your father when you were a little boy and that you had a bad experience with your boss in your first and only job, but are you going to talk about it for the rest of your life? You have had plenty of time in therapeutic community and lots of opportunity to get rid of your anger about your past. Now it is time to do something else."

THE SIXTH STEP: FURTHER ONGOING THERAPY

Most of the patients who finish their treatment in the therapeutic community and its three weeks of aftercare usually do not need further treatment. According to some district psychiatrists in Prague, the patients who went through Lobec asked less for psychiatric help and did not demand medications from general practitioners for their neurotic symptoms.

Some of them who needed further help stayed in our care. In the past, we have experimented with different kinds of treatment. At first we often continued with therapy close to psychoanalysis, except that the patients did not pay. We came to the conclusion that our involvement as therapists in the therapeutic community did not interfere with continuing individual treatment, and that the thorough knowledge about the patients collected during their stay at Lobec was a great asset to further treatment. It became clear to us that beginning with long term individual therapy is highly uneconomic, since treatment in a therapeutic community as the first step saves months, or perhaps even years, of individual treatment. This does not diminish the importance of individual treatment; as a matter of fact, we found that when treatment at Lobec reached a certain plateau, an extension of the stay did not help much. In some cases, we were able to achieve satisfactory results by providing consecutive individual therapy. However, without the model situation at Lobec, this would have been impossible because the patients needed to be confronted with their behavior, which the other patients did, and which could not be done in individual therapy.

Gradually experiences from Lobec infiltrated into all other elements of integrated psychotherapy so that both Lobec and other settings were changing their form constantly.

Presently we consider the most efficient form of treatment of patients who need to continue after going through the therapeutic community to be a group of four patients meeting once a week with the therapist for four hours. This treatment is limited to three months. Various verbal and nonverbal techniques are used. Significant persons are invited when it is considered useful by the group. The norms are different from those of the day house, in that the patients can meet outside the group, but, of course, must report it. One group met regularly with good results during the therapist's vacation. A detailed description of the technique of these groups is beyond the scope of this book.

THE SEVENTH STEP: THE CLUB OF FORMER PATIENTS

The club is run by a committee of former patients of the system and is open to them, their family members and partners, and invited guests.

The day center supplies physical facilities. One of the therapists functions as a resource person. The elected committee organizes all activities going on in the center or outside in the community. One member of the committee or other responsible member is always present. The club functions several hours a week, mostly in the evening. There is no structured program, but various activities, social games, dancing, and sports are available to the participants. In the club, former patients find old friends from the time of their treatment, get emotional support when depressed or lonely, or have the opportunity to offer their interest and support to others in need. People who have gone through the same therapeutic experience, even if treated at different times, mix easily and form friendships. Visits by partners and friends are also encouraged. Visiting the club, discussing personal problems with others, or informally with the therapist present, may be an important factor in either helping a person to master his problems or to seek professional help if needed. A few visits to the open group or to the day center, recommended and scheduled by the therapist, may help the person overcome a personal crisis and get back into normal life. The club may become the center of a volunteer network offering a wide range of nonprofessional mental health services.

NOTE

12. The outcome study of the treatment in Haney Forestry Camp

The therapeutic community in the Haney Forestry Camp was part of a research project, the aim of which was to compare the outcome of treatment in three equalized groups of neurotics in three settings: The Haney Forestry Camp, day care (improvised predecessor of the Day House), and the inpatient unit of the university hospital. The research was conducted by the first author, by G. Reith, Ph.D., and J. E. Miles, M.D. and supported by a National Health Grant and by the British Columbia Government Mental Health Branch.

The results, based on a multivariate analysis of variance of over twelve independent assessments, showed that there existed consistent statistically significant reduction of symptomatology in the invariant order: Haney Therapeutic Community the most; Day Care second; and inpatient treatment the least. Furthermore, it was found that scales measuring anxiety, self-acceptance, self-confidence, and sense of hopefulness, indicated equally consistently that the inpatients not only improved less but often were more anxious and less hopeful upon discharge than the other two treatment groups. (F. Knobloch, G. Reith, J. E. Miles 1973). The costs of the treatment were in reverse order to the efficiency.

If the cost of the inpatient treatment is taken as 100 percent, the cost of the day care treatment was 32 percent, and the Haney treatment 18 percent. Of the 118 patients, 84 were followed up in terms of one and two year evaluations. (Reith, Knobloch, Miles 1974).

The evaluation of psychopathology by a structured psychiatric interview and three independent psychological assessment inventories using a multivariate analysis of variance indicated that the Haney Therapeutic Community patients maintained their initial gains to a statistically significant degree, followed by day care patients; the inpatients showed the least gains.

Evaluation of social adjustment proved also to be an important dimension. *Social adjustment* involved measures of external situational adjustment such as financing, housing, etc.; the degree of self-acceptance; and the relationships with friends, children, spouse, etc. A *behavior performance adjustment* factor measured acceptance of personal habits and hobbies. A multivariate analysis of variance of all four factors for each of the three treatment groups yielded a greater than .0001 probability significance level for the Haney treatment; a .006 probability level for day care and an insignificant probability level of .626 for the inpatient treatment modality.

Chapter 8

DAY HOUSE IN VANCOUVER

Day House, a psychiatric day care center part of the university hospital, is located separately in a house on its own grounds. It was fortunate that the building, a former fraternity house, was in rather neglected shape when the Day House staff took it over. Rebuilding and remodeling of the house and developing the grounds offered a wide range of indoor and outdoor tasks for the group.

In 1971 one of the authors, as clinical supervisor, established two day care centers in two different locations forming a homogeneous group of patients with similar therapeutic needs in each. One center treats patients who have needed hospitalization recently. They usually come to the day center directly from the hospital, and the majority also continue in pharmacologic therapy. The program is similar to that in the other center, with less strict norms. The other center, the Day House, admits patients mainly referred from outside, from clinics or private therapists. Day House patients are people seeking help for various neurotic symptoms, often of long duration, or people wanting to change their behavior pattern. The candidates for treatment must be motivated and able to make a serious commitment to observe the norms of Day House.

A MINIATURE SYSTEM OF INTEGRATED PSYCHOTHERAPY

Day House accomplishes, in one unit, most of the functions of the original system of integrated psychotherapy. It screens and assesses new patients, functions as a day center, involves the patient's significant persons in the therapeutic process, and operates an aftercare group for patients who have completed the daily program. Some patients, who in spite of good motivation did not improve satisfactorily, have an opportunity to continue in small groups or in individual psychotherapy. Friends of the Day House is a club of former patients. As does the original system, Day House functions as a treatment setting as well as a teaching and research facility.

The Day House daily program runs from nine to four five days a week. The eighteen to twenty patients and the therapists spend most of the time together either in one group or divided into three small groups called "families." Their time is employed in various group sessions, work, and sports. They also have lunch together. The patients usually stay for six weeks. Only in special cases is the stay prolonged for up to eight weeks.

STAFF

In addition to the clinical supervisor, Day House has three full time therapists. At present, the senior therapist has a masters degree and a wide background in psychology and related fields; the second therapist is a certified nurse; the third, a work therapist, is a college graduate experienced in working with people, but without formal mental health training. The personal qualities of the staff—their emotional balance, high stress tolerance, mutual loyalty, ability to lead without being authoritative, capacity to take full responsibility for and at the same time always be a part of the patients group, their interest in work, and their dedication—are more important than an educational background. One or two residents in psychiatry work regularly in the Day House and after the necessary orientation function as therapists.

THE SCREENING

Every Friday, several old patients leave and new patients arrive. Before this point, the new patient had to go through a three step screening process:

1. Orientation group

Each Monday all new candidates for treatment are invited to the Day House, where they meet as a group with one Day House therapist or psychiatric resident and with the chairperson of the group.

After having greeted new candidates and introduced everybody, the therapist in charge begins the session with general information about the Day House. A short instructive film, especially made for this purpose, is shown. The candidates then have an opportunity to ask questions. After the questions are answered, the therapist suggests that each candidate take a turn and talk about him or herself and about his or her problems and reasons for coming. Essentially this is a dialogue, in front of the group, between the new candidate and therapist. The therapist may ask questions to clarify various issues; he has to determine in a short time the character of the candidate's symptoms and identify such factors contraindicative to the treatment as the history of psychotic symptoms or any serious dependency on drugs or alcohol. The therapist also has to properly evaluate the candidate's capacity to make a serious commitment and keep the therapeutic contract. He must be willing to complete the full six-week treatment plus three weekly aftercare visits. For the candidate, this may be the first opportunity of speaking about private matters to others in a group and at the same time a test of how far they are able to go in their commitment to treatment.

After all candidates have had their turn, the chairperson may say something about his or her experiences in the Day House (Appendix E). By the end of the session, the candidates must decide whether they want to continue and whether they are seriously interested in the treatment. Some may stop at this point, realizing this was not what they had expected and wanted. Others may be interested in treatment but find it hard to commit themselves, especially if that means having to control their drinking or drug taking by giving them up completely during treatment. Those still interested who decide to continue are invited to individual interviews if no contraindications have been found. They are also given a package of written material—a booklet about the Day House; two lists of norms, "Program Expectations," and "Day House Rules"; and instructions on how to write their own self-description (see Appendix E). In the time between the orientation and the individual interview, candidates write their own self-descriptions; they bring them to the individual interview. Following the interview, and before starting the group, each candidate must have the approval of his physician to participate in strenuous activities. Since group members are expected to participate in all parts of the program including sports, only people physically fit can be accepted.

2. The individual interview

The candidates meet with one of the Day House therapists or with the resident. If the candidates have decided to undergo treatment, they are asked at the beginning of the interview to sign their consent.

The interview then follows, but not rigidly, the self-description the candidates have written and brought with them. The therapist reads, discusses, and clarifies it with the candidate, one item after another. As the self-description has been written following the same order as the Problem Goal List (Appendix E), the therapist, by going through the self-description and obtaining the necessary information or asking for additional information, can then fill out the candidate's Vancouver Problem-Goal List as well. At the same time, the therapist obtains material enabling him to compile the candidate's complete history. Of course, the therapists may explore certain areas in more detail or open other avenues of exploration, if they consider it necessary. They can also ask additional questions about the candidate's previous treatment.

The interview takes about one and a half hours. At the end, the therapist completes the draft of the patient's history and fills out the problem-goal list in close cooperation with the patient. All fifteen parts of the problem-goal list have to be filled out. If the candidates do not have any problem in a certain area it is left with 0, if they have a problem those have to be identified using simple language which describe facts rather than interpret. Each problem area—symptoms, for example—is first discussed with the candidate, then formulated with their cooperation, and finally written on the form. At the end the candidates are asked to score the Problems-Goal List, practicing with it for the first time with the therapist's help. Later on, they will score it regularly every week during their treatment.

3. The group interview

Candidates found suitable in the previous step of screening and who are willing to cooperate further, are invited into the Wednesday morning group. The chairperson presides over the session, one therapist is present and takes the floor if necessary. The candidates have been given a slip of paper with questions they will have to answer during the interview. The chairperson has a list of various routine questions which he or she asks the candidates. After having greeted the candidates and introduced everybody present, the chairperson addresses each candidate asking the following questions (the questions have been included in the committee book and are available to the committee):

If you are accepted by the group—

1. Are there any health or other physical problems that would limit you in any way from participating in fairly strenuous sports and swimming?
2. Do you have any commitments, appointments, and the like that would fall in the six weeks of your stay in the group?
3. Do you, or have you habitually used any drugs or alcohol—including aspirin, tranquilizers, neocitron, or nose spray? Are you prepared to completely abstain from the use of any drugs regardless of how you may be feeling?
4. Are you prepared to return after the six weeks on three successive Wednesdays for aftercare?
5. Are you willing to make a sincere effort to encourage significant persons in your life to come on Tuesday evenings before the group?
6. Do you understand that your commitment to the group allows for no exceptions, nothing held back, no time off, that it is a total commitment?
7. Are you prepared to type an autobiography for presentation to the group on the Tuesday of your second week?
8. Are you aware that failure to follow group rules and actively contribute may result in probation, and if not corrected, discharge?
9. Have you arranged to support yourself financially during your stay here?
10. Are you aware that medical certificates, pictures, and a self-description must be turned in before you can join the group, which would mean this coming Friday?
11. Are you aware that according to your commitment and the rules subgrouping and forming sexual attachments with group members during the six to eight weeks plus the three weeks of aftercare is prohibited? (Subgrouping means discussing problems and meeting with group members after Day House hours.) (Sexual attachments means becoming sexually involved with a group member during your stay at Day House)
12. What concrete goals while at Day House do you have that would result in, or be, real changes in your life?

13. How motivated are you to make a solid commitment to change while attending Day House, e.g., what are you willing to give up?

Each candidate has a turn answering questions and explaining his situation and problems. The patient group is friendly, but direct in questioning. The group members are open in expressing what they think about the new candidate. At any time the therapist may give an opinion about the appropriateness of the candidate and thereby influence the group. At the end of the session after all candidates have had their turn, the patient group and the therapist vote about each candidate by acclamation. If the candidate gets a majority of votes he is accepted. If the group rejects the candidates, the group members explain openly why they voted against their admission. Mostly, the reasons given are that the candidate lacks serious commitment or underestimates the difficulty and stress of the treatment and shows lack of readiness, or minimizes his drinking and drug problem and fails to convince the group he will abstain. Rejected candidates are approached individually by the therapist to arrange an alternative referral.

THE FAMILIES

The whole community in the Day House is divided into three subgroups called *families*. The families, about five or six patients and one therapist, are small groups which involve no prescribed roles and should not be mistaken for simulated families. New patients admitted into the Day House are usually placed into a family having a vacancy and stay there during the entire treatment.

Each family nominates and elects a leader to be a member of the committee. Thus, for example, the chairperson or the work coordinator is leader of a family. The leaders change with each weekly election. (The duties of the family leader are described in the committee book, see note 8). The family usually functions as a team in the work program, being responsible for certain domestic or work projects. Each family has one therapist as a member who always stays with the same family. The family meets regularly three times a week for over an hour. The therapist is always present, except on the Friday session.

The main advantage of families. The techniques used in family sessions are the same as those in the big group. The main advantage of having families consists of having more time for therapy if the treatment occurs simultaneously in three sections instead of one. There is more time to work intensively with individual patients in the group. In the family certain therapeutic actions can continue if interrupted when the big group runs out of time; this is especially true of actions using abreactive techniques. On the other hand, therapeutic actions start in the family and can be elaborated on further in the big group session.

Families function as subgroups, not as independent units. "Families" are useful in the therapeutic community only if they do not isolate themselves but remain part of the whole group. Anything that happens in the family has to be transferred back into the big group, into the whole community. Not every detail must be reported but none of the essential facts must be held back from the big group. Families must not create their own secrets that they could not or would not share with the whole community.

If the families are to function as subgroups, continual communication has to be established between them and the whole community. In the Day House there are several formal and informal channels.

The family compiles a report each week that is written up by the leader and presented to the committee. The committee incorporates it into their weekly report and posts it one day before the big group session, usually the Wednesday afternoon group, led by the clinical supervisor. In discussing the report, events in each family are presented to the big group.

The family leaders report about their families in separate committee meetings and inform the leaders of the other families. The therapists report about the "families" they are members of at the staff meetings. The clinical supervisor usually attends one different family session each week.

The situation and events in each family are informally discussed whenever the group meets together—at lunchtime, during sports, or in the work period. The material from each group sometimes finds its way into the Friday afternoon play, written and played by the patients. Therapists share their differences about, and impressions of patients' progress throughout the day over lunch or coffee. They thereby gain support and encouragement for their work and keep information about the group flowing.

Disadvantages of families. We do not recommend introducing small groups like the family when a therapeutic community is just beginning. There are always significant dangers involved in dividing the community. The staff working with families have to be well experienced in subtle and sophisticated methods for keeping constant communication between the small groups and the whole community and for encouraging patients, mostly through the committee, to bring all important material back to the community. If an inexperienced staff tried to report directly to the whole community what happened in the small group, they would be considered watchdogs and become targets of patient resistance. They would be unable to handle the group. If there were no appropriate communication between the small group and the whole community, the small group would easily begin to function as an independent unit, with its own secrets and complicated ties of loyalty among members. Elsewhere, we have seen this kind of division undermine the unit's capacity to function as a therapeutic community.

DIARIES

Every day, even on weekends, the patients keep diaries. During the first years of Lobec we left it open to the patients to write what they wanted. Later we introduced the following instructions. The patients should report in their diary the three most significant events of the day in order of importance. They may write about other things too if they wish. The writing should be clear and use simple language which stresses facts and avoids professional language or theoretical discussion. The diaries are collected every morning by the member of the committee, the diary dealer, who is responsible for them. Each therapist reads the family diaries of and comments upon them if necessary.

Therapeutic significance. Writing the diary, in a certain way, complements the therapy. Patients go over the events of the last day and recollect their experiences even after the end of the therapeutic session. Each entry in the diary represents a direct communication between the patient and the therapist—one going in both directions since the therapist often comments upon it. The therapist does not reveal information from the diaries to the other patients or to the group but usually encourages the writer of the diary to do so and to bring it to the family. The patients know and also agree that other therapists in Day House may read their diaries and use the information in evaluating the mood of the group and in preparing therapeutic plans.

In the diary the patients may first write about what they find difficult to reveal in front of the group. Encouraged by the therapists' comments, the patients then present their problems in the group more easily.

The structure of the diaries makes it easier to use them in research as well.

NORMS

The basic norms from Lobec have been transferred to Day House. The group through elected members, the committee, is the main body fostering norms. The system of positive and negative sanctions is well elaborated and we describe it in the following sections.

THE COMMITTEE

The committee is responsible for the smooth running of the program, and is deeply involved in all parts of the community life and in the whole therapeutic process.

The committee not only organizes all domestic routines, checks on attendance and punctuality in the program, but it also plays an important role in fostering norms (basic and others) by generating the group's approval and disapproval and by regularly evaluating the patient's therapeutic progress.

The committee book

All of this is best illustrated in the committee book, a booklet describing the function of the committee and its individual members and instructing them how to act in various situations when performing their functions. The committee book has been compiled by several successive committees in cooperation with the therapists; it is handed to the current committee by the previous one who had fully agreed to it. Let us stress here that it would be false, when they start building a new therapeutic community, if the staff introduced to the patients such a booklet as presented here. Presented from the administrative authority, such a booklet would produce mostly negative reaction. On the other hand, in the Day House, the booklet, handed to the new committee by the members of their peer group, not by the therapist, became part of the tradition.

The committee consists of chairperson, work coordinator, and diary dealer. It includes always the leader of each of the three families. The roles and responsibilities of the committee members are described in detail in the committee book (Appendix E).

The committee elections. The day before elections, the chairperson asks for nominations to the new committee. Everybody in the group, including the therapist, can make a nomination. Once the nominations are made, posted (usually at lunchtime) and accepted by the nominees, the campaign starts. People usually accept nominations. If not, this becomes the subject of further discussion and analysis in the group. The usual reason is lack of confidence, but it may be a symptom of resistance toward treatment. In either case, further analysis usually supplies important material for the therapy.

On the day of nominations and on the following day of elections (in the Day House, this takes place on a Friday), there are posters everywhere, the nominees wear self-made pins and encourage others to vote for them. The atmosphere is usually playful, but at the same time it is clear that the group, as well as individual members, consider elections a serious matter. The nominees are aware of the responsibility of the position in the committee and of the special significance to them. This is also shown in the entries in the patients' diaries:

> Peggy nominated me for work coordinator. I very much want the job. It would help me speak up with people and in big groups. It would help me to be more responsible and to stop putting things off. I hope also it may help me to learn how to lead people and deal with them if they need help.

Another entry:

> It was good to get nominated. Now I realized that the group really trust me.

A group member may make nominations for others as well as for him or herself. Campaigning gives people an opportunity to speak for themselves, to assert themselves, which may be quite a new experience for some. This offers training and experimentation in new social skills and unfamiliar social roles.

The criteria for nominations. It may be evident to the staff that the committee members should be people with certain personal qualities—people able to do the job, respected by others, therapeutically well motivated, people who already have made certain progress in their own therapy. But voting is the decision of the whole group in which the therapist has only her or his voice. How do we convey these criteria to the majority of the group?

In a less cohesive group, such as that during the first period of the therapeutic community, the staff introduces their views about new candidates in meetings with the committee, by discussing various candidates at the group session, or by making their own nominations and subsequently explaining the reasons for their choice. When further cohesiveness and the therapeutic capacity of the patient group increases, the group accepts criteria mentioned as its own.

At Lobec it was mainly the committee that presented the criteria for nominations to the group. In the Day House the expected characteristics of a well functioning committee member have been included in the committee book. (see Appendix E). Before the elections the chairperson presents these criteria when informing the group about the responsibilities of the newly elected committee members. This usually happens the day before elections. At first the nominations are made for two positions only—for the chairperson and for the work coordinator. Since the small group families were introduced into Day House, each family has to be represented in the committee. If the first two committee members elected belong to different families, the group nominates the third committee member from the remaining family. If they belong to the same family, two other candidates from each of the remaining families have to be nominated and elected. Thus the final number of committee members is either three or four.

The candidates nominated give a speech before the group and in the speech they must explain why they want, or do not want, to get the position. The candidate is elected by a simple majority of the group including the therapist present.

Being on the committee: patients' reactions as shown in the entries of their diaries

Chairperson writes:

Most of the day I kept dreading sitting up in front of the Group and visitors and leading family night. [Tuesday night meeting with the patients' significant persons in the patient group.] I made myself more anxious and felt desperate. When I first sat down in front I was so nervous but as I saw me doing okay I was alright. At supper I told the Group I was afraid. Usually I won't tell people so feel alone with my worry. No-one said much but they knew. It made a difference. By the end *of the evening I felt natural and genuinely had something to say. I was proud I was able to do it* and wondered what I was so afraid of. The quotation "if you do the thing you fear the death of fear is certain" kept coming into my head all day. *I would never have learned this lesson if I hadn't taken the Chairperson position.* After the Group was leaving I told Sara how pleased I was that though I was afraid to sit in front of the Group I did okay. Sara asked my mum if she was surprised I did well and mum said no. I wish I could see myself as others see me. I am so young for my 27 years.

Another entry:

I felt strong and decisive today. I originally thought committee work would harm my therapy. It's working to the opposite. My involvement has increased my interaction with the people at Day House, both negative and positive. I've also done a lot of work and done it well.

Another entry:

I am enjoying *being on the committee*—the responsibilities and the becoming more aware of people is good. I enjoy being a family leader and co-ordinating and directing the others—it gives me a feeling of confidence and responsibility which I like. I feel it is good for me and helps me to finish things and become more organized.

Another entry:

As Chairperson I have very mixed feelings about myself. The responsibility I feel comfortable with. I also enjoy the position for the way it brings me closer to individual group members, for I consciously "look out" to those I think are feeling on the edge of the group or seem particularly upset. I view the group more for what it is—a functioning unit depending upon each of us and from which I and every other member is depending greatly. On the other hand, I feel very inadequate—unable to project my voice or my decisiveness; thus I see myself as looking and sounding very stupid. That I can roll with this is something for me—usually I try to do a job perfectly and pressure myself to do so. If I don't succeed (in my terms) I berate myself terribly. I'm glad I'm able to be realistic about being Chairperson. I still try my best but my "failures" I'm filing away as object lessons, considering the experience beneficial no matter how imperfect. Still, my self-consciousness has me pegged as an idiot a lot this week—i.e. I'm sure all the Group thinks I'm an ass—okay, I should ask—I will, but not today! That's immature, but I fear hearing from them what I sometimes feel about myself.

PROMOTING THERAPY THROUGH SOCIAL APPROVAL AND DISAPPROVAL

We will describe in this section formalized rewards and costs designed to speed up the process of psychotherapy. In dispensing these rewards and costs the whole group or the committee is involved.

Positive points

Once a week the group discusses the therapeutic progress of each group member. What the patients are doing in all areas of the Day House program, as well as in their life outside, is evaluated from the stand-point of how this promotes the therapy. The patients also discuss their progress regarding the accomplishment of special tasks to which they committed themselves upon entering the Day House (changing their life style, exposing themselves to situations they were afraid of). The person's progress is first discussed in the family. The family leader then makes the final ratings of positive points following instructions in the committee book:

Ratings in the following categories: Rate from 1 to 6—6 highest, 1 lowest

1. *Successes*: Points are given for changes in behavior which occur out-side the group. These should be clearly seen by the group as prog-ress—some new step which shows improvement in relation to the goals set by the member in coming to Day House. For example, if a member who fears meeting women or men, speaking to parents, crossing a bridge, or riding a bus does what he fears, he gets a high score. Other positive actions might be getting a job, doing a new activity, enrolling in school, or making a friend. This category indi-cates how the member is using his therapy and emphasizes the im-portance of carrying through on changes made in the Day House. The older members in the group are expected to make greater steps in this area than newer members.
2. *Therapeutic progress*: Points are given for changes occurring in Day House which are the result of therapy: achieving new insight, some visible improvement in symptoms, a change in feelings and behavior including having courage to express feelings openly, more assertive-ness, a change in appearance, a new attitude and relationship toward other group members, or some progress with guests at family night.
3. *Help*: Points are given for helping individuals and the group by sup-

porting rules, participating actively, and encouraging others in their therapy. Points are deducted for those members who undermine morale (see negative points).

4. *Work*: Points are given for performing a job carefully within the time period. Efficiency, creativity, involvement, initiative, and cooperation should be evaluated. In addition, the supervisor should be rated for his organization of work and members, and his skill in giving orders to others.

5. *Merits*: Points are given for special contributions, including bringing or making something special for the group and doing an extra good job as chairperson or on the committee. No points are given here for an average job on the committee.

Each member gives to the committee in writing on Monday evening accomplishments for the previous week to help the committee make their evaluation. A card is filled in for each group member where the positive (as well as negative) points are regularly recorded. This is the role of one of the committee members, usually the diary dealer.

Awards

Each family may suggest one member for a positive and one member for a negative award. But it is entirely up to them to do so. Sometimes a family suggests only one award or none.

The *awards* are small objects, that could be pinned up, and must be made, usually by the family leader, not purchased. The awards are meant as gifts, characterizing the reason for the reward. For example, a group member, who is getting much more confident, might get a small backbone made of wire and paper as a positive award. Another patient might get a small wood block as a negative award, suggesting that she still carries a chip on her shoulder.

In addition to positive awards dispensed by the family, a group member may obtain a grand award from the committee for an exceptional achievement.

The group members take awards seriously as a sign of the group's approval or disapproval. This is evident in their diaries.

Entry in a diary:

I felt very good when I received the positive award although I had some mixed feelings too. I have always been able to receive, and wanted to receive, criticism of one sort or another, but when very

positive reaction is given to me, I have found it difficult, even embarrassing to receive, as I never thought I really deserved it. However, today I could accept the positive response with more comfort
than before, yet with some embarrassment still present.

I never have received praise with comfort. I've even been apolo-
getic about it. I've never felt worthy enough for it, and almost want
to ask, "What do you see in me?" Probably because I don't really
see/feel what others see in me.

It's strange—and undesirable; I can criticize others, others can criticize me, and that is comfortable when in the process. Yet I find it
difficult to praise others, and squirm when others praise me.

Well, it seems a change in that script is occurring. It is strange, and
new, but I desire it, and need to learn how to handle it.

I've been too long in the habit of philosophies, and am presently
faced with the opportunity of experiencing. The discomfort of that
is a minimal cost for the rewards. I hope I can uphold that.

Another entry:

I was really glad to win the positive award today. I worked at it and
I think I deserved it.

Another entry:

I did work very hard this past week and I think wanted the award.
At the time of presentation, I felt sure I would be getting the negative
award. As is typical of me, I find it very difficult to accept good things
even when I have worked for them.

Another entry: (The patient was nominated for an award.)

Dan and Jill, the other members of the committee both felt I should
get the Grand Award and I said I would accept it, though I was afraid
I did not deserve it. In fact, Tuesday night when I was lying in bed
I was thinking about the awards ceremony and I was afraid the group
would rise up in disapproval of my having been chosen and demand
to know why someone else, like Dan, hadn't gotten it instead.
This afternoon when prizes were being awarded, I was fully prepared
to receive the negative prize for "family" 3 because I have not opened
up at all and have been afraid to say much in group about anyone

else because I might say the wrong thing. I feel very apart, physically because I am tall, and emotionally because I have never felt close to people in all my life, except to Paul and Bob and I can hug them and be relaxed with them. I am very afraid to find out what others in the group think of me and even more afraid that they don't think of me at all.

Negative points

Through negative points, the group expresses its disapproval of a patient's acting destructively against the treatment. The definition of destructive acts and the rating scale is presented in the following section of the committee book:

Only easily identifiable acts of breaking the contract, which the patient made with the community and on the basis of which was admitted, are included. They all are destructive to the treatment of the individual and a threat to the morale and successful work of the group. Of course, having no negative points does not itself guarantee successful treatment.

Guidelines to Follow:
1. Missed time (being late, leaving, etc.), per minute   1 point (3¢ per minute)
2. Diary not delivered   100 points
3. Autobiography not delivered, each day of delay   420 points
4. Breaking rules and individual commitments   50—100 points
5. Not signing in   15 points

Negative points accumulate during a member's stay. They are separate from the weekly ratings as a measure of each member's allegiance to the community and the rules as a whole.

The total number of negative points that have accumulated during an individual's stay should appear on the weekly report and on individual cards kept up-to-date by the diary dealer. The record of negative points should be taken into consideration in all decisions concerning a patient—whether the question is an extension of stay, aftercare treatment, or consideration for discharge.

When members do not fulfill commitments they may be asked to do makeup by the committee to compensate for time lost or for failing in their therapy. Makeups can include making coffee in the morning, coming in early, doing extra work, making a special project or wearing a sign, remaining silent for a day, eating alone, or something the group or committee feels is appropriate.

Makeup is a sanction that can be administered faster then negative points or awards, usually the following day. In suggesting makeup the committee has to use its creativeness, as well as proper judgment, as to what measure would be proper punishment for a certain person.
Entry in a diary of a patient who got negative points and makeup for breaking the rules:

> I felt very low in receiving negative points for makeup for breaking Day House rules. The more I think of my foolishness in going to Pat's house [Pat was another patient of the Day House.] I become angry with myself. I should have stayed home, expressed my feelings with my family for that is where it stemmed from. I am wondering if this what I may do instead of admitting my feelings directly to the person at that time. I smother them and run away. I feel there was no need to go to Pat's house for I deserve my makeups and negative points. It has made me aware of my doings.

This episode refers to subgrouping—when two group members meet secretly.

Probation
The committee can recommend probation for a group member who has consistently broken group rules, or failed to make sufficient progress. The group votes on this with therapists present. Probation is usually for one week during which time the member is expected to follow all the rules and work on their problems. He or she is subject to discharge if this isn't followed. Again the group would discuss such a step.

THE PROGRAM

Day House works on a weekly schedule (Appendix E). In the following section we describe its essential parts. Since elements such as work and the autobiography can be used separately in other settings, we describe them in more detail.

Work as part of the therapeutic program
Monday afternoons and part of Wednesday and Thursday mornings

are reserved for work. In the Day House, work consists mainly of improving the inside and the outside of the house, working in the vegetable garden, and a weekly car wash.

Physical work

We have had the best results in therapeutic communities with physical work, if possible outdoors or partially outdoors, with as many group members as possible working together. There may also be difficult group tasks and stress-producing situations. The function and the goals of work should be clearly defined. At Lobec, the patients work outdoors all year long—in the fields in summer and in the woods in the winter. At Haney, patients worked in the forest planting trees, clearing the woods, cutting heavy logs, and repairing tracks.

There seems to be a special advantage to physical work in psychotherapy. Physical work regulates the physical functions which have often been neglected by people suffering from neurotic symptoms or which are overtly disturbed in those having psychosomatic symptoms. Physical work shows the person's dysfunctions in posture and movement, making the patient and the others in the group aware of the special muscular inhibitions which are a part of his or her whole character (character armor: W. Reich 1949). Physical work breaks through the motor inhibitions directly and this often releases strong emotions like anxiety and anger. The patients become more expressive both verbally and nonverbally, and their problems become more accessible to the psychotherapeutic process.

What may otherwise be achieved by complex procedures of sleep deprivation, starvation and exposure to unusual experiences and rituals (procedures which often use complicated artificial devices) is achieved here in a simpler and more natural way. Work, as an ongoing activity, offers much more. People can experiment with new postures and motor patterns, and this calls for new attitudes. Patient's relatives and friends often comment on the facial expression which result. If a person moves differently, more freely, if his facial features become less rigid and more expressive, all of this influences his behavior toward others, and also induces changes in other's reactions to him. This is a mutual process; changes in other people's reactions (such as becoming more close and friendly) reinforce the changes in the patient.

The influence of physical work itself would be, of course, transitory if it were not part of the psychotherapeutic process.

Reactions to physical work in the patients' diaries. A diary entry:

The work project today was very good. I really dig sawing, and I would have enjoyed staying at the site all day. I felt free of my tension after work.

Another entry:

When cutting wood today, I almost didn't make it—my arms nearly fell off—but I wouldn't quit and when I finished I had a really good feeling of satisfaction. I enjoyed the feelings in my muscles and the rest of my body during the work.

Another entry:

The chopping and cutting of wood was fun. I enjoyed it and the more successful I became the more I enjoyed it.

Another entry:

Worked in the vegetable garden. Put a lot of effort into this work as I found it important and relevant.

Another entry:

I fixed drawers in the kitchen desk. I enjoyed it. I realized that I like doing things that involve coordinating my mind and body, just about anything like that. I think it gives me a sense of self-satisfaction and worth. Plus knowing someone else benefited by it makes me feel good.

How work is organized. One therapist, a full-time member of the Day House staff, is responsible for work as part of the therapeutic program. The therapist plans the work ahead, organizes it into group tasks, takes care of the material and tools, works with the patients during the working period, and often personally sets an example by tackling strenuous and unpopular tasks.

The therapist responsible for work is always in close contact with the other staff, reporting to them regularly at staff meetings and listening to their reports. Informal, but most important, communication goes on in the short breaks between various parts of the program. During these breaks the therapist who has finished his session briefs the one who will take the group over, on what has happened. Thus the therapist responsible for work has to be well acquainted with the therapeutic plans and able to understand the meaning and importance of whatever happens in his session. In Day House, the work therapist often helps in other sessions and in reading the diaries and commenting on them. In addition, the same therapist organizes sports and such related activities as hiking trips or visits to the public swimming pool. He often has lunch with the patient group and supervises their filling in of their problem goal lists and other questionnaires (charting).

Every week one of the three members of the elected patient committee becomes a work coordinator. The committee and the group as a whole support the elected work coordinator in various actions he undertakes appropriate to his function. The work coordinator meets regularly with the therapist, discussing plans for the next work period, defining group tasks, and also talking about his or her feelings and the problems which may be involved in performing the function. Although the therapist supports and encourages him, it is mostly up to the work coordinator and the family leader to organize the work of the group during each work period and to select people for certain kinds of jobs. They may ask for volunteers, control work done, motivate the group to greater effort, praise or criticize on the spot, or suggest positive or negative rewards at the end of the week. The therapist in charge is present or close by, but he lets the work coordinator do as much as possible in the practical organization of work.

It is imperative that work be considered as important as any other part of the therapeutic program. Being late for work, or skipping the work period, is considered as serious an offence as being late or missing the Wednesday afternoon session, or not doing autobiographies. Most work coordinators take their function seriously, and it often shows in their diaries:

> Mike and Cindy worked poorly before coffee. They resisted when I told them to work harder but were better after. I feel *helpless* and *frustrated* when I couldn't get them to work harder—I am frustrated by Cindy trying to avoid work. I think there is nothing I can do to change this. *I hate myself for not trying hard enough* to overcome these situations like the one with Cindy.

The work coordinator who does not take his function seriously enough may be criticized by the committee as well as by the group. Part of the weekly report of the committee:

Although the group seemed to be pleased with Ted's performance and Ted felt people worked well together, it was the committee's feeling that Ted somehow avoided being in an unpopular position of authority by deviating from the work schedule and by being generally too permissive.

Therapeutic significance of work. In general, working on group tasks and completing them efficiently, increases the cohesiveness of the group. And cohesiveness is needed if the group is to develop substantial therapeutic potential.

Creating real-life situations is the most important function of the work in the therapeutic community. There is always a task which must be accomplished despite such difficulties as fatigue or rain. It is a shared task, where group cooperation is needed. Here people reveal in a short time their specific patterns of giving and taking. The simple situations encountered in primitive living show such patterns best. If the person responsible for the fire in a therapeutic camp does not prepare enough wood for the fireplace, the whole group may freeze during the night session. When people work together in a group, various interpersonal tensions and conflicts emerge which may be related to their outside problems. All of this introduces important material into the psychotherapy. It may start with a simple episode such as described in the diary of a woman patient:

When working—fixing the fence—I got very angry at Mike [another patient], coming and going and not working. I used to do that at home. If I were busy I would not say anything feeling somebody should offer help. Then suddenly I would explode—yelling at Mark, take a broom and threaten Sue, feeling frustrated and rejected [Mark and Sue are the patient's teenage children].

Another patient wrote in her diary:

I was pleased that I handled the vegetable sale o.k. I made the effort to stop all the people I could to buy the produce and also to announce it to them all in the Cafeteria—twice. This is a very different me from just 2 months ago—at that time I was even afraid to wear something new and different to work for fear of being noticed and singled out. I felt safe in the blue uniform I wore every day. I am gaining in self-confidence and the knowledge that the world won't cave in if I assert myself once in a while. I want to keep the line drawn though between standing up for myself and being too aggressive.

Work provides the opportunity to be a leader or a follower and to switch from one role to the other. Many patients are elected work co-ordinators during their treatment. The opportunity is even greater in residential therapeutic communities such as Lobec or Haney where the working circumstances make it necessary for three or four groups to work on different tasks at the same time.

For some patients, becoming work coordinator may be a new experience in leadership and provide training in roles they have not been used to. In others it may evoke conflicts from work outside—conflicts, for example, in relation to authorities or subordinates. To switch between both complementary roles, being a follower at the beginning, then becoming an elected leader, then switching back to a follower may be, for many people, a useful experience. This shows in the diaries:

> I was excited being appointed work co-ordinator because I wanted to prove I can lead people without antagonizing them. I'm enjoying the group I have and really feel confident about being a good leader.

Another diary:

> I felt very comfortable in the role of work co-ordinator today. For one of the first times in my life, I felt like I didn't have to try extra hard to make myself liked. In fact, truthfully, I really didn't care if I stepped on anyone's toes, although that situation didn't arise. It was quite a new feeling for me and a good one.

Diary of a woman starting as work coordinator:

> I found it extremely difficult to lead the group today. I did not do much, although I had a pretty good idea what should be done. I somehow expected people would know what to do and became frustrated when the group did not co-operate consistently and finally did a rather poor job. It is the same as at home. I do not show directly what I would, I am always afraid to be considered bossy and unfeminine.

One patient's comment about another patient's performance in the role of work coordinator:

> I felt May was a good co-ordinator, although perhaps overzealous. She didn't seem to want us to take a break at all and this frustrated me a bit.

Being chosen as leader of a working team:

> I had mixed feelings about being chosen as leader—I was glad to know that I work well, but I usually take the role of follower rather than leader—I think I am afraid of responsibility.

Switch in leader-follower role (diary of a patient at the beginning of treatment):

> Work was fine, but I found I didn't like having a work leader tell me what to do.

The same patient writes after two weeks:

> I like being a work co-ordinator. Betsy seems a slow worker but when she gets going she works well. I haven't said anything to her yet but we'll see if it continues first.

Being a leader evokes certain specific problems the patient has in his job outside:

> When my work crew complained we had a pretty "nothing" job, I felt helpless to defend the job. I sort of then began to wonder if it was a work co-ordinator's job to defend the work. My crew seemed to work better after I told them that perhaps even though they thought this way, it was our job and if we got on with it and quit complaining, it might go easier.

Another example:

> I was quite tired today. And I also could not help thinking about my wife and the letter I got from her, suggesting divorce. I tried not to let it show. I was quite surprised in group today when we were talking

about the foreman, when Bea said she sort of felt I was tired. I *felt* it was *important not to show personal worries when acting as leader,* but obviously the workers realize that you can feel bad too and they don't seem to mind it.

Therapeutic strategy. The therapist responsible for work follows the same therapeutic plans, but he uses different tactics than those used in other sessions. If a conflict which needs further analysis arises during the work period, or any other event, the therapist does not interrupt work and does not start role-playing and psychodrama or other actions. The work has to continue, the group tasks have to be completed. But at the same time the event should be noticed as important for the therapy and the material should be transferred to other sessions for further analysis and working through. This is mostly done by the work coordinator, or by other group members, who introduce it in the family or in the big group session. The therapist may comment on it only briefly after the work period, or informally when talking with the work coordinator; nevertheless, at the same time, he mentions it to the colleague who takes the group over. The other therapist is thus alerted and may be more sensitive to pick up the material if it comes out in his session.

If, for example, patient A gets angry at patient B and has an argument with her, this may be recalled in the family session and replayed by the persons involved with other group members doubling for both. Patient A, replaying the recent conflict with patient B, may also reexperience another conflict with a significant person in his past. Recalling and reexperiencing the conflict, with his mother for example, experiencing at the same time its strong emotional component (when abreaction and other techniques have been used), he may achieve a step in the corrective experience and some of the one-sided assumptions in his mother schema may be influenced. Such change of attitude may, in turn, influence his present marriage.

Such a process, although it starts in the work period, continues through the other sessions. The therapist responsible for work is informed about the process in informal discussions with the other therapists and in regular staff meetings; he may sometimes even be present in a group session where the action has been focused on patient A. The therapist may then better understand the patient's behavior in his own session—for example, patient A's reaction to a new female work coordinator.

There is a weekly forty-five minute group to discuss the week's work and evaluate the work of the members and the performance of the work coordinator. Conflicts and observations arising from this group are further developed in the family and big group.

The right work atmosphere. Work should serve as a model of real life with stress, tension, and conflict. At the same time, the group as a whole, as well as individual members, should have an opportunity to work steadily and gain satisfaction from the work and from accomplishing group goals. One of the work therapist's most difficult tasks is to keep a proper balance between these two objectives. The appropriate atmosphere is always somewhere between the following extremes: no problems at all, efficiency in work is everyone's only concern; and too much conflict, no time for efficient work.

1. The group works hard, efficiently; everything goes smoothly; there seem to be no tensions or conflicts; and everything is fine. People seem interested solely in work, talking about it all the time, not revealing any personal thoughts, experiences, feelings, or observations about themselves—or others. They claim they don't have anything important to say about themselves, and they do not see anything unusual in others. This is usually a sign that something has gone wrong. Too intensive a preoccupation with work and its success has become a way of avoiding other more painful therapeutic experiences. This is a symptom of resistance and should be handled and analyzed as such. This flight into work may develop in a majority of the group members, or in one or two only. For example, a newly elected work coordinator starts to invest all of his interest and effort into performing his function and "does not have any problems". The analysis of his resistance might start with a short comment from the therapist at the end of the work period such as "You work pretty hard and do a good job, but I am wondering, does the group know you well enough?" This may stimulate the next family session to focus on the work coordinator. If flight into work becomes a general pattern in the group, the combined effort of all the therapists in all ongoing sessions is necessary to effectively handle and analyze it.

2. The group is torn apart. People are too angry, crying or not talking to each other, to be able to cooperate in group tasks. Such situations also need immediate analysis and action, which may start briefly at the end of the work period by defining and clarifying some of the interpersonal problems, and continue into the "family" or Wednesday group sessions.

Therapists need to be trained and experienced in special methods and techniques used in a therapeutic community, as well as to have certain personal qualities if they are to keep a proper balance between these two extremes mentioned. The therapist must constantly discriminate between serious effort and signs of resistance, and act flexibly.

The therapist responsible for work may find himself in conflict, seemingly acting against his own immediate interest. He is interested in having the work go smoothly and efficiently; it is then much easier to lead the session. However, he knows that if the helpful, efficient, hard-working work coordinator becomes the focus of the group's attention and his intensive preoccupation with work is analyzed as resistance, it is good for the final progress of his treatment even though he will probably be less helpful as a coordinator for the next few days.

In a therapeutic community, the therapists, no matter what conflicting thoughts they may have had, must always act to promote therapy and not to jeopardize it. The therapist's interest goes far beyond the action of his or her own sessions. The final improvement of patients is the therapist's main concern and the reward he or she gets for hard work.

Of course, many enthusiastic therapists working in traditional settings have the same main interest, the improvement of the patients, but the fragmented structure and organization of services make it impossible for them to cooperate with all other staff members in any systematic way. They, therefore, see little result from their efforts. In a therapeutic community, such cooperation is a significant characteristic of the therapists' work and function and at the same time a *condition* for efficient functioning of the therapeutic community.

How work here differs from occupational therapy. Let us now compare work in a therapeutic community, such as Lobec, Haney, or Day House, with occupational therapy programs in established psychiatric settings.

Work in therapeutic community:	Occupational therapy in traditional setting:
This is real work. Its purpose is well-known to patients and considered relevant. The group cooperates in various tasks. The efficient completion of work is acknowledged as an important group goal.	The patients consider occupational therapy mostly as a way to spend free time or as training in individual skills. The staff of the unit may vary in theory and in verbal approach, but in practice, they conceive of occupational therapy as the patients do.

The organization:

The therapist responsible for work functions more or less as a resource person. The patient group, through elected committee members and work coordinators, organize the work in practice.

The occupational therapist alone organizes most occupational therapy. He has no responsible members of the patient community to help him. Some patients may volunteer to help the occupational therapist, but they do not have the authority and social power to organize others.

Fostering norms:

Work is a group task. Individuals are bound by norms to participate in the group tasks and to overcome obstacles such as physical discomfort and fatigue. The transgression of work norms meets with the same consequences as transgressions in other parts of the therapeutic program. The group as a whole, acting through its elected members is the main body fostering norms.

There are usually no formulated norms beyond some basic rules of social conduct. Attendance and participation in occupational therapy is voluntary and uncontrolled. The patient may be advised by his therapist to attend occupational therapy, but his attendance and experiences there are not discussed further in individual interviews. The occupational therapist is left alone to take care of patients' attendance at his sessions.

Skipping sessions or poor performance is commonly used by patients as a resistance toward the therapy and the hospital establishment.

In some departments, there are problems over who should prepare and escort patients to O.T. A well-trained occupational therapist with the best ideas and intentions may then spend his session with one or two patients instead of the fifteen to twenty expected. Meanwhile other patients arrive, leave, and interrupt. The unit may be at the same time full of patients sitting in the lounges, smoking and eating.

The general status of work or O.T.:

Work is considered by the entire staff to be of the same importance as the other parts of the program, including other group sessions or individual interviews.

Other staff members consider occupational therapy generally a less important part of treatment than individual interviews or verbal group. This may not be expressed but nevertheless is clearly communicated to the patients.
Although the therapist may emphasize the importance of O.T. to his patient, the patient knows that he may be called out of O.T. any time the therapist he is assigned to comes to see him. Patients are regularly sent for laboratory tests and physical examinations during times reserved for O.T.

Contact with other staff members:

The therapist responsible for the work program is a full-time member of the staff. He is regularly informed about what has been happening with the patients in other sessions and informs them about what happens in work. All staff members follow the basic therapeutic strategy, even though they use different tactics. The therapist responsible for work receives attention and

The occupational therapist works separately from other staff in the unit. He or she usually organizes sessions for patients from several different wards or for the whole clinic. (This is considered the only way the occupational therapist can be fully utilized.)
Patients whom the O.T. meets will have been assigned to many therapists weekly. It is practically impossible for an O.T. to come

help from other staff when in difficulty, for example, when he encounters episodes of high resistance in the patient group. The therapist has an opportunity to observe the progress of his patients in other sessions and to see the results of his efforts.

into contact with all the other therapists. Even if he succeeds, the patient in which he is interested may not come any more.

If the O.T. contacts another therapist, he may not be able to communicate with him properly. The other therapists have differing philosophies and therapeutic approaches, and things one O.T. considers highly important may seem trivial to another therapist, such as one deeply involved only with his patient's early infant period. It is highly unlikely for the O.T. to obtain information about a patient's behavior and progress in other therapy sessions.

Even if the other therapists are pleasant and friendly, they can be of little help to the O.T.

The situation provides great opportunity for patients to act in resistance by antagonizing one therapist against the other. Misunderstandings so created can rarely be cleared up. Occupational therapists may be the persons who suffer most, since they are more dependent in their work on the presence of patients and on their cooperation in the sessions than other therapists who work with their patients mostly on an individual basis.

Neurosis and unrealistic attitudes toward work

We have found work, in the psychotherapeutic process, eminently important in treating certain patients in whom a rigid, unrealistic attitude toward work constitutes a significant element in the vicious circle of their personal unhappiness and their neurotic symptoms. Whether such people like or dislike a certain type of job or other activity depends more on a certain pattern of their group schema than on the real circumstances of their work. Let us first explain what we call a realistic or unrealistic attitude towards work. We should stress that we are talking here about a category of patients seeking help for neurotic symptoms. We are not talking about people or groups of people who have been deprived of a work experience because of social circumstances; the remedy in their case lies mainly in social and economic measures, not in psychotherapy.

Realistic and unrealistic attitudes toward work Let us look at an example. A little boy is taught to swim by his father. Unpleasant factors involved in the training, costs such as fear, may be well balanced by rewards such as receiving his father's attention, identifying with him, and pleasing him. In the beginning, the little boy may go swimming mostly to please his father and to enjoy his attention. Later on, the boy develops an independent realistic attitude toward swimming. He may go swimming and enjoy it because it produces a comfortable body feeling, or because he likes to compete, or because he likes to go to places like the seaside or lakes. Or he may dislike it because the water is polluted, his eyes get sore, or he does not feel confident enough in his bathing suit. But his attitude toward swimming no longer significantly depends on his relationship to his father.

How an unrealistic attitude to work fits into the vicious circle of neurosis. Those having an unrealistic attitude to work, due to certain patterns in their group schema, often miss or actively avoid training and acquiring work habits and skills. They also avoid and do not properly learn to plan their own personal goals and satisfactions. When they work, their lack of training and skills limits them to categories of work which are less attractive and rather boring; this reinforces their negative attitude to work. They then develop a dissatisfying life style full of boredom, which may be an important factor in their depression, feeling of worthlessness, and other symptoms.

Such people may talk freely about how much they disagree with their parents and yet not realize how deeply their disagreement influences their lives. They often see their attitude to work and their life style as fully dependent on external causes and consider them either irrelevant to their neurotic symptoms or a simple consequence of them. Their attitude to work is neither a cause of their neurosis, nor a simple consequence of their illness. But it is an important factor in the vicious circle of their neurosis. Let us demonstrate this in an example:

Paul, a twenty-three-year-old man, enrolled by the Day House program referred by his family doctor. Paul complained of fear of open spaces, sex problems, depression, and feelings of inadequacy and worthlessness. During treatment, it became clear that his life style and his attitude toward work and any other goal directed activities were significantly affected by his rebellion against his father and the values of the group to which his father belonged.

Paul's father was a hard-working carpenter who had built his own business. He was a man of strict moral principles and had a rather authoritarian disposition. He stressed hard work as man's most important duty. He wanted his son to go to school and achieve a better education than he had. He also expected that Paul would finally step into the family business and develop it further. Paul dropped out of high school when he was seventeen and left home for good. Ever since he had drifted around, working once in a while at odd jobs. He worked only if he could not find support otherwise. As he happened to live in a highly developed country, such situations rarely occurred.

Paul's father very likely enjoyed his work and drew great satisfaction from it, although the side of his work that he presented to his son consisted exclusively of duty, hardship, and struggle. Paul recalled his father coming home from work tired and irritated, especially if there had been business troubles.

When he started treatment, Paul said he could not recollect ever enjoying working. At school he felt pushed by his teachers and worried whether he could satisfy his father's high expectations. When helping around the house, he felt tense and unhappy and had difficulty meeting the standards his father set for almost every domestic activity. There were rules for how to sweep the floor and how to cut wood for the fireplace.

When his father sent him for swimming lessons, he stressed physical exercise as preparation for the hardship of adulthood. Paul skipped most of his lessons and in his early twenties he still was a nonswimmer. Paul's father often wondered why Paul was never interested in sports. The father had been a good soccer player.

Paul also believed that the family life style, full of duties and hard work, contributed to his mother's premature death of a heart condition in her late forties when Paul was sixteen.

Paul's treatment showed that working to him meant accepting the principles and values of his father and those of the social group to which the family belonged. Mostly out of rebellion against his father's principles and values he finally confined himself to a life of inactivity and leisure. He did not make plans and avoided setting any future goals.

Paul saw nothing unusual in his life style. He knew many other people around him living the same way, but contrary to most of them, Paul was not enjoying his life style. Most of the time he felt bored, he found it hard to fill the hours of the day with anything interesting. Sometimes he woke up in the morning feeling that he would barely survive the long hours until going back to sleep. He tried to occupy himself with music, experimented with drugs, became temporarily involved in meditation, but found no satisfactory solution in any of them. Once he attended an encounter workshop and returned home feeling he was an intelligent, valuable person, but this pleasant feeling of self-confidence and worthiness lasted only a few days.

In the Day House, Paul undergoes various corrective experiences at the same time. He has an opportunity to change his father schema as well as to develop a new, more realistic attitude toward work—an attitude based on direct experience. He will then be able to separate his attitude toward work from his father schema. Before coming this far, he must relearn neglected skills and acquire new ones. He starts working on his family's group task. The main incentive for his working will be that he accepts his peer group's tasks as his own, and not that he obeys the commands of an authority similar to his father's. True, there is an authority in the family, the family leader, but he or she is a different kind of authority, being elected for one week only and usually being more of a permissive person. In the first period of adjustment, Paul may not like work and may even come into conflict with the work co-ordinator and receive negative reactions. But the support and approval of the family will compensate for this and temporarily keep the balance of rewards and costs he draws from the whole work situation. Later, after he renews his skills and acquires new ones, he will be able to directly acquire satisfaction out of work.

If Paul started psychotherapy elsewhere, his attitude toward his father might also become the subject of analysis. But his life outside the therapeutic session might not enter into psychotherapy at all. Paul might continue in his boring life style and feel more and more worthless. This

féeling might not be a symptom of illness; he might not be doing anything worthwhile for himself or other people. But this would increase
his depression and finally lead to hospitalization.

Or the therapist might recommend that Paul be more active and look
for work. Then the impulse would be similar to that in his past; he is
asked by a person in authority to do things and associates this suggestion
with his father schema and rejects it or acts rebelliously to it in various
ways. Paul's willingness to be more active and look for work would depend then on his transference relationship to his therapist and could
follow its fluctuations to the positive or negative extreme. Even if he
starts working, Paul might not stay long but find the first period of
adjustment to schedules and the other strains of work too difficult.

SPORTS

Several times a week about one and a half or more hours is reserved
for sports. The patients play various games, go swimming, hiking or
skiing, depending on the season and opportunity. The work therapist
is responsible for sports. It is essential that the same norms and the
same sanctions apply to sports as to any other part of the therapeutic
program. Sports help to supply such important elements of the real-life
model in the therapeutic community as stress or competition. Patients
take sports seriously and react to it in many ways, often typical of their
problems, as is clearly shown in their diaries.
Diary entry:

I enjoyed the swimming and found that I won a lot of races sheerly
out of the enormous amount of energy I have for competition. But
I certainly could handle not winning, and winning didn't make me
want to judge myself or others at all. It was nice to feel comfortable
with it.

Another entry:

Was very angry over sports this morning. I have found Mattie uses
sports to get rid of her anger by using physical violence. I am covered
in bruises from her slugging me, kicking me and shoving me around.
I also noticed how uptight she made Bruce by doing the same things
to him. I spoke about it in "family" later on as several people were
angry about it also.

And what Mattie says about the same episode in her diary:

> I play sports hard, I do my best. I get a lot of anger and frustration out that way. But afterwards I feel guilty: *I'm too rough for a girl!* Oh, it's always been that way, and I shouldn't beat guys at sports, or at anything else for that matter. And I feel *guilty* about being good at things. Maybe it's all-important whom you match yourself with. I prefer to play against people who are a little better than I . . . but if someone asks me to play ping-pong, for example, and turns out not to be very good, and I can't *help* beating him (try though I may), I feel terrible.
>
> The roughness came out in soccer today. I throw myself around trying to get or block the ball. I'm competitive, but I don't want to hurt people. It came out once before that I feel better playing against people who are bigger and stronger than I so I won't hurt them. That's a sign of my explosiveness and energy, and after it's over I invariably draw back into myself. And that, come to think of it, is part of a pattern for me. Keep cool, don't lose control—and when I do I get frightened.

Another diary:

> I love playing soccer, any kind of sport for that matter. I always hated team sports before I came to Day House. I felt too self-conscious to enjoy it I guess. After I found out in my first week, that nobody laughed at me or got mad when I did something wrong, I started to enjoy it. When I was young, I used to fantasize I played on a real soccer team. Me as being the only woman on the team. I saw myself walking off the field at the end, covered with blood and preferably a few broken bones.

Another patient's diary:

> I didn't want to go swimming because I was still embarrassed about being seen in a swim-suit. Sheila and Kay encouraged me and I did feel much better. I discovered it wasn't all that bad and soon forgot all about it. It was fun and games in the water and I was really touched when Martin and Ron hugged me. I felt wanted and almost cried. I could cry now thinking about it.

Another Diary entry:

> I enjoyed bucket-ball this morning. I was always terrible at basketball at school, so it was very satisfying to be able to get some balls in the bucket. I felt I was actually a contributor to the team, rather than my usual ineffective nothingness. It gave me a *feeling of belonging.* Just writing that last sentence gave me a start—the extent to which belonging to a group is important to me hasn't occurred to me before. *I have always considered myself a loner by choice,* but *I see that* that *is not so*—I have spent much of my life wanting to belong and not succeeding. I don't feel secure enough in myself, I guess, to stand confidently alone.

AUTOBIOGRAPHIES

On Tuesday afternoons the group session in the Day House is reserved for autobiographies. If the group has more than fifteen participants, it may be divided in half, each half having the autobiography of one of its members. (In the last twenty minutes of the session, the group reunites and the final resumes are pooled for the others to read.) One of the group members presents his life history which he has prepared in writing. First he reads it and afterward works on it with the group and the therapist in charge. The other group members listen to it and then contribute by asking questions, volunteering in role playing, psychodrama, fantasy tasks, and various other verbal and nonverbal techniques. The action of the group moves flexibly between the past and the present, between reality and fantasy.

For example, Bob, after having read his life history, may play an episode which he experienced with his father many years ago as a little boy. After a while he may have an imagined argument with the same father telling him for the first time in his life what he really thinks and feels about him and about their mutual relationship and experiencing sadness, fear and anger. This second encounter never took place in reality in the past, and may never happen in the same form in the future. The father may already be dead. But open discussion with his father imagined in fantasy, involving cognitive as well as strong emotional components, may become an important step on the way to corrective experience in Bob's treatment.

How to write an autobiography

In the Day House, at Lobec, and in other places where a patient's autobiography constitutes a regular part of the therapeutic program, the new candidates for treatment have been informed in the admission, and in the patient group interviews, that they are required to write their life histories and present them before the group, usually in their second week. The new patients understand this as part of the therapeutic contract and accept it as such.

If the new patient wishes he may discuss various points of his life history beforehand with the therapist assigned to him. This rarely happens in the Day House because people usually start talking about their lives and also about their problems in writing their life histories in the families.

Better than any written or verbal instructions for new group members is their presence at a session where others who are more advanced read and act their autobiographies. At the Day House, the new patients have an opportunity to witness several autobiographies before they present their own. They listen to the reading, take part in the group actions and may even be asked to represent somebody's significant person in psychodrama.

The patients in preparing their autobiographies soon realize that the therapist and the patient group expect facts written in simple language; that the group is neither interested in general talk nor in interpretations following any theoretical model; that the history should start by describing the situation the patients were born to, the parents or other persons in their role, the social and economic background of the family, and continue in this way up to the present time. No periods in their lives should be left out regardless how insignificant they may seem. Authors of autobiographies, of course, usually go into more detail describing periods and facts they consider significant. They have to mention their previous medical and psychiatric treatment, but the group is not interested in discussing the treatment, other institutions, or other therapists. Instead, the group may ask them to be more explicit in describing their social and economic situations, their life styles, their relationships to other people in periods prior to and during the time they had symptoms and needed treatment.

For example, if Sheila said in her autobiography that two years ago she became depressed and started to see a psychiatrist, the group would first ask how she had felt when she was depressed, what she had been doing, and how she had lived at that time. Was she living alone or with somebody? Was she single or married? What was her partner or husband doing? What was their mutual relationship? Was she employed, supporting herself, or was she dependent on somebody else? Who? Did she have financial troubles? What plans did she have at that time? But the group would not ask for any details of her treatment either about methods or medications. If somebody tended to do this, other group members or the therapist would bring the discussion back to the points mentioned previously.

The patients also describe in their autobiographies their basic life philosophies, their life styles, and their plans for the future. They must mention what they expect from the treatment, whether they expect this to change their lives, and how.

Therapeutic goals

As in other therapeutic methods and modalities, therapeutic goals depend on various factors such as the general character of the setting, the selection and therapeutic potential of the patient group, the training and capability of the therapist in charge, the personality of the person giving the autobiography, and the special character of his problems. The therapeutic goals may vary widely.

In Day House as well as at Lobec, the therapeutic goal may encompass a corrective experience. In their autobiographies, patients may reexperience certain significant situations in their lives that they were not able to master before. Under more favorable circumstances, with the help and emotional support of the group and the therapist, the person may finally master them. The use of special techniques such as psychodrama, guided imagery, psychomime, and abreaction, increases the sensitivity of the person to react to various social cues more intensely than in the past.

For example, Susan, a twenty-five-year-old woman, was referred to Day House seeking help for neurotic depression. A college drop-out and unmarried mother of two, Susan had been going from one personal crisis to another in the past few years. She lived with several men in succession who were heavy drinkers, had been involved in criminal activities, took money from her, and finally left her when she became pregnant. After Susan read her autobiography in the group session, she wrote in her diary:

> Today for the first time I was able to tell my mother how I hate her. I really felt the anger of all those years with her and the hurt in me, talking to Dorothy (who played my mother). I always disagreed with Mom's moral standards and expectations she had for me, but never was able to tell her directly, and to stand up for myself. And that was

the reason I left home for good. Now after that work out I feel free. I don't think I care any more what she does or what she thinks of me. And I also realized, that although I was really unhappy when Mike went to prison and Tim left me when I was expecting my first child the idea flashed through my mind: "How will Mom suffer having her only daughter involved with criminals and expecting her child unmarried. What a punishment for her."

It became obvious that before her treatment, the idea of punishing her mother was the main incentive in leading Susan into her self-destructive way of life, although she was not aware of the significance of this idea and would probably deny it if told. Punishing her mother occupied a high place in Susan's hierarchy of values. The episode described in her diary was only one of many moments of corrective experience that Susan underwent while at Day House. Development of transference relationships toward the female therapist and other older women in the group also contributed in this respect. Only then did it become possible for the satisfaction that Susan had been drawing from her mother's punishment to drop in her scale of values. It made a place for other less ambivalent and more realistic values such as satisfaction from her own work, self-improvement, or a more satisfactory relationship with a partner.

The use of the autobiography as a technique may also be appropriate in settings with a less cohesive group and lower therapeutic potential—in outpatient groups, in mental health centers, in a therapist's private practice, or in inpatient units in traditional settings.

By preparing their life histories and thereby reviewing their own lives, the patients take the first step in identifying their characteristic patterns—the repeating features of their relationships to other people such as partners or family members. Or preparing their life histories may give them the first glimmering of insight into the processes that contribute to some of their life worries.

Sharing information about themselves with others usually brings the members closer and makes them feel more accepted. For many people, speaking before the group openly about their weaknesses, feelings of inadequacy, and guilt represents an intensive experience which is usually followed by relief of tension. Of course, revealing personal matters is a common occurrence at therapeutic sessions. But doing so in an autobiography as part of the regular program makes it easier for patients to start. The group supports and encourages them.

For example, Mark, a forty-four-year-old member of an outpatient group, said after the session:

> For the first time I could tell openly in public how weak, how afraid of the future I feel. All my life I had to pretend I was strong, capable and efficient and had a hard time to live as such. This I had to pretend to my mother who expected this from me and I continued pretending the same to my wife and children. I believed nobody would accept and love me if I showed any weakness.

Martin, a twenty-two-year-old member of an outpatient group changed significantly his previous withdrawn and rather unfriendly behavior, becoming more open, talkative and sociable. This was after he revealed in his autobiography that at the age of twelve he tried to kill his step-father whom he hated and by whom he felt mistreated. Martin constructed a primitive trap, which in fact did not work, and if it had would probably not have done the stepfather much harm. The stepfather never knew, but Martin always felt guilty about it and considered himself a potential killer.

Autobiographies of individual members increase the cohesiveness of the group and its therapeutic potential. Sharing information about life fosters mutual trust, and relationships based on transference easily develop.

The therapist's role

The therapist in charge of the session is responsible for the therapeutic plan. He or she suggests what episode to recall, play or imagine, taking into consideration suggestions made by the author of the autobiography as well as by other group members. At Lobec or Day House, the therapist has an opportunity to read the life history before the session and get a first impression of the problems involved. However, he never makes any rigid plan beforehand. Having the main strategic lines in mind, the therapist has to react quickly and flexibly to the situation as it develops during the whole session, beginning with the reading. Certain points may be accentuated by the reader and accompanied by strong emotions during the reading. Like a chess player, the therapist always has to plan the action several steps ahead, taking into consideration several possible options.

Techniques of the autobiography session

Many avenues stay open for action after the reading of the autobiography has been accomplished. We usually prefer to start with acting rather than with questions and discussions. Only rarely does brief discussion and clarification of certain points of the life history become necessary to avoid misunderstanding. Let us describe some of our preferred openings:

Selection of significant persons. The therapist asks the patient who has read his autobiography to choose people among the group members to represent significant persons in his life and bring them to the center of the room, or to the stage.

For example, Harry, a thirty-three-year-old man, brought his parents, his wife, and his six-year-old son. The therapist then asked Harry to have a short talk with each of them, starting by describing the person and then characterizing their mutual relationship. At the beginning he also had to speak for both himself and for the person playing his father, mother and other family members. To make it clear for whom he spoke, he had to change sides with the person he is representing.

Harry started talking to his mother (represented by Betsy, another group member).

"Mother, you are fifty-three, healthy-looking, rather on the heavy side. I feel close to you, we were both always very close. You are interested in me; you always find time for me if I need you. I trust you. Sometimes I am still your little boy."

Harry then changed places with Betsy and speaks for his mother. "Of course you are my boy. I love you. This is the way it should be. There is no other person like mother. Mother always likes her child. And what would you like to eat? Look what I prepared for you . . ."

Talking to his father, Harry said that he always felt distant to him. Answering for his father, he spoke about work, being busy all his life, and never having much time for his children.

Talking to his wife, he complained of distance between them and expressed a fear that they were growing more and more apart. Speaking for his wife, Harry did not tell us much about the character of their relationship. In his version, his wife was mostly interested in her job and night classes.

When he spoke to his son, Harry broke into tears. He told him that he was working hard in his therapy to get healthy and that he was looking forward to going hiking with him on Saturday and that he loved him. When speaking for his son, he expressed a lot of love and affection toward himself as a father.

Relate it in one sentence. The therapist may ask the person who is talking to and for his significant persons to characterize their relationship in one or two sentences, as in a slogan. For example, Harry characterized his mother as: "You are my boy. Mother always loves her children."

The happiest and the unhappiest episode. As a modification, the therapist may ask the person playing his autobiography to recall and play one episode when he felt the most happy in his life and another episode when he felt the most unhappy. He has to pick persons from the group and play a discussion or other psychodramatic scene with them. This opening may be useful in a short-term open group or workshop, in quickly defining the participant's important problems. If the patient has already worked hard on the various problems in his life and the group knows him pretty well, the therapist may start focusing the action on one specific point, such as the relationship to his father or mother.

How to find the right cue. Various cues usually emerge during the first few minutes of action. Let us go back to Harry. It seems that Harry is close to his mother and to his little son. Both are people of another generation than he. Harry did not mention any person close to him in his peer group.

The relationship with his wife was presented rather vaguely. Harry apparently does not know much about his wife's real thoughts and feelings, and yet he listed his unhappiness about the distance between them as his main problem. He was afraid the marriage would break up and his wife would leave him, although he did not seem to do much to prevent it. Harry said remarkably little about his job and his future plans. He did not seem to get much satisfaction from his work. At the same time he stressed his wife's interest in her job and in further training as contrary to a good marital relationship.

Considering all of these cues, the therapist found it useful to concentrate first on the marriage. Harry was supposed to talk for himself, and his wife was represented by the same group member as before. Other group members were encouraged to double for each of them. During the following dialogue, several group members, women as well as men, stepped in and talked for Harry's wife, expressing their own views on how they would feel in her place. Some group members doubled for Harry too. (female patients doubling—F 1, 2, 3, 4; male patients doubling—M 1, 2, 3)

Wife/F1, double: You are not a husband to me, you are a spoilt little boy, you expect me to compete with your mother. Which of us is more comforting and more devoted to you.

Wife/F 2, double: I am a person myself, I cannot be your devoted mother.

Wife/F3, double: You don't need me, you don't love me. You only love your son.

Wife/F4, double: What's wrong with me working? You dislike it, you complain that I am happier and more efficient in my work than you are. Why don't you do something about your job and training? Anyway, you know pretty well that I have to work, you are not able to support the family alone.

Another female patient, Barbara, speaking as Harry's wife, discussed practical, domestic matters. Criticizing Harry, she said that he was not fair and expected her to do much more by way of household chores and taking care of their child than he did. Harry seemed surprised and not properly informed about various simple household chores.

Harry/M1: I often think that I would rather be alone with my son than to live in all this tension with you. What do you want from me? Why are you not satisfied with me as I am? Why do you always want to improve me? (*Harry agreed with this impersonation.*)

Such an episode on a verbal level may be allowed to go on for several minutes, but should not go on for too long. The therapist must also be cautious not to allow the dialogue to slip into discussion of general matters such as the position of men and women in general, or who is right and who is wrong. Role playing, primarily, should broaden the person's points of view and give them an opportunity to consider various differing opinions, but it should not foster any definite solutions. There are several ways to stop the talking and switch to activity.

Boffer fight. At the end of the dialogue the therapist suggested that Harry have a boffer fight with his wife. Betsy volunteered to represent his wife. After hesitating for a while, Harry became more and more involved, especially when Betsy provoked him by shouting, "Come on, show how strong you are, you are weak, you are a spoilt little bastard." Harry fought back strongly, shouting "Shut up" and getting more and more angry.

The therapist may suggest playing out episodes to help the patient realize the significance of the various relationships in his life.

I am alone. Harry was asked to imagine that his wife had left him for good, taking their son with her. Harry was alone. He delivered a monologue about how he felt and what was going through his head. Harry was quiet for a while, then started complaining, repeating several times, "How could you do this to me?" At the end he was close to tears.

Harry might have thought that he would be happy living with his son. He might have been, but would it have been the right solution for both of them?

The son's monologue after ten years. Harry and the whole group were asked to imagine that Harry's wife had left him and that he has been living with his son, Steve, for ten years. The boy would be about sixteen now. He was to sit alone and think about himself and his father. Harry was not present in the episode, but listened to it with the group. Members of the group volunteered to speak for Harry's son, Steve. Various differing versions of the monologue were played by several group members who mostly acted out their own experience with their parents. Some stressed the love and attention they received from their fathers, others were rather ambivalent. "I know Dad loves me, he would do anything for me, but he also expects much in return. I have my own life to live. Why the hell didn't he remarry?"

Jeff, a 21-year-old man, was most dramatic and rebellious. He talked about leaving home and getting out of its "suffocating atmosphere."

Recall times you felt close to your father. The therapist focused attention on Harry's relationship to his father, previously presented as a rather distant dialogue. The therapist asked Harry whether he ever felt closer to his father than at present. Harry recalled an episode from the time he was about six years old. His father made a kite for him and both father and son hiked to a nearby hill to try it out. It was a sunny day and Harry felt happy. The episode was played with two other group members, one representing the father and the other representing the kite. (Animals and objects are also represented in psychodrama.)

Problems and pitfalls

Some people claim they cannot present their life history because there is a secret in their life they cannot reveal to anyone. This is most likely to happen in settings where the autobiography has been used sporadically and does not constitute a part of the therapeutic program. It is necessary to clarify the matter quickly, either in individual interviews or in group by asking the person to describe the nature of the secret. It is something that once revealed may harm the person's reputation, or that of others? Is it information connected with the character of his work and profession that is supposed to be kept secret? Most likely the person considers certain facts and episodes unique and damaging which in fact are quite common—for example, leaving a friend or partner in need, having abandoned a child, homosexual episodes, drug abuse, juvenile delinquency, or time in prison. After the person realizes that other group members have had similar experiences, his secret no longer presents a problem in preparing his life history.

People claiming to have professional secrets may be assured that nobody is interested in these secrets. But they are expected to explain and talk about how having kept secrets affected them and their relationships with others. Did they feel happy about having access to classified information? Did it help to maintain their self-esteem, did they feel it gave them power over others? Did they enjoy it? Had they felt, at the same time, alienated from their peers? Do they think that the fact that they were not allowed to talk freely about the details of their work with their spouses influenced their marriage? How?

Typical forms of resistance in autobiography

Insistence on having a secret may partly be a symptom of resistance toward the treatment. If this is not properly handled early enough, the patient may finally use it as an excuse and walk out of treatment. The autobiography can contain more subtle forms of resistance:

A very short autobiography contains facts and episodes enumerated without connecting them to the person's problems. A long history may dwell on irrelevant matters such as the climate which have no proper connection to his own person.

Sometimes the author omits certain periods and episodes of his life under the pretext that they were unimportant.

Discussing general matters is a common form of resistance in psychotherapy and may be unusually strong in discussing and acting the life history. The therapist has to be alert and bring this to the group's attention.

This is not a psychiatric case history

The therapist should keep in mind that the autobiography is not a case history. He does not discuss here diagnoses, prognoses, or methods of treatment, and must resist the temptation to answer questions addressed by patients concerning these matters. Also he must not give any interpretations nor offer any ready-made solutions. Of course, this is valid for all the kinds of psychotherapy described in this book. We emphasize it here because the danger that the less experienced therapist may fail in this aspect of handling the autobiography is greater than elsewhere.

Historical note

When we introduced the autobiography as a regular part of the program at Lobec, a ritual soon developed. The day of the autobiography became a day when the person was given the special attention of the whole group—as on a birthday. At the end of the session, after reading and acting the life history, the patient received little presents from the others. This spontaneous development was introduced initially by one of the patient committees.

FAMILY NIGHT: SIGNIFICANT PERSONS' NIGHT

Family Night is the name commonly used for Tuesday night group sessions, although other significant persons of the patient may be invited, such as friends, homosexual partners, or members of a small commune to which the patient may belong. It is up to the patients, as part of their commitment, to have their significant persons attend. The committee checks beforehand to see how many patients expect their significant persons so that each of them may have their turn during the session.

The chairperson presides over the session. After the preliminary introduction of all group members, therapists, and guests and the definition of the significant persons' relationships to the patients, the group usually divides into two sections. Each section works separately with one therapist. They rejoin at the end of the evening for a brief report from each section.

Each patient and his significant persons have their turn for about fifteen to twenty minutes. It is only because of the special methods used in this group that considerable therapeutic results can be achieved in such a short time. Let us present an example.

The overgrown nestling

Mike, a twenty-six-year-old, single, male patient at the Day House, invited his parents whom he had been living with all his life. In the last two years, he had spent most of his time at home. He had not worked and had isolated himself from people other than his parents. He never had a steady girlfriend. Mike suffered from depression and various psychosomatic symptoms. On Family Night, when Mike's turn came, the therapist asked, "Is there anything you wanted to tell your parents?"

Mike: Ahhh——
Dr. K: Or perhaps your parents would like to say something to you.
Mike: Well, I'd like to know what they think of the situation of me at home right now.
Mother: I think it's rather pleasant, he's found a new interest.
Dr. K: Since when?
Mother: Since he's been here. It seems to have improved his disposition a lot. I think he's much nicer.
Dr. K: How was it before? What did you miss before?
Mother: Well, he's a son, so it's always pleasant to have him around, but sometimes he has a little short fuse and didn't talk as much as I'd like him to. A little more conversation. Everybody has their own ways.
Dr. K: And father?
Father: It seems to be alright. I guess, it's an improvement since he started here. It helps a little bit, maybe the nerves cleared up a little bit. Seems to be alright.
Dr. K: You had a question?
Mike: Yeah, I wonder what you think of the situation of me living at home?
Father: It's alright, no complaints.
Mike: Sometimes you get mad and yell about it.
Father: The only time I get mad is when you do something wrong, that's all, which anybody would get mad if you do something wrong when you work all day——
Male 3: Like what?
Father: Well, when you work all day, I mean my nerves are on edge too, you know when you come home and there's something doesn't agree with you so you yell a little louder and they don't like it you know. Well every person is different you know, and you can't pat them on the back when they do something wrong.
Dr. K: Mike, how would it be if you would be in the place of your father? What would you be dissatisfied about with Mike? This is Mike now. (*Mike and his father exchange seats.*)

The following dialogue demonstrates the potential of a combination of patients and family (the technique of *amplified family*) in comparison with sessions of one family only. We maintain that in the fifteen minutes left at our disposal for this family, we achieved more than we could have in many sessions with Mike's family only. We intended (1) to find out why the parents seem so tolerant towards Mike when he is not doing anything and is being supported by them and (2) to determine whether their inhibitions stop them from expressing their dissatisfaction with Mike or whether they want to keep him at home forever like a little boy.

We knew that Mike accepted the opinion of the group that he should become independent, but he was hesitant. We wanted the parents to know clearly what the group thought.

First the therapist suggested that Mike and his father exchange their roles. They also exchanged their seats. Mike was now in the role of his father and his father in his role. (Role players and doubles will follow the name of the role represented.)

Father/Mike: Why don't you get out and get a job? Why do you waste all your time?

(The therapist picked up that a female patient is eager to double for the father's role.)

Father/Female 1: I've worked to support you all these years, now it's your turn to do something. Why don't you get a job?

Dr. K: Change places again; now Mike, you answer the father's question. (*Both change seats.*)

Mike: Ah (*pause*) I just don't feel up to getting a job right now, or I haven't felt up to it. And I've been unhappy at other jobs that I've had in the past, disappointed with the people that run it and the way they treat the workers.

Father: Hmmm——

Father/Female 1: How are you going to be happy and try and work out your problems if you don't try and get some work; if you don't try and go out and do something?

Dr. K: (*To father*) Do you agree with that question?

Father: Yes, yes.

Dr. K: She talks for you, so whenever you don't agree, say "I don't agree".

Father: Okay.

Mike: It's hard for me, I'm a little bit on the nervous side. I've done it before at work and sometimes I don't think it's going to be any different.

Father: Hmmm——

Father/Female 1: You know, it's hard for a father to see his son just sitting around. A father wants to be proud of his son. I brought you up and now I'd like to see you go out and try and do something, for yourself.

Mike: Well, it may have been easier if you'd showed more interest in my studies when I was younger.

Father: Hmmm——

Father/Female 1: Oh, I was always working hard, you know, providing for you. You did alright in school. I didn't have to——

Mother: What do you mean by more interest in the studies?

Mike: Well——

Mother: I always looked at all your work, asked if I could help.

Mike: Well, I wasn't doing so hot at school and you never really said anything about it.

Mother: I tried to encourage you. I spoke to the teacher; asked them what was the trouble. You wanted to be left alone.

Mike: Hmmm——

Mike/Female 2: I'm referring to Dad. He always started yelling at me the minute he came home and I felt he never gave any of us a chance. He was always very hard on us and very unfair.

Father: Well, I better speak up a little too. This didn't happen every day, I mean it's certain days that things didn't go right. So I spoke up and somebody whose head of the family has to speak up, to straighten things out, but I didn't go out and kill him or shoot him or anything, just bawled him out for what he did wrong. What else can you do? You gotta explain the good from the bad. You can't let somebody go ahead, and he's doing something wrong and just pat him on the back. So I guess maybe my nerves are bad too. After working all day you're on edge. I holler maybe a little too loud, but that, you can understand it too, I've been working all day and I'm on edge too.

The tactic worked. The father, encouraged by patients doubling for him as well as for Mike, spoke up.

Mike: Hmmm——

Mike/Female 2: Well, I'm a child and I have certain needs that were never fulfilled either. You never cared about me, all you did was come home and yelled.

Father: No, that isn't true. That isn't true, I——

Dr. K: (*To Mike*) Would you repeat it, do you agree?

Mike: Yeah.

Dr. K: So let's say it in your own words?

Mike: I was very unhappy being yelled at.

Mother: I know, but did you really think that your father—he always
  had to let loose, that's nothing, that's just a trait, a characteristic.
Mike: It's not enough.
Mother: Well, it is a fact that when he was growing up he never opened
  his mouth. They were told what to do, when to do it, and how to do
  it. So he found his voice and he screeched. Good preventative, you
  got to get it off your chest, you can't let it eat inside that has nothing
  to do with it.
Mike: Do you blame us for the troubles you had at work?
Father: No, no. Work had nothing to do with it. It's that when you're
  working you get tired and you get on edge a little bit, you're restless.
  When you do something that is not right it bothers me because I'm
  on edge too from working all day. So I gotta let you know about it.
  I can't just——
Mike: But you used to yell for hours without stopping.
Father: I know.

Here Mike expressed dissatisfaction and anger with his father. The
therapist did not encourage Mike to go too far with his anger at this
point. Although reawakening old conflicts with his father and expressing anger toward him was an important step in Mike's treatment, all of
this had previously happened in the patient group in Mike's abreaction.
Here at Family Night, in the presence of real parents, it was the therapist's main goal to move the parents to action, promote Mike's independence, even do a little pushing in that direction, so that the stress
was on the future, not on the past. Here the woman patient, Female 1,
helped by doubling for the father.

Father/Female 1: Mike, what do you want from me now, you can't change
  the past? You've grown up now and we can't change what happened
  then.
Mike: Well (*pause*) I don't know if I expect anything from you now.
Father: Well, I think you expect things from us.
Mike: So why didn't you help me?
Father: Well I got a job through a friend but I can't go to work with you
  and help you at work.
Father/Male 1: You got to improve yourself when you go to work. Something happens there, you gotta take the good and the bad, I mean
  not everybody gets——
Mike: You can't fight the whole company. The head foreman of the
  place was always on my back——

Father/Male 1: You just gotta show them you're better than the other man, by working but——

Mike: No one worked harder than me for the first six months there, and the guy was on my back every day——

Mother: So you tell him to take off and get another job.

Mike: I went to the union about a problem and the union didn't do anything about it, so what can I do?

Father: You gotta stick it out, because I worked all my life——

Mike: You don't have to stick it out.

Father: Well, when you gotta eat, you gotta work, and nobody's going to throw——

Mike: If you're in a rut why are you going to work your whole life? Why not get a better job, or get a trade or something?

Father: Yes, if you're well educated you would get a better job, you gotta go according though. I mean when you don't go to school, haven't a high school education well you gotta take what comes. And if you went to university or something like that, I would have helped you to go through, but you didn't care too much. I didn't go through school.

Mother/Female 2: Are you going to go to school now?

Mike: Yeah, I'd like to.

Mother: I know you started before and you quit. Are you going to stick to it this time?

Mike: Well I don't know, I'm not——

Mother: I know, you've told me that you weren't going to go and make me proud of you, that you want to be accepted for yourself. Well now, how about sticking to something. I mean that.

Mike: Yeah sure, it's not easy for me to sit in the classroom.

Mother: It wasn't easy for your father to stick this job.

Mother/Female 3: Sure Mike, you don't have to stick anything out because you can always live at home. I mean, you're my son. We can't throw you out, but you know, the time has come when you gotta do things for yourself.

Mother: It isn't that we want it for ourselves. I want you to be able to stand on your own two feet because you're capable. You've got the brain for it. You just don't want to. (*Mother takes the cue.*)

This episode shows how a therapist structures the whole action of the session by suggesting psychodramatic episodes to play and encouraging the patients to double for the persons involved, especially for the significant person. The therapist always watches the facial expressions of

the participants, being in a kind of nonverbal contact with the whole
group, like the conductor of an orchestra. With a little gesture, the
therapist then may ask patients to double, picking those whom he expects to act in a certain way. The therapist knows the patients and often
has previously witnessed, in the patient group, how they reacted to a
particular patient who is having his turn on Family Night. Often the
guests are also encouraged to contribute to the discussion. For example,
the therapist saw a smile on the face of one of the guests, the husband
of a patient, and asked him what he thought about Mike and the whole
family.

Guest (husband of a patient): I had a very overpowering father too, but
    Mike has, definitely as I can see, he has got to, he had the opportunity
    where I think I did not, to talk to his father. His father has shown
    openly that he won't pounce on him. If Mike wants to talk to him
    openly. Perhaps they can have a discussion and the mother can be
    present and offer suggestions.
    Certainly the mother is not 100 percent biased with the father. She's
    impartial. Perhaps if that is cleared then Mike can better feel more
    confidence in standing on his own two feet. As that member who
    spoke for Mike's father said, you've just got to get out and that's the
    whole beef. Don't be afraid of being kicked out. You're twenty-seven
    years old and you say, well it's a little too late. My friend, my father
    started life again in this country when he was fifty-five! And he started
    all over, from nothing.

The therapist must take the same precautions as always when cooperating with significant persons—assessing the reward-cost balance they
draw from the therapeutic cooperation and quickly intervening when
it seems the costs are too great, as when significant persons are too
harshly criticized. At the session the therapist may pick another group
member whom he considers more tolerant to comment upon the situation. Or he may stress some positive features of a significant person,
such as the fact that they came to Family Night and seem interested in
their partners or relatives.

Significant persons may get positive rewards out of the prospect that
the patient will be a healthy, more interesting person. In Mike's case,
although his parents were ambivalent toward his treatment at the beginning and wanted to have Mike at home, they eventually preferred
having a healthy son they could be proud of, instead of a little boy.

Sometimes the therapist and the group have to protect significant persons against too much criticism and aggression from the patient. Some patients, usually in the first period of their treatment, become unrealistically self-confident, feeling the emotional support of the group and may act in a way they would later regret.

THE PLAY

Once a week on Friday afternoons, the patients perform their own play. Lasting about one and a half hours, the play consists of several sketches written by volunteers from each family. The authors prepare a script which briefly describes the episodes in the play and the roles characterized. The actors then improvise, modifying the roles and adding various details to the scenes.

The play reacts in a joyful and often sarcastic manner to the daily life at the Day House and to the program. It alludes to the hardship of sticking to the norms and mocks the ways in which people avoid therapy, ridicules cliches, and often focuses on specific events of the week.

People usually volunteer for acting, although the family may encourage some members to play mostly in roles unusual to them and contrary to their nature. Acting in the play may become an important experience for a patient, as is indicated in the diaries:

Acted a part in our "family's" play today that is contrary to my character [an authoritarian and aggressive father]. Initially, I was reluctant to accept the role, due to fear of failing and appearing foolish. The "family", however, insisted I accept a part that would be difficult. I did so, and was relatively successful, which gave me a feeling of satisfaction to overcome such fear.

Another patient writes in her diary:

I took part in the play in front of a group which I found very hard to do. I felt I made an absolute fool of myself, but on thinking about it, at least I was able to do it. One small victory!

Acting in the play may stimulate a person to recognize some of his own maladaptive attitudes. This is illustrated in the following diary entry:

In the plays today I played an unloving father who demanded perfection from his children. I really got into the role and was a real bastard. Afterwards I felt frightened because I do think I am insensitive sometimes and can see myself acting that way towards certain people who make me angry. It taught me that I have to be more tolerant of people, especially when I think they are slow. Suzanne also pointed this out to me today, so I know that I act this way sometimes.

A male patient writes in his diary about his experience of being the author of the play as well as acting in it:

I was really pleased that the plays I wrote went so well and especially that Fran [the therapist] recognized the moral of the third "family" play. I was asked how I felt about playing a woman's part. I enjoyed it. I noticed while acting that I didn't have any visual sense of the audience. I could hear the lines and the laughter but don't remember seeing the other people. I hid within my part.

A patient volunteers to play a rather maladapted character only to realize that this is the role he plays in real life.

In plays I took the role of a sullen little kid. I was so busy being sullen that I missed a lot of the action across the "room". That's happened in real life.

Often the therapists join the play also, and enjoy it. Sometimes they are asked to play certain roles. The suggestion of a role may be influenced by an immediate stage of group resistance as when the therapist once played the role of a "dumb blonde, chewing gum and interrupting people with inappropriate comments." In the play, transference relationships become apparent, as in an episode described in the history of David (see chapter 9).

WEDNESDAY AFTERNOON GROUP

This is the meeting of the whole community led by the clinical supervisor. The aftercare patients (those who come once a week for three consecutive weeks) are also present for one-half hour.
Specific tasks This group session has the following specific tasks: The old patients meet with the new ones. The committee's report, posted the preceding day, is discussed, evaluating each member of the group. (Note 31). Awards are presented. The committee also focuses the attention of the group on those who are not snowing enough progress. The clinical

supervisor helps the staff to cope with the most difficult problems in the group.

The session usually begins with the aftercare patients reporting their progress during the last week and the new patients asking them questions. After a short discussion, the aftercare patients leave, and continue separately in their own group with another therapist.

The group then continues with a discussion of the committee's report and the week's scores of positive and negative points. Some group members are disappointed in their scores and oppose them; others may be surprised that they are evaluated so high. The committee then presents the positive and negative awards. After the awards have been presented, the group spends some time in evaluating the work of the committee.

In the second part of the session, the attention of the group is focused on individual members or families who represent special problems, usually related to resistance toward treatment. The whole group deals with them, using psychodrama, psychomime, or abreactive techniques.

The subtle techniques of leading this type of group go far beyond the limits of this book.

THE FEELING GROUP

Friday afternoon after the play, the staff meet with the clinical supervisor in a session much different from their regular meetings. It usually begins with music, expressive dancing, pantomime, or psychomimic activities; new nonverbal and action techniques may also be tried out. In this group, the staff have the opportunity to deal with various dissatisfactions, mutual tensions, or special individual problems. The group is not always led by the clinical supervisor; the other staff members also have an opportunity to try out new group techniques. The same techniques used in the patients' psychotherapy are used in this group and help the staff to get relief from the tensions and problems accumulated through the week and to catch up on their own mental hygiene. Needless to say, this demands high cohesion, balance, and mutual trust in the team.

BREAKING IN AND OUT

This is a ceremony that developed rather spontaneously at the Day House. Friday afternoons after the play, the group welcomes new members who have just completed their first week, and bids farewell to those who have finished their treatment at Day House. No therapist is present since the staff are simultaneously involved in their feeling group.

At first, new members have to break in to the group. Members of the group form a closed circle, holding hands. One after the other, the new members have to penetrate the circle. After they have succeeded, they join the group in dancing.

The other part of the ceremony is the trust jump. Each new member jumps from the stage into the out-stretched hands of all the group members.

The patients who are leaving present a written statement on What the Day House gave to me. In the statement, they summarize their experiences and the changes in their lives which they have undergone during their treatment. Afterwards, they go to each of the group members to say their good-byes. When all this is completed, the old patients get a trust lift, being lifted from the floor on the out-stretched hands of the whole group. The group then sings a song that has been adopted as the Day House song: "So long, it has been good to be with you," usually adding new stanzas such as "it has been good to cry with you," "fight with you," "dance with you," "play with you," etc.

Parting with old group members is usually associated with deep emotions and tears. Sometimes, when several popular members leave, the group goes through a period of sadness and depression, like mourning. In this regard, parting with old members represents an element in the Day House which models real life.

Chapter 9

DAVID: HISTORY OF A PATIENT TREATED IN DAY HOUSE

Our presentation of this case may seem unusual; some may wonder why we stress details from the patient's daily life that seem trivial or omit more detailed information about the patient's life before treatment.

In presenting this case, we want to trace and describe what really happens to a patient in the therapeutic community: what the patients talk about; what they really do if they develop a transference relationship toward other patients and the therapists; what the patients think; what they dream; how other patients react to them when their actions are biased by rigid, unrealistic father schema or mother schema; what happens if patients reexperience old conflicts from their past; what does it mean practically if a patient goes through a corrective experience.

We present here, first, a short summary from the patient's history, compiled and written at his admission into the Day House. In the main part of our presentation we have used the following sources of information:

Recordings of group sessions
Therapist's notes, written approximately every day, describing the patient's verbal as well as nonverbal behavior (the notes were written by different therapists, but always by the one in charge of the relevant group session or program).

The patient's diary

We have added our interpretations separately in brackets.

ADMISSION

From the therapist's notes. David, a twenty-three-year-old single man, was referred to the Day House by one of the district mental health centers. David complained of being tense and anxious with people, having little motivation to do anything, often being depressed, and always questioning why he did things. He also had a feeling of being inferior to others, was easily afraid of people, unspontaneous, had difficulties in developing closer relationships, experienced difficulty in sex, and suffered from insomnia.

From David's comments during the admission interviews

Father: Was nice to me when I was young. This changed when I got older at about ten to thirteen years of age. I had fear of him, fear he would spank me. It was when my father was fired or quit his job, I remember I avoided him. He was a creative man, he made beautiful kites. He did a lot of sailing. At present our relationship is terrible. I am unhappy about it.

Mother: I was closer to her than to my father, but I never fully agreed with her. She pushed me into activities such as reading, studying music. She got me into sports. I resented it. I felt I had to perform to please her and I hated it. She wanted me to be compassionate and understanding and I am not. I am hung up on myself.

I considered my parent's relationship to be good, but my mother told me that the marriage was a failure. I had mixed feelings towards my mother all my life.

Sister: Three years older. She was adopted. We fought a lot. She always bothered me in the past. Recently, I have started to understand her better.

Friends, schoolmates: I had many, but we moved often because of father's job and I always lost my friends and had to start from the beginning. Sometimes this was difficult.

Girls: I was always shy with girls.

Teachers: I cannot name a teacher I really liked. They were mostly unpleasant and bossy. I hated most of them, especially those in high school.

The therapist's summary at admission. David is a depressed, young auto-mechanic who has had no psychiatric treatment. He had sought a solution for his depression and anxiety through drugs, transcendental meditation and Eastern religion—all with no change. His depression has been chronic but is more severe at present since the failure of a relationship with a woman.

David felt rejected by his father in adolescence as he felt close to him as a child. He has little explanation except that his father had some employment difficulties when David was an adolescent. David's relationship to his mother seems quite stormy. She pushed him into many activities and seemed to have high goals which David rebelled against. He has good male friendships but has always been shy around girls. He feels unable to love. There have been a few relationships, none long term. He seems to choose women like himself, who fear intimacy.

In therapy, David can improve his self concept and his ambivalence toward women. He is a good candidate if he can make the commitment to the program.

Main Symptoms

Situation at Admission	Situation at Discharge
1. Tense and anxious with people, nothing feels enjoyable.	1. Much more relaxed with people and able to express what is on his mind to them.
2. Short attention span, questioning why I do things.	2. No more a problem. Good concentration.
3. Inferiority feelings, feels others are better.	3. More self-confident. Sees he has good qualities and is likeable.
4. Afraid with people, not spontaneous. Rationalizes.	4. Still present, but very mild.
5. Little motivation, little enjoyment, depressed. Life has no meaning.	5. No more a problem.
6. Insomnia.	6. No more a problem.

Working Situation

1. Unemployed.	1. Same. Looking for job. Sounds very optimistic.
2. Auto mechanic satisfied with his trade.	2. Same. Hard and conscientious worker (in the work program)

Sex Relationships

1. Shy amongst girls his age.
2. Avoids women he is attracted to.

3. No present relationship.

4. Sexual inhibitions.

1. Much more relaxed.
2. Able to express his feelings of affection and attraction to women he liked in the group.
3. Found a girlfriend. He is very happy but might need to face their relationship more realistically. Now he is too protective of new girlfriend.
4. Feels much better about sex. No more premature ejaculations.

Social Functioning

1. Exercise, enjoys sports, competitive.
2. Some close friends.
3. Shares suite with two other male friends.
4. Drugs since Grade 11. Some LSD, grass, chemicals.
5. Alcohol, occasionally to loosen up.

1. Same.

2. Circle of friends is expanding.
3. Same.

4. Not while in treatment. Doesn't want them any longer.
5. Not while in treatment.

TREATMENT

David received six weeks of treatment in the Day House, plus three weeks of follow-up care as an outpatient.

First day of stay
Therapist's note. David was punctual. He took part in the group but didn't talk much. Later when assigned to the car wash he worked well, silently. In sports very active. Not much talking with other people.

Fourth day of stay
Diary. Today in the family meeting, Ben told me to look people in the eyes, that I have a habit of looking away. It's something I've done all

my life. For the past year I tried to always look people in the eye, but I discovered in doing so I was trying to lay a trap on people to prove that I was better than them; it was a staring contest. I felt if they looked away first that I was better than them. So I stopped doing it. But in family I started looking people in the eyes again, without feeling it was a contest. I felt really good to have talked about it.

Fifth day of stay

Therapist's Summary from the small group session (the family). Cynthia and Delia [two young women patients] revealed that they felt irritated by David. They considered him aggressive in discussion as well as having a tendency to put them down. Cynthia compared David to her husband that she had separated from recently. The therapist asked both women to specify their remarks, presenting an episode or argument they had had with David recently. Cynthia suggested that they repay what had happened during the last work program. David agreed. The following episode was played.

David and Cynthia were working near to each other fixing kitchen shelves. Cynthia's hammer broke so she started to use David's. After a while David became annoyed and snapped at her "Stop it, the hammer is not of much use to you anyway." He apologized afterwards as he saw that Cynthia was embarrassed and almost in tears, but the tension between them remained. In the subsequent discussion Cynthia explained that she had felt the same thing in the past with her husband who used to criticize her and make derogatory remarks about her technical skills. David seemed angry but remained quiet and did not talk very much in the discussion. (He got more angry in subsequent fighting with Cynthia using boffers.) The therapist then asked David to have a monologue about what had just happened. David started slowly, saying that he often felt irritated by Cynthia, but did not know why. Later he said: "She is one of the women I feel uneasy with. They look so self-confident, active, easy talker, always interfering. They easily impress people. I often cannot find words, I feel inhibited in their presence, I feel inferior."[*Authors' note*: In a situation that is a model of real life—working with a group of people—David exhibits some of his maladaptive patterns in relation to women as peers and probably as sex objects.]

Therapist's note. David doubled spontaneously for Dorothy as she was playing a discussion with her father. He said to the father (played by Ben) that he was weak and did not care about him enough.

Diary. Cynthia and I shouted at each other in family. I felt afraid. Maybe it was because I was expressing a lot of anger and frustration and I am not used to expressing my feelings and I've always avoided other people who do. I know we didn't straighten out our conflict. I think she feels hostile and hurt. I feel uncertain about how to get straight with her. [*Author's note*: David continues working on his relationship toward women of his peer group. It seems that David's problems with women are related to his sister schema.]

After I came home I learned that Ken my employer is planning to buy a new truck on Monday. He owes me about $250.00. I thought of asking him why the hell he can't pay me even some of my money. But I did not call him.

At night I dreamed about it, that I demanded the money. He got out some paper and a pencil and started explaining his business plans to me and talked me out of the money. Then the scene shifted to P. in Saskatchewan where I was born and raised for seven years. In the dream I was at a ski hill with a friend Mike and his father standing in line for the tow. Mike told me father had bought two vans. Then my father roared by in a van. There was something unusual on that van. More like an armored car. My father smiled briefly at me but kept going. That's all I remember. In the past I did a lot of skiing with all my family (mother, father, sister) when I was young. [*Author's note*: David works toward more assertiveness with male authorities. First he tries it in a dream.]

Sixth day of stay

Diary. I went shopping downtown with Ted and Val (the people I share an apartment with). When we got home for supper I was feeling very uptight about how to tell Ted and Val how dissatisfied I was about how little of clean-up they are doing. Finally, I said nothing and decided to look for a place of my own. [*Author's note*: David realizes that he is still not able to speak up.]

Night dream. I am with a friend, maybe Ted and Val, we are just walking around, we see this girl a few times. She is always jogging. She has huge breasts and long brown hair. It is summertime in the country. We are strangers. She is not. She is from here. I forget what it is but I have asked her something, to do something with us, or go somewhere with us, but she says she's got to go to a music lesson. Then something changed in the scene, and I was at her place where she invited me for dinner. I don't remember whether Ted or Val is here. I am sitting at a big table with other people on each side. She is sitting on the same side. Her mother is across from me, I get about four plain fried eggs on my plate. Then the girl's mother makes one especially for me. I put it on my plate and notice it's twice as big as the others. Then I flip it over and notice it looks like the scrambled eggs Marion used to make me full of chopped chives and onions. Marion is a girl I lived with for five months last year. We are not on good terms these days. I haven't seen her in almost three months. I tried to work it out with her, but she didn't understand. I think she is very hurt. [*Author's note*: Important elements in the dream: A girl, feminine looking—she takes David into a family where *she* is *at home*, he is a stranger (David's sister was three years old when he was born). But the girl's mother serves *special food* to David. The association of Miriam (girlfriend) shows that there may be a connection between David's sister schema and his attitude toward women peers and sexual partners.]

Diary. Bette phoned after supper which made me really happy to talk to her. I met her about two months ago. We went out a couple of times, slept together twice, but did not have intercourse. She decided she didn't want to continue the relationship, that I had some problems to work out. She gave me a push I needed to get me to seek professional help. We've gone out together once since our split and talked over the phone a few times. I like her a lot. I intend to ask her to Day House.

Seventh day of stay

From the therapist's opinion of David during the group. Said nothing throughout session until end, though was attentively involved and watching Dorothy's abreaction. At the end of the session he said: "I hope I can work out my feelings like Dorothy did today."

Diary. In our family Dorothy had a really good workout. I felt it could easily have been me who was feeling all that pain and fear, anger and frustration, confusion. I know it's in me I have to get it out as well. So far I've felt that I don't want to butt into other peoples' valuable time. [*Authors' note*: Dorothy expressed anger towards her father in her abreaction. David identifies with her.]

Therapist's comment to the diary. Just go ahead, that's the reason you're here.

Diary. I got a letter from my parents today in which my father spoke directly and honestly to me for the first time in a long time. Both my parents have offered to do anything I want them to even as far as coming here to talk with "my psychiatrist." I felt my emotions welling up inside me reading their letter. I would like to invite Dad to Tuesday night. [*Authors' note*: David did not mention here that he had written a letter to his parents previously. He spoke about that letter the following day in the family meeting.]

Eighth day of stay

Therapist's report on the family session. David kept mostly quiet. Toward the end he expressed some frustration towards Cynthia for going around in circles without saying what she wanted. He said he wanted time but was always shutting up because he felt others needed it more and they were wasting it by going around in circles. Was told to stop arguing about it and use the little time left to say briefly what he wanted to say.

Diary. I feel a lot of warmth towards my mom and dad. Yesterday I received a letter from them and I felt and still feel like crying. I had written previously to them saying I wouldn't write them any more and I made them feel guilty for not giving me enough. Now my father tells me he is willing to come out here, but I am afraid to hurt him because I have an awful lot of anger towards him. I would like to have a work-out first.

Ninth day of stay

Diary. This afternoon [Saturday] Val who lives with me cut my hair. It feels really good. It is a lot shorter now, short enough so that it doesn't fall in my eyes. Before it was down past my shoulders and would almost totally cover my face if I let it hang down naturally. I had to brush it out of my eyes a lot, especially in sports. But I put up with it because I liked it. I had to wash it almost every day and it took about three hours to dry.

I first started growing my hair long when I was seventeen. I had wanted to before that, but my father refused to let me and I was afraid of him. At 17 though, he gave in. I guess he knew he was losing control of me and I began to rebel. Looking at myself in the mirror I keep imagining how people at Day House will react to my haircut. I smile inside when I think of all the attention they'll give me. And recently, I told Mike I felt better than him because he has short hair.

Eleventh day of stay

Diary. Today almost everyone complimented me on my hair cut. It was very flattering. I like a lot of attention like that. I feel I am liked. All the compliments made me feel warm inside. It was nice to brighten up the beginning of the day and the week.

Twelfth day of stay

Abbreviated record from the big group session where David read his autobiography. After David read his autobiography the therapist asked him to pick members of the group representing his parents, sister, and other significant persons in his life and arrange them on the stage. David placed himself between his father and mother and put his sister Bev far aside. Asked why he made it that way he said "I think she is not part of any relation to mother and father. She was rather blocking, interfering."

Therapist: Tell her directly.

David: You do not mean anything to me in my relationship to mom and dad.

Therapist: Tell her directly what you do feel about her.

David: I do not love you, but I do not dislike you.

Sister/Female 1: I am your sister, you should love me.

David: You are not a real sister, you are adopted.

Therapist: Talk to your sister. What is she like, what do you think of her?

David: (*Talking to sister*) You are an intelligent girl, you are tall, brown hair, blue eyes, rather strong. You are always doing good at school. You were given to me as an example—mom and dad expected the same from me, which I hated so much. You smoke a lot. You must feel insecure quite often. You are engaged to Dan—you are probably living with Dan. You used to tease me a lot. I had to fight you. I think I am beginning to understand you now. I hope you are well but I do not care much. You don't seem to care for me either.

Therapist: Now David, what are you to say to your father?

David: Dad, you are over 50, well built. You work hard, always did, you have a good position with your company. But you are weak. You never stuck to anything, you always chose the safe way.

Father/Ben: I think I did a good job taking care of the family and you too.

David: You did what was expected from you. You always followed the rules. But we can never talk. I am sorry. We can never talk. I realize it now. I love you dad, I wanted you to love me. I think you do, you just never showed me.

Father/Ben: We are men, men are not supposed to show love and affection openly. I often did not know myself how to react to you. I felt strange.

David/Peter, double: You never touched me, picked me up, held me.

Father/Ben: Boys do not touch.

David: And you drank a lot.

David/Peter, double: What were you hiding?

Father/Ben: I was insecure myself, I drank for the same reason you smoke pot.

Therapist: David you are so uptight talking to your father. What do you think, would you like to do something with your body? And what?

David: I have a feeling, I would like to hide in my position.

Therapist: You do not feel safe in front of your father?

David: (*Crosses his legs and stays quiet*)

Therapist: When I was young I was always afraid you would hit me, spank me, that I was doing something against the rules.

Therapist: Would you mind coming closer to your father? (*David approaches*) What would you like to do to him now?

David: Push him.

Therapist: Go ahead. (*David and father push each other, softly at the beginning and then getting harder and harder. David finally overpowers the father.*)

Therapist: How do you feel now?

David: Kind of silly—and guilty.

Therapist: Talk about it to your father.

David: I didn't want to fight you dad, I really didn't want to.

Therapist: Now let's bring mother in. Talk to your mother David.

David: Mother, you're close to fifty, slim, you have short grey hair. We have similar facial features. You work, you made a good career in business. (*David stops and after a while he continues.*) I feel sad thinking of the way you gave me love and attention and I didn't appreciate it. You loved me, but you always wanted to make me into somebody else, somebody you wanted me to be.

Mother/Dorothy: But you had great potential.

David: Maybe, but you didn't let me do things I wanted for myself.

Mother/Dorothy: I am older, more experienced, I knew what was best for you.

David: No you did not. Maybe you did if you trusted your instinct. You read all those books and picked up ideas from them on how to raise children, how to understand them. It was all wrong. And I just had to show you I wouldn't do everything you wanted.

Mother/Dorothy: You did not, you rebelled. But remember how often you returned home unhappy, desperate and expecting help.

David: That's true. But this was your fault, you made decisions for me, you made me dependent on you. (*David starts speaking louder and becomes excited.*)

Therapist: Try to express it in one sentence.

David: (*Speaking loudly and angrily.*) You are responsible, you did it, you fucked me up—yes, you really fucked me up.

Mother/Dorothy, Female 2 doubling: I had to push you, you wanted me to push you.

David: That's true. *(After a period of heavy breathing and bodily stimulations directed by the therapist, with the help of several other group members, David starts shaking and moaning.)*

Therapist: How do you feel now?

David: Like crying. *(After a while David starts talking, jerkily shouting.)* Dad, I'm afraid of you, I could not fight you, you made me fight. Can't you all see how weak I am? Dad, you never loved me enough. I want you to love me. Fuck off. Leave me alone!

Therapist: Who are you saying this to?

David: Mother. Fuck off mom, leave us alone. Dad and I are so weak.

[*Authors' note*: In psychodrama David recalls and reexperiences old conflicts with his parents and sister. Due to abreactive techniques this becomes an intensive emotional experience.]

Diary. This afternoon I read my autobiography. There were a few things I was very embarrassed to read about, mainly my sex life, but I read them. I felt relieved after I finished reading it. I told the group everything about me. It was an act of blind faith; I closed my eyes and jumped in.

When I finished reading it, Sara [the therapist] helped me do some heavy breathing and yelling. I almost fainted. For maybe 30 seconds I felt like I was stoned, like my body was spinning gently and I couldn't see straight. It was very pleasant. Then I lay on my back and yelled and roared. My legs trembled. I felt very detached from it. I was lying there, with everyone hovering over me, and I was really roaring. There were some incredible sounds coming out of me. I was really pleased to share these feelings of great sorrow, anger and hurt with the group. All my life I've had to share only my good feelings with people, and if I didn't feel good I had to pretend I did. [*Authors' note*: This entry confirms that David's experience in the abreaction was intense.]

Thirteenth day of stay

Diary. This afternoon in the play my role was a hysterical 16 year old girl in a hospital. [David refers to the weekly play, written and performed by the patients.] I enjoyed playing the part very much. I rolled around on the floor gasping, sobbing and shrieking. Doctors and nurses and others continually came to give me lots of attention. I enjoyed the attention a lot. I think, in a subtler way, I am always shrieking for attention, and rarely getting it. I've never allowed myself to be really hysterical or loud, because I thought people would disapprove, but I've always wanted to and doing it in the play felt really good. [*Authors' note*: The role of an hysterical person was the opposite of David's shy, unobtrusive behavior; he was, perhaps, experimenting in opposite roles, as well as evoking old conflicts about not getting enough attention from his parents?]

Another feeling I had in the play was extreme embarrassment when Edwin [the resident in psychiatry] as the doctor in the play talked to me. I have always been shy talking to Edwin since I've known him, because he doesn't smile much or show signs of friendship or acceptance of me, so *I feel rejection from him*. [*Authors' note*: David projected his father schema (a father who does not care enough, or rejects) on the male therapist and expected the same from him—rejection—as from his father. The therapist's not reacting in the way David assumed was an element of corrective experience.]

Twentieth day of stay

The therapist's summary in the progress notes (13th to 20th day of stay). David was elected a member of the committee, became work coordinator and took the responsibility seriously. He was active and flexible enough in resolving various problems connected with his function. He had open confrontations with several other members of the group and became able to express openly his positive as well as negative feelings towards them.

[*Authors' note*: David's success in being elected as a committee member and functioning well in the difficult position of work coordinator was partly due to some loosening up in his group schema. David no longer assumed all men in authority were rejecting him and all women were strong, competitive creatures trying to push or overpower him. This partial change enabled him to act more realistically with men and women in the group. There was an element of corrective experience involved. David originally bid for chairperson. He lost against another candidate, a woman older than himself, but he tolerated the defeat well and cooperated with the chairperson very well. This conflict recalled an old one in which his sister had defeated him, but he mastered this better than in the past, neither withdrawing nor rebelling.]

Nineteenth day of stay

Recording from the family session (therapist's summary). Family started by each member expressing themselves nonverbally, as to how they were feeling. David got up and walked around with his head down and arms flapping at his sides. Then sat down, crossed his legs and put his head right down, then came back and sat with the family.

Bess then expressed to him that if he hadn't shown this she would never have guessed that he felt down or unhappy. David then said that he didn't want to show that side of himself, that "people would reject him if he wasn't strong." Asked who had given him this message: "My mother—she would never let me cry." Then asked to walk around and express and show in his body what a strong person should be like. John walked up and down the room, very methodically, holding arms close and rigid to his body and looking down. "I must be strong—I musn't show others how weak I am, how lonely I am. I musn't show this to others."

I then asked other members to talk for David if they had similar feelings. Susan got up and started to walk around and around David, trying to look into his eyes—but he avoided looking at her. "Why won't you look at me—you are so tight." (David and Susan had discussed together in family on Friday their sexual attraction for each other. David had expressed fears at that time.) "Are you afraid of me? But you know I feel weak and frightened. I told you that." David: "No, I feel quite superior to you now that I know your fears. You don't threaten me any more."

Later on I asked David to choose who would represent his mother (chose Lyn) and tell his mother how he feels about her. David: "Mom, when I was little, before the age of five, I was always crying, I wanted you to pay attention to me. You kept telling me to stop being such a cry baby, be a man, grow up. You wouldn't let me show any weakness." David then went on to tell his mother of his great hostility towards her—blaming her for the way he is now. He wants to hurt her. Was hostile towards her when she visited him a month ago and has been hostile in his letters to her. Asked to express his anger using the boppers. Slow to get into it allowing Lyn, as his mother, to provoke him. Walking around her with a blank look in his eyes "Come on cry baby." Then started to strike without using words. The therapist said: "Tell her what you are feeling."

David: It's all your fault I'm the way I am. (Hitting very hard without many words. Asked to use the boxing bag—again striking without words—I asked others to help him, to double for him.)

Others: You expect too much from me.

David: Yes, you expected too much from me.

Others: Don't treat me like your husband.

David: That's right—don't treat me like your husband.

Others: I can't be the husband that you didn't get with my father.

David: That's very true—that's what you want—but I am not your fucking husband.

Asked to go into this more, but seemed unable to do it on his own, soon becoming silent once people didn't help him.

I asked Lyn, as David's mother, how she was feeling. Lyn started to talk to David expressing anger and frustration "Stop being such a cry baby, your sister is upset. I can't always be paying attention to you." David stood silent with the vacant look in his eyes. Finally he said "It's pointless. I can never tell you." Lyn continued to taunt him but he did not respond other than to look like a small child being told off—looking down and fidgeting his feet around.

After that I decided that was enough for the moment and finished the episode with David. Dorothy and John came close to David and comforted him. I asked them to stay with him for a while. The rest of the group suggested talking more about Lyn and her problems. [*Authors' note*: David recalled and reexperienced old problems he had had with his mother. Some elements of his mother schema became clearer—mother expecting too much, pushing him toward goals his father had not achieved, mother rejecting David if he did not fulfil her expectations.]

Diary. Today in family I spoke of how judgmental of people I am. I also spoke of how great a need I feel to be weak, to cry, to let go of my role as a cool, calm, and collected person, and also very strong.

Now it occurs to me that I would have got a lot more out of that workout had I put more effort into expressing the feeling; even if I felt it forced upon me at the start. I know now what to do. Next time I'll let go.

Twenty-third day of stay

Recording of family night (therapist's summary). David brought an old girlfriend, Marion, in. They had lived together for about five months and then decided to separate. David invited her to come as he felt obligated to bring a visitor. Talked of how he felt that they had both tried to make the other into the partner they fantasized about.

"You expected me to be strong." Asked to use another word—seemed to find it difficult. Then some said "confident." David: "Yes, over confident." Asked how Marion conveyed this request to him "I don't know." Marion also felt that David had expectations of her—that he didn't really care about her and she was fearful of any criticism from him.

[*Authors' note*: David seemed to apply his mother schema to his girlfriend, assuming she wanted him to be strong and confident and feeling obliged to behave the way she wanted him to—as his mother did. At the same time David was ironical with his girlfriend competing with and trying to overpower her. Perhaps his sister schema was involved also. This episode seemed to show some basic elements in David's problems with girls, especially in the area of sex.]

David was vague and hesitant. Asked what the relationship was now.

David: We don't see each other any more—actually I don't like your company.

Group Member: Why?

David: Well, I really think you are really quite a fine person, but I do feel tense in your presence. I feel inferior and tried not to show it. I tried hard to be superior to you.

Several group members then expressed that they felt the same that Marion must have felt, such as David being ironical, hypercritical and trying to show that he was better than they. But at the same time expecting attention, care and recognition. David listened attentively and looked resentful. Marion was surprised by how much the other group members shared her own feelings about David.

Diary. Marion came to Visitor's Night tonight. I explained to her my problem of judging people, that I tried to be superior to her. Sara [the therapist] pointed out that I do that in group too and as a result I am very lonely. I already know that, but I think it still really hit me. I feel terrible now, I want to sulk, I feel hopeless about changing myself, I need help.

I am really angry that nobody stood up for me, yet I know that nobody could honestly stand up for me on that point. I feel like withdrawing, like avoiding people completely, like never talking to anybody again. I want Dr. K. to help me.

Twenty-fifth day of stay

Diary. Today in family I said that I was very sad because I can't stop being so judgmental of people, because I hurt so much and I am afraid to let anybody know, that they might hurt me more, so instead I hurt them first.

[*Authors' note*: David was criticized by others in the family. Then the therapist asked him to go around and tell everybody in the group that he felt hurt. He cried and got a lot of support from the group afterwards.]

Mom and Dad are the ones who hurt, and they taught me to hide my hurt, so much that I can't recognize the hurt myself. This afternoon I felt the hurt, and expressed it. I cried a lot, something that is very hard to do. I shared my feeling with my family and then I began to see them more as people, just like me, people who have problems just like me. I have to work hard to remember this, to realize that I do hurt, and that I can share it with people, that I don't have to hurt or be hurt.

Twenty-sixth day of stay

Diary. In big group Tim expressed that he had to work something out with Nancy. He did and I realized exactly the same thing had happened to me, that Nancy had thrown her friendship at me and demanded mine back automatically with no allowance for spontaneity. I felt guilty about hurting her feelings so I went along with it, also because I wanted her approval. She manipulated me successfully. I was partially aware of it as it was happening and expressed it to her, but I closed my eyes to the whole truth in order to avoid hurting both of us. No, I realize this was a mistake.

I feel much more confident at Day House now. Before I was worrying about when and where and how to say things, but now I can express myself at the appropriate time easily.

Twenty-ninth day of stay

Diary. In family I was the centre of a circle in which everyone was about two feet away. They moved in on me gradually. At first I was afraid but then I relaxed and felt warmth so I put my arms around people and we formed a circle, arms around each other. I then felt a sudden warmth for Dr. K., and said it, and put my arms around him. It was a really tender warmth.

[*Authors' note*: David went through corrective experience in his authority schema; he could relate with warmth and tenderness to the man in authority, to the clinical supervisor. This was also contributed to his corrective experience with male authority.]

I got a letter from Mike, a friend I used to be very close to when I was about 16. In it he expressed thanks for a birthday gift I sent him recently. I felt a wave of emotion sweep over me as I read his words praising me. I guess it was warmth; that we gave each other something we need. I understand him and know that he needed to know somebody cared by sending him that gift and he understood that I need re-assurance back.

[*Authors' note*: David described his friend Mike in his autobiography.

He met him at a summer camp where Mike was a counsellor. Mike was older and a lot more experienced than David. In David's own words: "He questioned everything, argued everything and was very honest. He was very open about himself to other people. He did anything he wanted to. He was a martyr for all the oppressed people of the world. I shared no agreement with his values, but I took them on as mine anyway."]

Thirtieth day of stay

Diary. Lyn drove us together with Bert, Dorothy and Sue home. We were joking and all really merry. We cracked a few jokes about sex. I was amazed at how relaxed I was. I'm usually quite embarrassed talking about sex and shut right up, but tonight I enjoyed it and added to the conversation. [*Authors' note*: David feels more relaxed with women as peers or probable sex partners.]

Thirty-first day of stay

Diary. In big group Cynthia and I had a bopper fight. She directed a lot of anger for others towards me, which caused me to feel indignant. She said some things I thought were really stupid and which hurt me. She had a very good work-out, and there was an extremely noticeable change in her after. She was very relaxed and happy and seemed to feel very good about herself. I intend to talk more with her about a couple of things that still bother me about her.

Thirty-second day of stay

Therapist's summary of the mid-term (individual) interview with David
Therapist: What has changed?
David: I have felt happy now for at least a week. I used to feel guilty when I was happy, like I should be doing something more. I feel warm toward people in the group and am more open and less judgmental. Outside, I'm more open with my roommates and very active physically. I am less critical of their habits. I want to bring my parents. I'm angry with them. Always felt pressured from mother to do well, especially in school. Feel she is disappointed—still want to please her.
Therapist: Was she disappointed in father as well?
David: Yes, she was successful herself, worked her way up to head in business. I feel guilty.
Therapist: How does she still influence you?
David: Just by saying, for example, "Leave the possibility of university open." I feel uncertain about my decisions when she says that.

David says that he wants to call them and tell them all the ways that they hurt him and how angry he is with them. [*Authors' note*: This would antagonize the parents unnecessarily and hamper the future cooperation with them that David was basically interested in. The therapist interferes.] I suggested that when he calls he do something different and tell them a decision he has made about the next three months. He feels this would be a real change: "I never wanted to tell them anything."

We discussed who he wants to invite and with tears he says he really wants his father because he missed him. I encourage him to arrange it feeling this may be a quick way to get father and son together without mother to change the alliance in the family.

At the end I ask if he is seeing any women outside the group. He isn't. He says he feels good with the women here.

Diary. This morning I had my mid-term interview with Sara. I came away as good and happy that there were tears in my eyes. That was also due to our having talked about Dad, who I always get emotional about. Sara suggested some really positive courses of action for me to take with Mom, Dad, and girlfriends, and people in general.

In family I had a bopper fight and a shouting fight with Cynthia. Cyndy and Dorothy expressed a lot of anger at me too. I felt resentful. But I could see the truth in what was being said, that I was fighting with Cynthia the way I used to fight with my sister, and that I had been too aggressive and domineering; but I felt really hurt. [*Authors' note*: David was working further on his problems with women peers which related to his old conflicts with his sister.]

Thirty-fifth day of stay

Diary. I called Mom and Dad in Ontario. We arranged for them to call me back tonight. They called back and I told them all about Day House as I'd told them nothing about it, just that I was involved in some kind of therapy. I asked Dad to come out and help me with my therapy at Day House. He was eager to help and agreed; he'll come. It's the first time I've spoken directly to Dad in a long time; tears welled up in my eyes and I told him I'm very much looking forward to seeing him and doing things with him. It seems I haven't had a father for the last ten years or so. [*Authors' note*: Changes in David's father schema enabled him to approach his real father in a way more satisfactory for both.]

Tonight I went with Val to a party at his friend's place. I met Marsha. She is quite a beautiful girl. I was very attracted to her the moment I saw her. She seemed to be friendly and interesting and warm. At the party we danced and played some games together. Then I asked her to go for a walk with me. We talked about ourselves, our problems, and found we have a lot in common. She invited me to her place. We made love and slept together. I felt very happy with her, she is soft and warm and likes me a lot.

[*Authors' note*: Changes in David's sister schema and in his women peers schema made it possible for him to approach a girl and have satisfactory sex. He no longer felt threatened by a girl and he did not have to compete with her.]

Thirty-sixth day of stay

Diary. Marsha and I spent the day together. We made love twice today. I was open with her talking about my sexual inhibitions. We spent an hour in the park, cooked supper together, went to a movie. I am very happy that we love each other and enjoy each other so much. Tomorrow we are going to Harrison Hot Springs with another couple, Marsha's friends.

Thirty-eighth day of stay

Therapist's observation of David at the family session. Expressed feeling of happiness. Has met a girl, saw her over the long weekend. In a role-playing situation with Sue (female patient) playing the part of his girlfriend he was able to tell her how he felt about her and the relationship.

David: I feel we are pretty close. I have told you that I am in Day House and you have been able to tell me about yourself and your own anxieties.

They made love many times over the holidays and David said he had no problem with premature ejaculation. He was questioned by the group as to whether he might become very dependent on the relationship.

David: That might happen, but at present I am not afraid of that. I have told Marsha I want to play it by ear.

The group felt that the relationship sounded really good, but expressed some anxiety that it might interfere with his therapy here. David did not think so.

Forty-second day of stay

Therapist's comment. Following the session David approached me and said he wanted to tell me that if I hadn't asked him about meeting a girl outside, during the interview we had, he probably would have waited until after Day House—he said he was glad I talked about it. He took it as encouragement. I said I was happy that he had gone ahead and asked him to write about it in his diary. [*Authors' note*: This encouragement was given to David to move him to apply in practice what he achieved in therapy. This generalization of therapeutic change into normal life is an important aspect of integrated psychotherapy.]

Diary. Tonight Marsha and I talked a lot. I mentioned a few things that annoyed me about her. It didn't bother her, quite the opposite, she appreciated that I was telling her those things as nobody else ever did. I have a big hang-up about hurting other people's feelings—I mean people I like and feel close to—I am happy that Marsha and I are really working things out. [*Authors' note*: David was able to be more open with his girlfriend than he was before with other girls.]

Forty-third day of stay

Diary. In a big group this morning I was very angry with Bob—and had a bopper fight with him. I was surprised at how forcefully I expressed my anger. I hit very hard and rapidly and shouted very loudly. I think it showed some real change in me that I have much more self-confidence. [*Authors' note*: David worked more on his anger and resentment toward male authorities. Ben was much older than David and was chairperson of the committee.]

Forty-fourth day of stay

Diary. After we came home from a visit of Marsha's friends we had quite an argument. Marsha took valium and drank a lot. She got sick and rather stoned. I got worried she might not be alright, but she was. I told her I was worried she was becoming addicted to the tranquilizers and that if she did, I didn't think I could cope with it. She became very argumentative and stubborn. She told me to stop rationalizing so much, that I talk too much. So we had quite an argument, but we both felt relieved after. With Marsha I realize I don't have to explain myself all the time. We are learning to trust each other more and also being quiet, not talking at all. In the past, being with a girl I felt compelled to talk all the time. I found silence threatening. It is not so any more with Marsha. [*Authors' note*: David was now able to react realistically to a situation, to agree or disagree with his girlfriend, to speak up, to fight. He no longer confused his actual relationship with the attitudes and expectations he had toward his sister or mother. His sister schema and mother schema no longer interfered with his relationship to real persons in the present.]

Forty-fifth day of stay
   Diary. This afternoon Jerry read his autobiography. I felt many similarities with Jerry's problems and I told him I felt very close to him.

Forty-seventh Day of Stay
Diary: Sara asked me recently to write something about why my relationship with Marsha is working and others didn't, so here goes: Marsha and I have been honest with each other from the start. We've talked about all our problems: emotional and sexual. We've found them to be very closely related. Before I could never talk to anyone about my problems, and felt very insecure about them and therefore felt a need to act superior and put people down. Now I no longer feel that need, now that I can easily be open about myself. I learned in Day House I can tell people what's bothering me about them, without it being a big deal. I have been practicing it with Marsha, and it makes us stronger, to be able to survive direct criticism.
   Tonight Dad arrived from Ontario. It was very late and he was tired. We didn't talk much, but still went shortly over reasons he felt he came here and reasons I felt he was here. We were both friendly and hopeful about our relationship. After I dropped him off at his hotel I noticed a calm, happy feeling in me.

Forty-eighth day of stay
   Recording from the family session [Clinical supervisor, Dr. Knobloch, was in charge of the session.]
Therapist: (*Asking the group*) With whom are you most concerned?
Group: David.
David: Well, my father arrived last night and that's what I wanted to
   work on. My father is coming tomorrow to the Day House. I don't
   know what to do. I feel optimistic that we are going to work something out. But still, I think I should do something now, in the family.
   We haven't talked, my father and I, in ten years—well, we talked but
   we really haven't said anything important to each other. I lived with
   both my parents until I was eighteen. Last night we started to talk
   more directly. My father started talking about things he feels that he
   did wrong as a father.
Therapist: Like what?
David: That he was very insensitive. He is quite an emotional person,
   but he hides it.
Therapist: Did it start with you criticizing him?

David: He criticized himself. We were both kind of emotional and choked up when he first came.

Therapist: Let's see what you would like to tell him. Let's see if you can talk for both of you for a while. Imagine your father sitting here. Describe him. (*Ben, a patient, sat on the chair opposite playing David's father.*)

David: Father is fifty-three years old, average build, a little overweight. Medium short hair. He works for a B—— company. He is an active man, has many interests and hobbies. He builds kites and sails.

Therapist: What would you like to tell him?

David: Dad, I would like to say, to be able to be open with you. I don't know if I want to be your son or not, as much as I want to be your friend.

Therapist: (*Addressing the group*) What do you think about the way he talks now?

Lyn (A woman patient): Yes, it is so flat, not expressing any real feeling.

Another patient: He's sort of back to the way he was when he first came here.

David: I feel very emotional right now. Dad, I really feel close to you. I don't know how to express it. I was always afraid to come to you. I want you to be able to talk to me. I'm your son. You didn't even say good morning for about ten years. We lost out on a lot. I did and you did. But I feel confident that we can change it. If we can be open now, we can really help each other out. (*He stops for a short while.*) I feel like breaking down and crying. I want you to show your love for me. I want to change things with my father, but I don't know how to start. Dad, you could never tell me you love me. Never even touched me. I find it very hard to express my love for you. I don't know whether I love you, I know I need you. I need you Dad. I really need you. I need a father. I feel like I don't have a father. Up until I was nine I had a father. Something happened then. You became really cold and insensitive. I was always afraid.

Therapist: Who became insensitive, him or you?

David: Both. (*Speaking to the therapist*) I guess he got tied up on his job. He started out as a draftsman and worked his way to the top. He told me that last night. In fact, I never asked him before. (*Speaking to his father*) I wanted to come to you but I couldn't. I couldn't talk to you. I couldn't talk to anybody. I don't know, I was always afraid of you. I was afraid you'd spank me, as a kid. Couldn't get over that. I don't know what to do. I want you but I don't know what to do. I don't know what to do (*repeating loudly*). What can I do Dad? Tell me what to do. You don't know what to do yourself. You're weak. I don't want you to be weak.

Therapist: Compared with mother?

David: Yes, I guess. Talked a lot and dominated us both. I guess she saw she couldn't dominate you so she dominated me. You started doing things on your own the whole time. You have always been a loner.

Therapist: He was avoiding her?

David: (*To the therapist*) I don't know. They seemed happy. They seemed content to go their own ways and yet be happy. They seemed to have a good sex life when I was living at home. They are both very emotional.

David/Male 1, double: I never was happy.

David: I was happy when I was really young because you showed your love for me. We played together. Then it stopped. Why did it stop? Why did it stop?

Father/Ben, Male 1, double: I couldn't change things. I waited for you.

David: I didn't know what to do. You're my father, you should have known. You should have been able to help me. But you couldn't.

David/Female 2: I felt closer to you than to mom.

David: I feel closer to him now than I do to her. I don't want to be insensitive. I want to be able to be normal, to express my feelings and not be afraid of them. It's so easy for me to hide them. I feel hopeless, I feel hopeless (*repeats several times*).

Therapist: Hopeless in what?

David: In being able to express myself, my feelings, without being afraid that people will laugh at me.

Therapist: Do you blame your father for that? Or is it that you felt so strongly in the relationship?

David: Yes, it was because of him that I could never trust anybody, I could never talk to anybody. I would talk to my mother.

Therapist: You say it was because of him you couldn't talk to anyone? How was it connected?

David: I couldn't talk to him. I was always afraid. He looked so stern and he would get angry very easily.

Therapist: Let's have a talk with your father now as he visited you. Let father come closer here. (*Ben, representing David's father, comes closer.*)

Father/Ben: You called me over here and I came.

David: I've said it all Dad. I want you to love me. I want you to show your love for me. I want to love you. I want to be able to show you that I want to be your son and I want you to be my father and I don't know what that involves any more. It will be a whole new relationship and I won't understand anything about it at all. I'm afraid I'm sad and I missed something and you did too.

David/Male 2, doubling: You owe me something dad.

David: You owe me something. You owe me ten years. You wasted ten years of my life. I want my childhood. Fuck, you owe me so much. I want it, I really want it. But I don't know how to get it back. It's gone and I'll never get it back, the last ten years. I can never be ten years old again or thirteen. All those years I felt so shy and afraid of everybody. I needed help then and I didn't get it. I can't get it now for that. I'll never be able to get that back, never.

Therapist: And you're angry with him?

David: I'm angry Dad. You owe me something but you can't pay me, you can't give it to me. You can never replace that.

Therapist: Where is the anger? (*The therapist comes closer to David putting hands on his arms and shakes him several times.*)

David: I am angry. I feel hurt. I was hurt all the time dad and I didn't know what to do. I couldn't talk to anybody, nobody at all. Nobody. I could never talk to anybody. Nobody. (*Repeats yelling and crying*) I wanted to talk to somebody.

Father/Ben: Why were you afraid of me?

David: You were like a robot. You sat in your chair and read your paper.

Father/Ben: I never pushed you away.

David: I just felt I couldn't come near you at all. I was really scared to come up to you and tell you how I was feeling.

Father/Ben: Why do you blame me if you were scared?

David: You made me afraid from when I was really young.

Father/Ben: What did I do?

David: You instilled some kind of fear in me. I was always afraid of being spanked for one thing.

Father/Ben: I don't remember spanking you very often.

David: Not, not often, but whenever I did something bad. But I felt we had a lot of good times together up until I was about nine. But, at the same time I was always pretty cautious about you. There was a limit as to how far I could push you.

Father/Ben: Do you think that was wrong? It was for your own good. I was trying to give you directions. So why did you lose trust and confidence in me, I was there.

David: Maybe I could sense that you were.

Father/Ben: Sure, I was a little bit busier than I used to be. I had to work, I had to study to get through all that and reach the right position I wanted to achieve. I then didn't have much time to spend with you. I was tired when I used to come home from work.

Therapist: (*To David*) Are you still angry with him?

David: Yes, I'm really angry with you. You hurt me Dad. (Repeats yelling) Dad I'm really angry. I'm really fucking angry. Really angry. I'm angry at you Dad. Why couldn't I come to you? Why couldn't I talk to you? Why?

Father/Ben: What do you blame me for?

David: (*Crying*) Dad I really want to be close to you. I really need you.

Father/Ben: That's why I came over here. I left everything over there. I knew that something wasn't right anyway when you wrote to me and when you spoke to me. But I still don't know why you're mad at me. What *do* you want from me? Why did you move away from home? Why didn't you stay close to me?

David: I left home because I couldn't survive. I couldn't talk to anybody.

Father/Ben: Well, you never came to me.

David: I couldn't trust you. I was smoking dope and you just wouldn't understand. You still don't understand that, and you know about it.

Father/Ben: Sure, I still don't understand that, I don't know why you have to. And neither do you, I assume.

David: You think it's so evil.

Father/Ben: I never smoked it.

David: Well, you're a pretty heavy drinker yourself sometimes, and I think that is a hell of a lot worse.

Father/Ben: Yes, but I realize that drinking is a way to escape; you're smoking dope and I don't like that. We both do it for a reason.

David: We're wasting time. I want to be close to you. That's it. I'm afraid to be close to you.

Father/Ben: Why are you so afraid? I came over here.

Father/David, Dorothy, double: I am afraid to touch you. And yet I wanted for so many years to cry in your arms.

David: I feel really weird if I hug a man. I'd love to. Dad, I need you so much. (*David and Ben embrace each other*).

Father/Ben: Why don't you come home with me?

David: I don't know if it would be a good idea if I came home or not.

Father/Ben: Well, you said you wanted to be close to me. That's the only way.

David: I've been moving around so much lately, I've just got to get settled down. I've got to make a home for myself. I'm twenty-three.

Father/Ben: You know I never pushed you away. You're my son. I always wanted you.

David/Male 1, double: I am still angry with you.

David: I don't know what it is. I feel good about home. Looking at it objectively it looks like we've accomplished a hell of a lot, but I don't really feel it. We are closer now, but there is still a gap.

Father/Ben: I don't know what you want from me then.

David: I don't know what I want either. We just have to be with each other more.

Father/Ben: That's what I said, you could come to our side of the country. You could make your home. You don't have to live in my house.

David/Therapist, doubling: Yes, but we could live for ten years and it would be the same.

David: No, it's changed. We've started to talk to each other.

Therapist: (*Addressing the group*) I think we all feel it doesn't only have something to do with father, or sex. It is his relationship to people in general. Will you come and show it, and help him in what is still missing here?

Steve (a patient): I feel like I don't understand what is going on. Like, I thought it was my problem too. But I don't know now what David wants from his father. I don't understand what is happening now. It doesn't seem convincing to me. It doesn't seem convincing to me. It doesn't work.

Therapist: Come closer and tell him.

Steve: (*Speaking directly to David*) Well, you come here with the idea the problem is with your parents because something was missing and yet that doesn't seem to be it. No, well not to me. And I don't know if it's the way that I'm observing it or what. I sit here and think, Jesus, I must be fucked up. I don't understand what's going on at all.

David: That's how I am with you and Lyn——

Lyn (woman patient): Well maybe that's more important, how you've been reacting to us. Maybe things that are happening here at the Day House are the problem. Like you come here thinking I had to work out something with my parents. Maybe it's something with people and women in particular.

David: I know that. It seemed so obvious to me because of the way my father treated me that caused the problem.

Dorothy (patient): But it doesn't seem to me that he treated you badly. What did he do?

David: It was the fact that he was so insensitive and cold after the time I was nine years old.

Father/Dorothy, doubling: What did I do. You were growing up. You couldn't stay nine years old forever.

David: I couldn't talk to anybody.

Father/Dorothy, doubling: Why didn't you come and talk to me?

David: I was afraid of you.

Father/Ben, Dorothy: What did I do to make you afraid of me?

David: I don't know.

Father/Ben, Dorothy: So why are you blaming me if you were afraid of me. I didn't do anything.

David: You should have seen it in me and come to me.

Father/Ben, Dorothy: How could I see it in you. You don't show anything.

David: (Raising his voice) Well, fuck, I showed it when I was a kid. Cried a lot, didn't that show it?

Father/Ben, Dorothy: Sure I was talking to Mom and asked her what was wrong.

David: Why didn't you ask me, not mum?

Father/Ben: I was afraid to show my feelings, you never showed any.

David: Right. You never showed your feelings. You just told me last night that you were very emotional. You cried when Uncle Ted died. I didn't know you did things like that. You sit there and you're so goddam cold, paper in one hand and drink in the other. You are so cold Dad, you are so cold.

Father/Ben: But I'm happy this way. I don't want to change. I'm happy the way I am.

Mel (female patient): (*Spontaneously comes closer and starts talking to David.*) I am tired of your "Dad love me. Dad you never showed you loved me." How did you show love to him? And the mother. You said your mother loved you a lot. And what did you do with all of this? You didn't even invite her here. She must have had a difficult time with you. We all have.

David: (*Looking embarrassed*) Yes, that's true.

Lyn: (*Talking directly to David*) You had a lot of love from your mother. What else do you want? She talked to you all the time, she gave you attention.

David: Attention yes, but love no.

Lyn: Now you really confuse me. What do you call love?

David: Unconditional love.

Lyn: And what was it your mother was giving you?

David: Perform and I will love you.

Lyn: David, is that why you were angry all day lately? Do you think we like you only if you perform? And not for what you are as a person?

David: I don't know. I want to help myself. I want to change. I want to be happy, that's what I want to do. I feel self-conscious about doing all this in a group. I don't understand why nothing changes.

Lyn: You feel that nothing has changed by being here?

David: No, I feel a lot has changed.

Dorothy: And you feel there is still something missing you want to work on?

Therapist: (*To Mel*) Are you frustrated with David? Could you show it? (*Mel starts a bopper fight with David.*)

David: Well, you are really angry with me. Why don't you bring it out? Don't just stand there and swing your bat. Come on, let's get it over with.

Mel: Goddam bastard. I'll fucking well hit you any goddam place I feel like it.

David: Well, you tell me what you're so mad about?

Mel: Because you're a fucking, sulking bastard.

David: Just like you Mel.

Mel: Fuck off. You're just like my goddam father, sulking and hiding in corners. So bad that you can't stand up for yourself.

(*The fight went on for a while, both sides getting more and more excited and fighting with increasing vigor. Finally they stopped, tired and exhausted. Several group members came closer to David and Mel and showed friendly gestures, or sat close to them, and comforted them. The session ended.*)

[*Authors' note*: Both Mel and David experienced their conflicts with important persons of their group schema—Mel with her father, David with his father, mother, and sister. At the same time the episode occurred in a friendly supportive group atmosphere and thus offered elements of corrective experience.]

Diary. In family I worked out for about an hour. I expressed a lot of anger, hurt and fear towards Dad who Ben role-played. I found that I let out a lot but at the end I felt something was still missing.

Dad invited Marsha and I for dinner. Dad accepted Marsha very well and they both seemed to like each other. Dad talked a lot about himself, his parents and his early years at B——, where he grew up.

Forty-ninth day of stay

Recording from family session. [Mr. T, David's father was present. Inviting a significant person to the family session was an exception, made for

David's father. The group wanted to have longer time with him and this would not be possible at family night. After preliminary introductions and greetings the therapist addressed David's father.]

Therapist: So how has your visit been going so far?

Mr. T: Well, I've been saying to Dave it seems as though I've been here several days and I really came in on Sunday night. I've done a lot of things, including getting lost three times yesterday. I haven't been to this place for eight years and then it was on business and was very limited. I think our visit together is going extremely well. (To David) I think you'd agree with that?

David: Oh yes, really.

Therapist: From your point of view, what's been happening in the relationship?

Mr. T: From my point of view, I feel a hell of a lot better with David. Our relationship has been distant, there is no doubt about it I think, on both sides. I think it's coming very nicely. I wish I could stay longer here. We've done a lot of pretty plain talking I think.

David: Pretty straight forward.

Ben (patient): (Addressing Mr. T) Can you tell us more about it?

Mr. T: I haven't attempted to keep back anything that's critical. I said how I feel about Dave and Dave about me.

David: Well, I know we are both very emotional right now.

Therapist: Is that something that you've been talking about?

Mr. T: Did you tell people here about that, about crying?

David: Yes, they know that I do get very emotional when I think about or talk about Daddy. I think it's because we want to be close but before we didn't know how.

Mr. T: Yes, but I was telling Dave that I break up easily too. When I hear the bass fiddle play I get a big lump down here. And I easily get in tears at a funeral.

Therapist: What's happening between you and David that's so emotional? You feel like crying now David? Can you look at your father and tell him what you're feeling?

David: I think it's happiness that we're together and some sadness too that we've wasted a lot of time.

Therapist: Would you like to go close to him? Move your chair closer.

Mr. T: I think that's all over Dave. I think we've got it ahead of us now.

David: Yes, I agree.

Mr. T: And I think that's just great. I think geography accounted for part of it. For a long time we lived thousands of miles apart. I am

sure now there were many other things, I don't know what they were.
[*Author's note*: It seemed, both David and his father would continue in
a rather superficial friendly talk. The committee members intervened.]

Dorothy, (patient, member of the committee): Can you tell us more? Do you
    have any idea of what was happening, or how you remember things
    as David was growing up?

Mr. T: As I see it now, and I have been thinking about it a lot in the
    past few years, I was a rather authoritarian father.

Lyn, (patient): How was that?

Mr. T: I don't think there were many spankings, but "Daddy's king"
    sort of thing. David and Beverly are both grown-up now and that
    part doesn't matter, but I am not the same anymore.

Therapist: What would you do that you would describe yourself as au-
    thoritarian?

Mr. T: I think I would issue orders like the lieutenant-general of the
    army, sort of thing. Would you agree with that Dave? Do this, don't
    discuss it but do it.

David: Yes, I think.

Therapist: David, is it the same as your father describes it?

David: Yes, you were pretty stern and gruff and I was always afraid. I
    think I did question things every now and then, and I was always
    afraid of receiving, and I did receive sometimes, a really abrupt an-
    swer. Like don't ask just do it.

Mr. T: That's quite true, and I make no pretense at having even been
    a grade B father at that time.

David: On the other hand that's not the only part either. When I was
    very young, I thought you were a really good father to me. You spent
    a lot of time with me. You shouldn't just emphasize the negative part.

Therapist: Was there a time when you felt things had changed?

David: Yes, I have been talking about it here already, it was somewhere
    between the time when I was nine years old and thirteen years old.
    I was just changing from a little boy to an adolescent or something.
    Something changed in me at the same time.

Mr. T: We had five moves when kids were at home. From Saskatchewan
    to Ontario, to Nova Scotia, to Quebec and back to Ontario. I don't
    know how much this might have a bearing.

Ben, (patient): These moves were related to your work?

Mr. T: Yes. Right. Most of the time we all moved together and I believed
    at that time that we all looked forward to the new situation.

David: Except Bev, my sister. She did not feel good about leaving, and the same was with me. I was often unhappy losing my friends and starting in a new school.

Mr. T: I did not realize it at that time what it meant to you. You know how it is in big companies. They move people around, and when you have a responsible job, you spend more than eight hours a day at it, that sort of thing. You give a little time to your family. And I think at one period, in the sixties——

Therapist: Is this the time David was talking about also, from when he felt things had somehow changed?

David: Yes, I think so.

Mr. T: And I told Dave last night.

Therapist: Can you tell us now?

Mr. T: Yes. We were talking about the time when I was promoted to a position in Ontario. It was a pretty good job. But we did not move to Ontario. My wife was working in the old place, didn't like to leave her position before she was able to get something similar in our new place. David and Bev were going to school. I lived five days in M—— in Ontario and came home for weekends only.

Ben: What work do you do?

(During the next five minutes Mr. T., describes his work with a big industrial company and talks about himself. Ben, Dorothy, and other group members ask questions, compare their own experiences with various jobs. This is a kind of genuine interest in David's father, and the group also offers David moral support).

Mr. T: (Continues) I would come home on Friday night and I would bring a briefcase full with me and I certainly wouldn't work all the weekend but I did work on Sunday. I think I was not only neglecting David, I was neglecting Betty, my wife, and Bev, my daughter, at the same time. But that's all over and done with and I have a good job now and it is much less demanding. Of course, that doesn't matter now, you and Bev aren't there.

Lyn (patient): Do you miss your son not being there?

Mr. T: Yes, I miss not having done things with him when he was a teenager even when he was at home. We drew apart for whatever reasons. I am fond of sailing. I have a sailboat and I miss David not sailing with me. I felt I could ask you a couple of times and then I couldn't ask you any more.

David: I never really enjoyed it. Like tennis, volleyball, badminton, anything, I just didn't want to be with you. We always did a lot of things together on the weekend. In fact, we skied all the time together, and we played tennis together sometimes too. But I guess I enjoyed being with my friends more than being with you.

Mr. T: Should we mention Mike?

David: Well, I mentioned him in my autobiography. Mike is a close friend of mine still, although we do not see much of each other these days. I met him at a summer camp several years back. He is quite a radical. He doesn't have a family and he's travelled to South America, and going to university, and living very haphazardly in down-and-out places. We started doing a lot of things together. I was going through a sort of value conflict between home, which is very middle-class and Mike was very lower-class expounding about the values of social concern and social injustice, and things like that. I don't think I was ever really sincere.

Therapist: Why did you bring Mike up? What did you think?

Mr. T: We feel that Mike was a divisive force between David and family, not just Dave and me. We're not saying Mike is wrong in any aspect, but we're saying this is how we felt about it. I mean, my wife and I. He was for everything, as what we as middle-class people were not. I suppose we felt that way because both my wife and I are children of the last depression and material things probably mean more to us than they should. I don't know. It was not only that. Work, achievement meant something different to us, than to people like Mike. And it was going the other way with you, Dave, I think you felt material things should mean less and less.

Ben: And how did this all influence your relationship with David?

Mr. T: I think David and I were very much alike in several ways. One of them being obstinateness, if that's a word, or stubborn.

David: I think I'm stubborn.

Mr. T: If you don't like what I'm saying then I'm not going to talk to you about it. We'll just leave it under the table forever. Do you figure?

David: Yes, that's true.

Dorothy (patient): So things that you would disagree with you would just avoid talking about. Just like my father.

Mr. T: Yes. We never talked about drugs, we never talked about sex and we should have. When I say we I mean my wife and I. We should have made a point of getting through to you what——about even conversing about them, whether or not you would ever agree, or we would ever agree.

Therapist: Are these the types of things you have been able to talk about since you have visited? What's changed in this visit?

Mr. T: I've been able to talk about it. We were talking about sex the other night. How can I say, we were being man to man, comparing notes sort of thing on a joking basis. I could never have done that two or three years ago. Now I don't know whether you could or not.

Therapist: Is it something different in David? What's changed that you can see now?

Mr. T: I think we're both making a much greater effort. When I say effort, after the first handshake, it really wasn't an effort. But I came out here with the idea that I could say anything and I gather, or infer, that you're feeling the same way.

David: It used to hurt so much to talk about anything except the weather. I don't know why it was so painful, I just wanted to avoid it all the time. Now I get emotional about it, but it seems to come out easily. I think it's from being here at Day House and learning to talk quite openly with a lot of people.

Therapist: David, let's see what would happen if you would— Do you want to take your father's hand? And just hold his hand and close your eyes and just talk about how it feels.

David: I just feel sad. I think you're afraid of my getting close to you Dad. I can feel it in your hand. You're tense.

Mr. T: I'm applying pressure equally to your sort of thing. Dave brought up a point.that there has been very little physical contact between he and his mother and between he and I over the course of his upbringing after he was mobile. I don't know how to explain that except that Betty and I, I suppose, just happen to be like that. We are not really demonstrators of physical affection.

Therapist: How is it now that David is holding your hand? How do you feel?

Mr. T: I don't feel sad. I feel that here's David, and if he has a problem I'm here to help him and in no way do I dislike him holding my hand.

Therapist: Because part of you is still sitting facing the other way, and I wondered did you want to take your hand away?

Mr. T: No, no, I'm just comfortable this way.

Ben: Why do you look so sad David?

David: The wasted years. We can never have it back. I want to keep trying anyway. There is no sense in crying over spilled milk.

Mr. T: Just look ahead.

Therapist: Is there something you feel would stop you from having the relationship that seems to be happening now?

David: (Crying) I just wanted to be open about it. I don't think it will
stop us.

Mr. T: Dave, there is nothing now that I won't talk to you about. I have
a little bit more understanding now, or sensitivity, however you want
to put it.

Therapist: When you said it was difficult in the family to show affection,
was that how you put it? What was it on your part?

Mr. T: I didn't mean difficulty. It wasn't difficulty. I think it's the way
Betty and I are built probably. We have a good marriage, a happy
one, but I think we are the type of people that don't physically touch
our kids. I'm not saying this is right or wrong, I'm just saying that
was perhaps the way it was. I don't think we showed much affection
for either David or Bev. We were both, with my wife, busy people
and work always meant a lot to us. My wife is a career woman and
enjoys it. Although on the other hand we were talking about it recently and it came out when David was born we didn't leave him
alone, Betty stayed at home with him until he was a year old.

David: Dad, I would like you to stand up straighter. You look like you're
afraid. And I think it's all right to be afraid but—somewhat, not as
my father.

Mr. T: What do you mean, right now? When I'm walking? I don't feel
afraid. Well, openly speaking, I did not feel comfortable at the beginning, coming as a stranger into your place and sitting together
with all of you, but it's gone. I feel fine.

Therapist: David, why did you think your father is scared?

David: It's more the things I would like to tell him, things I have done,
I think would really hurt him. (*To father*) Do you want to hear it?

Mr. T: Sure. I've been around for a long time.

David: I'm just afraid you're going to break or something.

Mr. T: Take a chance.

David: I did LSD a couple of times.

Mr. T: I figured that.

David: I just thought you wouldn't figure that.

Mr. T: I don't pretend being happy about it. I hope you're out of it.
But you're twenty-three, you are an active young man. You're living
right in the drug scene or whatever you want to call it. I didn't know
that you did that but I figured the odds were that you did. If I had
been your age I probably would have done the same thing. That
doesn't shock me. Try another one. I guess this isn't the place to ask
you how you acted?

David: I don't mind telling. There are hallucinations, pretty patterns. I became very withdrawn on LSD. It made me realize that I was very afraid and so I stopped doing it quite a while ago.

Therapist: You talk in a very low voice, David.

Mr. T: I think you always have, haven't you?

Dorothy: He used to talk so at the beginning when he first came over here. He would talk to you at home like this also?

Mr. T: Most of the time.

Therapist: What is your impression of him when he does?

Mr. T: I don't know how to describe it. I have to say that I am, or have been, a very active man. And David I think is less active, physically a little slower. Maybe you're going to live longer because of it. There was a time when automatic doors weren't fast enough for me, sort of thing. I was very impatient. I think I would get impatient with you because you seemed slow to me. Now, I think you weren't as made up, if that's the word, as I was.

Therapist: You mean you were impatient with David and probably showed it if David wouldn't do things quickly enough. Or, as quickly as. you might have wanted him to.

Mr. T: Yes, but I wouldn't tell him directly.

David: I'm really glad you told me that.

Mr. T: It just came. If I had thought of it sooner I would have told you.

David: Yes, I think that was part of it. I felt, during this visit, that you didn't want to say anything bad about me. You wanted to take the blame.

Mr. T: I don't feel that I should take all the blame Dave, I think I should take some of it and your mother. We talked about it before I came out. And I don't know any perfect parents, I'll say that in our defence.

Therapist: How did you see it? How was David's relationship with his mother?

Mr. T: In my opinion, it was considerably closer than David and I. But perhaps not so much towards the last, as before you came West, would you say?

David: It was close, but it was also distant at the same time. We talked easily.

Mr. T: Betty has the capacity for talking things out much easier than I have.

David: I also think she manipulates easily. I never felt satisfied after talking to her. She was getting answers out of me that were pleasing to her and I never really had the guts to say——to tell really how I was feeling.

Mr. T: That could be, I don't know.

Therapist: Did you have the same difficulty with your wife as David?

Mr. T: No, I don't think so. We had our fair number of fights that any married couple have. Disagreements. But we always presented a solid front to the kids whenever a decision came along. We believed that was the right thing to do. Now, thinking about it, maybe this shouldn't be done when you have a growing family. When mother says one thing and father thinks another, you should say it in front of the kids. But this was our way of bringing up kids, mother and father always together, sort of thing.

David: This is the way I remember it. I remember one or two times being different. I remember once mother saying Bev and I could stay up late to watch a TV program. Then after you came home and she talked to you she changed her mind. Then you stated in front of us that if she told us before we could that she should stick with it and we were allowed to stay. I remember being quite surprised and a sort of hurt, that you were divided on it. I didn't like the feeling of tension. Now I think that was the right thing to do, I just didn't want to face it. I felt afraid, insecure.

Dorothy: Do you remember your parents fighting?

Mr. T: I told you we made a point of not showing that kind of activity in front of the kids. But we had our arguments.

Dorothy: Such as?

Mr. T: Well, you know, at home I used to be a pretty authoritarian guy, I'm king and all that. At the beginning my wife tolerated it but later, when she became more involved in her job and as I see it now, more self-confident, she objected. And she decided that this was going to stop and she was going to be equal as anyone, that kind of women's lib. I think it was fair enough, but it took me several years to learn to accept this. She would have some pretty hard thoughts about how narrow-minded I was, and I would have some pretty hard thoughts about, well what the hell, she's my wife. But we're over that now. We even have a kind of division of labor, in household chores.

Therapist: (*To David*) Do you have any recollection that something was changing in your parent's relationship?

David: No, I wasn't aware of it at all. I realized Mom having sort of liberated opinions and getting out of the house and having a career, but I never realized there any conflict between the two of them.

Lyn: How was David around the house as you remember him?

Mr. T: Shortly before he left, I remember him as really coming in to eat and sleep. I think that's a pretty fair description. He did certain chores that he was asked to do, you may have considered ordered to do. You would get as mad as hell when I didn't put things in the bag in time or the way you wanted.

David: Yes (*laughing together*). Well it was because I didn't put the garbage out on time or the way you wanted.

Mr. T: I remember you saying, damm once and that was a pretty big shock to me. There was my son saying damn. But that was when he was still very young. And I remember we had a lot of fun together when he was younger. Do you remember how we built a ping-pong table and played together?

Therapist: Is there anything you would remember about how he was, his mood?

Mr. T: I think he was a happy kid until mid-high school.

David: I was pretty happy I think until we moved to O—— But I was kind of afraid all my life about my ears and being ridiculed about them.

Mr. T: Were you really?

David: Of course.

Mr. T: I had them as a kid too.

Therapist: Are there other things that you didn't tell your father that embarrassed you?

David: Well, I was really shy with girls. Just really, really shy. I had pimples all over my chin and I was pretty embarrassed about that. You said if I stopped eating so much candy I would get rid of them. I remember once when I was smoking cigarettes and did tell you about it, it was very unusual. I was really afraid then. We were sitting in the living room after dinner. Eventually you began to notice I was troubled.

Mr. T: Yes, I did. You were quiet for a long time.

Therapist: What were you afraid of?

David: Being yelled at or being called stupid. I know I shouldn't be smoking.

Therapist: Your father would yell at you and call you stupid?

David: Not yell, but speak very gruffly, sternly.

Therapist: Could you do it as you would in the past? Could you show us how it was?

Mr. T: That's funny, that brings a thing to mind that was completely ridiculous. I was sitting on the floor. We had a new carpet. And you had a little piece of meat and just laid it on the carpet for the dog, a little piece. I said something like "for heaven's sake, Dave don't smear the carpet." And you looked scared, took the piece and the dog and walked out of the room. I had forgotten about that.

Therapist: Could you say it as you might have then?

Mr. T: It's kind of silly.

Therapist: Please, it's important.

Mr. T: Dave, for heaven's sake don't do that.

David: Say it more sternly.

Mr. T: (*Repeats it.*)

Therapist: What would you answer him?

David: It's not that important. Okay, I will clean the carpet.

(Therapist then asks them to repeat this back and forth.)

David: I just felt happy that I could answer.

Mr. T: You mean talk back.

David: Yes. I wouldn't dare when I was little.

Therapist: (*To Mr. T*) Does it feel like he is talking back?

Mr. T: No, not at all. I mean now. He's a man. If he were that high (*showing*) and I felt as I did at the time he was that high. I would probably feel he was talking back.

Therapist: But now you accept? But do you feel that David, that you can say that to your father?

David: Yes (*in a low voice*).

Therapist: But you go back to talking in a low voice. Are there things that you are angry with him about?

David: Yes. I feel like really yelling at you, not hitting you but, yes I am very angry at you. I don't know what about. I'm afraid to show you but I will. Like when I told you about the LSD I was really surprised. I expected a much more severe reaction.

Mr. T: Well you can see how I've changed.

David: Yes, you're not going to break. I think you can take criticism.

Therapist: What would you criticize him for?

David: I would really like to have a bopper fight with Dad.

(Both start fighting with boppers.)

Therapist: So, say what it is.

David: (Fighting) I needed more from you and you didn't give it to me and I didn't know how to ask for it. (Shouting) I needed a father and I didn't have one.

Mr. T: I don't know what to say. Did you try to approach me?

David: No, I was too afraid. I don't want to hurt you. I love you (crying).

(They continue in fighting for a short while and then stop.)

Therapist: What were you so afraid of?

David: I thought you wouldn't understand any of my fears.

Mr. T: I might not have then but I will now.

David: I was so afraid of being ridiculed for having large ears. I think you would try to talk to me without asking you a couple of times, you and Mom, you would say it's nothing, you'll grow out of it. I thought, okay that's the way it is. But I was really hurt. Well, tell me how you're feeling now.

Mr. T: Yes, I was wondering. Could we try to look ahead and not back? Is it possible Dave?

David: I think it's possible. I just have to let out this frustration and I really feel bad about letting it out on you but I feel it has to come out. But I do want to look ahead.

Mr. T: I think what I want is a relationship of two adults now. I want to be able to write to you and get letters from you. To telephone and talk to you. This sort of thing and that's why I'm here.

David: Yes, I know. I really appreciate the effort you've made. But I'm afraid if I'm too hard on you you won't be able to take it.

Mr. T: I mean if people are going to throw very personal questions at me very quickly and expect fast answers, that scares me. My personal life as far as you are concerned is wide open. But if someone tonight is going to say go back when you were ten years old and tell me how you felt.

David: And you don't feel it's anybody's business but ours?

Mr. T: That's right, I am a very private guy. I'm too private.

Therapist: How do you mean?

Mr. T: I haven't talked enough with David and Bev for that matter.

Therapist: How did your wife feel about you coming out here?

Mr. T: She was very glad. I asked her how she felt in relation that David had asked for me and not for her. She wanted to come. She felt that I was more important to David, and we talked about this. Because we felt that for the last few years while David wasn't very close to either of us, that he was probably farther away from me than her. So we were delighted when Dave wanted me to come. It was with some trepidation, because you're going into something you don't know anything about.

Dorothy: What do you hope for David in the future?

Mr. T: Well, I hope you can live your own life, a happy one. I hope for you that you can come home sometimes, write home, call home. Live at home if you should ever——

David: Are you disappointed that I didn't go to university?

Mr. T: I certainly was at the beginning when you could have gone first. Understand my point. Here's me, a guy who never got to university because there was no money. Now we've got the money we can educate our kids.

Therapist: So, you had hoped that David would?

Mr. T: Yes, but I don't think we ever pressured you.

David: Well I felt a lot of pressure. A sort of expectation. And I began to test you. This became the most important issue. Whether I could get away with not going to university.

Therapist: Do you want to say anything about how you see things in the future David?

David: Well for the immediate future, I would just like to let things lie for a couple of months or so, and just think about it. I would rather you not expect me to work on our relationship hard and fast with me calling.

Mr. T: No, it's a thing that has to come in stages.

David: (*Comes closer to his father and embraces him.*) This is something I wanted so many times.

Therapist: (*To Mr. T*) Is it something you missed as well?

Mr. T: Yes, I did. I guess this is probably about twenty years since this happened.

David: You used to kiss me goodnight until I was about six or seven and then I felt I didn't want to do it anymore.

Mr. T: You were a boy. Boys were sissy to do that. Even at my age I can remember feeling that way.

David: I felt that way with mom too.

Mr. T: You never knew my father, but he was a very undemonstrative man.

(Both David and his father have tears in their eyes. Several other group members such as Ben, Lyn, Cynthia burst out crying expressing how good it feels to see this and how much they would want their father to do the same. Jerry, a patient, expresses some criticism about the whole thing and says, "I don't believe this is real.")

Diary. Today in the "family night" Dad and I each said things we've held back before. At the end we embraced and expressed our love for each other. I cried freely for the first time in about fifteen years. It felt really good. I told Dad everything I wanted to say to him; I held back nothing. I told him about my LSD trip, about my anger towards him, about things in the past and anger about something he said tonight. I didn't think he could take it, but he did. I felt very happy about it.

Fiftieth day of stay

Diary. Dad came to dinner at my place, with Marsha. We all had a very pleasant evening together. It was much more personal than eating in a restaurant. And we were much more relaxed and at ease than at our first dinner. Later I drove him back into his hotel and said goodby as his plane leaves early in the morning. Today several people in Day House told me they liked my father. I told them that he seemed pleased. I wrote him that people in Day House told me about him and that they liked him.

CONCLUSION

Before treatment, David carried the following unrealistic hypotheses about people in his group schema:

Father Schema. David assumed that men in authority were demanding and expected too much from him, but showed him little attention and easily rejected him if he did not perform satisfactorily to their high expectations. David felt shy in front of men in authority (he could not speak up with his boss) and would usually withdraw from them. David built his father schema mostly out of experiences as he saw his father in a certain period of his life, probably in early adolescence. David could not trace any specific incidents with his father and it seemed that David's feeling that his father had rejected him had been accumulated during a long period of time when David's father experienced difficulty in his job and gave less attention to his family than before.

Mother Schema. David assumed women in authority were demanding and pushed men toward goals they prescribed for them, that women easily rejected him if he did not perform to satisfy their expectations, and that they let him feel a failure. This schema developed during a certain period of David's life with his mother, who probably had high expectations of her son and pushed him into activities and a career. She might even have expected David to fulfill some of her needs such as warmness and empathy that her husband did not satisfy (not during a certain period of life). This all happened at a time when David, for reasons that had not been fully identified, was not able to fulfill all mother's expectations and therefore felt a failure.

Both parents seems to be average people, without any unusual or pathologic personality features. A special combination of inner and outside factors in the family made David develop such an unrealistic role schema of male and female authorities.

Sister Schema. David assumed that women in his peer group, and also women as sex partners, were strong and dangerous, that he must compete with them all the time and try to overpower them. He often tried to put them down with irony and feelings of superiority. This schema developed in David mostly during his experience with his sister, who was three years older. She was a strong, bright girl, doing well at school. She was probably getting more of the parent's attention. We may speculate that the parents had special problems in raising together an adopted and natural child, and out of fear of not loving the adopted daughter as much as their natural son, they might have gone overboard and offered so much attention to their daughter that David felt rejected. His sister schema complicated David's relationship with girlfriends. He was eager to have a girlfriend, but, due to his sister schema, he was rather suspicious and afraid of girls. Therefore, he tended to choose those who were shy, distant, and had problems similar to his, which made it difficult for both of them to achieve a real closeness. Also, David tried to dominate the girl, being ironical and feeling superior. Such relationships were full of tension. David developed premature ejaculation and this reinforced his feeling of being a failure. A vicious circle developed in David's sex problems.

During the treatment, David reexperienced his old problems with his parents and his sister. He also expressed emotions, such as anger, that had been associated with these conflicts in the past. He experienced all of this in the friendly and supportive atmosphere of the patient group, and at the same time he had the opportunity to develop various transference relationships to persons in authority, both male and female, such as the therapists, the chairperson and other members of the committee, older group members, and women in his peer group. This way David was able to master the conflicts he had had with his parents and sister but had not been able to handle in the past. This helped him change his rigid hypotheses about certain people and about his father, mother and sister schemas. His behavior toward other people became more relaxed and more realistic. He developed a satisfactory sex life. His relationship with his father improved into one between two friendly adults.

David's treatment, like all treatment in the Day House, is covered by the health insurance program supported by the Provincial Government of British Columbia and the Federal Government of Canada. In David's case, the hospital received for the initial interview, his six week treatment in the Day House, and three aftercare visits $782.00 from the health insurance program and $37.00 from David himself. Comparatively, one day of treatment in the Day House cost less than a one-hour session with a psychiatrist.

Chapter 10

ELEMENTS OF INTEGRATED PSYCHOTHERAPY IN ESTABLISHED SETTINGS

This chapter describes in detail our experiences in introducing elements of integrated psychotherapy into a rather traditional aftercare clinic in a large North American city.

When we arrived, the clinic had been functioning for more than twelve years. A few months previously it had been joined to the university psychiatric hospital—originally one of the large state hospitals on the outskirts of the city. The head of the university psychiatric hospital planned to consolidate most of the mental health services in certain districts, combining the inpatient unit of the hospital and outpatient facilities of the aftercare clinic. This plan, though never realized, became the object of many discussions and created much tension. It also interfered with the already established mental health services of the city. The director of the aftercare service, as well as most of the staff, resented being placed under the supervision of one of the inpatient unit directors, who had become supervisor of the whole area. Previously the aftercare clinic had operated much more independently.

The aftercare staff were offered a chance to participate in the university hospital's educational seminars. Teachers from the psychiatric department of the university were invited to the aftercare clinic to teach the staff and have them improve their methods. Jirina, a visiting professor at the time, went to work at the aftercare. It was clear from the beginning that the aftercare staff were not interested in being instructed and taught in any kind of formal teaching or experiential workshops. They felt they needed help because they could not cope properly with their heavy caseload. Some of the staff members were unhappy with the routine and thought that the structure and methods of service had to be changed.

There was a typical division of roles between medical and nonmedical staff. Doctors, mostly psychiatrists trained in academic psychiatry, came for several sessions a week, assessed new patients and followed-up old patients with one or three month appointments. The treatment was almost exclusively pharmacological. Doctors with caseloads of several hundred patients felt overburdened. Their schedule was filled with ten or fifteen minute interval appointments and they sometimes saw fifty or more patients a day.

The psychiatrists' work was completely separate from that of the nonmedical staff—social workers and nurses. The same patient might have been referred to the social worker from an outside agency and yet seen by the psychiatrist separately; the two of them never exchanging a word about the same patient. The psychiatrist would discuss symptoms with the patient and prescribe medications, while the social worker carried out the patient's case work, often offering a lot of time, sympathy, and interest. Often, the efforts of various categories of the staff were duplicated and contradictory; one worker jeopardized the efforts of another.

INTRODUCING THE SYSTEM

Jirina intended to introduce certain elements of integrated psychotherapy into the network of services but realized from the beginning that first of all she had to develop a proper relationship with the staff and the patients in that area. To start as a consultant, introducing new methods without offering help in a way that the staff would understand would only have created bad feelings and isolated her from the outset.

At first Jirina offered part of her time to see and assess new patients and to take over the caseload of a colleague who was temporarily absent. She explained her plans to the director, to her colleagues and to the supervisor of the social workers.

Staff relations
Firstly, Jirina tried to develop mutual loyalty in relation to the other doctors. She made it clear she had no intention of interfering with their

work or criticizing them, and she expected the same from them. She did not expect them to be interested in her teaching.

Secondly, she tried to develop a relationship of mutual trust and co-operation with the supervisor of the social workers, Mrs. S, one of the most important people in the aftercare structure. The clinic adhered strictly to the traditional civil service policy, with every category of employees having its own system of supervision. There was very little direct professional contact between the members of various categories.

If, for example, a doctor wanted a social worker to work with him on the same case, he had to discuss it first with the supervisor. The supervisor then appointed a social worker to that particular case. When working on the case with the psychiatrist, the social worker had to report regularly to the supervisor and receive suggestions from her.

It is true that in many mental health departments the atmosphere is more open and friendly between various segments of the staff than the situation here, but the differences may only be superficial. The nurses, social workers, occupational therapists, and psychiatrists may well sit together in long conferences, but usually each service also has separate supervisory meetings where therapeutic plans are discussed, therapeutic results evaluated, and special measures taken without the knowledge of the other services. The final fragmentation of treatment may not differ much from that in the aftercare clinic described in this section.

The supervisor of the aftercare social workers, Mrs. S, was a middle-aged woman who had been working in the field of social work in that particular area of the city for many years. She was experienced and interested in individual case work and was an expert on the complex network of various social agencies and services in the city. She was a very capable, dedicated, hard working woman. She had never been trained in group psychotherapy and displayed a very cautious attitude toward group treatment. It became apparent later that she adopted this attitude mostly because of personal experience with some previous representatives of group therapy at the clinic.

During the first few weeks at the clinic Jirina, on several occasions, explained her therapeutic plans and ideas to Mrs. S. She also invited Mrs. S to work with her directly in the treatment of several new patients where Mrs. S's special professional knowledge and experience became useful. Later, when Jirina began working directly with social workers, crossing staff lines, Mrs. S did not feel threatened and was supportive. The social worker who worked directly with Jirina continued reporting to Mrs S, as supervisor, but Mrs. S did not interfere with any suggestions in cases where psychotherapy was used. On the other hand, Jirina greatly respected Mrs. S's professional and human qualities and benefited from their discussions and from her cooperation. Mrs. S's reactions and the information she was willing to offer were of great help to Jirina in orienting herself in the setting, structure, and culture of the whole area.

Starting as a small team

Jirina began to work with one social worker and one nurse as a team. All new patients assessed by Jirina, and those referred by different channels directly to the social worker or the nurse, were seen and then reported on to the other two therapists. This took place most of the time in the open group which the team of three therapists had started and attended. All new patients were invited to attend the group at least once, the only exception being patients who were unfit to take part in a group.

All three therapists agreed on the therapeutic plan of each patient. The plan was then carried out by the one assigned to the patient. Attending the open group was a part of the plan, either for a short or a long time, but the working team was flexible enough to adopt a variety of other modifications in the treatment. For those patients unable to take part in a group—such as those who were grossly disturbed or had brain syndromes—individual interviews, home visits, or interviews together with their significant persons were arranged. Patients who were considered to benefit from medications, almost exclusively psychotics, had them prescribed by the medical therapist of the team. The staff tried to avoid the traditional approach in which, for instance, patients go to the psychiatrist to have their illness or their brain cured by medication but go to the social worker, or other nonmedical therapist, to get help with their practical problems. The patients in these traditional settings expect, more or less passively, that something will be prescribed or given to them. Very often they will also receive contradictory messages. A depressed housewife whose children are about to leave home may receive a suggestion from the social worker to consider taking a job at the same time the psychiatrist is telling her, "Just be yourself, do not overstress yourself, and keep taking the Tofranil."

The question of medications

The medical therapist would never prescribe medications for the other two therapists' patients without their knowledge and agreement. The staff's attitude toward medication was practical and may be freely formulated as follows:

Clinical and research evidence confirms that medications may be useful in decreasing or relieving some symptoms of mental disturbance. Medications were prescribed particularly if the symptoms hampered persons in realistically perceiving their environment and in making correct judgments about objects and people around them. For example, patients who suffered from visual or auditive hallucinations for a long time might have been unable to pursue goals they wished to achieve, to develop satisfactory interpersonal relations, or to adopt social roles appropriate to their age, sex, mental capacities, and background. Even after symptoms such as hallucinations had been relieved such patients still might have had difficulties like a lack of social skills or a deficiency in their group schema. They could, therefore, benefit from psychotherapy. On the other hand, all symptoms were not treated by medication. Sometimes the patients were asked to tolerate some of their symptoms—such as fear, tension, or depression—in the process of psychotherapy. In a good therapeutic relationship between patient and therapist, a basic trust is expected to develop, and the patient then understands that the therapist has valid reasons for prescribing, or not prescribing, medications.

No general or theoretical discussions concerning medications were encouraged or carried on during the therapeutic sessions, but individual feelings and reactions toward medications were freely discussed, thus forming part of the same psychotherapy as other problems in life. In practice, there were very few attempts to discuss medication in the aftercare group. If new patients in the group began a general discussion in that area, the more experienced members brought the newcomers back to their own reactions to medication by asking them direct personal questions.

There was another reason why the participants of the group did not often discuss medications. In a traditional setting, medical and non-medical aspects are separated; patients complaining of symptoms and medications indicate their need to be seen by the psychiatrist or other medical person in an individual interview. In some places, this is the only way for a patient to be seen individually by a psychiatrist. The general philosophy of such settings traditionally considers individual interviews with the medical therapist as the most valued form of therapy. Thus patients are subtly encouraged to have such complaints. In the aftercare group, the medical therapist's attention was given to patients in or out of the group, but bore no direct relation to their symptoms.

A TYPICAL SESSION

The open group was in session the same afternoon each week for about two hours. Most of the sessions were recorded by the stenographer, a member of the aftercare clinical staff. We present here an original recording of one session together with additional information about the patients present at the session. Surnames were preferred by the patients in this group. Of course, the names have been changed.

Members of the group, present at the recorded session

Mrs. Lowensten. A fifty-five-year-old widow who was referred to the clinic after a short stay in the hospital, Mrs. Lowensten suffered from severe street phobia, never having walked alone on the streets in five years. She had to be accompanied either by her married daughter or by her son-in-law. She was able to drive a car without much fear (occasionally borrowing her son-in-law's car), but not without discomfort. She had been in individual psychotherapy with a private psychiatrist for the past four and a half years. Shortly before her arrival at the clinic she discontinued the treatment due to her lack of finances. At first, her attitude toward the clinic could be characterized as What can you offer me after individual treatment? At the outset of the group she spoke of her symptoms, being rather vague about herself. From the beginning, however, she was interested in others, and was friendly, helpful and always ready to make a comment or a joke. Later, supported by the group she decided to look for a job. She found a suitable job and started working. Her symptoms decreased and finally disappeared completely.

Mr. Weintraub. An elderly man and a chronic patient of the clinic, he had been in the hospital many times with episodes of depression. He lived alone and in the past it had often been difficult for him to keep regular appointments with the doctor. His attendance at the group was punctual, but the majority of the time he sat there quietly. The group was a place for him to belong, to make simple social contact, and relearn some of his social skills. The therapist prescribed his medications. Later he found his way to the Fountain House, a special day center for mental patients.

Mr. Perez. This man, over forty, had been treated many times in the hospital for psychotic episodes. He presented a typical rigidity of thought and used to jump to conclusions on the basis of superficial associations. He lived with his aging parents, and there was constant tension between the three of them. We did not expect any big changes in Mr. Perez's condition. We would have been satisfied to take him out of the complete isolation of his home, relieve his parents, and keep him on regular maintenance medications and out of the hospital as much as possible. Treating Mr. Perez in the group, the therapist always had to keep a proper balance between a tolerant attitude toward him and placing certain limits on his activity. When he would start to talk in cliches, he tended to make long speeches on general matters which were referred to as his preaching.

Mrs. Cohen. A widow and retired teacher, Mrs. Cohen had had several episodes of depression with paranoid features. She suffered from eye trouble and expected to be operated on for cateracts. She was interested in others in the group and liked the group as a place where she belonged. She was especially helpful in discussing various, often unrealistic, plans of other group members concerning their future education. To this subject, she brought a realistic approach and factual information. The group supported her emotionally during the difficult time she waited for her operation. Mrs. Lowensten and other members visited her later when she was in the opthalmologic department.

Mrs. Bagarosa. A fifty-two-year-old, married woman, Mrs. Bagarosa worked as a supervisor in a department store before her hospital treatment. She was brought into the hospital depressed, having attempted suicide with sleeping pills. Her behavior in the hospital was diagnosed as a deep psychotic depression with delusions that her son, who had been reported dead in the Vietnam war ten months earlier, was still alive and had returned home. She was diagnosed, in some reports on her chart, as having a belated mourning reaction. Mrs. Bagarosa lived with her husband, a small businessman who suffered from a heart condition and had to spend long periods of time unemployed. Their only son had lived with them until voluntarily enlisting in the army without his mother's knowledge. He was reported dead after twenty days of service at the front. His death was a great blow to Mrs. Bagarosa. She could hardly believe it and started to daydream and think that it was a mistake and that her son was still alive and would return home in the future. She was easily won over by a fraudulent scheme that operated at that time. A woman approached her and suggested that Mrs. Bagarosa's son might not be dead, but held prisoner by the enemy, and that the woman was a member of a team who could bring him back. Naturally, a substantial amount of money was needed to bribe the authorities and pay for all the expenses. Mrs. Bagarosa withdrew, without her husband's knowledge, most of their mutual savings, and paid it to the imposter. Shortly after it became known that the whole scheme was a large scale fraud, she became ill and attempted suicide.

Mrs. Bagarosa spent several months in the mental hospital, and was later discharged to the aftercare clinic. Her husband was told of his wife's involvement in the affair, and also of the loss of his savings, by the doctor at the hospital. The couple never discussed this openly, as the doctor in the hospital had suggested to Mr. Bagarosa that his wife must not be disturbed by reminding her of the past events.

Returning home from the hospital, Mrs. Bagarosa faced difficult problems. Her relationship with her husband had deteriorated rapidly in the past ten years. Mrs. Bagarosa had invested more and more in her relationship with her son, the son being the closest person to her. She spontaneously remarked at a group session, "What really hurts is that my husband was in the war for four years and *he came back*. My son was only there for seventeen days." Her twenty-two-year-old son's voluntarily enlistment may have been an attempt by him to escape from this close relationship. It was obvious that the husband was full of rage, and he must have felt that his wife's credulous wasting of money was directed against him. But because she was so ill he kept this to himself, and the couple hardly talked to one another for fear of touching on any controversial topics. The atmosphere at home was tense and unhappy. Mrs. Bagarosa still wore black two years after her son's death, and many people around her considered it natural that she had to be sick and depressed because of the loss of her son. It was obvious that Mrs. Bagarosa was in a dilemma, even though she was not aware of it. To be treated as mentally ill, relieved her from facing the problems at home and with her husband. The husband tried to be nice and did not complain. However, being mentally ill also meant a limitation in Mrs. Bagarosa's life style, as well as a substantial limitation of income if she were to stop working indefinitely. To be considered cured, healthy, able to enjoy life, and able to work meant that she must face her husband's rage and the unsolved problems of her marriage. She felt guilty and responsible for her husband, who was partly an invalid, and she did not want to leave him. In spite of the ambivalence of this marital relationship, the other partner was still the closest person for each of them, now that the son was dead.

During the treatment of Mrs. Bagarosa in the group, the strategy was adopted of encouraging and helping her to find some realistic basis in her future life with her husband. Mr. Bagarosa was eventually invited to take part in the group and their mutual problems were for the first time discussed openly. After several months Mrs. Bagarosa recovered completely.

Mr. O'Keefe. A bachelor in his early fifties, Mr. O'Keefe was a heavy drinker who became a patient of the aftercare clinic after a hallucinatory episode several years previous. He also suffered from epileptic seizures and was on antiepileptic medications. He was referred to the group by his psychiatrist, who worked in the aftercare clinic, with the idea that the group might help the patient to regulate his drinking and stay away from the hospital. We did not expect to change Mr. O'Keefe's drinking habits and his personality in that kind of an outpatient setting, and he apparently did not intend to stop drinking or to change his life style significantly. However, he was afraid of his hallucinatory episodes and wanted to be with the clinic. After starting the group he became interested and stayed there for several months, although his attendance was not always punctual.

Mr. O'Keefe had a long work record as a janitor, a member of a building maintenance crew, and was a member of a union. At the time of the group recording the union was on strike and he was temporarily not working. He was a friendly, jovial man who was always ready to make a remark or a joke. He was also able to offer a practical knowledge of many areas of manual work in a big city. His comments were useful to many other members of the group in their reality testing. The group did not moralize about his drinking, but once or twice when he came to the group in an intoxicated state, he was shown out. Although we did not have any high therapeutic expectations of him, we thought it might be useful if he developed some kind of relationship that was different to his superficial barroom friendships. He had much to offer as a member of the group. He was a realistic, hard-working man, free of any psychotic symptoms while he attended the group. He did remember his own episodes of illness and this made him tolerant of others who were sometimes on the verge of psychosis, such as Mr. Perez. In this group, with people of other cultures, he represented a kind of reminder that as Mrs. Lowensten aptly expressed, "You can be a person of proper color and proper accent and still be in trouble."

Mrs. Warwich. Although present at the session, Mrs. Warwich did not speak. Her history will be described in detail later.

Mrs. Ramos. A thirty-three-year-old, married woman, Mrs. Ramos's history will also be described in detail later. Her husband and some of her children were also invited into the group.

Mrs. Simpson. Mrs. Simpson attended the session only once and shortly afterwards returned to the hospital.

In addition to the members present, the group session was also attended by the therapist, Dr. Jirina Knobloch; three observers, Mrs. K, Mrs. A, and Miss E; and by the recorder, Miss B.

The Session

Miss E: We can begin the group. Is it necessary for you to have a leader?

[*Authors' Note*: At first we often started the group by introducing new members. At this session, the group had been going several weeks and a nucleus of members had developed who often started discussion spontaneously and showed mutual interest before the therapist came in. Miss E, a social worker attending the group as observer, unnecessarily felt compelled to start.]

Mrs. Lowensten: The first time I came here, I said I would just sit and observe, and the second time I would talk.

Miss E: Did this happen?

Mrs. Lowensten: No. I didn't want to talk the second time, but Dr. Knobloch began telling me to push my chair in and close up the circle. She got me to the point where I was in the middle of the circle. Then she said "Let's hear about you." I said to myself I had better open my mouth and I did.

Miss E: Did you feel as though you were on the spot?

Mrs. Lowensten: Yes, because I am basically a very shy person.

Mrs. Cohen: I thought you were very outgoing.

Mrs. Lowensten: That's just a cover-up. (*To Mrs. Ramos*) What happened to your husband last week? Is he sick?

Mrs. Ramos: He had to go to the hospital. He had an appointment with the doctor today.

Mrs. Simpson: How is your daughter?

Mrs. Ramos: She's fine.

Mrs. Simpson: Is she home?

Mrs. Ramos: I keep her at a friend's house. My friend said that she would like my daughter to stay and keep her daughter company.

Mrs. Lowensten: I tell you, when you have little children you have little problems. Bigger children, bigger problems.

[*Authors' Note*: Several members, such as Mrs. Lowensten, Mrs. Cohen and Mrs. Simpson showed interest in Mrs. Ramos's family and continued a discussion from the past session in which various problems of Mr. and Mrs. Ramos had been discussed.]

(Dr. Knobloch, the therapist leading the group, enters with Mrs. K.)

Mrs. Lowensten: (*To the therapist*) I was just telling about how you put me on the spot. Do you remember the time you had me move my chair until I was in the middle of the circle?

Therapist: Yes, I remember. How did you feel that time?

Mrs. Lowensten: I felt on the spot.

Mrs. Cohen: Sometimes you have more to say than at other times.

Therapist: That is true. I am interested in what made you nervous at the session two weeks ago.

Mrs. Lowensten: I don't know. It was just a sensation, but I said to myself, you're going to sit here and take it even if it kills you.

Therapist: What?

Mrs. Lowensten: I was talking to myself. Eventually, the feeling passed away. It really puts me up against the wall.

Mrs. Cohen: (*To Mrs. Ramos*) Is your husband coming today?

Mrs. Ramos: He had an appointment with the doctor today.

Mrs. Lowensten: Mrs. Johnson said that your husband was sick last week.

Mrs. Ramos: He had to go to the hospital.

Mrs. Simpson: Does he have to stay in the hospital?

Mrs. Ramos: No. He had an accident about five days before that and had to go to the hospital also. They gave him medication.

Therapist: Your husband brought one of your daughters to the clinic last week.

Mrs. Ramos: Yes, I couldn't come because I had a cut on my leg.

Therapist: How is your family?

Mrs. Ramos: My daughter is leaving on vacation Saturday. My husband went to see the doctor today. Evelyn, the one that ran away, is staying at my friend's house. My friend offered to have her stay there and keep her daughter company.

Therapist: Does she like it there?

Mrs. Ramos: Yes.

Mrs. Lowensten: Is her daughter the one that ran away with your daughter?

Mrs. Ramos: No. This girl's mother won't let her out of the house.

Therapist: The girl that ran away is at your friend's house, but you have other children at home.

Mrs. Ramos: One boy and one girl.

Therapist: Did you talk to your daughter?

Mrs. Ramos: I keep asking her why she ran away. She was showing me around St. Mary's park and we were talking. She wanted to show me some place and I got cut with the glass.

Therapist: She spent time in this park?

Mrs. Ramos: They spent a night there. She did not get to sleep because they were listening to music.

Mr. Perez: Does your daughter belong to the Weathermen?

Mrs. Ramos: What?

Mr. Perez: Is she a hippy? [Mr. Perez's comments are characteristic of his jumping to conclusions and his general rigidity of thinking—all related to his mental problems. During his participation in the group, the other members developed a kind of tolerance toward him. Only if they felt his comments might be too embarrassing for someone, as for example for Mrs. Ramos, did they offer correcting remarks such as those of Mrs. Lowensten.]

Mrs. Lowensten: Hippie is a loose term. Just one thing could be not right and right away the people are hippies.

Mr. Perez: She is a hippie. She likes rock music and goes to the park for the festivals.

Mrs. Ramos: This is the first time she did such a thing.

Mrs. Lowensten: Did she say why?

Mrs. Ramos: She didn't have any right because we did nothing to her.

Mrs. Lowensten: That has nothing to do with it. She made up her mind to run away. She must have had a reason.

Mrs. Ramos: When she was trying to show me the place where she slept, I got cut. I told her that it was her fault because I was so excited.

Mrs. Lowensten: Yes. I once saw a woman at the supermarket. Her little boy was crying and she went to hit him, but he was standing in front of a brick wall, and instead of hitting the boy, she hit the brick wall and broke her finger. You see, they punish us, even if they do not mean to.

Mr. Perez: How come all these hippies talk about peace and they do not want to go and fight the war?

Therapist: See, the preaching is beginning already. [This relates to a discussion from one of the previous sessions. The therapist had to stop Mr. Perez talking. She did it in a friendly but firm way by calling his talk preaching.]

Mr. Perez: The hippies are going to turn this country over to the Commies. They are the people who are making trouble in this country. They burn buildings, take LSD, but they do not want to fight.

Mrs. Lowensten: Would you? If they told you to go fight, would you?

Mr. Perez: Why not? I love this country, but I'm too old to fight.

Mrs. Cohen: If they sent all the old men over to Vietnam, the war would be over tomorrow.

Mr. Perez: Some hippies are nice, but they are going to destroy this country by turning it over to the Commies. They listen to the Communists and destroy buildings.

Therapist: I think you are reading too many newspapers.

Mrs. Cohen: Let me tell you something. I know you are going to think that I am a hippie too, but I do not think there is any real necessity for this war. This society is poorly planned. Some people can have millions of dollars, but the poor people have nothing.

Mr. Perez: The hippies also sell LSD drugs.

Mrs. Cohen: Why do they take these drugs?

Therapist: I am not really interested in political discussion.

Mr. Perez: This country is in bad trouble.

Therapist: How long have you lived in this country: [It became obvious that Mr. Perez's talk was a message; the therapist tried to distinguish from general matters. She was trying, through questioning, to bring Mr. Perez back to talk of himself, to let him describe the situations, events, and people who made him feel unhappy and discriminated against him. It was not possible at that moment to separate fact from fiction in Mr. Perez's talks. Both were important messages saying that he felt unhappy, isolated, and unjustly treated and that he sought attention. The therapist and the whole group were ready to give it to him.]

Mr. Perez: Twenty years.

Therapist: How is it with you now? Tell us something about how you live now.

Mr. Perez: Now, I have been through a lot of discrimination. They always call me a black man.

Therapist: Who?

Mr. Perez: People call me a black Puerto Rican. I do not care what the color of a person is. I once went to a hospital and the lady there—she did not know what she was doing—put down my description as a black man. This is how people make me feel.

Therapist: But why do you say this country is beautiful, if things like that happen?

Mr. Perez: It is the people.

Therapist: Why not speak about your problems, not the country's.

Mr. Perez: I have certain rights as a United States and Puerto Rican citizen. I am entitled to these rights.

Mrs. Bagarosa: Why are we discussing politics? When my son was in the country, he was proud to fight.

Therapist: (*To Mr. Perez*) When was the last time you felt bad?

Mr. Perez: This had happened to me many times. When I worked in the factory, I was called a black Puerto Rican and a spic.

Mr. O'Keefe: This happens all the time. Years ago, if you were Irish, they called you a donkey. I say So what.

Mrs. Lowensten: Things were always like this.

Mr. Perez: That is the problem with the country. We should live in peace.

Miss E: Mrs. Ramos's daughter has run away and spent the night in the park. You called her a hippy and this is upsetting her. [The interesting and typical reaction of an observer who cannot tolerate tension and has to interfere. Miss E was not supposed to make any comments interpreting or reprimanding the group member. Even had she been in the position of a therapist, she should have waited until somebody else (Mrs. Cohen or Mrs. Lowensten) corrected Mr. Perez, or until she had asked for other group members' views first. Miss E's "nursery governess" approach exposed her unnecessarily to Mr. Perez's negative feelings.]

Mr. Perez: But it is true.

Mrs. Lowensten: Maybe she is just a nature lover.

Mrs. Bagarosa: (*To Mrs. Ramos*) Did you find your daughter?

Therapist: Why did your daughter run away from the house? You must be interested to know the reason.

Mrs. Ramos: I do not know. I guess she wants to be free.

Therapist: Free from what?

Mrs. Ramos: From so many people telling her what to do. Free from me.

Therapist: Do you think it is necessary to tell her what to do all the time?

Mrs. Cohen: You aggravate them that way.

Mr. O'Keefe: This happens once they get to be a certain age.

Mr. Perez: I say not all hippies are bad persons. I was a hippie myself once about twenty years ago. I want her daughter to come back to her (*Mrs. Ramos*) and have a happy life. Hippies have a miserable life.

Therapist: How was it with you? Twenty years ago there were no hippies.

Mr. Perez: I was a beatnik. The beatniks drank alcohol. We drank some, but we never used LSD drugs or went to demonstrations. Hippies understood better then. [Mr. Perez started to feel more insecure and tried to get closer to the group, contributing to the discussion in his usual way by mixing reality with fantasy.]

Therapist: What did you do twenty years ago?

Mr. Perez: I was a beatnik. It was much better.

Mr. Bagarosa: How did your parents feel?

Mr. Perez: I never ran away from the house.

Mrs. Bagarosa: What did your parents think of you?

Mr. Perez: I behaved good in my house. I used to be a beatnik. I dropped out of school on account of drugs. They offered me pot and I said no I quit school. I went to work. I had a lot of trouble in school, but it was not me, it was the other kids.

Mrs. Lowensten: "It was not me, it was the other kids."

Therapist: Is it not so?

Mrs. Cohen: They should get the pushers. The ones who make the millions.

Mrs. Bagarosa: I think this war has something to do with it. The big shots have a lot of money invested in it.

Therapist: You are always talking about the war. How will this help us? We asked Mrs. Ramos to tell us things. We are very concerned about her daughter. (*to Mrs. Ramos*) What other things concern you besides your daughter?

Mrs. Ramos: Everything. Sometimes you can not tell.

Therapist: Try. You must have the time. Your husband is not here now. [This was said more or less as a joke. The husband had been there at previous sessions and the group had spent a long time with him and the whole family.]

Mrs. Ramos: I have a headache for three days. I can not sleep.

Mrs. Bagarosa: Maybe you're nervous.

Therapist: You went through a bad time.

Mrs. Ramos: My husband is leaving for Puerto Rico on the thirtieth.

Therapist: He has finally decided to go? What do you expect will happen?

Mrs. Ramos: I do not know. I am afraid.

Therapist: What are you afraid of?

Mrs. Ramos: That he's not going to make out.

Mrs. Lowensten: So he'll come home.

Mrs. Ramos: I can not tell him this because he gets excited.

Mrs. Bagarosa: Holler back.

Mrs. Ramos: I'm afraid. I would rather suffer than get into trouble.

Mrs. Lowensten: It eats you up inside.

Mr. Perez: We don't want women's liberation.

Mrs. Ramos: Everytime I think about him (*Mr. Perez*) when I'm home, I start laughing.

Therapist: (*To Mr. Perez*) Please do not start about it.

Mr. Perez: There is a lot of trouble between men and women.

Therapist: (*To Mr. Ramos*) I am not sure that you can speak openly to your husband.

Mr. O'Keefe: She is afraid.

Therapist: Mr. Ramos does not like to listen?

Mr. O'Keefe: He likes his own way.

Therapist: What are you afraid of? What will he do if things are unsatisfactory?

Mrs. Ramos: He has been there four times and he says the same things. Things just do not seem to work out. Why should they work out this time?

Therapist: Why don't you tell him this?

Mrs. Ramos: I tell him to go to work here and forget about Puerto Rico. If we go we will starve. Right now I have six rooms, I know I am safe. I don't want to go to Puerto Rico and suffer. I do not know how it is going to be. I might suffer. Nobody would blame me if I did not go. Nobody would be with me there.

Mrs. Lowensten: It is a big step.

Mrs. Ramos: He keeps saying things are better there and he will work and get a house, but I tell him that some families have been there a hundred years and things still have not worked out. I am afraid he is not going to succeed.

Mrs. Bagarosa: If he can not get a job here, forget about it.

Therapist: It is not necessary to persuade her.

Mr. O'Keefe: At least you can get a job in a big city. You might not do what you want to, but at least you can work.

Mr. Perez: Do not let your husband boss you. Get it off your chest.

Therapist: Come into the center Mr. Perez. Pretend you are Mr. Ramos. [The therapist picked Mr. Perez for the role of Mrs. Ramos' husband because he was the only man speaking Spanish; she was aware he did not otherwise fit the role. Mrs. Ramos was too vague to choose somebody herself. The idea was that a more spontaneous emotional reaction might enter into the dialogue if it were spoken in the mother language.]

Mr. Perez: (*To Mrs. Ramos*) I think you are a nice lady.

Therapist: I doubt this is the way Mr. Ramos talks to his wife. (*To Mrs. Ramos*) I think you do not speak openly to your husband. Imagine this is your husband. Tell him now what you would like to tell your husband, maybe in your own language. What do you speak at home? Spanish?

Mrs. Ramos: But my husband does not act like that.

Therapist: Yes, but this does not matter now, try to imagine your husband in Mr. Perez's place and talk to him.

Mrs. Ramos: I can not.

Therapist: I think you can.

[After a while, Mrs. Ramos starts talking in Spanish to Mr. Perez. Both sit in the middle on two chairs. Mrs. Ramos starts crying. The discussion continues awhile.]

Therapist: Now, can you repeat your discussion in English just briefly?

Mrs. Ramos: I told him——

Therapist: Please, Mrs. Ramos, talk to him directly. [It is important not to let the person playing a dialogue step from the first person approach. The therapist had to insist on her speaking directly to the other partner in dialogue.]

Mrs. Ramos: (*To Mr. Perez*) I told you may times already, I won't go there, I do not know how it is going to be. I do not want to leave my home. This is my home. This is my home here. I feel safe here. And you always tell me you will find a house there, get a job, send for us. It won't work, I know it.

Therapist: And what does your husband say. Say it also there, I am afraid. Mr. Perez will not be able to answer for your husband.

Mrs. Ramos: He does not answer, he hollers——

Mrs. Lowensten: Who, your husband?

Mrs. Ramos: Yes.

Mrs. Lowensten: Everybody thinks that Mr. Ramos is a quiet, polite man. He is quiet and polite when he is here, but when he is out of here I think he is different.

Mrs. Ramos: He says it is my problem if I do not want to go, it is my fault. I tell him that nobody will blame me.

Mrs. Lowensten: Of course nobody will blame you. He deserted you.

Mr. Perez: Does he ever beat you up?

Mrs. Ramos: I would hit him back.

Mrs. Bagarosa: How do the children feel?

Mrs. Ramos: The children want him to go.

Mr. O'Keefe: He went four times before and nothing happened?

Mrs. Ramos: I feel like he wants to get away from me.

Therapist: Tell him why you think he is going away. (*Mrs. Ramos and Mr. Perez are still sitting in the middle.*)

Mrs. Ramos: You do not love me any more and want to get rid of me.

Therapist: What would your husband say to it.

Mrs. Ramos: He says that this is not true, he says he is only going to make me happy. But I tell him——

Therapist: Tell it directly to him.

Mrs. Ramos: I tell you, you can make me happy here.

Mrs. Bagarosa: Maybe he liked somebody else.

Therapist: Do you think he would do this?

Mrs. Ramos: I do not like to say things like that. He is worried and says he wants to help me.

Mrs. Cohen: She says she has six rooms. I think she should not leave them. I live with other people because I cannot find an apartment on my own. I know somebody who went to Israel and wanted his mother-in-law to come with him, but I told her not to go because she should come back, she would not have a place to live.

Mr. Perez: (*After speaking with Mrs. Ramos in Spanish*) I was just saying that she loves her husband and her husband loves her, so there is nothing to worry about. [One of Mr. Perez's fast conclusions without grounds. The therapist corrected it but for Mrs. Ramos it may have been useful to listen to such a statement, reminding her of some of her unrealistic beliefs about her marriage.]

Therapist: But how do you know that? She is not sure herself whether her husband loves her, so how can you be sure?

Mrs. Ramos: Sometimes people get tired of each other.

Mrs. Lowensten: Take a vote with your whole family and see if they want them to leave.

Mrs. Ramos: The girl that ran away wants him to go. I want my husband to have a good job and to take care of us. He says that if we go to Puerto Rico everything will be all right and the daughters will be married, but what if they do not get married? I do not want to go.

Mrs. Bagarosa: He has no feelings for anybody.

Mr. Perez: I give my support to her. (*After speaking with Mrs. Ramos in Spanish*) She is afraid we will tell her husband next week.

Mrs. Simpson: We would not do that.

Therapist: There is nothing here that we do not know already or that Mr. Ramos would not know. I wanted Mrs. Ramos to tell us things because I feel she must express something. She does not tell her husband things. Do you tell him openly that you will not go there even if he is successful? Did you ever tell him you would be afraid? Instead, you are sick and have symptoms. You have no proper discussion with your husband.

Mrs. Ramos: I talk with him every night.

Mrs. Lowensten: Let him go.

Mrs. Bagarosa: I feel sick. I want to see the doctor. I feel depressed. [Mrs. Bagarosa was seeking attention in her typical way, talking about depression and asking for a doctor. The therapist was not satisfied with her explanation "depression" and tried to go into Mrs. Bagarosa's interpersonal problems.]

Therapist: Tell us why.

Mrs. Bagarosa: I see so much that brings back memories. This time of the year my son was on leave. He said he would come back.

Therapist: There must be some other reason. There must be something else. Something happening right now.

Mrs. Bagarosa: I have not been feeling well. I had a breast operation when I was in the hospital and when the weather is like this it acts up. I cannot leave my room and they said I cannot receive disability. [Mrs. Bagarosa offered another physical symptom as explanation—a probatory surgical operation on the breast, the cancer was not confirmed.]

Therapist: This is a nuisance.

Mrs. Bagarosa: It gets me very upset. Even the sleeping pills do not help.

Therapist: What does your husband think of this. [The therapist leads the discussion to Mrs. Bagarosa's present situation, especially the relationship with her husband.]

Mrs. Bagarosa: He is a help. I felt bad last night and could not sleep, so I watched the news. He spoke to me and said that I should not watch the news because it only upsets me, but I do not know what to do with myself.

Mrs. Cohen: You have financial difficulties now?

Mrs. Bagarosa: I owe a lot of money, but they said I could pay it back whenever I have it. I have to depend on my husband's veteran's pension and social security. I cannot get anything for myself.

Therapist: Can you get disability later on?

Mrs. Bagarosa: Yes.

Mr. Perez: When your son died and they notified you, did they send you any money? Maybe your son is still alive.

Mrs. Bagarosa: Don't say that.

Mr. Perez: I've heard of cases like that.

Mrs. Bagarosa: A woman once told me that my son was alive and she could bring him to me. I gave her $40,000 because I really thought my son was alive. They would not open the casket for me.

Therapist: (*To Mr. Perez*) You always give advice. (*To Mrs. Bagarosa*) I am sorry that you feel so bad.

Mrs. Bagarosa: They say time is a healer, but it only gets worse.

Therapist: You were working before?

Mrs. Bagarosa: I think I should go back to work. I go to my daughter's house. Her children look so like my son.

Therapist: But you are not happy. How is your husband? He was very ill once.

Mrs. Bagarosa: He had a heart condition.

Therapist: You worked hard when he was ill.

Mrs. Bagarosa: Yes. My son worked too after school.

Mrs. Cohen: I lost a brother two years ago and I found that going to the temple helped a lot.

Mrs. Bagarosa: But it is not the same as losing a child.

Mrs. Cohen: His death put me in the hospital. Go to the church and you will find some comfort. You lost your world, but you have to build a new one.

Mrs. Bagarosa: It hurts very much to lose a child. What really hurts is that my husband was in the war for four years and he came back. My son was only there for seventeen days. [This is an interesting statement from the point of view of Mrs. Bagarosa's family relationships.]

Therapist: Were you worried about your husband and if he would come back?

Mrs. Bagarosa: I used to think of my son as a lucky baby. I would never have married again if my husband had died. At least I had something to live for.

Therapist: But now you have your husband. He must feel unhappy because he is unable to help you stop thinking about your son all the time.

Mrs. Cohen: I hope you do not think I am minding your business, but you should do your best for your husband's sake.

Mrs. Bagarosa: I have this terrible habit. We live in a garden apartment and when the children were younger I used to sit by the window and watch them play. Now I still look out the window and whenever I hear a knock on the door I feel that my son is coming back.

Mrs. Cohen: You should go back to the hospital.

Mrs. Bagarosa: I keep going back to the past and what that woman did to me.

Mrs. Ramos: I had a boy that died too. I had another boy that looked just like my boy does now, but he died. He was three months old. He suffocated and they said it was my fault. They said the baby had pneumonia, so I gave him his bottle and laid him down. I went to check on him later and he had suffocated. I went crazy and I have been nervous ever since. Nobody helped me. The family used to say it was my fault because I laid him down. They said I killed him. The doctor said that he died from bronchitis with pneumonia.

Mrs. Lowensten: But that was not your fault.

Mrs. Ramos: I got over it because I had another boy. He will be thirteen this year.

Therapist: Your husband has decided to leave. What do you expect will happen?

Mrs. Ramos: I do not know. I cannot tell.

Therapist: Did he leave you any money.

Mrs. Ramos: He says he is going to work and send me money, but I want proof.

Therapist: You will get some financial help here?

Mrs. Ramos: Yes.

Therapist: You will be partly supported. But you will expect him to send money and are afraid none will come.

Mrs. Ramos: A lot of things to through my mind. I am afraid.

Mrs. K: What are you afraid of?

Mrs. Ramos: That he won't get any house.

Mrs. Lowensten: He has everything here.

Mrs. Ramos: I told him that even if he went with a lot of money it would still be hard. He always said we should live there. He could never save money. I cannot work myself, I wish I could.

Mrs. Bagarosa: Why don't you get a job and let him stay home with the kids and see how hard it is.

Mrs. Ramos: On his vacation he stayed home and helped me. One day I hit him. I was going to hit my daughter for something she did and he got in the way so I hit him instead.

Therapist: He told us that when he wanted you to feel good he made you something to eat. Whenever we asked him how he could make himself happy he mentioned food.

Mrs. Ramos: He also likes photography. That is the kind of work he did, but he got fired because he fainted in the darkroom once.

Therapist: He usually went to Puerto Rico on vacation. Perhaps that is why he likes it so much.

Mrs. Lowensten: It is quite different when you are there on vacation.

Mrs. Ramos: He knows many people who have studios. He has a friend who wrote him and said he could work in his studio in Puerto Rico.

Mrs. Lowensten: You have to let him go.

Mrs. Ramos: If I saw proof that he was doing something, I would go there. But if I go there and we have to come back, I would have lost my apartment. I will go if I know he has something, but I cannot just go like that. I want to be happy.

Therapist: I do not think your husband is happy at home.

Mrs. Ramos: No one is happy.

Therapist: (*To Mr. O'Keefe*) What is new with you?

Mr. O'Keefe: Nothing much. I have not been feeling well for the last couple of days. Indigestion or something.

Therapist: How are you doing financially?

Mr. O'Keefe: Well, the strike is still on, but I am not worried about it. As soon as the strike is over, I'll get a job. I need something to keep me occupied.

Therapist: How is the man you are living with?

Mr. O'Keefe: He is now on vacation. He is up in Yonkers with his niece.

Therapist: Now you can bring your friends to your house and not be surprised by anyone.

Mr. O'Keefe: There is no one to talk to.

Therapist: You can drink as much as you like. Have you been drinking very much?

Mr. O'Keefe: Since last Wednesday. I feel sick. My drinks keep coming up.

Mrs. Lowensten: What a waste of good liquor.

Therapist: (*To Mrs. Simpson*) And you? How are you doing?

Mrs. Simpson: Pretty good. They took me off medication and I got nervous, but I am alright.

Therapist: You feel better?

Mrs. Simpson: Yes.

Therapist: You are planning to go to Fountain House?

Mrs. Simpson: I never heard of Fountain House until the man talked about it last week.

Therapist: I thought you were planning to go to it.

Mrs. Simpson: No. I have a dog. I walk her twice a day.

Therapist: Who took care of the dog while you were in the hospital?

Mrs. Simpson: My son, but he moved away two years ago, so now it is just my dog and me.

Therapist: What is your dog's name?

Mrs. Simpson: Toby.

Therapist: (*To Mrs. Ramos*) Life is difficult for you now.

Mrs. Ramos: Yes, my mother is sick. I have to take her to the hospital. My mother-in-law is jealous of this, I think.

Therapist: Not only do you have the responsibility of the children but your mother and mother-in-law as well.

Mrs. Ramos: I have a sister in California who has written me a letter asking if she could come to New York and stay with me, but I cannot let her come. I have not answered it yet.

Mrs. Lowensten: Tell her you'll be in Puerto Rico.

Mrs. Bagarosa: Could not some other relative take care of your mother?

Mrs. Ramos: There is nobody else. My mother was once in a mental hospital six years ago. She has nobody else but me and she always says this to me. The rest of my family is in California.

Mrs. Bagarosa: You have no enjoyment out of life.

Therapist: You feel you have missed something?

Mrs. Cohen: We all did. If we had to do it all over again we would do different things.

Mrs. Lowensten: No, we would do the same things.

Mrs. Ramos: I would.

Therapist: Well it is three o'clock. I hope you will all come back next Wednesday.

MEMBERS DURING THEIR TREATMENT

Mrs. Ramos and her family

Mrs. Ramos, a rather handsome thirty-three-year-old woman of Puerto Rican origin, had moved to the United States at the age of thirteen. The couple had six children, the eldest being a girl of sixteen. Mrs. Ramos was referred to the clinic from the regional mental hospital where she had been treated for an episode of mental disturbance diagnosed as mania. She recovered quickly in the hospital and was released to after-care. When we had looked into her hospital file and knew more about the whole situation, we came to the conclusion that Mrs. Ramos's episode was probably more an acute hysterical symptom in crisis than a mania.

Mrs. Ramos's stay in the hospital had two important consequences. First, the four weeks spent in the hospital was her first opportunity during her marriage to stay away from home, family, and the responsibility of the household. It was the first time in her life, since early childhood, that someone had cared for her, cooked and served her meals, and expected her to do nothing. She enjoyed it as the first holiday of her married life. She had been pregnant when she married at the age of fifteen and a half. Her mother summoned the father of the child before the court, and he was sentenced at the same time he married the patient. The couple had already wished to marry, but the whole dramatic situation created tension and a feeling of mistrust in their future life. This we realized later during the therapy.

The second important factor was a change in the family balance as Mrs. Ramos shifted from a respectable wife and mother into the position of a sick and irresponsible member of the family. She felt this was true, and it was obvious at the beginning of treatment that her husband also had this attitude.

It was in the group that Mrs. Ramos first experienced that she was not alone and that there were many others, some of whom were very respectable people, who were treated in the mental hospital. The therapist and other members of the staff present in the group expected her to continue in her daily duties as before, even encouraged her to take more responsibility.

As marital and family problems seemed important in Mrs. Ramos's life, especially during the period after her inpatient treatment, the therapist suggested that first Mr. Ramos and later on, if necessary, other members of the family visit the group. Mr. Ramos had been seen once by the therapist, together with his wife, at admission. At that time he had acted as a sensible, healthy husband would, presenting his mentally unbalanced, sick wife. The therapist hoped that this attitude would change more readily in the group than in individual marital therapy and make it possible to go into the real problems of both partners. Mrs. Ramos and the group agreed to the invitation of Mr. Ramos and his further participation in the group.

In the group Mr. Ramos was treated with friendly respect. At first, he tended to talk about his wife's symptoms, her treatment, or the doctors' opinions of his wife's illness. He soon realized, however, that the group was more interested in him as a person, in his work, occupation, money problems, and in the whole family. He was treated as an equal with his wife and with other members of the group. His attitude that he was a healthy husband slowly disappeared without any direct correction and recommendation. At the same time he was treated as a respectable member of the community by other group members—people with different backgrounds but the same problems.

After a while, both of the Ramos's started to talk about other immediate family problems. At first, they talked of their sixteen-year-old daughter who had left home and decided to live with a girlfriend. This was a shock to them, especially to the father.

Mr. Ramos had a typical conflict. He had been raised in the tradition in which a man as the head of the family protected and provided for his wife and children but controlled them in a patriarchal way and expected obedience. However, he could hardly play this role successfully in a poor neighborhood in a big American city. First of all he could hardly be a good provider since he had no qualifications and earned very little in the small laboratory of a friend who owned a photographic shop. He had been out of work in the past, at which time the family had lived on welfare. The eldest daughter, who dropped out of school before finishing the twelfth grade, worked as a waitress and sometimes earned more than her father did. Twice in the past ten years, Mrs. Ramos had returned to Puerto Rico for several months, expecting to find a job and an easier life there. Not succeeding, he had returned home even more tired and depressed than before. His wife was more realistic about his dreams of "the sunny country where you can always find something to eat or grow your own vegetables and oranges." Mr. Ramos tried unsuccessfully to exert his authority over his growing family. He was very strict in his control; for instance, the girls had to be home at seven o'clock at night. He also controlled the household finances, doing all the shopping, even grocery shopping, so that Mrs. Ramos never had any substantial amount of money in her hands. When Mr. Ramos was in Puerto Rico, the eldest daughter took care of the money.

Mr. Ramos received various reactions from other members of the group—criticism as well as emotional support. Another man recalled his own troubles in looking for a job and difficulty with money; no one criticized him for not making more money. Many other members of the group did not agree with his authoritative, patriarchal attitudes toward his family.

The daughter was also invited to the group, during which time she told them of her plans. She made a good impression on the group, presenting herself as an intelligent and sensible girl. In the discussions, it became clear that moving out from the family home was nothing exceptional for many young girls. Mr. Ramos's main concern was that his daughter would get involved with men and become a disgrace to the family by having an illegitimate child. At first, Mr. Ramos did not openly admit what he meant by disgrace, but the matter was soon clarified by the experienced Mrs. Lowensten who blandly formulated it and he agreed. The Ramos' daughter had a boyfriend, but this did not seem the most important reason for her moving out of the home. The Ramos's had heard in the group about other families having teenage children who had boyfriends and girlfriends with no immediate consequence of pregnancy. We did not go into this matter any further, knowing that it would be hard for the Ramos's to tolerate any kind of discussion about contraception. However, after the group, we were quite happy when the daughter became involved in a friendly talk with one of our social workers about contraception and accepted a referral to the family planning clinic.

Although the daughter was a sensible girl, we did meet her at a crucial moment when she had already started to rebel against the strict family structure, especially against her father. During the past two months, she had left home twice for several days, spending the time at her girlfriend's place and allowing her father to call the police to look for her. Acting out of this rebellion, she could easily hurt her father the most. We have seen, in many similar cases, girls who get involved with men and become pregnant, even though they are not especially interested in sex. Although the reward they would get for hurting their parents might be the most important goal for them at the time, it would cut them off from other goals in their young lives.

The group helped, in part, to relieve the tension between the parents and the daughter. Although Mr. Ramos never agreed to his daughter's action, he became less firm in his ideas about family discipline and family life in general and became less of an authoritarian. The daughter did not return home, but no longer rebelled against her father, feeling more pity for him than hate. The reward for rebellion had lost most of its value for her. She was able to invest her effort and energy into other matters, such as planning to obtain a better job, and finishing her schooling by attending evening classes.

Mrs. Ramos, the original patient in the group, went through several steps during her therapeutic experience. First, she realized she was not alone, she was not indefinitely labelled sick, and she was able to return to her daily life. Then, the real marital and family problems came to the surface. During the treatment we were able to reconstruct the situation leading to Mrs. Romas' admission into the hospital. The family had had financial troubles. Mr. Ramos earned less and less and also complained that the atmosphere in the laboratory was full of chemicals and that he could tolerate it no longer. He decided once again to return to Puerto Rico, renewing his fantasies about a sunny, happy country. Mrs. Ramos was unhappy about this decision. She was more realistic about the life in her native country than was her husband, and was in contact with many of her countrymen who had already come from there.

At the same time, the daughter had started to rebel against her father and left home. Mr. Ramos thought his wife was partly responsible for the girl's actions and complained that she sided with the girl and did not help him to handle their daughter properly. This was partly true, as Mrs. Ramos sympathized with the girl and considered her husband's attitude inappropriate in the contemporary situation.

One evening, her husband told her that he had finally decided to return to Puerto Rico and started to make plans about how, in a short time, he would earn enough money to build a house and then send for the whole family. She started to shout at him. She also threw china at him and finally locked herself in one room of their apartment and cried, not letting anyone in for several hours. Her husband called the police, and Mrs. Ramos was brought into the hospital. She became composed after two days in hospital and also recovered from the influence of a heavy dose of tranquilizers she had received on admission.

Mrs. Ramos had been raised in the same tradition as her husband. She expected the husband to be the head of the family, to be the authority, and she was ready to obey and please him. She expected the husband to be a good provider, to support the family, and to successfully handle family matters, including disciplining the children. She was willing to give up the freedom that other women in other cultures had for the security of a well ordered and well provided family. However, such was not the case. Mr. Ramos could hardly be a good provider under the circumstances. He could not protect his wife and family from troubles and worries. At the same time, both partners adhered to an old schema of family structure. Mrs. Ramos became scared as to what would happen if her husband left. She was not encouraged to become more active or to gain more confidence. She did not even shop for groceries, as this was her husband's task, and he was insistent upon it because controlling the household gave him a feeling of confidence.

The eldest daughter, who had been a support to the mother, had left for Puerto Rico several months earlier, and her second daughter was now leaving too. Mrs. Ramos was caught in the middle. She could not draw any feeling of security from her traditional feminine role, and she was not prepared to take responsibility in the role of a more active, independent woman. In fact she did not know many simple things, such as how to shop, how to open a savings account, how to complete simple forms, even though she was an intelligent woman. This was partially due to the fact that she felt her husband did not approve of women doing such things.

During the treatment, the relationship of the marital couple changed.

At first, Mrs. Ramos was encouraged by the friendly, supportive atmosphere of the group and expressed some of her complaints not only about life, circumstances, and illness in general, but about some of the particular attitudes and actions of her husband. This began when he was not present at the group; she was asked to have an open dialogue with another member of the group playing the part of her husband. Later she criticized her husband directly. The therapist tried to maintain a balance between the criticism the husband received from the wife and the emotional support he was receiving from the group, in order to keep him sufficiently motivated to attend the group. For example, when his wife was very direct and strong in her justified criticism, the therapist asked and encouraged other members' comments, picking those who might be expected to feel empathy and special understanding of the husband's problems.

The freedom to criticize and express anger at her husband was a necessary, but not a final, step in Mrs. Ramos's treatment. To throw words and gestures of anger on her husband at the therapeutic session was far better than throwing china at home and was more useful for Mrs. Ramos. The final goal concerning the marital relationship was to enable the couple to understand each other better and to come to some workable solution about their future relationship. The therapist and the group had no preconceived ideas as to what the final solution had to be; whether it would be a closer relationship or a separation. Let us summarize the effect of the open outpatient group on Mrs. Ramos and her family.

   The group helped Mrs. Ramos and her husband to cope with the immediate consequences of her hospitalization in the mental hospital.

   The group treatment prevented a typical vicious circle from developing: family crisis, development of hysterical symptoms in Mrs. Ramos, action under the influence of symptoms leading to hospitalization. The stay in the hospital was a relief to her—getting away from family problems for a while, receiving more attention from her husband and others. Returning home, she would play the role of a sick, partially irresponsible wife and therefore would become less able to cope with the original family problems, and would easily be prone to new symptoms. This might have easily led to further hospitalization. Once a person has been hospitalized and a file started with a diagnosis of mental illness, a person is easily hospitalized again.

   The group treatment helped to change the relationship of the marital partners. Mrs. Ramos was encouraged to act more realistically in the complex family situation and both partners became better able to solve their problems.

Mrs. Warwich: the little depressed lady

Mrs. Warwich, a sixty-three-year-old, frail looking widow, who lived on a small pension, came to the group after one of her many depressive episodes. For the past ten years, she had lived alone in a small apartment in an old house which belonged to her distant relatives. The rest of the house was constantly rented, mostly to transients. The neighborhood of her home had changed a great deal in these ten years, which is usual in large American cities. All the friends and neighbours she had been associated with in the past had moved long ago, and Mrs. Warwich had no ties with the new inhabitants, considering them strange and often mistrusting them. She lived an isolated life. She bought her groceries in a big supermarket close by, with automatized, impersonal service and hardly exchanged a word with anyone for weeks. Her only contact with the aftercare clinic was a formal appointment every two or three months with one of the doctors, often a different one, who prescribed her medications—most of which were antidepressants. Some of the doctors tried talking to her, showing their interest, but she remained monosyllabic and they finally found her uncooperative and resistant and put this into her file. She probably viewed them as strange and inquisitive and mistrusted them. Sometimes she skipped her appointment, stayed at home for several weeks, neglected and starved herself, and had to be transferred to the psychiatric hospital.

Mrs. Warwich attended the group punctually for several months. She sat quietly, hardly speaking a word unless she was questioned. When she did make some of her rare comments, it was obvious that she followed and understood what was going on. Watching the expression on her face seemed to reveal that she was often interested and even enjoyed listening to others. Generally, she presented herself as shy, polite, and rather timid, and we did not push her into any more active participation. After she had attended three months, the group was canceled for one week. (There were too many bomb scares then, and we canceled all afternoon activities for several days.) The following week Mrs. Warwich spontaneously said something about how strange she had felt the previous Wednesday, staying at home after lunch and not going to the group. The group was slowly becoming a part of her life. It had been many years since her husband had died and all the people she was close to had disappeared. Thus the group had become the place where she wanted to go, where she was willing to accept the interest of others without too much mistrust, and it became the place where, to a certain degree, she belonged. She expressed it as so, and we considered this an important step in her treatment. Before summarizing the therapeutic goals we expected Mrs. Warwich to achieve, let us first take a look at her case.

Mrs. Warwich was one of those chronic patients typical of the majority of the caseload of an aftercare clinic. She had been diagnosed as melancholic, or melancholic depressive—her episodes of acute illness always having been of psychotic character, often with paranoid features. She was reported as responding positively on medications, especially on antidepressants. We had no other information or grounds to change her diagnosis or make substantial changes in her pharmacologic treatment. Mrs. Warwich belonged to the type of patient who come for medication only, are ambivalent in taking it, and have no other relationships other than to the clinic. They resent being pushed into such activities as occupational therapy or bus excursions by young, active members of the staff and dislike being objects of their enthusiasm and charity. The majority of the staff consider them uninteresting patients, unpleasant, ungrateful, not motivated for any type of psychotherapy, and resistant. In seeing these patients, the doctors often try to do something beyond merely prescribing medications. Many doctors resent their role as machines for prescriptions in that type of clinic and try to involve patients in conversation, activities, and outside interests, but it does not work. The doctor's office and the individual interview does not seem to offer enough stimulation to change the old, well-trained pattern in those patients. This pattern follows the well known schema—coming into the office for a specific appointment, talking a little about symptoms, and getting a prescription for the next two or three months.

First of all, we wanted to break the stereotype of Mrs. Warwich's contact with the aftercare. It was arranged that she would have medications prescribed by the therapist leading the group, but after every third group session. In that way, she could discuss any problems she may have had with the medication. The group session was a good opportunity to observe her from the point of view of side effects, or other signs related to the medications. We also asked her to watch her supply of pills and report if she needed a refill. We did not rely on her and were ready to remind her if she did not mention it herself. After three months, she started to ask for medications quite regularly.

Second, we wanted Mrs. Warwich to come out of her seclusion and develop some ties to the outside world—first to the group, but this was only the initial step. The idea was to expose her to experience, in the supportive atmosphere of the group, which would increase her interest and trust in other people and encourage her to develop mutual interests with them. We expected that association with some group of outside people would expose her further to natural experiences; everyone needs to retain, or improve, their social skills and prevent them from deteriorating. The simple act of living in seclusion as long as Mrs. Warwich had might lead anyone's social skills to deteriorate.

Mrs. Warwich eventually found her way back to church (she had previously been a member) and took part in social activities there. This had been suggested to her many times previous to the group treatment, but it had not worked, as it does not work with many similar chronic patients, or otherwise emotionally disturbed people—those who need a special therapeutic experience before they can follow beneficial suggestions and arrangements. The group may offer a special kind of stimulation to recollect and rehabilitate an old skill. Let us mention an episode with Mrs. Warwich.

One afternoon Mrs. Ramos, another member of the group, began to complain about her sewing machine. Mrs. Ramos had always wanted a sewing machine, but the family could not afford to buy a new one. Finally, her husband bought her an old model from the thrift shop. The machine worked but Mrs. Ramos found it hard to manage. When Mrs. Ramos was describing the machine and the trouble she was having with it, the therapist saw an expression of interest on Mrs. Warwich's face and asked her what she thought about it. Mrs. Warwich explained in her slow, hesitant way that she remembered how she had had the same type of sewing machine from her husband shortly after they were married, forty years ago, and how happy she had been about it. "It was a good, up-to-date model then," she added, smiling.

The old sewing machine helped to develop a type of relationship between Mrs. Warwich and Mrs. Ramos, people who were otherwise very distant from the standpoint of age, background, and culture. One day, Mrs. Lowensten, the only person in the group to drive a car, offered to take Mrs. Warwich to Mrs. Ramos's house to have a look at the machine. As reported later, all three ladies enjoyed a technical conversation about the advantages and disadvantages of the sewing machine and had coffee in the Ramos's living room.

FINAL COMMENTS ON THE PROJECT

Using methods of integrated psychotherapy in traditional settings may be helpful in the following respects:

In overcoming the fragmentation of approaches and services in a particular department

In helping the staff, as well as the patients, to give up the medical model of mental disturbance and move toward an understanding of the person within the network of his interpersonal relations as a social being

In making it possible for the therapist and his working team to develop, on a small scale, more efficient patient treatment and gain more satisfaction from their work, much more quickly than any substantial changes in departmental structure could be achieved

In starting the project, Dr. Jirina Knobloch was aware from the beginning of its limitations. She arrived at the aftercare as a consultant with no real power to change anything in the structure and methods of work. The fact that she was recommended by the head of the psychiatric department who supervised the aftercare was rather a disadvantage in the eyes of the aftercare staff. She was able to proceed in the project only after she developed a good personal relationship with the director of the aftercare and with the supervisor of the social workers and after having instituted a relation of respect and nonintervention with the other psychiatrists.

The team worked with a heterogeneous population of patients. The patients enrolled in the group also differed in their capacity to understand what was going on and to observe the group norms. Only some of them were able to fully utilize the methods used. We would have preferred to form two heterogeneous groups, each with different therapeutic goals and norms, and each using different therapeutic tactics, but the circumstances did not allow it.

The aftercare functioned only for patients discharged from the mental hospital. Only later were patients who were referred directly from the community admitted. The team working on the project invested additional effort in keeping the project going despite various obstacles typical of the contemporary mental health scene. Let us mention some of them.

Despite the generally positive attitude of the staff, they nevertheless

easily interfered with the treatment of the project patients. The following episode with Mrs. Ramos represents a typical example.

Once, in the middle of her treatment, Mrs. Ramos walked out at
the end of the session still in tears and obviously anxious, but more
active than ever before and in the right mood to try to be more active
in her life. She decided to apply for a part-time job, and the other
group members gave her some good tips about this. Her husband
was away at the time visiting his relatives in another part of the state.
The following week, the group, with great interest, asked Mrs.
Ramos to tell how she was doing in her new job. Mrs. Ramos, who
had come late to the session, which was unusual, and looked tired
and sleepy, was rather hesitant at first. She then explained that she
had postponed going to work as she realized that she still felt too ill
and weak to do anything but her housework. She said she did not
know why she felt so sick; nothing unusual had happened to her.
It took some time before the group got the whole story from her
and the therapist realized what had happened to Mrs. Ramos. Leaving the session the week before, she had met a friendly social worker,
Mrs. M, whom she had known in the past. Mrs. M invited Mrs. Ramos
to her office for a cup of coffee and a friendly chat. This social worker
was interested in Mrs. Ramos's life and her present problems and
gave her some advice as to how to solve them. Seeing Mrs. Ramos'
red eyes and finding her excitement unusual, the social worker suggested that Mrs. Ramos take something to calm her down. And in
her quick and efficient manner, Mrs. M obtained a prescription for
Valium from the psychiatrist in the next office and had the aftercare
pharmacy fill it. Mrs. Ramos took the pills without a moment's thought;
she had been used to accepting social workers as authorities since
early childhood. As the Valium took effect, Mrs. Ramos felt relief
from immediate tension and anxiety for a while but was still not
strong enough to look for work.
Mrs. Ramos did not realize at first that the whole episode had any
significance. In the past, it had often happened that a friendly social
worker had offered her a cup of coffee mixed with various forms of
advice. Neither did Mrs. M, the social worker, consider the episode
important. She did not see anything wrong in her friendly attention
to Mrs. Ramos. She even recommended that Mrs. Ramos attend the
group industriously. It took several diplomatic talks with the project
staff, over lunch, to make the staff members realize the significance
of such actions.

Let us use Mrs. Ramos's case to consider a typical unfavorable feature of the contemporary situation in mental health care. In the two weeks prior to the episode mentioned, there were various forces working in Mrs. Ramos's mind, each influencing her actions in varying directions. There was a wish to change her life and her role at home to a more active one, with less dependence on her husband, who was not able to fully support her. These forces were moving her toward making a decision about various domestic and family tasks and about looking for a job. On the other hand, there were forces moving her in the opposite direction: fear of unknown situations; a temporary disagreement with her husband, who was adjusting rather slowly to her increasing activity even though he accepted it eventually; and also the recollection of pleasant feelings when she was hospitalized and everybody, including her husband, had cared for her, plus other rewards for being an ill and irresponsible wife who did not have to worry about the children. There was a precarious balance between all these forces, and the day Mrs. Ramos left the session, before meeting Mrs. M, the balance was probably tipping toward constructive action.

Events such as the episode described happen all the time in the contemporary mental health scene. Often patients undergoing psychotherapy are just at a point similar to that in Mrs. Ramos's case when they get impulses from different sources. Other psychiatrists, social workers, nurses, reward them and direct them in opposite directions. The final outcome often is, as is common in physics, the cessation of movement. For the patients this means a reversal back to the passivity of the illness.

Let us assume a similar situation occurs with a patient having a heart condition. Any time this patient meets a doctor, a nurse, or a medical assistant, they prescribe medication, X-rays and exercises, and disregard what the patient has already been taking and doing as prescribed to him by those doctors and health workers he has met before. Such a patient would die within a few days of an overdose or from the imcompatibility of various therapies. Patients treated with psychotherapy usually do not die so easily, although they may sometimes commit suicide.

The patients in a systematic psychotherapy such as the therapeutic community must be treated by the same team and should not be seen by outside therapists during the course of their treatment in order to avoid interference in the balance of rewards and costs.

Let us now imagine what would happen with some of the patients treated in the project if they had an opportunity to be treated in a fully developed system of integrated psychotherapy. Mrs. Lowensten and Mrs. Ramos would probably be treated in the residential therapeutic community (step 3), after having attended two or three sessions in the open group (step 2). They would then go as far as step 5 (the aftercare of the system). Mr. Ramos would be invited to cooperate in steps 4a and b. The therapist in charge of Mrs. Ramos would probably see her with the whole family in one or two sessions after she left the therapeutic community. This may have been what both patients needed. The entire duration of treatment might be fourteen to fifteen weeks. Mrs. Bagarosa would probably benefit most from the treatment in the Day Center for about three to four weeks, in addition attending a couple of sessions in the fourth step along with her husband.

Most of the other patients in the group and the majority of the aftercare patients would have benefited most from attending sheltered workshops and having supportive group meetings once or twice a month. Such meetings could be informal, for example, a picnic or a hiking trip.

Appendix A

PHILOSOPHICAL BACKGROUND

Many interested in integrated psychotherapy may not be concerned about its philosophical background, yet without it, integrated psychotherapy cannot be fully understood. Integrated Psychotherapy as a program of unification took its inspiration from a much broader attempt to unify knowledge: the program of unified science represented by the great philosophers of this century, Moritz Schlick and Rudolph Carnap, and by the many other contributors to that monumental work, the International Encyclopedia of Unified Science, Neurath, Frank, Morris, Russell, Bohr, Dewey, Brunswik, among others.

Progress in any field of science is dependent not only upon the discovery of new facts, but also on the systematization of knowledge. In the field of psychotherapy, such systematization is impeded by the fragmentation of psychotherapeutic schools and behavioral sciences, each developing its separate language. This fragmentation is caused by their separate historical developments; it also has deep philosophical roots in the traditional mind-body split, anchored in language and fixed by persuasive visual metaphors.

In psychotherapy, the concepts have been growing like trees in a wilderness. Overlapping and frequently vague, they form illusory dichotomies and divide people with similar views and identical practice.

For example, the philosophical difference between psychodynamic and behavioral schools seems to many irreconcilable (Franks 1974), yet conceptual analysis points in our opinion to their unification. No progress in this unification can be achieved without first clearing away some of the confusion by means of conceptual analysis.

The general idea of the unity of science was admirably expressed by Freud (1933):

> The *Weltanschauung* of science . . . assumes the *uniformity* of the explanation of the universe; but it does so only as a programme, the fulfilment of which is relegated to the future. . . .
>
> It asserts that there are no sources of knowledge of the universe other than the intellectual working-over of carefully scrutinized observations—in other words, what we call research—and alongside of it no knowledge derived from revelation, intuition or divination. It seems as though this view came very near to being generally recognized in the course of the last few centuries that have passed; and it has been left to *our* century to discover the presumptuous objection that a *Weltanschauung* like this is alike paltry and cheerless, that it overlooks the claims of human intellect and the needs of the human mind.
>
> This objection cannot be too energetically repudiated. It is quite without a basis, since the intellect and the mind are objects for scientific research in exactly the same way as any non-human things. Psychoanalysis has a special right to speak for the scientific *Weltanschauung* at this point, since it cannot be reproached with having neglected what is mental in the picture of the universe. Its contribution to science lies precisely in having extended research to the mental field. . . . If, however, the investigation of the intellectual and emotional functions of men (and of animals) is included in science, then it will be seen that nothing is altered in the attitude of science as a whole, that no new sources of knowledge or methods of research have come into being. Intuition and divination would be such, if they existed; but they may safely be reckoned as illusions, the fulfilments of wishful impulses. It is easy to see, too, that these demands upon a *Weltanschauung* are only based on emotion. Science takes notice of the fact that the human mind produces these demands and is ready to examine their sources; but it has not the slightest reason to regard them as justified. On the contrary it sees this as a warning carefully to separate from knowledge everything that is illusion and an outcome of emotional demands like these.

Since Freud wrote these words, behavioral sciences and neurophysiology made considerable progress, and yet very little progress seems to have been achieved in the scientific attitude and thinking of the average psychotherapist. Surprisingly, there is a widespread mood among many psychotherapists who explicitly deny the importance of scientific knowledge, sometimes even introducing an artificial dichotomy between humanism and science. We will not deal with different varieties of openly anti-scientific and irrational views so common in North America. We will rather draw attention to those who do not deny the importance of science, but who limit it in such a way that it interferes in our opinion with the progress of psychotherapy. We will quote only those who themselves in one way or another made scientific contributions to psychiatry—otherwise their choice is random and their widespread views represent opinions rather well. Harry Guntrip, a psychoanalyst, says:

> There is clearly a growing call for a nondeterministic, non-Positivistic, teleological theory, what C. Taylor called a "psychological psychology." . . . In particular, prediction and validation as found in the physical sciences are not relevant to psychic reality. (1973).

Here Guntrip strips psychology of its basic scientific attributes. Since what is the purpose of any empirical science? It is to *know* in order to *predict*; to predict in order to *decide*; to decide in order to *control*. If the statements cannot be validated and psychology does not contribute to causal explanation, it is difficult to see what it has to do with science.

More cautious, but similar is the view expressed by Robert Holt who contrasts deterministic and humanistic point of view in Freud's work. He concludes:

> In many details, the mechanistic image is sharply antithetical to the humanistic one. . . . The mechanistic image of man is most familiar to all of us, of course, in the various transformations of behaviorism or behavior theory. Even in its modern guises, S-R theory is antihumanistic, seeking always to view man as a machine. (1972).

We agree with Holt that Freud's physical models of personality are grossly inadequate, but that is not the point which Holt wishes to make. He contrasts humanistic and causal explanations of human behavior (which he calls deterministic, mechanistic, machine-like, and which makes free will, according to him, an illusion).

Both authors quoted differentiate psychology from other sciences because of their philosophical position of vitalism. This does not seem to be the case with Elliot Slater who nonetheless sees insurmountable barriers for scientific psychology:

The scientific method can only concern itself with the real world, the world outside us, which we can to some extent study objectively. There is also the world within us, forever the domain of subjectivity, forever beyond the reach of science, the territory of the arts and humanities. . . . Despite its inaccessibility to science, it yet contains the possibility of greater understanding. This is a world the psychiatrist cannot ignore and in which the psychoanalyst seeks his understanding. (1972).

Since Slater does not see the possibility of interindividual confirmation of self-observational statements, he consequently denies the scientific status of observations of the "inner world". As we shall see, the position of the unified science (physicalism, methodological behaviorism) is sharply different.

TWO THESES OF UNIFIED SCIENCE

The first thesis of the unified science is the thesis of unified language. This does not require that all terms of different sciences can be mutually translated. It is sufficient that there is a common basis of terms to which all terms of all the sciences are tied. Such basis is observational language of every day with its simple terms describing objects and properties (hot, blue, large, small). It can be shown that all concepts of sciences such as physics, chemistry or biology have a direct or indirect connection with these observational terms. It is true that the theoretical terms cannot be derived by means of operational definitions from observational terms, as it was believed in the past (P. W. Bridgman, R. Carnap) and as some psychologists still believe today. It is sufficient that the theoretical terms appear in general statements which together with other statements lead to predictions in observational terms and these predictions can be interindividually confirmed. We can ask about any statement, whether an observational statement or general law: How would the world look if the statement is true, or if it was not? What observations can contribute to its confirmation, either positively or negatively? If there is no way that the statement could be confirmed in principle, the statement is meaningless, it is a pseudostatement. It still may have an emotional, prescriptive or appraisive meaning, but it does not contribute to our knowledge. Pseudostatements mislead us sometimes, so that we regard them as statements. Pseudostatements have an important role in the history of philosophy and form the bulk of metaphysics (Carnap, 1959). There is little disagreement that simple observational language is all we need as confirmation basis for the sciences mentioned. We will postpone the argument that this is possible for psychology also. A corollary to this thesis is the assertion of the unity of the scientific method. In any branch of science, inductive and hypothetico-deductive methods are the same, despite the variety of special scientific techniques.

The second thesis of unified science states that all laws of empirical sciences can be deduced as theorems from physical laws as postulates. Both theses—and particularly the second one—go far beyond our present knowledge and have to be understood as heuristic programs. Though not clearly formulated, they were leading ideas in the development of the sciences and were extremely successful. Fields of science which seemed completely disparate—such as mechanics, theory of magnetism, light, heat, electricity, chemistry—were unified. Despite strong emotional resistance, successively more and more processes in organisms have been explained in terms of physics and chemistry. The version of unified science in the past—for example, in its primitive form as mechanistic materialism of the eighteenth century—created the vision of the world as a coherent causal network with people as parts of that network. The modern version of the unified science is also called physicalism (or, if applied to psychology, methodological behaviorism).

PSYCHOLOGY IN UNIFIED SCIENCE

There are three possible sources of psychological knowledge about a subject: *statements about behavior, self-report statements,* and *physiological statements*. There will be perhaps little disagreement that behavioral and physiological statements are interindividually confirmable in the same way as statements in the physical sciences—that is, that the basic language of confirmation is the everyday observational language, describing objects and properties. The trouble starts with the self-report statements. If there would be no way of interindividual confirmation of these statements, they would have to be excluded from science, as Slater suggests. This was the position of radical behaviorists, such as John B. Watson, and in a less clear way, B. F. Skinner.

We shall start with the self-report terms. Can they be tied to the terms of the interindividual observational language? They must be, in some way, otherwise there could not be self-report terms in common language, that is, language understood by different people. Take, for example, how a child learns a self-report concept such as being tired, angry, or sad. The parents take the child for a long journey and on the way home the child displays certain behavior symptoms—moves sluggishly, has a limp body, whimpers, or wants to be carried. From the child's behavior and from the parents' own experience of being tired, they say, "Now you are tired." In this way, the child learns to say in similar situations, "I am tired." The child designates the same state of its organism as the parents do, yet their experience is quite different. The child *feels* tired and the parents *observe* his behavioral patterns. But the parents do not *identify* the behavioral patterns with the state of being tired as some behaviorists do (note 7). They regard these behavioral patterns as *symptoms* of the state of the child's organism.

It may be objected that the child's experience of being tired is different from that of the parents observing the child. That is true, but it is not necessary that people must have the same experience in order to designate the same things correctly. To use an example of an astronaut, in principle I do not need to go to the moon and have his experience to confirm his observations. I can see pictures of the moon's surface or take some measurements. Or to give another example, a color-blind physicist never sees the color red as other people do, yet he knows what "red" means. By means of instruments, he recognizes when a substance turns red, and he can explain it better than we can. How can we confirm that he really knows what "red" is? The crucial experiment is that he, with whatever tools he uses, reports "red" when and only when we see that substance turn red. Here we point to the important distinction between *experience* and *cognition* or *knowledge*. This distinction, when neglected, leads to serious misunderstandings. The color-blind physicist has, no doubt, a different experience when seeing the color red than most other people have, yet in the sense that is most important for science, "red" has the same designative meaning for him as for all others. It may have a different emotional meaning, but that is irrelevant here. And what is so striking here is true about other concepts in interindividual language: people may perceive things differently, connect different emotions with different concepts, yet they understand each other, they designate the same things with the same terms, and it can be confirmed that they do. Without efficient interindividual language, the tremendous development of science and technology would have been impossible.

In a manner similar to that of the color-blind physicist, the parents of the child are "color-blind" to his being tired, that is, they do not experience his being tired and yet they can say in most cases by observing his behavior and knowing the situation, when the child is tired. Sometimes, they may be wrong, and at other times the child may claim to be tired when it wants to avoid an unpleasant task. Behaviorists were right in that self-report is especially unreliable; but it is not useless. Comparing the report of the child with its behavior and the whole situation, the parents may come to the conclusion that the child is only pretending to be tired. Psychoanalysis, by showing the unreliability of certain parts of self-report, unwittingly paved the way for behaviorism.

We conclude that such elementary terms of self-report (psychological or phenomenal or introspective) such as tired and angry, can be reduced to the observational language which designates simple physical events in everyday life and which is the common observational basis of all science.

There cannot be any useful term introduced into interindividual psychological language which does not have, in principle, behavioral and situational characteristics. That does not mean that these characteristics have to be present all the time. You can sometimes feel tired, angry, or sad, and nobody notices it. Such terms as being tired, sad, or angry also cannot be *defined* in behavioral terms, but they can be sufficiently explained by them (reduction statements; Carnap, 1938, 1956). If used critically, that is enough to make them useful in common language and psychology.

It is reasonable to conclude that interindividual confirmability as a criterion of scientific meaningfulness can also cover self-report statements. *Whatever can be confirmed privately, can also in principle be confirmed interindividually.* Although I have a unique experience about myself, somewhat similar to that of an astronaut who has a unique experience which nobody else has, my self-report statements can be, in principle, confirmed interindividually, by observation of my behavior in certain situations, or physiologically. "In principle" means "under suitable conditions." A storm at the North Pole cannot be studied if nobody witnesses it, but under suitable conditions it is observable.

As you have noticed, we do not ask questions such as: are mental processes really physical processes or vice versa? Is the world one? With Carnap (1938, 1963), we doubt that there is any theoretical content in

316 INTEGRATED PSYCHOTHERAPY

the way this problem is discussed in the philosophies of monism, dualism, or pluralism. We ask, instead, whether the self-report language can be tied to the observational interindividual language and whether the self-observation statements are interindividually confirmable. The answer is yes—under suitable conditions. We shall enlarge on this in the next chapter.

The view presented here states that whether I say "I am angry," or somebody else observes the symptoms of my anger in my behavior, or a physiologist observes a combination of characteristics typical for anger, all three statements denote (refer to) the same microevents in my organism. Here some readers may object: my anger is a qualitatively different experience from the experience of the observer of my behavior, or the physiologist who would observe my brain. That is true. However, the same events may cause different experiences and yet they may be identical. For example, people had for centuries two different experiences: seeing the Morning Star and the Evening Star. And yet the two experiences refer to (denote) the same object, usually the planet Venus. It is rather a complicated mental process to arrive at the identity of the two concepts, Morning Star and Evening Star. Similarly, is it not curious that "that beautiful blue color" and "electromagnetic waves of 450 millimicrons" are the same? True, these two concepts have not the same meaning (what is called in logic "intension"), but they have the same denotatum or reference ("extension").

Here we will quote two slightly different versions of physicalism, first that of Feigl:

> The solution that appears most plausible to me, and that is entirely consistent with a thorough going naturalism, is an *identity theory* of the mental and the physical, as follows: Certain neurophysiological terms denote (refer to) the very same events that are also denoted (referred to) by certain phenomenal terms. The identification of the objects of this twofold reference is, of course, logically contingent, although it constitutes a very fundamental feature of our world as we have come to conceive it in the modern scientific outlook. Utilizing Frege's distinction between *Sinn* ('meaning', 'sense', 'intention') and *Bedeutung* ('referent', *'denotatum'*, 'extension') we may say that neurophysiological terms and the corresponding phenomenal terms, though widely differing in *sense*, and hence in the modes of confirmation of statements containing them, do have identical *referents*. I take these referents to be the immediately experienced qualities, or their configurations in the various phenomenal fields. (1967)

Carnap formulates physicalism somewhat differently, as apparent from his reply to Feigl (1963b):

> Although I agree with Feigl in the position itself, I have some doubts about his way of formulating it. The identity statement mentioned is a sentence of the object language; this fact may mislead the reader into believing that the controversy about identity view concerns a question of fact. This impression may be further strengthened by Feigl's reference to certain facts as "evidence" for the identity view. It seems preferable to me to formulate the question in the metalanguage, not as a factual question about the world, but as a question concerning the choice of a language form. Although we prefer a different language, we must admit that a dualistic language can be constructed and used without coming into conflict with either the laws of logic or with empirically known facts. However, in the dualistic language, the identity statement is false; the philosopher who uses this language is therefore justified in denying this statement. Those facts which Feigl proposes as evidence for the identity view are perhaps better regarded as reasons for preferring a monistic language, e.g., the reistic language containing psychological thing predicates. In a certain version of this language, on the basis of suitable postulates and rules, the above identity statement is true. . . . To sum up, I am willing to call my position an identity conception in the following sense: in agreement with Feigl I prefer monistic language, and like him I believe that the evidence available today provides good reasons for the assumption that this language will also function well in the future.

"Copernican revolutions" in the development of unified science The thesis of the unity of science is the scientific counterpart of previous philosophical attempts, particularly materialism, to see the world explained in a unified way. It evokes the same reluctance and emotional resistance which Freud commented upon. We present his view, amplified by Brunswik (1952) and Carnap (1959b).

What is the background of this resistance? The "Copernican revolutions" are blows to human pride and grandeur, and, as Freud said, the history of science is one of "retreating narcissism." Copernicus dethroned man as the center of the universe. Darwin dethroned man by showing his descent from animals. Marx relocated the basic causal factors in history from the realm of noble ideas to that of basic material needs. Organic compounds, which were believed to be produced only in living organisms, were produced artificially. Freud dethroned the conscious and rational self as the true representative of human motivational dynamics, arguing that "man is not master in his own house."

The pursuance of goals (teleology, finality), regarded as an exclusive feature of organisms, particularly human beings, and believed to be directed by a supernatural principle such as entelechy (Driesch) or élan vital (Bergson), has been simulated in servomechanisms. The thesis of a unified science (methodological behaviorism)—putting psychology and the social sciences together with biology and physics—is for some an offensive idea. The irrational, emotional reaction against these threats to narcissism is often as strong as those in the past against heliocentric and evolutionary theory.

What has been said, however, does not mean that the thesis of the unity of science does not have its difficulties and problems. The mind-body problem has been in recent years the subject of renewed interest and heated controversy among philosophers of science (see, for example, Borst, 1970).

Radical behaviorism versus physicalism (methodological behaviorism). We have briefly described the position of unified science, sometimes also called—perhaps less appropriately—methodological behaviorism. Some behavior theorists and therapists, such as Mahoney (1974), were turned recently to methodological behaviorism, as opposed to the radical (or metaphysical) behaviorism of Skinner. We will deal here with Skinner's views, because of Skinner's important contributions to the behavior sciences and his influence, and to clarify the differences between radical behaviorism and physicalism (methodological behaviorism). This is not easy, because of Skinner's fluctuating position. Originally, Skinner was programmatically neglecting what went on inside the organism (mediational processes, self-report) and identified emotions with overt behavior. Some of his recent pronouncements (1968, 1971, 1974) are puzzling. He repeatedly ascribes to methodological behaviorists and logical positivists the very views which he proclaimed earlier and on some occasions still proclaims, and which have repeatedly been rejected and criticized since the twenties by Carnap and other logical positivists.

We have listed in the left column Skinner's criticisms of methodological behaviorism and logical positivism. The right column demonstrates that he should criticize himself, not logical positivists such as Carnap and Feigl.

Skinner (1971): What is called "methodological behaviorism" limits itself to what can be publicly observed; mental processes may exist but they are ruled out of the scientific consideration by their nature . . . many logical positivists in philosophy have followed a similar line. But self-observation can be studied, and it must be included in any reasonably complete account of human behavior.

Skinner (1974): Methodological behaviorism and some versions of logical positivism ruled private events out of bounds because there could be no public agreement about their validity. Introspection could not be accepted as a scientific practice. . . . Radical behaviorism, however, takes a different line. It does not deny the possibility of self-observation or its possible usefulness, but it questions the nature of what is felt or observed and hence known.

Skinner (1974): Logical positivism or operationism holds that since no two observers can agree on what happens in the world of the mind, then from the point of view of physical science mental events are "unobservables."

Skinner (1974): Mentalism kept attention away from the external

Skinner (1953): The objection to inner states is not that they do not exist, but that they are not relevant in a functional analysis.

Skinner (1974): The mentalistic problem can be avoided by going directly to the prior physical causes while bypassing intermediate feelings or states of mind.

Skinner (1953): We define emotion—insofar as we wish to do so—as particular state of strength or weakness in one or more responses induced by one of a class of operations. . . . In the end, we find ourselves dealing with two events—the emotional behavior and the manipulable conditions of which that behavior is a function—which comprise the proper subject of the study of emotion.

Skinner (1953): Our "independent variables"—the causes of our behavior—are the external conditions of which behavior is a function. Relations between the two—the "cause and effect relationship" in behavior are the laws of science. . . .

Skinner (1953): If this state is purely inferential—if no dimensions are assigned to it which would make direct observation possible—it cannot serve as explanation. But if it has physiological or psychic properties, what antecedent events which might have explained behavior by seeming to supply an alternative explanation. Methodological behaviorism did just the reverse: by dealing exclusively with external antecedent events it turned attention away from self-observation and self-knowledge. Radical behaviorism restores some kind of balance. . .

Skinner (1974): Most methodological behaviorists granted the existence of mental events while ruling them out of consideration. Did they really mean to say that they did not matter, that the middle stage in that three-stage sequence of physical-mental-physical contributed nothing—in other words, that feelings and states of mind were merely epiphenomena? The view that a purely physical world could be self-sufficient had been suggested centuries before, in the doctrine of psychophysical parallelism, which held that there were two worlds—one of mind and one of matter—and that neither had any effect on the other.

role can it play in a science of behavior?

Carnap (1963a): If . . . I make the statement "I have a toothache" using an intersubjective language, there is a possible behavioristic symptom for the toothache . . . if no other, then at least the utterance of the sentence mentioned. I emphasized that the state of a person designated by a psychological term is not identical with his overt behavior, the latter is causal consequence of the former and may therefore be regarded as a symptom.

Carnap (1938): In psychology, as we find it today, there is, besides the physiological and the behavioristic approach, the so-called introspective method. . . . Much of what has been said about it, especially by philosophers, may be looked at with some suspicion. But the facts themselves, to which the term "introspection" is meant to refer, will scarcely be denied by anybody, e.g., the fact that a person sometimes knows that he is angry without applying any of those procedures which another person would have to apply, i.e., without looking with the help of physiological instruments at his nervous system or looking at the play of his facial muscles. . . . Anger is not the same as the movements by which an angry organism

> reacts to the conditions in his environment, just as the state of being electrically charged is not the same as the process of attracting other bodies. In both cases the state sometimes occurs without these events which are observable from outside; they are consequences of the state according to certain laws and may therefore under suitable circumstances be taken as symptoms for it; but they are not identical with it.

Whereas Skinner rejects the concept of "meaning" as mentalistic, logical empiricists show that it can be formulated in behavioral terms.

Skinner: I think an analysis which deals with verbal behavior without appealing to mental concepts such as meaning is a step in the right direction. (Evans 1968)

Morris (1946): Since the factors operative in sign-processes are all either stimulus objects or organic dispositions or actual responses, the basic terms of semiotic are all formulable in terms applicable to behavior as it occurs in an environment. Semiotic thus becomes a part of the empirical science of behavior.

We will conclude with the words of Carnap and Feigl. Carnap (1956) says:

> In a way similar to the philosophical tendencies of empiricism and operationism, the psychological movement of Behaviorism had, on the one hand, a very healthful influence because of its emphasis on the observation of behavior as an intersubjective and reliable basis for psychological investigations, while, on the other hand, it imposed too narrow restrictions. First, its total rejection of introspection was unwarranted. Although many of the alleged results of introspection were indeed questionable, a person's awareness of his own state of

imagining, feeling, etc., must be recognized as a kind of observation, in principle not different from external observation, and therefore as a legitimate source of knowledge, though limited by its subjective character. Secondly, Behaviorism in combination with the philosophical tendencies mentioned led often to the requirement that all psychological concepts must be defined in terms of behavior or behavior dispositions. . . . In physics great progress was made only by the construction of theories referring to unobservable events and micro-entities (atoms, electrons, etc.). In psychology analogous developments have begun from two different starting points. The one development began with the introspective approach. . . . The other development began with the molar behavioristic approach. . . . Both these approaches in psychology will probably later converge toward theories of the central nervous system formulated in physiological terms.

And Feigl (1967) says:

. . . as soon as the *peripheralistic* type of behaviorism (as for example, in the outstanding work and basic orientation of B. F. Skinner), is supplemented by theories about the central states and processes within the organism, and especially in its nervous system, it is on its way to the kind of physicalism which forms the frame-hypothesis of the present philosophical analysis.

Self-report, behavioral, and physiological methods complement one another

We believe that the thesis of a unified language of science is reasonable and suggests a vast program of exploration to the psychotherapist. It calls for cross-checking of data obtained by all three methods: self-report and behavioral and physiological observation. We have stated so far that this is possible in *principle*, but specific methods have to be worked out in order to accomplish it. The field is barely touched, and tremendous developments in diagnostic psychological assessment can be expected, not limited to paper and pencil tests as has been mainly the case. Here, only a few possible approaches, each capable of being developed both qualitatively and quantitatively, will be enumerated.

Consistency of self-report statements. Self-report sentences inform us about the states of the organism. They themselves are part of behavior which is causally connected with the interaction of the organism with the environment. They have to be regarded as are such other expressions of the organism as movements of a leg, yet they are sentences in the same language in which our psychological report is written.

How do we increase the degree of confirmation of self-report sentences? One way is to study the *consistency of self report statements*. As an example approaching an ideal method, let us take an audiologic test designed to check whether a person lost hearing in one ear as the person claims. Such problems have to be solved for the purpose of military service or in compensation claims. The person is asked to say whether or not he hears sounds produced in series. On the basis of the test procedure, it can be safely confirmed or disconfirmed whether the claim of the person is honest. The test is designed in such a way that even a physician knowing the test would not be able to simulate onesided deafness. Here, the consistency of self-report statements is based on the distribution of yes-no statements. In psychotherapy, we are far from having such tests.

The study of the consistency of self-report statements was developed by Freud and his followers and was used for identifying the patient's repressed thoughts, feelings and impulses. No doubt, there are limits and risks of misinterpretation if this method is used uncritically, yet it is a very valuable method, especially if used in connection with other methods. It is broadly and often successfully used in daily life. If a child claims to be so ill that he cannot go to school, but at the same time wants to go and play with other children, the parents can use this inconsistency to explore the actual state of the child.

Self-report and nonverbal behavior. Comparing self-report with nonverbal behavior is always valuable and often used successfully in daily life. Sometimes, the patient is surprised when the discrepancy between verbal and nonverbal behavior is commented upon. For example, the patient compliments the therapist and at the same time pounds his fist. When asked, he definitely denies any anger. But then he reveals that he came with tremendous anger toward the therapist but, as he entered the office, forgot about it completely.

The comparing of verbal and nonverbal spontaneous behavior has been utilized and thoroughly studied by psychoanalysts and other psychotherapists, but the situation of an individual interview or of a patient lying on the couch provides limited opportunity for observation. A comparison of Pavlov and Freud seems to us appropriate. As Pavlov fastened his dogs, Freud "fastened" his patients to the couch. Both had good reasons, and both were helped to discoveries which they would not have otherwise been able to make. Later as the classical Pavlovian school had resisted leaving the study of fastened dogs, the school of classical analysis resisted giving up the couch as the only situation. We do not want to deny the couch's usefulness; and we use it ourselves sometimes. However, for studying a patient, we need a much broader basis of exploration.

Empathy of the therapist. Therapists can use empathy for formulating hypotheses about their patients. There is nothing mysterious about empathy. Therapists, using the verbal and nonverbal cues from the patient, put themselves into the patient's position and observe their own reactions. They use themselves as a model and from their own reactions make hypotheses about the patient. To the degree that the therapist is similar to his patient and takes into consideration the variability of people's reactions, he can make empathy an important tool of psychotherapy.

So far, we have described methods of exploration used in traditional psychotherapy. All of these methods are severely limited both in the material they can gather and as confirmation procedures. The necessary step for the therapist is to expose the subject to a broad scale of situations. The person is now led not only to talk about symptoms (marriage, etc.) but is now induced to reexperience his problems in the present. The interview with the therapist becomes a diagnostic interaction. The patient's interaction with other people—members of artificial groups (other patients) or of natural groups (family, friends, coworkers, boss) or of both artificial and natural groups—is observed. The patient and other members of the therapeutic group or family participate in psychodrama or other action techniques and physical exercises. Complex environments such as a therapeutic community are structured both as a model of daily life (the patients work, and have other group tasks, participate in sports, plays, and games) and as a model of surplus reality—environments where a broad scale of fantasy situations can be created in a playful manner (Moreno). The patients act mutually as observers. The wealth of direct observation being significantly larger than one therapist could make leaves him with the problem of how to make useful generalizations from it.

In our opinion, all the different techniques of psychotherapy mentioned will lead from paper and pencil tests to new personality tests which will measure personal and interpersonal variables. However, the development of such tests has to go hand in hand with the development of a theory of the individual's functioning in a social field. This book presents some preparatory work toward such a theory by attempting to sweep away the conceptual rubbish which interferes with its building, and by developing and integrating techniques of exploration, confirmation, and behavior change and relating them to a model of personality functioning.

We believe that psychotherapy offers such a unique opportunity for the theoretical study of individual and small groups that it deserves attention from theoreticians of vastly diversified fields, from ethologists to social psychologists.

Physiological data. We started with the notion that there are three possible sources of psychological knowledge: observation of behavior, self-report, and physiological data. Practical psychotherapeutic use of physiological data is in its beginnings. As an example, electroencephalography and electromyography can easily disconfirm the patient's complaints about insomnia, and also show that a nurse's observations, although more reliable, are still grossly deficient. A lie-detector has a certain (limited) usefulness. There is also reasonable hope that biofeedback will become a useful tool of psychotherapy.

UNIFIED SCIENCE AND FREEDOM OF WILL

> The pseudo-problem of freedom of will . . . is really one of the greatest scandals of philosophy. Again and again so much paper and printer's ink is devoted to this matter. (Moritz Schlick 1939)

If we accept the theses of unified science, we visualize human beings as embedded in the causal network of the world. Does this in any way limit human freedom and responsibility?

The problem is usually formulated as follows: If human mental life is causally determined, man cannot make a free choice, and free will is an illusion. If so, I am not responsible for my acts. Therefore, moral responsibility presupposes freedom and exemption from causality. We seem to have a difficult dilemma: either we accept causality in which case people are not responsible for their behavior, or we accept freedom of will and thus exempt mental life from causality.

Fortunately, we can easily solve this dilemma by analyzing it carefully. It will turn out that this is a pseudoproblem, stemming from the philosophical misuse of a harmless word *free*. *Free* is used in ordinary language without special difficulties. A prisoner is not free to leave his cell because the door is locked. Freedom means the opposite of compulsion: a man is free when he is not hindered in his choice between alternatives.

If his stay in prison is mandatory or if he is held on the floor by a strong man, he is not free.

But such compulsion has nothing to do with causal determination. Let us suppose that you have a choice between two meals and you decide to take meal A. You could perhaps tell us immediately why you prefer meal A to meal B, telling us of your past experience with both meals. It is quite possible that if you think about it more or talk with somebody about your choice and free associate that you yourself would be surprised at the complex motivation of your decision, which might have a long history going back into your childhood. But when you find that your choice was motivated, that it had determinants you were not aware of at the time of your choice, what difference does it make to the question of whether your choice was free? Did you feel compelled to choose meal A because of your motivation? Your answer is no, you were free to choose, although we found some cause for your choice. (Whenever we say *cause*, we mean *partial cause*, since in psychology we rarely know all the conditions necessary and sufficient for an explanation—and even those we discover are often tentative.)

The problem of free will arose because of the confusion of *compulsion* with *causal determination*. The confusion of the two concepts—compulsion and causal determination—carries with it the confusion of their contradictory opposites. The opposite of *compulsion* is *freedom*, and the opposite of *causal determination* is *not subject to the laws of nature*. Because of this confusion, the problem of free will is a pseudoproblem and both positive and negative answers are pseudoanswers. Therefore, we regard as meaningless both the *positive* answer that "the will is free," given by those who declare indeterminism in order to save human freedom, and the negative answer given, for example by B. F. Skinner:

> The hypothesis that man is not free is essential to the application of scientific method to the study of human behavior. The free inner man who is held responsible for the behavior of the external biological organism is only a prescientific substitute for the kinds of causes which are discovered in the course of scientific analysis. All these alternative causes lie *outside* the individual. (1953)

But what about *responsibility*? We cannot agree with Skinner when he says, after explaining that both involuntary and voluntary movements are determined,

When we recognize this, we are likely to drop the notion of responsibility altogether and with it the doctrine of free will as an inner causal agent. (1953)

As explained, the doctrine of free will is a pseudoproblem and, therefore, the empirical question of responsibility has little to do with it. Whatever the usefulness of the concept of responsibility in future may be, it is an empirical concept; it is an imprecise concept, but so are most concepts used in everyday life. Certainly, if you have a serious car collision, you want to know who is responsible. It may sound surprising, since it is opposite to what the adherents of free will and indeterminism say, but *responsibility presupposes causality*. When a judge tries to determine the responsibility of an accused person, the more motives there are, the greater the responsibility. If somebody premeditates killing a person for a long time, it is regarded as a more serious crime than if he kills as a reaction to a quickly developed situation. If the behavior were not to be causally determined, that is, if it can not be explained by any laws and is, therefore, unpredictable, the behavior of people would radically change every minute without any reason. There would not be any point in asking for a reason or motive, and it would be impossible to make anyone responsible for anything. From everyday life we know that it is not so. The behavior of people, to a certain degree, is predictable despite all the unpredictable changes of environment which influence behavior.

Punishment aims at individual and general prevention and is based on an estimate of how a motive can be implanted in the delinquent and others, which would prevent repetition of unlawful behavior. It involves assumption of causality.

There have been attempts to support free will and indeterminism by atomic physics: there are indeterminate quantum jumps which are, according to what most physicists believe, random. There are different opinions as to whether a single jump could influence human decision. It is not likely (Carnap 1966). If it were so, it would only inject randomness into human decision-making; there would be decisions which would be principally unpredictable. They would be random, jumpy, surprising to the subject himself, but not free.

For further discussion, the following reading is recommended Schlick (1939); Frank (1957); Carnap (1966); F. Knobloch (1941).

Appendix B

PSYCHOTHERAPY AS A LEARNING PROCESS

Learning, in its broad sense used in psychology, means *change in probability of behavior patterns as a result of experience.* It covers not only, as in the common-sense meaning, acquisition of new knowledge or skills, but also acquisition of inappropriate fears or harmful habits. It is widely believed that neurotic and similar disorders are, at least to a large degree, the result of learning. If this is so, then psychotherapy is basically a process of relearning and new learning. Stressing the importance of learning in behavior disorders does not exclude the importance of other factors, genetic or others. Psychotherapy could be even for some time the leading method of treating disorders where the genetic factor would be the most important one, assuming that the genetic factors are not accessible to change and where some learning is possible.

Although learning has been the most studied subject in psychology, no unified theory of learning as yet exists. The starting point for behavior therapists were paradigms of simple learning, known from animal experiments, whereas schools of dynamic psychotherapy, dealing with complex learning, did not have any systematic theory of learning, and no such theory exists still today. The difference between behavior therapists and dynamic psychotherapists can be understood essentially as a difference between two learning strategies. We will use two examples from other fields of learning, one from the field of piano playing (but it could be learning of other skills, such as tennis or skiing), and from learning mathematics.

A piano teacher admits a new advanced student who, however, has not been taught properly and who has many habits which put limits on his technique. There are two ways the teacher can deal with the problem. One possibility is to let the student continue to play on the level he reached, and to help him to relearn his false habits one by one. The other way is to advise the student to stop playing Beethoven or whatever he plays completely, and to train him only on finger exercises for many months. The choice of one of the alternatives depends not only on the specific problems of the student (how "deep" they are) and on his goals, but also on the goals, beliefs and flexibility of the teacher.

Another example is a student failing in advanced mathematics. The new tutor finds to his horror that the student lacks elementary knowledge in mathematics and that without it he cannot understand the present level. In this case, the student cannot stop studying on the present level, otherwise he would fail the whole year. Some compromise has to be found so that the student can work both on the present level and at the same time learn what he missed on the past levels.

Correspondingly, the difference between behavior and dynamic psychotherapists seems to be essentially the difference of teaching strategies. When dealing with a phobia, behavior therapists showed in some cases that you can deal efficiently with the phobia alone, whereas the dynamic psychotherapists were impressed by the deficiencies on "deeper" levels. "Deeper" means for us deficiencies in social learning, which lead to unsatisfactory social relationships, building an inadequate group schema, and adoption of subgoals which cause suffering and chronic conflicts. But both alternatives are in the field of learning and the question which strategy to choose is a practical one, as with the teacher of music and mathematics.

Behavior theorists and therapists have moved recently into the field of cognitive processes and self-control (e.g., Mahoney 1974, Thoresen and Mahoney 1974). It can be hoped that the connectionistic (stimulus-response) and cognitive theories of learning will fuse in future and with the help of animal and machine models a unified theory explaining processes of complex learning will emerge. In the meantime, disparate pieces of knowledge of learning processes have to be collected and used by a psychotherapist. Both the conceptual framework and clinical rules of this book have obvious relationship to the learning models of this

chapter, yet we have not commited ourselves to the language of any of
them.

We will present different types of learning, starting with the best
described ones, known today as *classical* and *instrumental* conditioning.
These were identified at approximately the same time—at the end of
the nineteenth century, by Pavlov and Thorndike, respectively.

TYPES OF LEARNING

Classical conditioning

In Pavlov's classical experiment, a hungry dog salivates (unconditioned reaction, UR) if it receives the meat powder (unconditioned stimulus, US). If an indifferent stimulus (acoustic, visual, or tactile), not
eliciting that reaction by itself, is introduced just prior to the presentation of the meat powder (US), it will elicit the salivation by itself after
several associations. It is then called the conditioned stimulus (CS). In
this way learning has taken place, since CS elicits reaction R which it
had not elicited before and which had been elicited only by US, the
meat powder. Roughly speaking, classical conditioning is *stimulus substitution.* To make the conditioned reaction stable, the CS has to be accompanied and reinforced from time to time by the US, that is, by the meat
powder, otherwise the reaction to the CS will disappear; *extinction* will
take place.

If a tone was used as a conditioned stimulus, another similar tone
could elicit the same reaction by the process known as *generalization.* But
if two tones are presented, so that one is systematically reinforced and
the other is not (even if the difference is so small that it is less than a
quarter of a tone), *differentiation* takes place: the dog reacts to the reinforced stimulus and does not react to the other one.

Especially resistent to extinction is fear reaction. Using the idea of
classical conditioning, Watson and Rayner (1920) experimented with a
little boy Albert. They used loud noise as an unconditoned stimulus
producing fear and presentation of a white rat as a conditioned stimulus.
Albert was not originally afraid of white rats, but he started to be after
the rat was associated with the loud noise. Watson and Rayner proved
in this way that fear can be learned. But how to get rid of such a fear?
Unfortunately, they had no opportunity to study it in Albert.

The problem was further studied by Mary Cover Jones in Thordike's
laboratory in 1924. Another little boy, Peter, was afraid of rabbits. Since
extinction of fear is very slow, Jones used counterconditioning. White

gave Peter his favorite food, a rabbit in a cage was brought into the room, but at such a distance that Peter continued eating. The cage was gradually brought closer, until finally the rabbit was released from the cage while the child was still eating. The basic idea of counterconditioning is that the positive experience of eating, and the negative experience of fear, are incompatible and the weak fear of the rabbit can be inhibited by the positive experience of eating and will gradually disappear. (Jones also let Peter observe other children playing with a rabbit: observational learning will be described later.)

A treatment for phobias, introduced by Wolpe (1954) as *systematic desensitization*, is based on the same idea. The phobic patient, with the help of the therapist, prepares a hierarchy of feared situations. He is then trained in relaxation, and in that state is instructed to imagine himself in the feared situations, starting from the least feared. As relaxation and fear are incompatible, the fear is gradually weakened. Transfer to real situations is the task of the patient himself. (About the theoretical dilemmas of how to explain systematic desensitization, see Yates 1975.)

As mentioned, classical *aversive* conditioning is used in the treatment of alcoholism and other maladaptive habits in which the autonomic system plays an important part. In the treatment of alcoholism, nausea is chemically induced (emetin, apomorphine) in the patients, so that they vomit when they taste alcohol. The treatment is based on the expectation that the nausea will occur later whenever the patient tastes alcohol. According to the extensive study of Skala (1971), the aversive treatment is insufficient in itself, but is a valuable adjunct in the complex psychotherapeutic treatment of alcoholic patients.

Instrumental conditioning

If organisms could learn only by classical conditioning, there would be no new responses. The only difference would be that the responses would be elicited by new, that is, conditioned, stimuli.

But there is another way of learning whereby the animal's behavior (action or refrained action) is instrumental in producing the reinforcing unconditioned stimulus, or *reinforcer*, SR. The reinforcer is contingent upon certain behavior patterns, and in this way the animal exerts some control over its environment. A hungry pigeon in a Skinner box, by random trial-and-error, presses a lever and obtains food. Gradually, its ability to press the lever whenever it is hungry will increase. If pressing the lever produces food only if some previously neutral stimulus (visual, acoustic, etc.) is presented, the animal learns to react only after the presentation of such stimulus, the *discriminating stimulus*, SD.

The systematic study of instrumental conditioning began with Edward Thorndike (trial-and-error learning, law of effect) in 1898, and was developed by B. F. Skinner in particular; *operant conditioning*, as he calls it, is a variety of instrumental conditioning. In Russia, Bekhterev was one of the early contributors. From Pavlov's pupils, Yerzy Konorski and others studied instrumental conditioning.

Skinner distinguishes positive and negative reinforcers. Positive reinforcers, S+ (approximately: rewards) reinforce by being presented. Negative reinforcers, S− (approximately: aversive stimuli) reinforce by being terminated. A response can be reinforced (increased) by presenting a positive reinforcer, or by terminating a negative reinforcer.

Reinforcer	Postive S+	Negative S-
Presented	increase	decrease (punishment)
Removed	decrease (punishment)	increase

Punishment means the presentation of a negative reinforcer, or the removal of a positive reinforcer. According to Skinner, punishment is not a very efficient way of preventing responses from occurring. It is true that punishment is often useful in stopping undesirable behavior, but it is not reliable in preventing it from happening later.

In instrumental conditioning, there is one finding of tremendous practical importance. If we remove the reinforcing stimulus (reward), the instrumental response will disappear after some time. But its resistance to extinction is much stronger if the response is reinforced intermittently or partially—that is, not after every successful accomplishment, but only from time to time. The total number of responses is actually greater with intermittent reinforcement than with continuous reinforcement. This was systematically explored by Skinner and his pupils. There are four basic types of reinforcement schedules. In a fixed interval schedule (FI), after the first successful response is emitted, reinforcement comes at the end of each interval, as, for example, in FI-20, after every 20 seconds. It is often observed that the animal slows down in its responses at the beginning of the interval and as the time for reward approaches, its responses become more frequent (scalloping). In a fixed-ratio schedule (FR), the organism receives the reinforcement after a certain number of successful reactions, for example, in FR-20, after every 20 successful reactions. Other basic types are the variable-interval schedule (VI), and the variable-ratio schedule (VR). These basic schedules can be combined in different ways (multiple schedules of reinforcement), and this has been a subject of very intensive study, especially in animals. In general, the variable-ratio schedule is the most effective if we want to achieve a rapid and steady response and a high resistance to extinction. Children are, of course, far more suitable for experimentation, as they are more accessible to such simple rewards as candy.

From what has been stated, it is apparent that it is easier for a therapist to intensify behavior which the patient exhibits anyway, than to stop it. We do not want, and cannot use, punishment forever, and undesirable behavior is persistent since it has most likely been reinforced intermittently. The best way to help a patient stop smoking is to find another activity incompatible with smoking which the patient likes better. The trouble is to find such an activity.

Through operant conditioning, Skinner was able to make animals perform complicated sequences of behavior, which they would never have performed without training. His technique is called *shaping* and is based on the reinforcement of a series of approximations. The experimenter reinforces approximate responses, but in the trials that follow, he reinforces only those responses that are increasingly similar to the desired response. If the animal has to learn a chain of responses, the experimenter may start with reinforcing the last link.

The amazing performances of circus animals are obtained through operant conditioning. Operant conditioning is also essential for human motor skills, as they involve voluntary responses of the striated, skeletal muscles.

In the past, the instrumental learning of visceral responses was generally regarded as impossible. However, there were some, such as J. H. Schultz (1932), who, in his *autogenic training* based on hypnosis and meditation, defended the possibility of the voluntary control of visceral processes. In recent years, it has been claimed that self-control of many functions, such as heart rate, blood pressure, and brain alpha-rhythm, can be achieved through operant conditioning by using biofeedback. The feedback consists, for example, of an unpleasant sound when the undesirable state is present, which disappears when the desirable state is achieved. Biofeedback has been met with enthusiasm and exploited by business. Objective assessment of its practical value has not yet been forthcoming, though it is reasonable to expect it will be helpful in psychotherapy.

It is of great practical importance for psychotherapy that immediate reinforcements are more effective than delayed ones (gradient of reinforcement). This difference can be used as an explanation of some cases of the "neurotic paradox" (a person repeats, again and again, self-damaging behavior which he later regrets). One explanation is that the pleasure comes first and is more effective for learning than the punishment, which comes much later. If punishment is to be effective in learning, it has to come soon after the undesirable act.

If classical conditioning is the primitive form of the cognitive process of induction, operant conditioning goes a step further in learning about the world. The organism not only reacts, but actively manipulates the environment and accumulates knowledge about the causal relations in the assumptive world which embraces both the organism and environmental objects. The individual gains partial knowledge about itself as causal agent of its own destiny. This knowledge may exist to differing extents even in animals. One animal is unable to escape from painful shocks coming from a charged grid, whereas another animal learns to operate the switch and create for itself a comfortable environment.

Similarly, people receive stimuli which are either independent of or dependent on their previous behavior. Successful treatment often changes the patients' perspective; many stimuli which they regarded as independent turn out to be dependent on their previous behavior. Their control of their environment and of themselves increases.

Habituation

Habituation—changing behavior because of repeated experience—can be regarded as the simplest form of learning. If you tap the side of an aquarium, or a terrarium, many animals will react to the first few taps but will stop reacting later.

There have been suggestions that systematic desensitization could be explained by habituation.

Observational social learning

Learning by observing others plays an essential role in the growth of animals and man. However, the study of observational learning was neglected for a long time by the learning theorists because it is difficult to reduce satisfactorily to conditioning. For example, talking birds sometimes learn to imitate complicated verbal and melodic structures. It seems impossible that they could learn this merely through shaping. Another reason for this neglect may be that those who have dealt with imitation in the past stressed its instinctual nature and a strong dislike of instinctual interpretation has developed since the 1920's, especially in North America.

One of the early laboratory experiments in vicarious classical conditioning is that of V. I. Kriazhev, 1932 (cited by Bandura 1969). One animal in each of seven pairs of dogs was conditioned to stimuli presented in conjunction with food or electric shock, while the others merely witnessed the procedure. The observing dogs rapidly developed anticipatory salivation responses to the signal of food and conditioned agitation and respiratory changes to the signal of electrical shock.

Observational learning was used by Masserman (1943) for extinguishing responses acquired through classical conditioning. He produced strong feeding inhibitions in cats by pairing food-approach responses with air blasts. Later, the inhibited cats observed a cagemate, who had never been aversively conditioned. The cagemate approached the food without fear. Some cats lost their fears, but some of them became fearful again when their models were not present.

Although the notion of observational learning is old, its intensive study is new. Bandura (1969) in particular represents this new trend. Provisionally, the following concepts have to be regarded as synonymous, or overlapping: observational learning, imitation, role-taking, identification, contagion, social facilitation, vicarious learning, and modeling.

Observational learning plays a basic role in all human learning. Without it the socialization process of the child would not be possible, particularly the acquisition of language.

In group psychotherapy, situations are created conducive to observational learning on a much broader basis than the therapist alone can conceptualize and plan; if all goes well, peer learning significantly enhances the therapeutic process.

Cognitive learning

Classical and instrumental conditioning are based on repeated stimulus-response (S-R) connections. However, we can remember the face of a person, or remember a sequence of words, or remember how to go around a new city after only one exposure. This seems to indicate that stimulus-stimulus (S-S) connections are learned, since no reactions and reinforcements are apparent. (Whether they are or not is subject to controversy, and does not concern us here.)

Wolfgang Kohler was the first to study *insight learning* in apes. One of the situations involved an animal and a banana which could not normally be reached. However, there were boxes scattered in the cage to enable the animal to climb up and get it. First the animal exhausted the usual methods of reaching the banana. It then stopped all activity—apparently it was thinking—and finally, with sudden insight or "cognitive restructuring" of the situation, solved the problem.

Tolman, in his study of rats, showed that when they learned their way through a maze, what they did learn was not a rigid sequence of stimuli-responses but a cognitive map of the maze. When they had to change their activities, to swim instead of run, they were able to pursue their goal. When one alley was closed, but many alternatives available, they did not choose the alley next to the one that was closed but another which seemed to be a short-cut to their goal.

Self-conditioning

Bandura (1969) states: "Until recently, self-reinforcement phenomena have been virtually ignored by psychological theorizing and experimentation." This is not quite so. George Herbert Mead, a largely ignored "pivotal figure in American philosophy of behavioral sciences" (Morris 1946, 1964), repeatedly stressed in 1922 that the use of symbols allows man to become a self-conditioning being, and complained that the existing doctrines of conditioned response failed to account for self-conditioning.

You plan a trip and condition yourself in advance to different routes. Driving the next day, you are conditioned to avoid the first route and take the second. In preparing the trip, verbal and imaginary (especially visual) mediators played an important role. Without language and post-language symbols (a concept introduced by Morris), human behavior could not achieve such consistency as it often has. This consistency is a tool mostly useful for the individual and has apparently developed in evolution as a species-preserving mechanism. It may also become detrimental as the consistency thinking of a paranoic shows.

Skinner, in controlling behavior, relies upon external stimuli and avoids the inner states. He says, "The objection to inner states is not that they do not exist, but that they are not relevant in a functional analysis" (1953). They are, however, relevant; not only does the environment control, or more precisely codetermine, behavior, but the organism's behavior itself also cocreates, or codetermines, its environment. The usual objection against inner states is that they are private, covert and inaccessible to checking. As we tried to show, this privacy is relative, and some techniques described in this book are capable of increasing the degree of confirmation of statements about a subject's inner states.

Because of the continuous interaction of the organism with the environment, the circuits of the self-control mechanisms often go through the environment. For example, a person exerts self-control by setting an alarm clock for the morning, creating environmental conditions which later control his behavior. In another case, there are no environmental consequences, but the person produces self-evaluative reactions. For example, he imagines himself not smoking and compliments himself for this. Generally, control by images and other private experience, both rewarding and aversive, is of tremendous importance. As we saw, it has a basic role in the group schema. It helps to understand why neurotic or psychotic behavior can be, to a large degree, under inner control.

It is apparent that the simple S-R theory is too limited; it has to be complemented by the concept of mediating responses. They modify or redirect the responses, so that there is not a one-to-one relationship between stimulus and response. As Bandura states:

> The process of behavioral change will be conceptualized quite differently depending upon whether one assumes that responses are regulated predominantly by external stimulus events or partly by mediating symbolic events. In nonmediational interpretations, learning is depicted as a more or less automatic process wherein stimuli become associated with overt responses through differential reinforcement. By contrast, in mediational formulations the learner plays a far more active role and his responsiveness is subject to extensive cognitive determination. On the basis of salience of environmental events and past learning experiences, persons select the stimuli to which they will respond; environmental events are coded and organized for representation in memory; provisional hypotheses regarding the principles governing the occurrence of reinforcement are derived from differential consequences accompanying overt behavior; and after a given implicit hypothesis has been adequately confirmed by successful corresponding actions, the mediating rules or principles serve to guide the performance of appropriate responses on future occasions. (1969)

Integrated psychotherapy tries to apply all available knowledge to facilitate therapeutic learning. For example, the therapeutic community is a closed system for rewards and costs (which can be understood in terms of reinforcement contingencies). It differs from token economy systems (Ayllon and Azrin 1965) in that it systematically uses social approval and disapproval as main reinforcers. In addition to their informal use throughout the system, they are partly formalized as a system of positive and negative awards given by the community and by self-ratings. Competition between subgroups (families) is also used.

SOME DILEMMAS POSED BY THE THEORIES OF LEARNING

Behavior therapy is sometimes defined as "methods of treatment which are derived from the modern theory of learning" (Eysenck 1968). Unfortunately, as many have pointed out, there is not one theory of learning. There are many interpretations, even of the same learning process, and different learning theories. At present, psychotherapists are not yet in a position to take a stand in the discussion, based to a large degree on animal experiments. Therefore, the exposition will be brief. However, all progress in the theories of learning is of central importance for the further development of psychotherapy.

Innate-learned: mixture or intercalation? Whereas most American authors and some ethologists believe that learning enters into all kinds of behavior, other ethologists, such as Lorenz, Hess, Eibl-Eibesfeldt, and Koenig, do not believe so. "If we consider learning as a specific function achieving a definite surviving value," says Lorenz, "it appears as an entirely unfounded assumption that learning must necessarily 'enter into' all other neurophysiological processes determining behavior . . . innumerable observations and experiments tend to show that modifiability occurs, if at all, only in those preformed places where built-in learning mechanisms are phylogenetically programmed to perform just that function" (1965). Lorenz talks about "instinct-training intercalation"; that is, instinctive and learned behavior "come in chunks" which are integrated; the learned components lend flexibility to behavior.

The correctness of one or the other view can be of considerable consequence for the theory of mental disorders and the practice of psychotherapy. Let us take neurotic behavior and the episodic breakdown in voluntary control, such as hysterical seizure, compulsive act, tic, obsessional idea, or phobic panic. Could it be that they represent fragments of fixed motor patterns (instinctive patterns to be explained later)? It could be objected that they are not completely automatic and out of voluntary control, but that is true of almost any human activity, be it breathing, yawning, laughing, sobbing, or sexual intercourse.

Connectionistic (S-R) learning or cognitive learning? Whereas the S-R (stimulus-response) learning theories ask what the individual has learned to do, the cognitive theories ask, How differently does the individual perceive the situation? Whereas the connectionist theories talk in terms of S-R connection, the cognitive theories talk in terms of perceptions and beliefs. The gap between strict S-R and cognitive theories can scarcely be overcome; however, the connectionist theories acknowledging mediation and cognitive theories can converge. Mediational theories deal with internal responses which intervene between stimulus and response. If it is accepted that internal responses (including symbols of language) can function as cues and can produce such stimuli as cognitive maps, conditions are present for the convergence of connectionist and cognitive theories.

The function of reinforcement. Inside the connectionist camp, the reinforcement theorists assumed the presence of reinforcement in all learning. The contiguity theorists, although not denying the importance of reinforcement for performance, regard contiguity (the occurrence of two events together) as essential for learning. If we want to know what a person will do in the future, we have to look at what he does now, as he will be likely to repeat it under similar circumstances.

In addition to the various interpretations of reinforcement derived from animal experimentation, new problems are posed by the goal-directed machines and machines which can learn. There is no parallel to reinforcement in guided missiles, although, to be sure, there would be no difficulty in principle to simulate reinforcement mechanisms in a machine. The question of whether learning can take place through feedback without reinforcement is discussed by learning theorists (see Annett 1969).

It may be fortunate for the future of learning theory that psychologists have moved to behavior therapy and are faced with the complexities of human behavior. Although some stick to S-R models, others are initiating new developments, using both animal and machine models; this will likely speed up the convergence of connectionist and cognitive theories. Thanks to such psychologists as Bandura (1969, 1971) and Mahoney (1974), and others, the atmosphere is changing.

How far the theory still has to go can be seen in the issue of systematic desensitization, which theoretically seems relatively simple. Yet, as Yates shows, each component of the procedure can be removed and the method still seems to work. "Although systematic desensitization apparently 'works', the critical factors involved remain unclear and the theoretical explanations are conflicting and indecisive" (1975). The difficulties increase as we move to more complex kinds of treatment. Therefore, given the present state of knowledge, we are not committed to any particular learning theory but use as our basis the more global framework of social group processes. For the same reason, we are not committed, like some social psychologists (Homans 1961, for example), to the interpretation of social exchange in terms of operant conditioning.

Appendix C

THE INNATE BASIS OF HUMAN BEHAVIOR

The innate basis of human behavior is of great importance for the theory and practice of psychotherapy. Unfortunately, the knowledge of innate behavior in human beings and even in animals is limited and there are considerable differences of opinion among specialists. Nonetheless, the topic cannot be avoided in any attempt at integration of psychotherapy, for several reasons. Firstly, hundred of books are published each year which repeat Freud's view about instincts; these views have great influence not only on psychoanalysts, but many other psychotherapists. The concepts of Freudian instinctual framework—such as Eros, destructive instinct, Thanatos, psychic energy, psychic forces—do not appear in any laws which would be empirically confirmable. Although a thorough analysis of Freud's views is not intended here, we will give examples of his views which in our opinion are clearly misleading.

Secondly, we believe that ethology, even in its present stage, is a source of valuable inspiration for psychotherapists. In the field of psychoanalysis, Bowlby (1969) attempted a synthesis of psychoanalysis and ethology in the field of mother-child relationships. Here we will present briefly some concepts of classical ethologists who have continued in the work of Darwin (1965) such as Konrad Lorenz (1965, 1966, 1970-71). It is, however, necessary to keep in mind that there is a whole spectrum of views among students of animal behavior, ranging from Lorenz to completely opposite ones minimizing the influence of innate factors in higher animals and in people. A cautious and moderate view is represented by Hinde (1970, 1974). It is our belief, based on the recent development of nonverbal techniques, that psychotherapy in the near future will be in a unique position to make a direct contribution to human ethology.

ARE THERE ANY INSTINCTS IN MAN?

After the deficiencies of the concept as used at the beginning of the century were pointed out, many psychologists denied instincts completely. Ashley Montagu said:

> If there should be any instincts in man at all, they consist perhaps in the automatic reaction to a sudden noise or to the withdrawal of some support; otherwise man has no instincts.

On the other hand, ethologists, particularly Lorenz and those close to him, recognize the instinctive basis of human behavior. For example, Hess writes:

> For several decades behavioristic psychologists in the United States have strongly resisted the very notion of innate behavior in man. . . . However, ethologists believe that it is possible to apply many of the same concepts they have developed with respect to the study of animal behavior to human beings. Darwin (1872), of course, had an ethological approach to human behavior. (1970)

Koenig, a coworker of Lorenz, writes:

> The opinion is often expressed that the high intelligence of human beings is founded on the burying or complete loss of so-called instincts. However, comparison with many different species shows that man possesses many innate movement, or fixed action, patterns. Man possesses more innate behavior patterns than any other animal. This, however, does not lead to rigidity, but increased plasticity. An apt comparison of innate movement patterns is to building blocks. The greater the number of building blocks and the smaller their size, the more it is possible to build different and finer patterns. . . . To choose

various combinations correctly relative to different situations, there is a need for considerable abilities of attention, learning combination, and integration. (1971, our translation)

The differences may be partly due to semantic confusion.

A false opposition of the "instinctive" to the "learned" has tended in the past to prevent us from seeing these common features of human behavior and from recognizing that they must result, much as the instinctive behavior of rodent and carnivore does, from (a) the way we are made and (b) the universal features of the human environment. (Hebb 1972)

Hebb says about instinct:

What we conclude is that instinct is the neural organization, over and above paths, which is common to a whole species: determined by a common heredity and the common features of the environment. (1972)

This seems to be a view closer to that of Lorenz (1965), who criticized Hebb for his earlier views.

Man is a self-domesticated primate who developed, as the other animals in evolution, through the process of differential survival by natural selection. As Charles Darwin states, and modern ethology documents in detail, evolution concerns not only body structure and functions but also behavior. Present day man, compared with the time stretches of evolution, is only a recent development. Man's body structure and functions resemble closely those of higher animals, and it would be surprising if the same did not hold for the "programming," neural mechanisms underlying man's behavior. To have a grasp of the time proportion of evolution, let us imagine that the first animals on earth appeared one month ago. The first primates would have appeared on the last day of the month, the apes departed from our common ancestry in the late afternoon, the Australopithecus developed in the last hour, and modern man (homo sapiens) emerged in the last minute.

There is little dispute that some behavior patterns in animals and men are relatively stable under normal environmental conditions within the species. For example, all animals deprived of food will periodically engage in goal-directed activities, starting by paying selective attention to edible objects, then vigorously trying to overcome obstacles, and finally when the goal is reached, consuming food. The activities are often highly complicated and yet, to a high degree, specific for the species, for example, the way of predation. An observation made by Eibl-Eibesfeldt provides an impressive example. Squirrels reared in isolation and never given any objects to handle nevertheless attempt to bury nuts or nutlike objects in a bare floor upon their first encounter with them, making scratching movements as if to dig out earth, tamping the object in the floor with the nose, and finally making covering and tamping down movements with the front legs. Eibl-Eibesfeldt concludes: "The entire behavior sequence therefore is preprogrammed as phylogenic adaptation" (1970). Similarly, there will be little dispute that there are invariant patterns of behavior within the same species, such as eliminative behavior, shelter seeking, sexual behavior, care giving, and care soliciting behavior, agonistic, contagious behavior, and investigative behavior. Such behaviors are often called instinctive. The differences of opinion occur when, proceeding from a description of behavior, theorists draw conclusions about underlying innate mechanisms (innate programming) in the organism. Although everybody agrees that behavior can take place only if there is an organism, its environment, and their interaction, the differences of opinion beyond this point are tremendous.

SOME CONCEPTS OF ETHOLOGY

A typical innate behavior sequence starts as appetitive behavior becomes more and more specific and ends with the consummatory act. The consummatory act is usually based on a fixed motor pattern (stereotyped and coordinated motor actions) and on taxis (movements steered in a certain direction). The fixed motor patterns are brought into action by innate releasing mechanisms, brain mechanisms released by environmental stimuli called releasers or sign stimuli (if the stimulus is a characteristic of the body or behavior of another animal, it is called a social releaser). An example will clarify the meaning of the concepts mentioned.

When, in the breeding season, a three-spined stickleback female appears in the territory of a male, the shape of her body is a social releaser for the male who answers with a zig-zag dance. This in turn releases a special display movement of the female. He then leads her to the nest. She follows and he shows the nest entrance and she swims into it. Then he repeatedly butts at her tail which still protrudes from the nest; she spawns and swims off. He enters the nest and milts. Each of these social releasers can be imitated by a dummy. If the level of the hormones responsible for sexual behavior in the male is increased, the dummy of the female can be more and more dissimilar to the real female and yet successfully function as a social releaser.

According to Lorenz (1970-71), all instinctive processes in animals which are not fully activated nonetheless manifest themselves in a rudimentary form of behavior (Heinroth's *intentional movements*). This behavior, if understood by an observer, can inform him what emotional state the other animal is in. If the observer is an animal of the same species and starts by chance to react in an appropriate way, this may be a new device with survival value for the species. Through the process of natural selection, rudimentary forms of instinctive behavior through modification, elaboration, and ritualization became innate social releasers of paramount importance for the individual and the species. It is of advantage that an animal, without complicated learning, reacts appropriately in different situations to such significant members of its own species as parent, child, sexual object, or rival. Social releasers are composed of simple sign stimuli—visual, acoustic, olfactic; the reaction to a social releaser is a sum of reactions to various sign stimuli (the law of heterogenous summation, according to Tinbergen 1951). This means that isolated sign stimuli release partial reactions which the complex social releaser would normally release. This is strikingly different to reactions acquired by learning complex stimuli; there the isolated partial stimuli may not release any reaction at all.

Ethology makes many of Freud's speculations about the sexual basis of instincts unnecessary. For example, let us take Freud's observation that a baby sucks for pleasure and not just because of hunger. "The baby's obstinate persistence in sucking," says Freud, "gives evidence at an early stage of a need for satisfaction which, though it originates from and is instigated by the taking of nourishment, nevertheless strives to obtain pleasure independently of nourishment and for that reason may and should be termed *sexual*." (1940) Freud's assertion that a baby enjoys sucking and does not suck just for nourishment is beyond doubt, but this does not justify regarding it as sexual. Ethology knows many drives like that; Lorenz calls them "little servants of species preservation." For example, Paul Leyhausen gave cats which were keen hunters one mouse after the other. First the cat stopped eating but killed a few more mice leaving them untouched. Next, the killing bite disappeared, but the cat continued to stalk and catch the mice. Later still, when the movement pattern of catching was exhausted, the cat did not stop stalking the mice but always chose those furthest away in the opposite corner of the room and ignored those that ran over its forepaws.

The example shows that the cat's goal in performing the pattern of prey catching is not just that of feeding. To a degree it is a goal in itself which probably developed under the selection pressure of evolution. The ancestors of cats were able to survive better if they took special interest in prey-catching and took pleasure in developing this skill.

INTERFERENCE OF DRIVES

There are genetically programmed behavior opposites, such as fight and flight; fear of new environment and curiosity to explore it; enjoying vigorous activity and resting; searching for food and rejecting it when satiated.

Sometimes incompatible drives are stimulated simultaneously. The result is either some form of ambivalent behavior, redirection, or displacement. All perhaps have analogues in human behavior. Ambivalent behaviors are described, particularly in neurotics, by Freud as different kinds of compromise solutions of neurotic conflict. *Redirection* perhaps would be called in psychoanalytic terms *displacement*. For example, a male baboon threatened by a higher-ranking animal does not challenge him but redirects his aggression against a lower-ranking one, who in turn passes it on.

Displacement in an ethological sense is interesting. In certain conflict situations, animals show behavior patterns which do not belong to either of the conflicting drives; this is called displacement. For example, when a rooster's drive to fight is about as strong as its drive to flight, it begins to peck intensely on the ground, shaking its beak often; such cleaning movements as wiping and bathing appear as displacement activities. Ethologists believe that displacement activities can be observed in man. A speaker, they speculate, is sometimes in conflict, whether to deliver his message or run away. The displacement reactions fall into such categories as bodily care (wiping, rubbing, and scratching movements, bringing the open hand around the neck and nape of the neck; stroking the beard, even if no beard is present; scratching the head, eating (biting, chewing, sucking on objects like pens; spontaneous chewing movements; licking and swallowing), and many others, some of them learned (fondling of the tie; rhythmic pushing of the button on a ball-point pen).

HUMAN ETHOLOGY

There are tremendous differences of opinion about the ethological concepts explained and about their applicability to people. Lorenz and those close to him, such as Eibl-Eibesfeldt and Koenig, believe they are applicable.

Most broadly accepted is the innate character of such neonate behavior as babies in their rhythmic search for the nipple—a search replaced in a few days by an oriented search for the breast (i.e., when the mouth region is touched, the infant turns toward the stimulus object). Both spontaneous and answering smiles are regarded as instinctive patterns. The latter seem to be elicited by the sight of the human face as a social releaser as observations and experiments with masks seem to indicate (studies of R. A. Spitz and K. M. Wolf; see Wilson 1975, Hess 1970).

To an adult a baby's smile seems to be a social releaser for caring behavior, especially to the mother. It is speculated that this was of vital importance to the baby's survival under primitive conditions. Lorenz also regards babyishness (typical proportions of the body of an infant, especially the head) as a social releaser for adults.

For adult persons, the shapes of the male and female body are believed by ethologists to be innate visual social releasers. The ideal shape of male and female bodies, as represented in Greek statues and regarded as beautiful throughout the ages, indicates sexual maturity and hormonal balance—features favored by natural selection.

In this connection, let us make a speculation about dream symbols. There seems to be reasonable clinical and some experimental (Kline 1972) support for Freud's assertion about sexual symbols: male genitals, or sexuality, being represented by objects like sticks, umbrellas, poles, and knives, whereas female genitals, or sexuality, are represented by hollows, caves, boxes, doors, gates, etc. It could be speculated that the dreamer, if sexually aroused, activates an image of a social releaser geometrically simplified as an object which can penetrate or be penetrated. The same can be speculated about some Jungian archetypes such as mother, child, and hero.

As the elements which compose the innate releasing mechanisms are relatively simple, the releasers can be imitated. In fact, experiments with dummies became an important part of the study of social releasers in ethology. According to Lorenz, people also react to dummies of social releasers and cannot help misinterpreting certain characteristics of animals in terms of innate releasing mechanisms—seeing an eagle or camel as noble and proud. Bizzare forms of clouds or rocks can be anxiety producing, if they remind one of the aggressive attitude of another man. This is, according to Lorenz, the explanation of the "physiognomic perception of objects," which plays a role in primitive mythology, but also in visual arts and perhaps in music (musical sounds imitating human voice as a social releaser).

SOCIAL BONDS: ETHOLOGY VERSUS FREUD

One of the basic deficiencies of Freud's theory of instinct is his belief in the irremediable antagonism between the demands of instincts and the restrictions of society. According to Freud, social bonds develop secondarily. For example, the attachment of a baby to its mother is a result of her satisfying its needs (feeding and oral pleasure). He also says:

We have admitted, too, that in spite of all our pride in our cultural attainments, it is not easy for us to fulfill the requirements of this civilization, or to feel comfortable in it, because the *instinctual* restrictions imposed on us constitute a heavy psychical burden. Well, what we have come to see about the sexual instincts applies equally and perhaps still more to the other ones, the aggressive instincts. (1933)

In contrast to Freud, ethologists believe that, again and again, social life developed under the pressure of selection in different species including primates. Innate or instinctive programs to form bonds are structured as strongly as innate programs of feeding behavior. The selection pressure has molded the instinctive heritage of many species to form social units which have contributed to their survival. Bonds are formed, like mother-young, sexual pair, and subgroups of males, females, and siblings. Some social activities, like the triumph ceremony of wild geese become goals in themselves. Social releasers and reactions to them—performed by innate releasing mechanisms and fixed action patterns—secure the coordination and integration of social units. Even intraspecies aggression secures the survival of the species according to Lorenz; it helps even out the distribution of the animals of a particular species over an inhabitable area, and it selects the strongest animals for reproduction through rival fights—fights very rarely lead to killing or serious injury. In some higher vertebrates, it is instrumental in establishing ranking orders as an organizing principle in group living. Lorenz believes that part of the redirected aggression contributes to positive emotional bonds.

W. Smid, studying the releasing capacity of typical human expressive activity (human laughter), found that it is composed, as other releasers are, of a small number of sign stimuli. "This fact", says Lorenz, "beside many others, supports strongly the contention that the reactions of man to expressive movements of his fellow men are to a large extent caused by the innate releasing mechanisms" (1970-71). According to Lorenz, the innate releasing mechanisms are "the rigid structural elements of human society."

Lorenz observes that the basic themes of literature and theatre from the ancient world to this day (sacrificing oneself for one's friend, manly courage, love of homeland, love of husband and wife, love of children and parents) have a counterpart in the animal world. Two wolves may be fighting each other, but when a predator attacks one of them, the other will fight for his fellow, even to death. Lorenz believes that people's positive value judgments of such acts are outlined by innate releasing mechanisms.

Harlow (1971) distinguishes in rhesus monkeys five basic kinds of love: maternal, infant, peer, heterosexual, and paternal. These kinds of love are interdependent so that heterosexual relationships, maternal behavior, and adult-adult peer relationships are grossly impaired in individuals who were deprived of infant-mother and peer relationships. It is interesting that the lack of infant-mother relationship can be partially compensated for by infant-infant peer relationship (for discussion see Hinde 1974). The attachment to mother was shown to be more dependent on intimate body contact than on breast-feeding.

FUNCTIONAL PLEASURE AND PERFECTION-REINFORCING MECHANISM

In contrast to Freud's *nirvana principle*, K. Buehler, a famous Austrian child psychologist and theoretician, stressed *Funktions-lust* (pleasure of functioning) for functioning itself. Lorenz sees functional pleasure as a subjective aspect of the perfection-reinforcing mechanism, which supposedly exists in animals and people. He speculates that this mechanism reinforces economical perfection in motor skills independently of the ultimate biological goal in whose pursuit the learned movement is developed. Lorenz says,

I still believe and claim that I can see something particularly en-
trancing in a raven's playful soaring antics, in a gibbon's amazing
gymnastic stunts, and in the streamlined flourishes of a porpoise, and
that I saw it long before I had realized that these movements con-
tained an exceptionally large share of individually acquired skill. The
most convincing argument in favor of my speculative assumption lies
in the fact that acquired motor skills of this type, more than any other
types of movements, are forever being performed for their own sake
in the obvious absence of any other motivating or reinforcing factors.
Indeed, the very concept of play is based on this fact to a large extent.
(1965)

Lorenz points to human activities such as dancing, skating, or skiing
which we perform for their own sake for the enjoyment they give us.
He further thinks that this is also at least part of the motivation for all
human arts.

If Lorenz is right, the perfection-reinforcing mechanism could be
regarded as one of the biological roots of Maslow's self-actualization.
This topic is of great interest for psychotherapy.

Traditional psychotherapy has been known to sometimes influence
the patient's posture, walk, gestures, and emotional expression and make
them harmonic, rich, and creative. But much more striking changes can
be achieved when psychomotility itself is made the target of change
during psychotherapy. This happens in dance, expressive dance, sports,
or in relaxation training, psychomime, or abreactive techniques. In some
of these activities, weakening of inhibitions leads to the discovery of the
functional pleasure of movement never experienced by the patients before. In turn, the functional pleasure in movement powerfully enhances
the motivation for psychotherapy. The functional pleasure of free
movement in space in a group inspires the creative seeking of new life
solutions. This can be most convincingly demonstrated in a therapeutic
community of the type described in this book—a therapeutic community
such as Lobec.

MAN AND DOMESTIC ANIMALS

Man shares with domestic animals some disorders of health rarely
found in the wilderness, such as obesity and its consequences. One of
Lorenz's examples is the intake of sugar. For prehistoric man, sugar was
valuable as an energy source, and so evolution put a prize on its attractiveness. Man has not adapted to an abundance of sugar in the envi-

ronment, and if there is an abundance, it leads to obesity, dental cavities, etc. Lorenz believes that both animals and people may have problems if they live in situations for which they are not phylogenetically prepared.

As an example, we will present a study of abundance in a species not phylogenetically adapted to it. The ethologist O. Koenig (1971) from the Biological Institute in Wilhemingberg, Austria, experimented with egrets. The birds were abundantly supplied with all they needed for feeding, drinking, and nesting. There were no enemies, no weather catastrophes, no external problems. This resulted in what Koenig calls "waywardness out of luxury." The young did not make themselves independent and leave the parents when adult but begged to be fed by the parents although food was within their reach. They did not build their own nests but brooded together with their parents. In one nest there were eggs from several pairs—a condition which led to competition about the care of the eggs. More eggs than usual were destroyed so that in some nests only two were left. The defense of the nest was weak so that it was easily possible to take all of the eggs away. Neighbors fought fiercely, whereas in the wilderness they usually avoid such fights. There were also rapes of neighboring females and youngsters. Apparently the luxury led to a deterioration of social life.

In our civilization some people may find themselves in a situation where they cannot or do not want to put effort into pursuing any goals. They suffer from lack of stimulation and their self-esteem is low. Since they do not achieve anything, they often come as patients, but we find difficulty in helping them if they are accommodated to the situation and do not want to change it simultaneously with being treated. Some of them are very rich; others live on welfare.

Lorenz counts among civilized man's eight deadly sins "the waning of all strong feelings and emotion as a result of overindulgence."

> The process of technology and pharmacology furthers an increasing intolerance of everything inducing the least unpleasure. Thus human beings lose the ability to experience joy that is only attainable through surmounting serious obstacles. The natural waves of joy and sorrow ebb away into an imperceptible oscillation of unutterable boredom. (1974)

Bad rearing of animals

Wild animals in captivity suffer deprivation. If they are young, they display easily recognizable disorders of phylogenetic mechanisms according to Lorenz. He calls this brand of deprivation simply *bad rearing*. Some fixed motor patterns, releasing mechanisms, and social inhibitions are particularly sensitive. Fixed motor patterns, such as fighting or activities belonging to the reproductive life, are diminished or uncoordinated. For example, the process of building a nest is often interrupted. Carnivorous and omnivorous animals when breeding in captivity are prone to eat their own young.

We will describe the observations made by Paul Leyhausen (Lorenz and Leyhausen 1973), which may be of great theoretical importance for psychotherapy. Leyhausen described several wild cats in captivity which were unable to give a killing bite—a very definite movement sequence regarded as a fixed motor pattern. In these animals, the killing-bite pattern can be elicited by electrical stimulation of a certain point in the hypothalamus; however, this experience does not help the animal to use the killing bite with prey. They observed most closely a female wild cat named Freda, of the Serval species. She missed exposure to the releasers during her sensitive period and was unable to make a killing. Many attempts at eliciting her fixed pattern of killing bite by situational hyperstimulation, stimulus therapy, were unsuccessful. Yet finally they succeeded. A more experienced conspecific attacked the prey animal, and in competition with him, the killing bite was released in Freda and has functioned since then.

Can the behavioral deficits of some of our patients be explained in a similar way? It is true that children do not live in cages, but in their assumptive world there also may be bars erected by their parents through restrictions and instigation of fear and guilt. These patients are unable to respond emotionally to social stimuli, be it with warm feelings, or anger, joy, sadness, or assertiveness. They are unable to laugh, get angry, cry, engage in sexual courtship, or accomplish sexual intercourse. Sometimes the inhibition affects only some sectors of the motor and autonomic patterns, sometimes it is generalized.

When the highest psychic functions are inhibited, primitive psychomotor patterns rise to the surface. Kretschmer (1952) called them *hypobulic* mechanisms (as the counterpart of primitive cognitive processes, which he called *hyponoic mechanisms*, approximately identical with Freud's *primary processes*). We see crying and laughter in a sleepy child; rhythmical movements (from rocking and drumming with the fingers in relaxation of thought to stereotypies in hysterical twilight states and schizophrenias); and motor storms and convulsions (in panic, hysterical seizures, ecstatic states). All these phenomena can be observed in hypnotic states and during abreactions.

Kramer (1968) suggested that fixed action patterns may be inhibited in neurotic patients and can be released by abreaction. He gave examples of abreactions which happen during therapeutic LSD intoxications.

We arrived at the same hypothesis by extensive experience with guided abreactions, described later. These abreactions, provided they are part of a complex psychotherapeutic plan, lead sometimes to instant changes of expressive behavior which become permanent if working-through continues. Abreactions are usually connected with the memories of situations when the patient was hurt, physically or mentally, felt fear, anger, grief, loneliness, and cried for a caring and loving person. In abreaction, the situation or a series of similar situations is reproduced together with the appropriate affect, which often in the original situation was inhibited.

It is not essential whether the concept of fixed motor patterns—which is not generally accepted—is used in the explanation of abreaction. In any case, the abreactive phenomena deserve behavioral and neurophysiological study and their analysis may be, as we believe, the psychotherapist's contribution to human ethology.

Appendix D

ACTION TECHNIQUES

Verbal behavior is only one of the sources of information about the patient. Observing his behaviour in a variety of situations is also necessary to obtain a broad picture of the patient's personality and the problems involved. Furthermore, talking on its own is not sufficient to change an individual's behaviour. We do not learn to play tennis, drive a car, master a new language by talking only, but by acting, often in model situations. Psychotherapy, whose aim is to change the personality and life style of the patient has to provide a variety of situations in which unsolved problems and traumatic events from the past can be relived and new patterns of behavior can be tried out and trained. Learning by doing does not, of course, exclude thinking and feeling, they are interconnected.

Let us take the example of a young man who is generally inhibited, particularly toward male authority figures. He has poor posture, has a functionally uneconomical distribution of muscle tonus (some muscles being too tense and some too relaxed), mumbles, and is generally unexpressive. Let us suppose that through the transference relationship in long-term psychoanalytic treatment, he releases his anger, which he has never dared express toward his father, an important, disturbing figure of his group schema. This would take a long time, even if the treatment were relatively successful, and would probably not be sufficiently reflected in his overt behavior. His overt behavior is important, because, this is what people react and respond to with complementary counterbehavior. In this way, the old circuit of his group system was initiated. By receiving further reinforcement, this aspect of his group schema—one not easily changed in the first place—is maintained.

The young man's patterns of posture and movement are an effective barrier to the expression of anger. He represses also the proprioceptive (kinesthetic) signals which would make him aware of the tension in his body and the nature of his emotional state. He may not even know that he is tense all the time and may also have such autonomic symptoms as speeding up of the heart rate and sweating.

If we see the patient's repressed anger not only as a conflict of ideas in his head but more broadly as the state of his total organism and as a style of interaction with his environment, we will ask whether it is possible to intervene at several points of the pathological circuit. We can help him become aware of the tension in his muscles, for example, and induce relaxation by massage or by suggested movement. This may elicit fear which can then be explored. He may be pressed to talk loudly, and this may elicit fear also. He may be induced to observe the tension in his muscles to reestablish his kinesthetic awareness. Or he may be instructed, as in psychomime, to do certain movements which go counter to his postural and motor rigidity, and this may lay bare, unexpectedly, his feelings. He may be instructed to interact in a model situation with a person or symbolic object, or to use tools such as boppers to express anger, or if he does not feel any, to fight with them which may eventually release repressed anger. Finally, we may observe and guide his interaction with people in his life—father, coworker, girlfriend. These possible approaches can be combined.

One of the first who saw the total involvement of the organism in neurosis and talked about the identity of *character armor* with *muscular armor* was W. Reich (1949).

> Every neurotic is musculary dystonic and every cure is directly reflected in muscular habitus. (p. 343)

> The armor makes the individual less sensitive to unpleasure, but also reduces his libidinal and aggressive motility, and with that, his capacity for pleasure and achievement. . . . The character armor consumes energy. (p. 342)

We use techniques suggested by Reich and further developed in *bio-energetics* (Lowen 1975). We use relaxation, according to the system of *progressive relaxation* of E. Jacobson (1970) or more comprehensive *autogenic training* (Schultz 1966; Schultz and Luthe 1959ab). Valuable techniques to change kinesthetic awareness have been contributed by Elsa Gindler and her followers (Stolze 1959, in Germany; Goldberg in Israel; and Shatan in the United States). Imagination is used in Leuner's guided imagery (1969) and in Schorr's *psycho-imagination therapy* (1972). Though less well known, Malamud's attempts to combine imagination with encounter exercises, known as *Self-confrontation* are excellent.

Sometimes expressing fantasies with materials like paper and colors, clay, papier-maché, and dough can be very revealing and can release strong emotions. We will mention here only G. and U. Derbolowsky's *Lambano therapy* (1966). Other nonverbal techniques used in Germany, not well known in America are described in H. Petzold (1974).

Integrated psychotherapy does not usually employ special sessions for psychodrama, psychomime, or other action techniques. They are used as the situation seems to demand. Their use when the families of patients are present is facilitated by other patients.

We shall deal with *psychodrama*, the first action technique, which influenced most of the others. We shall describe *psychomime* which we developed, and finally, *abreaction*.

Each technique introduced by the therapist may be used as resistance by the patient and the therapist must be constantly aware of this. Psychoanalytic conservatives point to these risks. However, we have persuaded ourselves that on a higher level—especially for someone with psychoanalytic experience—the danger can usually be minimized and the results repay the risk. As is often the case, the saying, nothing ventured, nothing gained, is valid here. In the future, we hope to increase the precision of the application of action techniques through outcome and process studies.

PSYCHODRAMA

Psychodrama was the first action technique introduced into modern psychotherapy. It is also the most important, and has both directly and indirectly influenced gestalt, encounter and some abreactive techniques, to name a few. As psychoanalysis is associated with the name of Sigmund Freud, so psychodrama is associated with that of J. L. Moreno (1946, 1959). The important implications of Moreno's ideas are absorbed in the theoretical framework of this book.

Psychodrama has both *fact-finding* and *therapeutic* value. Even in the initial interview, patients may use role-playing to show exactly how they and their significant persons behave. Of course, the data must be critically evaluated, but much more information on a patient is gained through role-playing than through an interview alone. In addition the process of reexposure, if it is appropriate, can begin during the first session.

Since many examples of psychodrama in clinical situations were described in part IV, we will give here only the simple classification of the psychodramatic situations we have been using in our work. Only four variables are introduced—*role, time, reality character*, and *communication means*—each with three alternatives. This provides eighty-one possible psychodramatic situations. More variables can be easily instituted, but those mentioned are sufficient for an initial orientation.

Role: One's own   *Reality of represented events:* real
Other complementary   possible
Other unrelated   fantasy (dream,
                                                     hallucination)

Time: past   *Communication means*: verbal only (role-playing)
        present   nonverbal only (psychomime)
        future   both (psychodrama)

Role

In psychodrama, persons can play their own roles, or the roles of others. In our notation, *roles* will be designated by small letters, *persons* by capital letters. For example, the protagonist P (the person who is in focus) plays his own role p and that will be designated "pP". If he will play the role of his wife, this will be designated "wife P". The other patients will be called *O1, O2, O3*, etc. The interaction of two or more persons is shown by a dash, and an arrow (→) denotes the sequence of dramatic episodes.

To illustrate, we will take a male patient in the Day House during Family Night, where his wife is present, and deal with their marital problems in front of the group. *P* is the male patient.

1. pP-wifeWife. The patient (protagonist) and his wife reenact the conflict which they had had at home two days before.

2. pP-wife O2. On the preceding day, the patient had discussed this conflict in the group and, according to his version, it was reenacted by

him and a female patient *O2* who felt angry with the protagonist and thought that she could empathize with his wife. The role of his wife had been played by the female patient *O2*.

Making a comparison of performances 1 and 2 is important since it reveals the differences in how the protagonist views his wife's feelings (a view which may be quite distorted), how another person views the wife's feelings, and how the wife herself actually feels about the conflict.

3. pWife-wife P. *Role reversal*. At Family Night, after the protagonist and his wife play their own roles as described in performance 1, they are asked to exchange roles and, at the same time, to exchange seats. It is very important that, no matter who plays a role, each role is attached to a specific place. This is not only a most efficient way of avoiding confusion and saving time in explaining who is talking for whom; it also facilitates taking the role of the other (perhaps even fusing one's body schema with that of the other). For example, the protagonist, when shifting to his wife's seat and talking for her, may have the strange feeling of identifying with her and this may lead him, to his surprise, to some realization of how she feels which may not have occurred to him before.

4. pO2-wife P. Just after the reenactment described in performance 2, the protagonist was asked to play the role of hiw wife W, to show the female patient *O2* how he thinks his wife feels.

Role reversal has both therapeutic and theoretical significance. It creates an opportunity to study the range of roles with which a person is able to identify and to what degree, and to explore the properties of the person's group schema.

5. pP-wife Wife, O2. *Doubling*. At the Family Night session, as the protagonist *P* and his wife W interact, a female patient *O2* is invited (or volunteers) to talk for the wife. For example, the female patient *O2* might feel that the wife W is not fully expressing what she thinks, perhaps because she is afraid of her husband *P*. The therapist asks whether the wife W agrees with the double *O2*. Sometimes there are multiple doubles. The doubling during Family Night saves a lot of time since the patients, as doubles, are capable of catalyzing a process which, in family therapy with one family only, would take a long time or would not have such an impact. We call this process *amplified family*. It is, of course, the responsibility of the therapist to continuously assess the rewards and costs for both the marital partners, and to go no further than is useful for the therapeutic process.

6. pP,O5,O6-wifeWife, O1O2O3O4. Both the protagonist and his

wife W have *multiple doubles*. Sometimes almost the entire group, including the visitors, become involved in doubling.

7. pP *Monologue*. The protagonist is asked to think aloud about his relationship to his wife. He may be asked to do this in her presence, but to turn his chair around so that he does not face her. He may also be instructed to talk directly to her, but when it is difficult to tell her something, to turn his head aside while saying it, which symbolizes that she does not hear it.

8. pPO5. *Monologue with a double*. The protagonist has a monologue, and another patient *O5* stands behind him, touching his shoulder when he/she wants to talk for him. Naturally, the protagonist can agree or disagree with the statements made by *O5*.

9. p*1* P-p*2* P. *Monologue—interaction of subselves*. The protagonist plays two or more parts of himself, shifting from one chair to another. For example, the protagonist has a moral conflict, and p*1* and p*2* represent two opposing attitudes with respect to resolving the conflict. The protagonist may also portray two aspects of his personality, for example, *strong me-weak me, coward-bold, whining me-despising my whining, feeling inferior-feeling superior*. This interaction of subselves can lead to the exploration of the origin of the disunity in the group schema. The interaction of subselves continues in interaction with role schemas, leading, for example, to an interaction between one's parents which had occurred in childhood.

10. pP-image. *Interaction with an imagined other* ("empty" or "auxiliary" chair). The protagonist talks to his father, who is not present (and may even be dead) but whom he imagines is sitting opposite him in a chair. He may simply talk to his imagined father, or he may express anger toward him, not just verbally, but by physically getting up and hitting the chair with a bopper. From this psychodramatic technique other techniques have developed, such as gestalt (used, for example, in reliving dreams) and various types of abreactive therapies (Casriel 1972; Janov 1970).

11. pP → oP → objP. *Autodrama*. The Protagonist plays, in succession, the roles of all participants—even, at times, including inanimate objects *Ob*. For example, a male patient recounts a dream in which he is standing in the open doorway of a bus. The bus driver shouts at him and then closes the doors on him, squeezing him; he feels that he is being crushed between the doors and tries with all his might to tear the doors apart. By having successive monologues for himself, for the bus driver *O*, and for the squeezing doors, *Obj*, he goes through emotions which

release his anger toward his father—the bus driver—whom he blames for having left home when the patient was a child, a circumstance which he feels destroyed his life.

Of course, in autodrama, the protagonist can switch constantly from his own role to another, and back again. For example, if the protagonist reenacts the conflict between himself and his wife, he plays both roles, switching from one seat to the other: pP→←wife P.

The technique of autodrama was a favorite of Fritz Perls, who used it with great virtuosity and inventiveness.

Time

In psychodrama, we can reexpose a patient to a situation from the *past*. It may be the recent past; an episode which occurred between two patients in the morning may be reexposed that afternoon. But it may be something that happened between a patient and spouse the day before their wedding ten years ago. Or it may be something that occurred in a patient's early childhood.

Psychodrama can also deal with the *future*. For example, during their last week at the Day House, we asked the three patients who were leaving to imagine that they would meet again in a bar in two years; they then asked each other how they were, and how they had lived over the two years. Or, to give another example, when a girl and her boyfriend are asked to talk to each other as they might in two years there are sometimes surprises for both participants and observers. It may turn out that the girl does not expect to be with her boyfriend in two years.

Reality of represented events

The events portrayed in psychodrama can be *real*: a patient may be asked to reproduce an event as exactly as possible so that we can explore in detail what happened (be it a marital conflict from the same morning, or a vague memory about an episode from early childhood which becomes vivid during the performance). Psychodrama can also deal with what has not happened, but what is *possible*. For example, we may ask a male patient, who is shy and has difficulty starting a conversation with a girl, to role play various approaches with different female patients. Another example is a psychiatric resident who participated in a workshop and who was in conflict at that time over whether to return to his native country, India, or to stay in the United States. Both alternatives were role played in detail—meeting his relatives and friends in India, leaving his friends in the United States, etc. The performance was designed to help him in making his difficult decision.

Finally, psychodrama may deal with a *fantasy*, for example, the dream mentioned earlier. Psychodrama can also deal with a daydream, a presently produced fantasy, or a hallucination. Moreno's favorite fantasy was *The Magic Shop*: Usually one of the therapists sets up a shop on the stage. The shop is stocked with symbolic items such as courage, love of one's friend, having been able to have a baby, and so on. The items are not for sale, but can be exchanged for values which the patient is willing to give up. The therapist, as the vendor, gives suggestions for the exchange. A thorough knowledge of the patient is necessary. This technique is very demanding for the therapist because, the therapist not only has to quickly produce ideas but must check their suitability as well: the offers for exchange can function as undesirable implicit interpretations. The therapist must be aware that even suggestions for psychodramatic activities are implicit interpretations. If successful, the method may throw light on the hierarchy of a patient's goals.

Communication means

Usually, in psychodramatic action, total behavior is used. But sometimes it is useful to leave out the verbal part. The participants can either interact in psychomime (described later on), or their interaction may be vocal but nonverbal—that is, they may speak in gibberish, or sing melodies without words.

Several outstanding features about psychodrama amaze those who witness it for the first time. First of all, there is often tremendous *emotional involvement* for the participants. Although all the participants know that this is a play, they often react as though it were real. For example, in performance 2, when the patient chooses a female patient who reminds him of his wife, he may become involved in a quarrel with her in which he seems to forget that she is not really his wife. He may get very angry, and she may react with tears (as his wife might have). When asked, she may explain that the episode reminds her of how her husband or boyfriend hurt her. This is not chance. When we ask a protagonist to choose a woman to portray his wife, he chooses (sometimes without fully realizing it) a woman similar to his wife. This is particularly amazing when the participants are strangers.

The second surprising feature is the broad scope of role-taking capacities. Spontaneously, without any rehearsal (which would diminish the credibility), people are able to take on the role of another, irrespective of age or sex. A male patient may be vague or reluctant to say how his wife reacts to him, but when playing her role, he may be swept completely into the role and may, for instance, reveal her very unfavorable opinion of him. Some of our dreams witness how well we are able to reconstruct the behavior of other people, but there is no better opportunity than psychodrama to systematically explore the capacity of role-taking, which seems to be important for mental health.

This capacity, of course, can be trained, and some psychodramatists train staff members as assistants (*auxiliary egos*, Moreno 1946). In our therapeutic community and groups, our patients are sufficiently trained, so that we do not feel the need for special assistants.

The third amazing thing revealed by psychodrama is how basically similar people and life situations are. For instance, in a group of strangers, a man volunteers to reveal some of his conflicts with his wife, played by a female participant whom he has chosen. After a while he exclaims in amazement, "She speaks exactly like my wife!" This can even be demonstrated cross-culturally: In our international workshop, which was arranged in conjunction with the III International Congress of Psychodrama, we composed simulated families of participants from various parts of the world. It showed both cultural differences (a Japanese "wife" bowed deeply when a North American "mother-in-law" arrived) and basic similarities in relationships.

A classical psychodramatic session has three phases: warming up, psychodrama, and discussion. The warming up phase is a group process, under the leadership of a therapist, from which a protagonist emerges as the focus of attention. The second phase, psychodrama, focuses on the problems of the protagonist, but scans all the participants. The task is to choose a protagonist whose problems can be shared and are important for the others too. A skillful psychodramatist—following the methods of the late J. L. Moreno—finds a person whose psychodrama would be lively and of interest to others. (A psychodramatist in this case is not unlike a hypnotist who has the skills to pick, from the audience, a suitable subject.) In a therapeutic community with twenty or so patients, and when everybody wants to do something, the right choice has to be based on careful consideration. Ideally, psychodrama deals with the present problems of everyone, so that for those who are neither protagonists nor auxiliaries, important observational learning takes place.

PSYCHOMIME

In psychomime (Knobloch, 1971, Knobloch, Junova et al. 1964, Knobloch et al., 1974, Junova et al. 1966), *the patients create through movement*

a fantasy world in which they seek solutions to their problems in playful ways.
The group, or an individual, is told to perform a certain task—for example to imagine the group is *shipwrecked on a desert island.* The instructions are standardized and broadly formulated so that the participants
can improvise and use their own solutions. The task is done in pantomime without talk. A discussion of the impressions and experiences the
participants underwent follows. Certain tasks are acted simultaneously
by the whole group; others, such as the *fashion show,* by individuals in
front of the group. Psychomime was designed mainly for groups, but
many tasks can be also used in individual therapy or when dealing with
couples.

From several hundred exercises, portraying basic patterns of various
life situations, the following will serve as simple examples:

1. *Dominance-submission.* After a few gymnastic exercises and competitive games, the participants are asked whether they regard themselves
as being *dominant* (assertive, not yielding easily) or *submissive* (non-asser-
tive, yielding easily to the demands of others). The ones who label themselves as *dominant* are sent to one side of the room; the *submissive* ones
to the other side. Partners are chosen so that every dominant faces a
submissive. All are then told that they must reach the other side where
their partner is standing, but that the way is not easy. Between them
and their goal is an extremely narrow path on which they must meet.
On either side of the path is an unpleasant area of mud and water, so
that if one yields and steps aside he or she will fall in, and certainly no
one wants to fall in.

Without talking, the partners meet and a variety of reactions follow.
Some pairs remain undecisive, watching each other for a long time;
others try to push their partners aside, sometimes using tricks; some
proceed with the idea they will yield, but seeing the aggressiveness of
their partners, begin to fight; and some try to cooperate and assist their
partners in getting to the other side by such techniques as crawling
between their legs or utilizing a modified form of leapfrog.

This simple exercise can quickly lead to the exposure of a variety of
intense emotions. Two men start fighting. A girl steps aside when her
male partner makes a commanding gesture, but regrets it afterward (it
reminds her of her situation in marriage). Frequently the discrepancy
between the person's opinion of himself and his behavior becomes rapidly apparent. One girl goes to the submissive group and this inspires
laughter in the whole group. She is surprised and protests that she really

is submissive in life. However, when she meets her male partner she becomes aggressive, tries to push him aside, and starts churlish fighting.

Another variety of this exercise is to divide the group into subgroups of about six and have the members of each subgroup line up one behind the other facing a wall. Initially, the arrangement in the line-ups is random; then the following instruction is given: "Please arrange yourselves so that each of you will find your place somewhere between the dominant and submissive extremes, with the one who is the most dominant nearest the wall, and the one who is the most submissive at the end of the line. Find the appropriate place for you in the line-up, and if that place is already occupied by someone else, then push him or her out of the way." This exercise can be used for other hierarchies: "Imagine that these are your siblings and you can choose whether you are the oldest, the youngest, or where you are in between." This exercise sometimes shows the remarkable difference between how people see themselves as submissive or dominant and how they act. Participants may classify themselves differently from the way they really feel, because they do not like to show their real feelings or because they do not take the exercise seriously. This can be recognized by further exercises.

It is not important whether the concepts *dominant* and *submissive* are clearly defined at the beginning. This is only a starting point whose aim is to elicit idiosyncratic behavior patterns and problems. In most instances, this occurs when participants by acting instead of talking are seduced into reacting to the exercise as if it were a real life situation.

Psychomime helps to find out what the problems are, helps to change the picture a person has about his behavior, and helps to show what reactions in others his behavior provokes. In exercises such as this, we usually focus on several individuals who show an especially apparent discrepancy between their self-concept and their behavior. Some pairs are asked to repeat the exercise while being observed by other members of the group and this may cause them to begin doubting their view of themselves. Others, for whom the exercise was seemingly only play without significance, spontaneously remember it weeks or months later, when they realize that it made them alert to a current similar situation and led to some discovery about themselves. They then indicate it as a turning point of some sort (new self-awareness, new decision, etc.).

For practical reasons, we have divided the psychomimic exercises into *easy* and *difficult*. The *difficult* exercises are designed to explore a particular problem—are pertinent to an individual, or to the group as a whole. The *easy* exercises are designed to warm up the whole group or a particular individual, to induce an optimal structure, or to create a playful atmosphere. It is useful to conclude group psychotherapy (psychomime infiltrated all our psychotherapy) with *easy* exercises which help the group to relax and induce an optimistic mood. Music—from baroque to contemporary dance music—is normally used at this point, according to the mood of the patients and therapist. Some exercises are reminiscent or identical with those used in sensitivity and T-groups.

Easy exercises

Walking. Walk anywhere. Walk as if moving from home to work. Walk as if returning home from work. Walk as if carrying a very heavy suitcase. Walk as if against a strong wind. Walk around carefully avoiding people. Walk around bumping or pushing people. Walk as if going somewhere you have to go, but do not want to go. Walk as if depressed. Walk as in pain. Walk as if anxious. Walk as if suspicious of everybody else. Walk as if angry. Walk as if embarrassed. Walk as if very self confident. Walk as if going for your first date. Walk without any noise. Walk as if you are coming home late at night and do not want to awake anyone. (This is usually less noisy than walking without any noise.)

Introducing oneself. In an initial meeting either in a psychotherapeutic group or a training workshop, considerable time can be saved if introductions are postponed until after the initial group exercises. Motor activity (of itself) and carefully chosen types of nonverbal exercises (including competitive ones) help to break the barriers and inhibitions. Introducing oneself can be made into a game. After saying his or her name, a person indicates by raising a hand how loudly the others should repeat the name, and this is then repeated three times. Names are better remembered. Introductions in a group are often a formality and a waste of time, since some names are not heard by everyone. With this game, we collect interesting observations about each person's self-evaluation.

Small decisional conflict. You leave home or walk somewhere and remember that you have forgotten something when you are quite far from home (represented as in the middle of the room). Show without words how you will go through your conflict, and whether you will continue or return. How will you decide? (One obsessional neurotic could not decide, so we had to interrupt his exercise.) In addition to the obvious parameters such as the length of time necessary to reach a decision and whether to continue or return, there are minute behavior signs emerging from all these exercises which we perceive intuitively and which have heuristic value for forming very tentative hypotheses about the person in question.

Persuading to join. One or two persons who feel self-confident volunteer to go to one side of the room, whereas the rest of the group go to the other side. These two persons want to persuade the rest of the group to join them. They can only use gestures—no force—in approaching the rest of the group. In a reverse variation, one person is on one side of the room and has to be persuaded by the rest of the group to join them. A useful subject for this exercise is a person who sulks a lot and goes through the motions of refusing the invitation of the group and being in the spotlight. Such a person is given an opportunity to understand his pattern, and others can point out details of his behavior which may be helpful in tracing his pattern.

Fashion show. One patient after another shows by gestures what he or she is wearing and talks across the stage as if in a fashion show. These exercises sometimes reveal behavior potentials which surprise us and which are hard to discover in other ways.

Zoological garden. Everybody chooses an animals to represent and behaves accordingly, making appropriate sounds.

Difficult exercises

Forbidden fruit.   A ball is placed on a chair in the middle of the room which symbolizes forbidden fruit. The participants are told, "There is something which you long for in your life, but you know you should not have it: it is forbidden. What will you do? Close your eyes and find out if there is any conflict like that in your present life. If you cannot find any, go back in your memory through your past until you find such a conflict in your life. How did you solve it? How would you solve it now?

After a few minutes, the patients are asked, one by one, to get up and move, without words, toward the symbolic object. Basically, behavior here is similar to that of experimental animals in the approach-avoidance conflict situation. Many patients start moving toward the object quickly, but the more they approach it, the more they slow down. There is some moving back and forth, as they oscillate between approach and avoidance, and there is a tendency to go around in circles. However, the considerable individual variations of this basic pattern reveal both individual styles and individual problems. In some patients, serious conflicts are reflected not only in motor, but also in autonomic reactions (blushing, getting pale, crying, sweating). In others, although no such reactions are apparent and they seem to perform the task without any involvement, this is not necessarily so. They may report later that they experienced an intense inner conflict. In some instances, they are not aware of any reaction, and it comes an hour or so later, sometimes in a dramatic way (trembling, sweating, crying, headache, etc.). What is especially interesting, and not without theoretical significance, is that some patients, especially those in a phase of resistance, start the task unwillingly and show by their gestures that this is merely an unpleasant, formal task, without any real significance. Their gestures are careless, and they perfunctorily perform the task. But after a while, going through the movements, they move, against their will, into a high degree of involvement and express personal problems.

One young woman in the residential therapeutic community at Lobec tried to find some solution to serious inner conflict over her relationship with a married man. Being at Lobec and away from her partner, she felt strong enough to end her suffering, as she called her relationship—a suffering which had gone on for years, without her being able to control it. During one group session, she decided to break up the relationship. The other patients sympathized with her solution but did not believe her, because of fine discrepancies in her behavior. They did not believe she had solved the problem as she repeatedly claimed, and suspected that she would not be able to break off the relationship after she returned to Prague. Their disbelief made her angry; she refused to talk about it and she said that for her there was nothing more to talk about, as she had made her decision. She began to isolate herself from other patients. In the forbidden fruit exercise she quickly rid herself of the symbolic object without any signs of emotion, as if this were a purely rational situation. But suddenly her behavior changed; she described her experience later: "I only followed instructions, not thinking about any particular conflict, and acting automatically. And then I suddenly felt in my body, especially in my knees, a sudden weakness and I felt dizzy. Only afterwards the image appeared and I understood what was going on. I felt near to the man I loved. But I knew that it was hopeless, as he was married and had two children. I knew that we had to part, but I did not have the necessary strength yet. For a while I felt like suffocating, and then came the mentioned spell of weakness. Nevertheless, I felt that I had really told him good-bye and that there was no way back to him. Before this episode, I tried to persuade others and myself that there was no problem for me any more. But only now I felt that I made it real and that I could not take it back again. This feeling continued for two days. I tried to persuade myself that nothing had really happened and that I had the freedom to decide after my return to Prague. Something happened so that I experienced the irrevocable parting."

Another female patient, a nurse, approached the forbidden fruit like a thief. She looked around and then quickly took hold of the ball and hid it under her sweater. There was something so unusual and strange in her behavior that the patients were curious as to its meaning. Although she said that it was "just nothing," a random idea which had occurred to her, this episode incited the group of patients—and staff—to look more closely at this patient who, they felt, was keeping something to herself. They discovered that the patient was a drug addict, which fact she had hidden, so far successfully, in the therapeutic community. She had stolen drugs in the hospital in which she had worked before, precisely in the way she stole the forbidden fruit. She had continued her habit in milder form even while at the Center. Her performance—similar to that of some of the other patients in psychomimic exercises—was a sort of confession compulsion, facilitated by the task.

Another male patient had no difficulty approaching the forbidden fruit and taking it immediately. He showed no sign of conflict. This was a patient who had many affairs with women but usually left them after a short time. He had been divorced twice, both times because of his behavior with other women. He had never been able to develop a deep and lasting relationship with a woman. During the affairs he was free of guilt, but it came later regularly. The neurotic symptoms which had compelled him to seek psychiatric help were connected with it. The exercise revealed the same pattern. He approached the forbidden fruit—thinking about a woman—directly, as if without any inhibitions, but two hours later he had anxiety attacks with strong autonomic accompaniment.

The king and his guards. The patients or trainees are asked to close their eyes for a few minutes and imagine a wish they want very much to be fulfilled. When they open their eyes, they are told that there is a fairy-tale king who can fulfill that wish. But there are four guards to guard the entrance to the castle. Four volunteers stand in two rows in front of the wall where the imaginary entrance is. Each patient, one by one, attempts to go to the king, but first have to persuade the guards, each separately, to let him in. However, the guards have instructions from the king not to let anybody in and risking severe punishment if they do so.

It happens only very rarely that the participants do not fully immerse themselves into the fantasy. Talking is not permitted, so everybody tries to explain in pantomime why he needs to see the king. It may be something he wants for himself (health or money) or for someone else (for a mother with a sick child or for mankind). A male participant might pretend to be a high officer and behave dominantly toward the guards; another might come assertively and show a document permitting him to enter; still another might try to bribe the guards with money or with alcohol. A female participant might arrive with a baby, another show that she is pregnant, and still another be seductive toward the guards (male or female). Some try to reach the entrance by force from the very beginning, others after they have failed with other methods. Usually force fails. Some, with great inventiveness, distract the guards' attention and then jump in. There is also broad variability in how the guards behave and whether or not they let anybody in.

One male psychiatric resident in a workshop, unable to obtain access, knelt before a guard played by a head nurse, and begged to be let into the castle. At a certain moment, it became apparent that the resident was no longer playing, that getting through the guards symbolized something very important for him. He was desperate, had tears in his eyes, and finally collapsed. (He later claimed that he lost consciousness for a short time.) The guard grabbed one of his legs and pulled him away. Another male resident became terribly upset and angry, and with tears in his eyes cried: "That bitch!" The same episode happened in another workshop with psychiatric residents in Canada. A female resident was attacked for similar behavior. This initiated a chain of insights for her during the process groups which followed. Fantasy games like this can cause strong involvement both in patients and trainees. (See also the description of forbidden fruit in the history of Anne, chapter 17.)

Shipwrecked on a desert island. Participants are asked to imagine they are on a liner on the ocean. They may do what they want. After a while a new instruction is given: there is a violent storm, and they become shipwrecked. There are two small islands to which the participants can swim, each island is only big enough for about fifteen people.

Some groups easily divide, and each half inhabits one island. Others start fighting for the island they imagine to be more attractive than the other.

In most cases, the inhabitants of each island quickly elaborate on their group fantasy, including the stresses of living, and the distribution of roles. They quickly develop a feeling of cohesiveness and become critical of the other island as an out-group. Some groups cooperate well, people are busy building shelters, discovering food, or signaling to possible rescuers.

In one training group of occupational therapists, somebody found a badly injured person and the group started to nurse him. In another training group, a resident in psychiatry attracted a lot of attention as he almost drowned and lost consciousness. He was saved by the others who succeeded in bringing him to life. In one group, a man invited a woman from the other island and she swam over. That made another woman close to him angry; she threw sand in his eyes and left the island. The participants of the play form small groups, get married, or build houses for their families (see the history of Anne, chapter 7).

Fancy-dress ball. The patients are asked to participate in an imaginary fancy-dress ball. In one variation of the exercise, they are permitted only a minimal use of additional clothing or accessories and are asked to portray their roles in turn, using gesture and nonverbal sound.

When the participants present their roles in brief turns, this is a relatively easy task; when they play them as longer episodes with the help of other group members, this exercise may lead to an intensive therapeutic experience.

A young man in the therapeutic community in Lobec choses the role of an executioner. He picked out the female psychologist as the subject for a pantomimed execution. The deed was performed with an imaginary axe, but done in such a ruthless and realistic fashion and with such apparent emotional indifference that the observing group members were horrified and somewhat frightened. The young man then rejoined the observers and sat smiling for the remainder of the session. He was inaccessible for discussion so that nothing was learned about his feelings.

This young man came to the therapeutic community because of recurring, peculiar attacks, the symptoms of which were facial pallor, tachycardia up to 200/minute and profuse sweating. He was aware of no particular emotion preceding or accompanying the state and believed (as did some physicians) that the problem was not psychological. He had come reluctantly to the therapeutic community.

In his autobiography, he described his childhood in a small village. His father, a hunch-back, remarried after the death of the patient's mother. According to the patient, the step-mother became domineering and cruel, both to the son and to his father. When the patient was fifteen years old, he made a decision to kill his step-mother. One day, he and a friend lay in wait for her near a path which she took through the forest each evening. His plan, however, was frustrated by the appearance of other people on the path at the same time as his step-mother and he never again worked up enough courage to carry it out. At the time of his treatment, the patient was still living at home and the situation was unresolved.

The other patients in the Therapeutic Community had not been particularly impressed by the young man's story as he originally told it. To them, it had seemed unconvincing and lacking in emotion. It was only after the enactment of his executioner fantasy that they thought about it seriously. During the dinner following the session, the patients were thoughtful and preoccupied with the preceding event, but the young man seemed to be relaxed and even gay. After dinner, the community met for another session. Suddenly, while another patient played psychodrama on the stage, the young man began to have an attack. For the first time, he became aware of its connection with his murderous impulses. This was confirmed by later developments and he soon lost his affliction.

Psychomime in training groups

Psychomime can be an efficient tool at the beginning of training groups to warm up the group and speed the formation of group cohesiveness. Later it may help clarify an individual's highly personal problems. Others can learn about some of the general features of the personal problem, and become deeply involved without knowing concrete details which the person in question would not like to share. They can connect the experience with their own problems. Psychomime can even be used with groups of psychiatric personnel who work together. After such a training group one or more persons regularly come to the leader and reveal some discoveries connected with highly personal insights.

In a training group composed of psychiatric residents in the United States, one man reacted strongly while performing the forbidden fruit exercise. Although it could be guessed that a conflicting relationship to a woman was in question, this was never established with certainty and neither the leader nor the participants tried to find out. Nonetheless, many members empathized with him and projected their inner problems on him as he, extremely tense, oscillated before the forbidden object not able to decide whether to take it or not. Many times it seemed that he decided to take the symbolic object; he touched it, but then withdrew his hand.

As he was unable to decide, the leader suggested that he explore what would happen if he kept it after he touched it. In another exercise, he was closely followed by three people who represented his conscience. One is again and again surprised how such a highly artificial situation can provoke strong emotions of guilt, shame, fear, and panic. The resident tried to withstand his conscience, but he soon gave up and tried to escape. A third exercise followed. The man stood before an imaginary court of justice, with judge, prosecutor, and defense attorney. This was a pantomimic procedure, but later the leader suggested that the participants talk.

Advantages of psychomime

Besides eliminating verbal cliches, psychomime has the following special advantages:

All participants can be active at the same time, whereas in a verbal group, only one can talk while others must listen. In a verbal group, a person with a serious problem is more likely to escape attention. Giving the same task to different people has the advantage of being partly a test: the therapist gets acquainted with all possible types of reaction to the same stimulus and can quickly estimate individual differences. The therapist structures various situations and then scans the group constantly for the most revealing reactions. With the help of further exercises or in the discussion which generally follows every exercise, the group later focuses on these reactions.

Psychomime has also a quasi-experimental character; psychodynamic hypotheses about a person can be studied through exercises. The therapist is not dependent upon the patient's verbal report but can compare it with the behavior elicited in the exercise situation.

Some exercises may serve as sociometric tests to show the mutual relationships within the group.

Various combinations of instructions can stimulate group action toward certain experimental goals, such as splitting the group or developing competitiveness as shown in the desert island.

In the system of integrated psychotherapy, psychomime can be flexibly employed in various settings and combined with psychodrama and abreaction. For example, the therapeutic session may start with several easy warming-up exercises. The problems revealed by the participants in the discussion which follows may then be played in psychodrama. After one of the participants in psychodrama becomes emotionally involved in the play, the therapist may suggest several abreactive exercises. The patient progresses into abreaction with the attention and help of the remaining group. After the abreaction, the session may end with more psychomimic exercises to relax the group.

ABREACTION

The explosive release of emotion in public is culturally sanctioned on rare occasions—the expression of grief on hearing of the death of a close person, pleasurable news (a father's learning about his child being born, winning a large sum in a lottery, a goal being placed by one's favored sports team, a rock music happening), or as part of a religious experience (talking in tongues). Funeral customs include abreaction as part of their mental hygienic functions; it ends mourning by its intensification and exhaustion and is followed in some cultures by a feast and dancing.

If we leave aside all the explosive emotions in psychotic individuals (a fascinating topic which Darwin (1965) had indicated as one of the important sources of information about innate mechanisms of emotional expression), then *the uncontrollable explosive release of emotion* constitutes such neurotic symptoms as panic reaction, crying spells, and hysterical seizures. As industrial civilization evolves, the symptoms are less dramatic (the neuroses shift to character neuroses and psychosomatic disorders). They become more intense again as war neuroses on the battlefield (about the Western experience during World War II, see Grinker and Spiegel 1945; about the USSR see Davidenkov 1950).

For therapeutic purposes, explosive release of emotion (abreaction) has been used from time immemorial by shamans, prophets, and priests. Abreaction, called *crisis*, was the aim of Anton Mesmer's magnetic treatment toward the end of the eighteenth century. Mesmer was the heir of the old tradition of exorcists who used abreaction in a religious context. The term *abreaction* was introduced by Breuer and Freud, inspired by the Aristotelian term *catharsis* (but with changed meaning, namely, an emotional release in the protagonist and not in the observers). Freud, although impressed by the power of verbal and nonverbal reliving of traumatic experience in leading to the release of the "strangulated affect," soon recognized not only the limitations of abreaction but also its

interference with the therapeutic process. Breuer with his patient, Anna
O., had reached an impasse, probably because the abreactions were part
of mutual involvement between patient and therapist and rewarding for
both parties. Greenson (1967) summarized the psychoanalytic view of
abreaction or catharsis as a non-psychoanalytic (auxiliary) method used
in psychoanalysis:

> Today abreaction is considered valuable in giving the patient a sense
> of conviction about the reality of his unconscious processes. Emo-
> tional intensity may vivify the details of an experience which might
> otherwise remain vague and unreal. The expression of affects and
> impulses may bring a temporary sense of subjective relief, but this is
> not an end in itself and, in fact, may become a source of resistance.
> (p. 48)

Despite the acknowledged usefulness of abreaction, psychoanalytic
method does not allow the therapist to provoke abreaction, only to use
it, if it spontaneously emerges.

When Freud gave up abreaction as an active method, others continued to use it, apparently with success, particularly, Ludwig Frank. In
1910, he asked his patients, lying on the couch, to concentrate on their
feelings and assisted them in reviving forgotten episodes from their
childhood and abreacting them. The famous psychiatrist A. Forel, regarded this method as the true, original psychoanalysis of Breuer, which
Freud had since distorted (Ellenberger 1970).

Abreaction was widely popular during both world wars. It was achieved
during World War II with the help of drugs (such as Sodium Amytal)
in the West and hypnosis in the Soviet Union. Grinker and Spiegel
(1945) regarded the abreaction in war neuroses as rarely helpful in
itself, but as a necessary step to insight. They added:

> Abreactions spontaneously lived through under alcohol are nonther-
> apeutic, as we have learned from our patients who, while drunk,
> explode terrific hostilities in neighboring pubs. (p. 392)

There can be no doubt about two factors which contribute to the
favorable impression both patients and observers have about abreaction.
One is an instant effect, that is, the pleasurable feeling after a socially
sanctioned abreaction. Further, the patients and observers witness a
treatment which is dramatic and supposedly intensive. As Jerome Frank

(1966) pointed out, there have been waves of enthusiasm and disenchantment about abreaction throughout history.

In integrated psychotherapy, we use abreaction, particularly in group treatment. It is used at certain points when we believe that intensive interaction with the role schemas can contribute to the corrective experience of the patient. For example, during psychodramatic performances, patients remember a traumatic episode from childhood, related to their parents or, less frequently, to other adults or peers. The most frequent episodes involve being alone and crying for their parents; being undeservedly punished or humiliated; being unjustly accused, criticized or ridiculed; or not being appreciated or loved. The parent is represented by another patient or a therapist or is simply imagined. The persons representing the parent are of secondary importance and can be replaced during the process or removed.

The feelings and attitudes which become manifest during abreaction are usually either missing from the behavioral repertoire of the patients, or they are unaware of their presence. For example, some patients never complain openly, but their faces express permanent suffering. Some patients are unable to be self-assertive. They complain that people do not take notice of their existence, but they hide themselves through their behavior and their lack of expression. Other patients are not able to express anger or even claim that they never get angry, and yet they signal anger by their nonverbal behavior. Some impress others as cold, but suffer from not being able to express their warm feelings. They are unable to date, to make friends, or even to socialize at a party.

The inhibited emotions and behavior patterns most often dealt with in abreaction are suffering and crying, grief, despair, fear, helplessness, anger and rage, disgust, guilt, assertiveness, affiliation (feelings of liking, closeness and love), feelings of emptiness, and a lack of emotions altogether.

In integrated psychotherapy, the use of abreaction developed gradually out of psychodrama and psychomime. With both, abreaction sometimes appeared spontaneously and represented an important step in the process of corrective experience. Therefore, we were looking for tools which would catalyze abreaction when it seemed appropriate. At hand was hyperventilation, which we had been using for diagnostic purposes for years. In 1966, we studied the ingenious techniques of the late English actor, Roy Hart, which consisted of singing, shouting, and repeating phrases. In 1967, Fritz Perls invited one of us to Esalen. Perls asked his patients to repeat phrases and that confirmed our experience of the impact of repeated words. In 1969, we studied the abreactions in the groups of Daniel Casriel (1972), who was inspired by Synanon.

The choice of phrases to be repeated is important and demands a great deal of empathy with each patient. Most of the phrases fall into the categories mentioned. As an example, let us give some often used:

Mum! Dad! Please come! Help me! Why don't you come? I am hurt. I am afraid. I am scared. Leave me alone! Don't touch me! Go to hell! I am angry. No, no! I kill you! Don't put me down! Be with me! I need you. I need love. I am lovable. I don't care what you think. I am a man. I am a woman.

The therapist suggests the sentences to be repeated on the basis of what the patients have revealed about themselves in discussion, psychodrama, or psychomime. However, as the memories unwind, the reaction to revived childhood situations often shift suddenly from one emotion to another. Crying for help shifts to anger, anger to guilt, then it goes back to anger, and ends with tender feelings toward the parent.

Besides repeating emotionally loaded sentences, the patients work themselves up into an emotional state through hyperventilation, by being instructed to make sounds or talk in gibberish. The therapist exerts pressures of different intensity to the epigastric region or produces pain by pressing one of the three branches of the trigeminal nerve at their outlets or pressing other painful points such as the sternum. The other patients are sometimes instructed to massage the neck, arms and legs of the patients, or to tickle them. Some bioenergetic exercises (Lowen 1975) also prepare the patient for abreaction. Some induce shaking which facilitates the expression of inhibited emotions. Among the tools often used, the boppers (foam rubber clubs) should be mentioned. They permit harmless fighting which provokes anger and hyperventilation.

Patients may abreact while sitting, standing, or moving from person to person in a circle, but the most favorable position is lying on a mat after some exercises.

An altered state of consciousness sometimes takes place in which the highest cortical centers are probably inhibited and the archaic motor-autonomic mechanisms (the hypobulic mechanisms of Kretchmer 1952) take over, manifesting themselves by motor storms, rhythmical movements, temper tantrums, laughing mixed with crying. These are associated with reliving childhood episodes or dream-like states characterized by archaic cognitive processes (the hyponotic mechanisms of Kretchmer or the primary processes of Freud).

Some of the comments from patients' diaries give an idea of the subjective experience during abreaction. Annette, detached and saying little about herself before abreaction, writes:

Somebody was talking how he was confused about love and hate. I started crying and I didn't know why. I don't know who had laid me down, but I felt like a kid again. A totally confused kid. Also I felt like as if I was in some kind of trance and I was just allowing this trance to take over. But it seemed as though another part of me was quite aware of where I was, and what I was doing. This part was embarrassed at the other part that was rambling on. I felt that by keeping my eyes closed then no one else could see me . . . I felt at times as though I was being crazy. I was letting caution fly to the wind. I got into some early feelings that I had for my father. Somehow love and punishment seemed to me to be synonymous. I heard my dad saying that everytime he punished us, he was doing it because he loved us. I was thinking "how I wished if this was love, he'd quit loving me." I resented that he looked only to my mother for affection, when there I was so ready, willing and able. But at the same time I was afraid of wanting that affection because the violence seemed to go along with it. I felt that I could not have one without the other. So I chose to have neither. To me being loved means being helpless and at someone else's mercy. I guess that's why I've always avoided anyone to whom I felt strongly attracted. And I've never been able to say to anyone "I love you" or "I want you to love me."

John writes:

At first I didn't think I could go through with it, so I faked it, but after a while I got into it. At one point I really was fourteen years old. Day House just faded away. I was surprised I had so much hidden anger toward my mother. Now that I realize that it's there I realize that there's still more. I felt really good afterwards, like I had dropped a weight that I had been carrying around for years.

Bill, a very inhibited fellow whose presence has not been felt in the group, writes about his abreaction:

Yesterday a feeling of hopelessness. Today, I was able to experience the fear I had of my father all over again, and it was like the feelings had built up inside me to such a point that I couldn't control them anymore. At one point I thought I was going crazy. When I finally calmed down I felt like all the tension had gone from my body and I felt very calm and peaceful. I was very aware of the rest of the "family" around me, and I felt a great amount of compassion for them. I really felt a need to hug them, and when I did, I did not feel at all tense about it.

Linn, 20 years old, has been controlled all her life by her parents. Her father is a professor, he and his wife married late and both are hypochondriacal and compulsive. Linn was referred to the Day House after one year of psychotherapy which did not lead anywhere. She is of athletic build and her muscle tension is visible. She is unexpressive, leaves sentences unfinished, and is uncertain and doubtful about anything she does or says to the degree that she impressed some psychiatrists as schizophrenic. There was no visible change whatsoever for four weeks in the Day House. Then, in her abreaction, while lying on a mat, she did not cooperate, refused to repeat any sentence suggested to her, and negativistically did the opposite to what she was asked. She was then asked to repeat "No!" while being physically restrained by the patients. Then suddenly, while repeating "No!", she went into a blind rage, resisting the physical force of the strongest members of the group. She revived episodes with her parents from childhood and raged at their restrictions. Her behavior changed instantly, which she felt as if she was breaking through the glass wall between her and other people. Although the abreaction was only an episode in her treatment, it seemed that it was a necessary step.

We believe that, once having witnessed an abreaction such as those described, one is led to compare these kinds of abreactions with Leyhausen's *stimulus therapy* and the release of blocked neurophysiological mechanisms, as described in the chapter on ethology.

Appendix E

FORMS USED AT THE DAY HOUSE

VANCOUVER PROBLEM-GOAL LIST

The Vancouver Problem-Goal List was developed by the first author. The *problem categories* are modification of his earlier scales. Of course all ratings have to be taken with caution, especially when compared inter-individually. Nevertheless, it still gives some orientation not only about progress but also about the whole group. For example, the therapist who has the scores of all patients on one form might notice that more patients had problems with mothers than with fathers and predict more conflicts with female therapists than with male therapists.

A guide to ratings in 15 problem areas.
  1. Mood, happiness, life satisfaction
    0: undisturbed by past, fully satisfied, optimistic
    1: *definitely* more satisfied than dissatisfied
    2: rather more satisfied than dissatisfied
    3: rather more dissatisfied than satisfied
    4: *definitely* more dissatisfied than satisfied
    5: extremely unhappy, depressed, pessimistic

2. Symptoms

Undesirable thoughts, feelings, impulses, physical symptoms of mental origins, inexplainable to oneself

0: *none*: no complaint

1: *minimal*: traces of symptoms, not distressing

2: *mild*: weak, rare, mildly distressing, rarely if ever limiting activities, rarely if ever apparent to others

3: *moderate*: weak and frequent, or strong but rare, distressing, partly limiting activities, occasionally apparent to others

4: *severe*: strong, frequent, distressing, seriously limiting, often apparent to others

5: "Can hardly be worse," strong, frequent, terribly distressing, incapacitating, usually apparent to others

3. Self dissatisfaction

Dissatisfied with myself, (not accepting, not liking myself) because of personality, habits, lack of talents, lack of effort, weak will, guilt, body build or how I look.

0: basically satisfied, optimistic about positive change, putting in effort

1: much more satisfied than dissatisfied, optimistic, putting in effort

2: somewhat more satisfied than dissatisfied, putting in effort

3: rather more dissatisfied than satisfied, putting in effort

4: definitely more dissatisfied than satisfied, variable outlook and effort

5: hate myself, blame myself, believe change not possible, no effort to change

4. Accepting my physical condition, disability, illness

Negative features of physical condition which cannot be changed and are a handicap in performance or social life.

0: optimally adjusted

1: somewhat concerned, does not affect life

2: somewhat concerned, mildly affects life

3: concerned more than necessary, moderately affects life

4: waste time by thinking about it, severely affects life

5: cannot accept, extremely affects life

5. Appearance, speech, expression

Behavior or effect on behavior which can be changed, recognized as problem: voice, speech, posture, stance, walk, hygiene, grooming, dress, etc.

    0: no problem
    1: minimally affects life
    2: mildly affects life
    3: moderately affects life
    4: severely affects life
    5: extremely affects life

6. *Work/study/money*

    0: satisfied with the present activity or have clear plan
    1: continue in present activity or have clear plan
    2: unstable activity, yet support myself, have plan for change
    3: unstable activity, support myself partly, vague plans, but concern is apparent
    4: no activity, no plans, some concern
    5: no activity, no plans, do not care

7. *Sex partner (and sex)*

    0: no problem, positive feelings, balanced give and take, perfect sex
    1: much more satisfied than dissatisfied in all three areas
    2: more satisfied than dissatisfied, or efficiently seek solution
    3: more dissatisfied than satisfied, initiating contacts
    4: bad relationship, or miss partner; weak attempts to find solution
    5: extremely bad or destructive relationship; or missing partner badly, not seeking solution, no sex outlet

8. *My children*

    0: no problem: good relationship, or happy to be without
    1: minimal problem
    2: mild problem
    3: mooderate problem
    4: bad relationship or miss them
    5: extreme problem or miss them badly

9. *Father (male authority)*

Total relationship to father disregarding whether he lives or not; how the relationship to father is reflected in relationship to other male authorities.

    0: positive feelings, independence, balanced give and take

1: the same, minimal frictions, or genuinely indifferent
2: mildly disturbed relationship
3: moderately disturbed relationship
4: severely disturbed relationship
5: extremely disturbed relationship

10. Mother (female authority)

Total relationship to mother disregarding whether she lives or not, how the relationship to mother is reflected in relationship to other female authorities.

0: positive feelings, independence, balanced give and take
1: the same with minimal frictions, or genuinely indifferent
2: mildly disturbed relationship
3: moderately disturbed relationship
4: severely disturbed relationship
5: extremely disturbed relationship

11. Siblings (peers)

0: positive emotions, independence, balanced give and take
1: the same with minimal friction, or genuinely indifferent
2: mildly disturbed relationship
3: moderately disturbed relationship
4: severely disturbed relationship
5: extremely disturbed relationship

12. Friends, people in general

0: good relations with friends (positive feelings, independence, balanced give and take) and people in general
1: the same, with minimal problems
2: some problems in relations with friends and/or people in general
3: unsatisfactory relations with friends and/or people in general
4: the same as 5—but not extreme
5: extremely bad or destructive relations with friends and/or people in general; or lack of relations and miss them badly

13. Daily routine

Is daily routine a problem contributing to unhappiness? How efficient it is? (Household chores, personal hygiene, etc.) Does it interfere with biological health? (Insufficient diet, overeating, alcohol, drugs, smoking, coffee, not enough sleep. Is it unnecessarily complicated because of neurotic behavior? (e.g., always being late.)

0: effective and healthy
1: minimal problems
2: mild problems
3: moderate problems
4: serious problems
5: extremely ineffective and/or unhealthy

14. Free time
Is it fun? Is it variable enough? Is it creative? Does it interfere with health? Do I miss hobbies? Does it give an opportunity to meet people?
0: no problem
1: minimal
2: mild problem
3: moderate
4: serious
5: desperate (unable to enjoy or make choice what to do), or interferes with health

15. Philosophy of life
Problems related to religion and parareligion, such as astrology, witch-craft, etc; to political attitude, to community, women's movement, mi-nority groups, ethnic origin, to moral values, to criminal activities, to nature.
0: no problem
1: minimal problem
2: mildly disturbing uncertainties and conflicts
3: moderately disturbing uncertainties and conflicts
4: as 5, but not extreme
5: extreme uncertainties, and conflicts, or interferes with important needs of others

INSTRUCTIONS FOR THE CHAIRPERSON (FROM THE COMMITTEE BOOK)

Chairperson's role in orientation
The chairperson's role in the orientation of new patients is to aid the therapist in explaining the philosophy, procedures, and rules of the Day House. This is the time that the new patients get their first look at Day House and, on the basis of what they learn in orientation, will make the decision whether or not to try to be accepted by the group. It must be remembered that the purpose of the orientation is not to deal with the new patient's problems, but to inform them about what happens at Day

House and how they can benefit from the treatment. They evaluate
their potential in the program, and the staff draws its first impressions
of them. It has been noted that in the past, a large number of people
that come for orientation decide that the program is not for them. The
chairperson must take care not to unnecessarily scare new people away
by trying to deal with their problems or by telling them how rough Day
House is. He is there as a source of information about Day House and
as an aid to the therapist.

INFORMATION FOR THE CANDIDATES FOR TREATMENT IN THE DAY HOUSE

Program expectations

1. The program is of six weeks' duration—Monday through Friday,
   9:00 a.m. to 4:00 p.m. You should not arrive before 8:30 a.m. nor
   stay later than 4:30 p.m.
   Following completion of the regular program, you are required to
   attend the post-group follow-up visits, which take place on three
   successive Wednesdays.
2. You are asked not to smoke and to try not to leave the room during
   the group; it can be disruptive to the therapy in progress. Leaving
   the group when upset is escaping. Stay and work it out.
3. Compose and read your life story within two weeks of your arrival.
   All the facts of your past and present life should be presented. A
   photograph and typed copy of your autobiography are necessary
   as part of your chart.
4. Acceptable absences are serious illness, an important appointment,
   or a special event. If it is necessary for you to be absent, ask the
   group ahead of time. If you are discouraged or depressed, don't
   stay home, come and discuss it in the group. If you are ill or late,
   report this by phone.
5. Lateness or unacceptable absence three times in one month could
   result in probation or discharge.
6. Coming into the group under the influence of nonprescribed drugs
   and/or alcohol may result in probation or discharge.
7. You are expected to participate verbally and physically, so wear appropriate clothing. Wear slacks and runners for sports; older
   clothing for working around the house. Bring your own facecloth,
   towels, and soap for showering.

Day house rules
Do you want to achieve maximum improvement? Do you want the same for others? Then you have to follow these rules:
1. Speak openly and frankly about everything in the meetings of the whole community.
2. Take care not to do anything which would make it difficult either for yourself or others to speak openly.
3. Use every opportunity to be with the whole community. Do not isolate yourself.
4. Do not form subgroups. Do not form any sexual attachments. Meeting group members outside is almost always harmful to the therapy. Use free time for meeting other people.
5. Help others to become members of the community as quickly as possible.
6. Listen to the opinions and recommendations of others, but take the responsibility for your own decisions.
7. You may not leave the program unless you first discuss it with the group. You are part of the program and your separation effects everybody.
8. While in the program, all medical care and drugs are given by the staff. Any appointments or drug use should be discussed first with the staff.
9. Keep your contract, which includes: full participation in the program, inviting relatives, and attending at least three aftercare meetings.
10. You do not have to believe in the therapy; just stick to the rules and see.

INSTRUCTIONS TO CANDIDATES FOR TREATMENT BEFORE THE INDIVIDUAL INTERVIEW

Self-description
Dear Friend:
A part of your commitment for your treatment at the Day House is "NO SECRETS FROM THE GROUP." This applies not only to information about your past, but also to everything during your treatment. Otherwise, your treatment cannot be successful and would be a waste of time and energy for both you and the group. Therefore, do not enter

into treatment at the Day House without making a firm decision about your openness!

Here is your first task: to tell us about yourself concisely, stressing that which is especially difficult for you to reveal. Use simple words, do not be vague! Your report should be typewritten, please type it or arrange to have it typed.

Using the following outline as a guide, please write your self-description on a separate page, noting both the numbers and titles of each heading.

Please do not leave any underlined question unanswered.

Complaints about:

1. *Mood, Happiness, Life Satisfaction*: Depressed? Discouraged? Has it changed recently? Why? Ever intended or tried suicide?
2. *Symptoms*: Mental or physical symptoms of mental origin, such as fears, cannot sleep, headache, fatigue, cannot concentrate on work, or thousands of others.
3. *Self-dissatisfaction*: Dissatisfied with yourself because of personality habits, lack of talents, lack of effort, weak will, guilt, body build, or how you look?
4. *Physical Condition, Disability, Illness*: List all illnesses, surgery, injuries you have had since childhood. Also all pregnancies, abortions, menstrual difficulties. Any consequences? Do you have physical conditions which cannot be changed, which handicap your performance, self-confidence, or social life?
5. *Appearance, Speech, Expression*: List any problem which you have.
6. *Work/Study/Money*: a. List last few jobs, your plans for future job or study; b. Present income; c. Debts and financial worries.
7. *Sex Partner*: Short history of your dating and love relationships. Describe your present relationship (marriage) and problems in it. If no relationship, why? Do you miss it? Short history of your sex life, including complaints, worries, deficiencies, abnormalities.
8. *Children*: Relationship with them. Do they live with you? If no children, do you want them in the future?
9. *Father (Male Authority)*: Either here or under Mother (10), describe where you grew up. Was your childhood happy? What is the worst you remember? Describe your father, his origin, occupation, your relationship with him since childhood. Remember episodes which influenced your relationship to him! What was his main advice to you? Do you have "unfinished business" with him?

10. *Mother* (Female Authority): The same as with father.
11. *Siblings (Peers)*: Make a schema of your brothers and sisters with age differences. Describe your relations with them.
12. *Friends, People in General*: Any problems with friends, or why you do not have friends. Problems with people in general.
13. *Daily Routine*: Is daily routine a problem? How efficient is it (household, chores, personal hygiene, etc.)? Does it interfere with your health (insufficient diet, overeating, alcohol, drugs, smoking, coffee, not enough sleep, etc.)? Is it too complicated because of neurotic behavior (always being late, etc.)?
14. *Free Time*: Is it fun? Is it variable enough? Is it creative? Does it interfere with health? Hobbies? Does it give you an opportunity to meet people?
15. *Philosophy of Life*: What do you believe in or sympathize with? Problems related to religion, or parareligion (astrology, witchcraft, etc.), to political attitude, to community (women's movement, minority groups, ethnic origin), to moral values, to criminal activities, to nature. Have you ever been involved in criminal activity?
16. *Hope*: What do you think has been causing your problems? What hope do you have that (a) your mental health can be improved, (b) you can change your personality, (c) you can change your life situation?

INFORMATION FOR FAMILY LEADER (FROM THE COMMITTEE BOOK)

Duties of family leader

As family leader you may also be sports coordinator, dairy dealer, chairperson, or work coordinator (or sports coordinator and diary dealer) so check additional duty instructions that you are assigned.

1. During work periods, each leader should do the duties listed by the work coordinator. Follow daily responsibilities as laid out in chairpersons' book.
2. Preside over family group and insure that members with problems speak up.
3. When your family is assigned to domestics, lead in delegating duties of same.
4. Check members to insure they carry out their responsibilities.
5. Keep the group informed of members' problems and commitments as they arise in family discussions. Write specific member com-

mitments on the black board. Bring the committee chairperson's
attention to the latter so he can include them in the committee
report. Keep the chairperson informed.

WHO FORMS THE COMMITTEE (EXCERPTS FROM THE COMMITTEE BOOK)

The Committee consists of:
2. A chairperson who also acts as family leader of one family.
2. A work coordinator who may also act as family leader of one
   family *unless* the work coordinator is in the same family as the
   chairperson; then the work coordinator does not act as family
   leader.
3. One family leader elected from a family that does not have the
   chairperson or work coordinator amongst its members.
4. If the work coordinator and chairperson are in the same family,
   another family leader is to be elected from the family not represented. This person will also be the sports coordinator.

Therefore the Committee would have a minimum of three members
or a maximum of four members.

They are members who the group feels have made progress, and who
are willing to make greater effort toward their progress by taking on
more responsibility.

They are committed to the program and the continuing progress of
the group.

They take initiative when things slow down and encourage others to
speak up.

They speak openly and set an example for others to do so.

They represent the group by welcoming and orienting new members
to the group.

They take the responsibility for insuring that new members completely understand their commitments to Day House.

They are to emphasize the seriousness of commitments and probation, enforce the disciplining of broken commitments, and report on
probations.

They evaluate and organize the group's activities daily.

They are required to jointly write a weekly report of the mood of the
group (committee report).

They are to do ratings of the group members.

They are to make a list of negative points for members of the group
who have them.

They are to evaluate whether group members are speaking plainly and honestly to each other—that is, not using cliche words or phrases that have obscure meanings.

They are to review Wednesday morning the committee report and the negative/positive point scale and to make the necessary adjustments taking into consideration Tuesday evening contributions (significant person's night), then return the report and rating scale to the bulletin board and Day House secretary prior to 11:00 a.m. Wednesday.

They are to support community rules and commitments, and they are to generate enthusiasm to increase the progress of the whole group. If the group is not functioning well as a whole; individuals do not make progress.

Before leaving Day House during the week, they are to make sure that all doors of entry are locked.

Chairperson

The chairperson is elected by the group and is a person in whom the group feels a sense of trust.

He or she coordinates the committee's responsibilities and makes certain all their tasks are completed on time.

He or she oversees the group with authority to insure unity and responsibility.

He or she chairs lunch discussions and Friday's elections, keeping order and making sure everyone contributes.

He or she encourages members to speak about their problems.

He or she assists new members by welcoming and orienting them to the group.

He or she assists new members with their questions and insures that family leaders are responsible to their members.

He or she with the other members of the committee writes the weekly report and ratings, and posts them on Tuesday morning.

Duties of the chairperson

Reads reports in the morning coffee breaks or at lunch.

Follows up on make-up assignments, probations.

Lists specific commitments people make on the blackboard.

Coordinates the committee.

Oversees the group activities and insures they function as a unit.

Keeps the group to a timetable.

Duties of diary dealer

The Diary Dealer's main responsibility is to aid the Chairperson.

1. Give diaries to new members, and collect and account for all diaries every day before the start of the first activity.
2. Call absent members. Phone.
3. Collect late fines and record them (3¢ per minute, not to exceed $3.00).
4. Count names on census sheet to see that all have signed in on time (8:58 a.m.) and fine members 15¢ if they have not signed in. Assign members fifteen negative points for not signing in on time.
5. Help to insure that new members arrive on time for activities.
6. Give out charts on Mondays (for regular filling of problem goal list.)
7. Collect diaries and pitfall speeches from members leaving the group on Fridays.
8. Enter commitments into commitment book and write them on the commitments black board.
9. Wednesday afternoon:
   a. enter negative points on file cards
   b. make file cards for new members
   c. write commitments on file cards
   d. take cards of members leaving the group to the secretary.

EXAMPLE OF A COMMITTEE REPORT

General mood. The group is withdrawing. Apathy prevails. There does not seem much effort to find out what other people are feeling. People must be angry but they do not show it. Also do not be afraid to show it if you are happy. Spread it around. Show your affection toward group members, do not wait until someone is down to show it. If it feels good do it. Toward the end of last week there seemed to be quite a bit of apathy particularly on Friday. F. and J. [therapists] were not there so perhaps the groups is becoming dependent on them.

Business is going over the twenty minute time limit. The committee will stop business after the 20 minutes allotted.

The committee would like to encourage people to bring in information about outside activities.

Successes should have the area of your success clearly identified as well as your name.

Group—Not supportive enough. Why is Anne always thinking of leaving? Does the group encourage her to stay? Susan speak up. We would like to discuss your fear concerning your thoughts about the depression in your family. Also the therapists will give you information. Barb you

	MONDAY	TUESDAY	WEDNESDAY	THURSDAY	FRIDAY
9:00					
9:30	SPORTS		INTERVIEWS	WORK	INTERVIEWS
10:00	BREAK				
10:30	FAMILIES		BREAK	BREAK	BREAK
11:00			WORK	WORK DISCUSSION	BIG GROUP
11:30					
12:00				LUNCH	
12:30	LUNCH		LUNCH		LUNCH
1:00				FAMILIES	
1:30	CHARTING	AUTO-BIOGRAPHIES	BIG GROUP		PLAYS
2:00	WORK				
2:30				BIG GROUP	BREAK-INS
3:00	BREAK				GOOD-BYES
3:30	WORK			BREAK	
4:00				SPORTS	
4:30		BREAK			
5:00		SPORTS			
5:30		DINNER			
6:00					
6:30		FAMILY NIGHT			
7:00					
7:30					
8:00					

are still just drifting through. Sue, have you made progress? What will you do with the time left? Ben are things different with you? What happens to you if Trudy leaves? What will Ben have left? We haven't seen much change. Pierre you can get close to people but don't let your feelings bottle up. Tell people what you think. If the closeness is real it will stick. Be honest.

Work—Work seems to be going well this week. Things are being done fast and well. The rain has slowed outside activities some but the projects are moving along swiftly.

"Family"I—Domestics is coming along smoothly. Steve and Martin are getting into their work more. We are impressed. Martin should work more with others. Pierre is a bit preoccupied with other thoughts. Joanne is interested and doing really well. Judy is holding back a bit. Barb is working well.

"Family" II—Projects are coming along well (with the help of "family" III). Rita is energetic and interested in her work. Good job on the seedling stand. Craig and Sue, a fine job on installing Kate's shelves (units 1 & 2). Alex doing well, enjoying his work this week. Linda great on logs and boppers. Henry does a good job though he should talk more while he works.

"Family" III—Janet and Susan enthusiastic and thorough on unit 3 of Kate's shelves. Carol works well but held back with logs. Jan is a super worker. Speak up if you think the logs should have been done another way. Mike is a good hard worker. Debbie, good work on the boppers. Ron was preoccupied with problems on Monday, usually a good worker.

The group thanks Mike for bringing his chain saw, it was a great help.

Sports—In swimming everyone was taking part and making an effort. Taking time for a free swim was a change and people were talking and playing games of their own. Yesterday the game was close and everyone enjoyed the competition. Pierre, we missed your good spiking.

"Family" reports

"Family" One: The "family" is helpful and supportive. Barb requested time but needs to ask for more. Anne is getting out a lot of her angry feelings towards her parents in workouts. Mike is speaking up more and it's good to hear from him. Everyone could speak up more. More participation in workouts benefits each of us. Let's go.

Mike: It's good to hear from you. Keep it up.

Anne: Stop analyzing your own problems and start sharing. Don't be vague.

Barbara: Ask for time. You've got support.
Stewart: Let's hear more about you.
Pierre: You made a good start. Keep sharing with us.
Judy: It helps to talk about it.

"Family" Two: Seem close and work well together. Craig is most active in "family". Alex always tries to be helpful. Rita is speaking up a bit more but not enough about herself. Simone is always ready to help others but should make more effort letting us know about herself, make some tie in "family." Linda is usually interested in other members but is far away at times. Tell us about it. Henry is slow to start his therapy but seems eager when asked.
Rita: Don't be so stubborn. We can't help you unless you help yourself.
Ben: We're worried that you aren't changing.
Craig: You're getting easier to approach and more consistent with your affections.
Linda: Start with one problem at a time. Take time in "family."
Gerry: Practice talking to women here; we're approachable. Start on your therapy now.
Nancy: Progress is slowing. Keep pushing.

"Family" Three: A nice family to be in. Everybody except Ron goes to each other for advice and support. Mike has particularly taken the opportunity to seek advice from the group. Susan is bringing things to the group—her fear of bugs. Janet is beginning to get support to look at her anger, her assertiveness and her dress. Jan is trying but is confused but the "family" has told her to tell them about her feelings. Debbie is very supportive and seems willing to discuss her problems.
Janet: Use your remaining time to work on anger and assertiveness. They are related.
Susan: What's behind the bugs you are afraid of? Keep trying.
Jan: Keep talking. If you are confused, let us help you.
Carol: Keep pushing. Keep looking for some answers.
Mary: Don't slow down. You are helpful and can be helped.
Debbie: Your openness helps us.
Ron: The group will listen now. Talk.

                    Signed,
                    THE COMMITTEE MEMBERS

GLOSSARY

Abreaction

Reliving of painful or conflict-producing experiences from the past, accompanied by explosive emotional discharge which was inhibited at the time of the original experience. Typically, a feeling of relief follows, often only transient. Abreaction appears *spontaneously* (e.g. displaced anger of a drunken man in a pub), or in different psychotherapies (e.g. in psychoanalysis where it is often welcome, but never induced, by the analyst), or *induced* by a healer, priest (in exorcism), or psychotherapist. Abreactive therapies rely on induced abreaction as their main tool, such as the "cathartic method" of Breuer-Freud, "scream therapy" (D. Casriel), "primal therapy" (A. Janov), etc. In Integrated Psychotherapy, induced abreaction has a definite but limited role.

Abstinence rule

"Analytic treatment should be carried through, as possible, under privation—in a state of abstinence" (Freud). The treatment should not offer substitute satisfactions which would divert the patient from his therapeutic goals; it also helps to prevent a premature "flight into health." See Rewards-costs rule.

Acting-out

A form of resistance to treatment. The patient avoids remembering crucial situations from the past and acts instead. The acts are often maladaptive, even self-destructive, and always complicate the treatment (though, in the long run, can be beneficial for the treatment).

Ambivalence
Contrasting attitudes towards an object, person or goal. (introduced by E. Bleuler).

Amplified family technique
A form of family therapy, in which the other patients are observers and "double" for the family members, functioning as catalyzers for the family interaction. Since one of the family members is in group treatment, he is known to the other patients who react to him as quasi-family members. Amplified family technique is part of Integrated Psychotherapy: it is efficient in terms of time economy, fact-finding and fact-checking.

Assumptive world (Cantril)
A coherent picture which everybody has about the world, which is to a large degree, formed by assumptions. Each new experience is interpreted in terms of this "assumptive world". For psychotherapy, the most interesting part of the assumptive world is what is called in this book—Group Schema.

Attractiveness of a group
For a member, the group attractiveness depends on the member's outcomes (i.e. how the rewards compare with the costs), and whether they reach or exceed the level that the person expects of "fair exchange".

Autodrama
Psychodrama in which all roles are played by one person (protagonist). This was the favorite technique of F. Perls in dealing with dreams.

Autogenic training
Self-hypnosis induced by a series of exercises (of heaviness, warmth, slow heart-beat, slow breathing, etc.). It was developed by the German psychiatrist, J. H. Schultz in the twenties, on the basis of extensive studies of hypnosis and meditation.

Behaviorism
Important movement to make psychology scientific by conceiving it

as a theory of behavior. *Radical behaviorism*, as formulated by J. Watson, excluded self-observational terms from psychological dictionary, rejected self-observation as a source of knowledge and stressed onesidedly the environmental determinants of behavior. Radical behaviorism, as formulated by B. F. Skinner: more sophisticated, but still biased in the directions indicated.

Methodological behaviorism: approximately synonymous with the position of unified science or physicalism (see unified science theses). Self-observational terms can be explicated in behavioral terms. Self-observation is an important source of knowledge and is in principle confirmable interindividually (by behavioral and physiological methods).

Body Language

Imprecise term designating non-verbal communication signs of all kinds. Although some of these signs are clearly part of language such as English or Chinese, and are learned in the same way as the verbal part, others are not (such as some expressions of emotions).

Body Schema (image)

One's awareness of the spatial extension of one's body at any particular time, based on self-perceptions, images, etc.

Catharsis

Therapeutic use of abreaction. In this meaning, introduced by Breuer and Freud.

Causal principle

The most general heuristic hypothesis that the world is predictable, that is, that laws can be formulated describing regularities of events. This is sometimes also called "determinism" (as in Freud's determinism). Two kinds of laws have to be distinguished: *deterministic*, making possible exact predictions, and *probabilistic*, predicting with certain probability only (e.g. most physicists believe that atomistic events can be in principle predicted with certain probability only).

COEX system (S. Grof)

A system of condensed experiences, manifesting itself by vivid memories from different life periods with one basic theme (e.g. fright, humiliation, rejection, physical stress endangering survival, etc.) which tend to appear together during psychotherapeutic LSD session (but also in other psychotherapies facilitating abreaction). The concept can probably be subsumed under the concept of "complex."

Cohesiveness
Group characteristic to have "we" feeling, to stick together, co-operate, and resist dissolution of the group.

Communication (information) theory (started by C. Shannon in 1948)
Developed by engineers concerned with the most efficient way to transmit messages, disregarding the content of the messages. (It deals with "selective" information only, not with "semantic" information). This is the only legitimate use of communication theory. Despite interesting observations about animal and human communications (Bateson, Jackson, Haley and others) behavioral communication theory does not exist yet.

Complementation
Taking complementary role, e.g. child-parent, teacher-student. Psychotherapist is concerned with maladaptive complementation. The broad categories distinguished in this book are complements to male, female supraordinate, peer, subordinate, sexual partner. As the other important category of role-relationships, see Identification.

Complex (T. Ziehen, C. G. Jung)
A cluster of inter-related ideas, usually unconscious, strongly charged emotionally. A complex has considerable influence upon attitudes and actions of a person.

Conditioning
Process of learning predictable connections between stimuli and responses.

Classical (respondent) conditioning. A neutral stimulus, CS, repeatedly followed by unconditioned stimulus, US, results in the capacity of CS to elicit similar response as US.

Instrumental conditioning. Responses to be conditioned are rewarded and their frequency increases. Instrumental conditioning is discrete-trial procedure. Its modification, free-trial procedure, is called *operant conditioning.*

Confirmability (R. Carnap)

Is a criterion of empirical meaningfulness of a sentence. A sentence (statement) is confirmable, if observation sentences can contribute either positively or negatively to its confirmation. *Testability* is a stronger criterion. A sentence which is confirmable by possible observable events is, moreover, testable if a test procedure can be specified for producing such events at will. See also pseudo-sentence.

Conflict

(1) *Interpersonal.* Two individuals or groups mutually interfere with their goals.

(2) *Personal (choice)* A person has a need to reconcile incompatible information, attitudes or goals, accessible to awareness in different degrees. Choice conflict can be *predecisionals* (before deciding upon a course of action, or *postdecisional* (F. Nietzsche: "I have done it, says my memory. I could not have possibly done it, says my pride and stays inexorable. Finally, the memory yields.") The main types of predecisional conflicts are: approach-avoidance conflict (e.g. love-hate relationship to a person), double approach conflict (choice between rewarding goals), double approach-avoidance conflict (a choice between goals, all of them implying some rewards but also heavy costs). Only conflicts involving avoidance and interpersonal relations (with real people and group schema) seem to be pathogenic and of psychotherapeutic interest.

Constancy

Object constancy. Capacity to recognize objects as the same or belonging to the same category, even if changed, and retain them as images and concepts even if they are not present.

Self-constancy. The capacity to recognize the self as the same, despite physical and mental and situational changes.

Contract

A contract is an agreement of a group (two or more people) to adhere to certain goals and norms, and sometimes also to commit oneself to a certain role. Contracts, though usually implicit and informal acts, are mutual agreements about rules of conduct and are part of most human relationships. Of psychotherapeutic interest are deceitful contracts, when a subject, sometimes not fully aware of his strategy, indicates agreement with a contract, or initiates contractual arrangements, but breaks them later. S. Potter and E. Berne described a variety of deceitful and confused contractual arrangements.

Therapeutic contract. Participants of the therapeutic process (patient, therapist and other patients) formulate the goals, norms and roles of the therapeutic process and express their willingness to adhere to them.

Corrective experience

Partial re-exposition to situations which the person was not able to master in the past, re-exposition under more favourable circumstances, so that successful mastery is achieved. Both cognitive and emotional aspects of corrective experience are important. (The concept was first used by F. Alexander as "emotional corrective experience".)

Costs

All non-rewarding activities and states which an individual has to go through as member of a group, and all rewards foregone because of not being a member of an alternative group.

Defense mechanisms

Systematically studied by psychoanalysis. In the frame of Integrated psychotherapy they are conceived as protective strategies which help to cope with interpersonal stress and conflicts (both with real people and the Group Schema), by avoiding, circumventing, or escaping from their productive solutions. Repression, denial, dissociation, displacement, rationalization and reaction formation are examples of such defence strategies.

Double (psychodrama)

When person A is playing his role in psychodrama, person B doubles, that is, shares that role and talks for A. The purpose is to bring into the open ideas and feelings of A which A is not fully aware of or hesitant to reveal.

Economic model of groups

All interactions among group members are conceived as social exchange of rewards and costs, similarly as goods and money are exchanged in economic transactions. Though economic model is limited, it is regarded in this book as a useful model (first approximation for a psychotherapist). See rewards-costs rule.

Ego

(1) Means "I" and since the English word is adequate, ego is not used in this book at all.

(2) (psychoan.) in Freud's model, ego, id and superego are three instances of the mental apparatus. Freud's model is based on a mixture of social and quasi-physical (energy, force) images. According to this book, it has outlived its usefulness, makes the description of interpersonal processes difficult, obfuscates phenomenal spatiality of mental events, and causes inflation of pseudoconcepts (desexualization, desaggressivization, etc.) In this book, it is replaced by the more parsimonious social model of group schema.

Ethology

A school of comparative psychology (K. Lorenz, Tinbergen, and others), continuing Darwin's ideas on evolution of species-specific behavior. The stress is on observation of behavior in natural habitat, but such observation may lead to design of artificial situations which elucidate particular aspects of behavior mechanisms.

Exchange, fair

Each participant in an interaction should receive rewards that are proportional to the costs he incurres in that interaction. Related are the norm of reciprocity of A. W. Gouldner and distributive justice of G. C. Homans.

Extinction

The progressive decrement of the intensity or frequency of a conditioned response under conditions of nonreinforcement.

Feedback

1. A method of controlling a system by reinsertion of the results of its past activity so that it influences its future activity. *Negative f.*: decreases the deviation of the achieved value from the desired value. *Positive f.* amplifies the deviation.

2. Synonymous with reaction (e.g. one leading textbook of psychiatry explains f.: Expressed response by one person or a group to another person's behaviour.) This fashionable, but incorrect use, should be discouraged, not only because it corrupts an important concept, but also obscures the patient's concrete ideas and feelings.

Fixed action pattern (ethology)

Genetically programmed sequence of coordinated motor and autonomic actions, performed without previous learning.

Group schema
Condensed experience with people in different roles: male-female authority, peers, subordinates, sex partner. It forms the basis of expectations about people, is a social training ground in fantasy, and supplies substitute satisfactions in fantasy.

Group, small
A system of two or more individuals each interacting with everybody, in pursuit of goals, some of which are shared.

Here and now principle
It is often not realized that it has a variety of meanings causing confusion.
1. Present relations with therapist or other patients, as model relations accessible to direct observation, are particularly valuable material for psychotherapy. This is broadly accepted.
2. From this, some therapists falsely deduce that the patients should be discouraged (even forbidden) to talk about anything else.
3. A view that whatever the patient talks about, is connected with the here-and-now situation. E.g. A patient talks about his suffering in childhood, but his motive is to have attention and pity of the group. While useful as a heuristic attitude, it has to be used critically.
4. A view expressed by G. C. Jung "I no longer find the cause of neurosis in the past, but in the present", later repeated many times by others. It had positive effect of drawing attention to situational factors keeping the neurosis going (including the neurotic vicious circle initiated by the patient in new environments again and again), but led also to some misunderstandings due to the usual ambiguity of causal terminology. Talking about the past is not travelling into the past, it is a present process which may or may not be relevant for therapy.

Homeostasis
A system keeps a variable within certain limits, despite the variation of the environment (e.g. body temperature).

Identification
1. Taking the role of another person, his characteristics and perspectives. It is used so in this book.
2. (psychoan.) As defensive mechanism, if the above reduces tension and anxiety.

Identity
1. "A is identical with B" means that A and B are the same. This is the way concept of identity is used in logic and also in this book.
2. In the process of rapid corruption of terms typical for present-day psychiatry, identity has variety of meanings, such as self-awareness, stability of personality, stability of goals in life, belonging to a group, etc. It is suggested that the patients are guided to use more informative words than identity.

Imprinting (ethology)
In many birds, relatively permanent attachment of a hatchling to an object presented to it, usually the mother, occurs after a short exposure. It lays basis for future social behavior, including sexual object choice. It is now regarded as a kind of learning. Opinions about the similarity of behavior changes in mammals and particularly humans to imprinting in birds differ.

Incorporation (psychoanalysis)
Fantasies of taking objects into one's body. With Schafter, we agree that it is the only term describing internalization which is useful to retain as a phenomenal description of some patients and can be easily accommodated in the group schema model.

Interaction
As in other empirical sciences, two bodies are in interaction if their reactions are mutually stimuli for the other. Particularly, we think about behavioral interaction, that is, mutual exchange of behaviors, which are often symbolic behaviors. No need is felt to introduce transaction as a distinct term from interaction.

Internalization (psychoanalysis)
The subject locates some previous regulatory object within some self-boundaries. ". . . internalization is a spatial metaphor that is so grossly incomplete and unworkable that we would do best to avoid it in psychoanalytic conceptualization." (R. Schafter). We agree.

Introjection
". . . introjection can only be a synonym of incorporation . . . it is redundant." (R. Schafter). We agree.

Narcissism (psychoanalysis)

The concept of primary and secondary narcissism is based on Freud's model of libido economy and since this concept is not empirically anchored, neither is that of narcissism. It is unfortunate that an attempt to describe a certain category of patients, who do not do well in psychoanalytic treatment (narcissistic personalities) takes the mythological concept of narcissism as its starting point.

Neurotic paradox (Mowrer)

A neurotic repeatedly creates situations which increase his misery, without being aware of his contribution. This was well described by Freud, Schultz-Hencke, and other analysts (neurosis of destiny). Whereas Freud's explanation was in terms of repetition compulsion, Schultz-Hencke was the first who refused this and interpreted it in terms of interpersonal interaction (the vicious circle). The causation of neurotic paradox is probably different in different cases. The mechanisms of operant conditioning (rewards coming first and punishments later), of cognitive learning (pseudoconfirmation of a false hypothesis), of avoidance of guilt feelings by self-deception (Mowrer) and other mechanisms have to be taken into consideration.

Norms

Rules prescribing what every member of the group is supposed to do and what not to do. To be distinguished: n. *prescribed, accepted,* and *performed.*

Object relations theory

Defined as study of internalization of interpersonal processes. It is the approach of the British psychoanalytic school (M. Klein, Fairbairn, Winnicott, Guntrip, Sutherland), or broadly of other authors also (Erikson, Jacobson, Mahler, Kernberg, and others). Obviously, there are common points between object relations and group schema approach. The difficulties of studying them systematically lie in the circumstance that the object relations theories are entangled in Freud's network of concepts needing radical revision (see Schafer 1976), internalization being one of them.

Outcome (social exchange)

Rewards received and costs incurred.

Phenomenal World

The world as experienced at any time, perceived or imagined. Phenomenal world changes profoundly in dreams, fever, under LSD, in psychoses, sometimes during psychotherapy. To disentangle the misunderstandings leading to false dichotomy intrapsychic/interpersonal, it is useful to understand the difference between the physical and phenomenal space.

Power (group process)

It is the capacity of person A to influence the outcome of person B. It is often limited by counter-power; that is, power of B over A's outcomes.

Pseudosentence

Although grammatically a sentence, it is cognitively meaningless (e.g. Heidegger: Nothing nothings.) According to R. Carnap and other philosophers of science, many philosophical problems are pseudoproblems. Both positive and negative answer to a pseudoproblem is meaningless (e.g. both answers to the question "is the will free?").

Psychomime

A psychotherapeutic, essentially nonverbal technique portraying everyday situations, in order to identify problems and maladaptive patterns of patients and trainees, and contribute to corrective experience.

Reference group (group process)

A group to which an individual relates himself and shares its perspectives, without being necessarily a member of that group. Family of origin is usually the first reference group, functioning as one of the reference groups for the rest of the life. The group schema is a common denominator of different reference groups.

Reinforcement

A stimulus that will increase the probability of occurrence of the preceding response. *R. intermittent*: not following each correct response. Intermittent reinforcement creates in instrumental and operant conditioning greater resistance to extinction. The schedules of reinforcement are: *interval* (after predetermined time intervals) or *ratio* (after a predetermined number of correct responses). Both interval and ratio schedules can be *fixed* or *variable*.

Rewards—costs rule of psychotherapy

The rewards and costs which the patient receives in therapeutic relationship have to be contingent on his behavior in such a way that the motivation for therapeutic change is maximized.

Role

Rules which do not apply to all, but only to one or a few members of the group. To distinguish: R. *prescribed, accepted,* and *performed.*

Role schema

A condensed experience a person had with people in the same role (e.g. male-female authority, male-female peer, male-female subordinate, male-female sex partner). Due to previous experience, the expectation of a person in certain role may be distorted and biased.

Self-schema

A concept overlapping with body schema (body image). Essential elements of self-awareness based on:
1. space boundaries of self
2. identity in time
3. unity
4. activity

The more complex self-reactions such as self-esteem, self-criticism, etc. are best understood if self-schema is regarded in the context of group schema.

Social releaser (ethology)

Behavior pattern of an individual which elicits species-specific response in another individual of the same species (e.g. triumph ceremony in geese, laughter in man, shape or smell of females ready for mating perceived by males in many species, etc.).

System

A set of objects forming a closed causal network as seen from a certain point of view.

Teleology (finality)

Explanation of processes by goals and purposes. *Metaphysical*: Teleological explanation is an alternative of causal explanation and cannot be replaced by it in principle. *Scientific*: Teleological explanation in living and some nonliving systems is a short way of describing processes which can be described in detail causally.

Transference (psychoanalysis)

Inappropriate repetition in a current relationship of interpersonal experience from childhood. Alternatively, it is an inappropriate interpretation in terms of a rigid group schema. The term transference should be used only if it can be stated *what* is transferred *to whom, from whom.*

Unified science theses

1. The terms of all the sciences can form one language such that the signification of the terms in all sciences can be formulated on the basis of some initial set of terms (e.g. terms of simple observation).

2. Laws of all the empirical sciences can be deduced as theorems from some set of laws which serve as postulates (laws of physics).

3. All the sciences employ, in spite of differences, a common method in obtaining knowledge of their subject matters. The theses go far beyond the present state of knowledge and have to be understood as heuristic principles which worked well in the past. Roughly equivalent names: physicalism, methodological behaviorism (R. Carnap and others).

BIBLIOGRAPHY

Adler, A. 1930. Individual psychology. In *Psychologies of 1930*, ed. C. Murchinson, pp. 395-405. Worcester, Mass.: Clark University Press.

Adler, K. 1959. Quoted in "Social Interest" by H. L. Ansbacher, In *Essays in individual psychology*, ed. K. A. Adler and D. Deutsch. New York: Grove Press.

Alexander, F., and French, T. M. 1946. *Psychoanalytic Therapy*. New York: Ronald.

Annett, J. 1969. *Feedback and Human Behavior*. Baltimore: Penguin.

Ansbacher, H. L. 1956. Social interest. *Journal of Projective Techniques* 20:.

————. 1959. Social interest. In *Essays in Individual Psychology*, ed. K. A. Adler and D. Deutsch. New York: Grove.

Arieti, S. 1967. Critical evaluation: the interpersonal and the intrapsychic. *International Journal of Psychiatry* 4: 522-524.

Ashby, W. R. 1954. *Design For a Brain*. New York: Wiley.

————. 1956. *An Introduction to Cybernetics*. London: Chapman and Hall.

Ayllon, T., and Azrin, N. H. 1965. Reinforcement and instructions with mental patients. *Journal of the Experimental Analysis of Behavior* 7: 327-331.

Bales, R. F. 1970. *Personality and Interpersonal Behavior*. New York: Holt, Rinehart and Winston.

Bandura, A. 1969. *Principles of Behavior Modification*. New York: Holt, Rinehart and Winston.

———. 1971. *Social Learning Theory*. Morristown, N.J.: General Learning Press.

Bartos, O. J. 1967. *Simple Models of Group Behavior*. New York: Columbia University Press.

Bateson, G. 1955. A theory of play and fantasy. *Psychiatric Research Reports* (American Psychiatric Association). 2: 39-51.

———. 1956. The message, "this is play." In *Transactions of the Second Conference on Group Processes*, pp. 145-242. New York: Josiah Macy, Jr. Foundation.

Berne, E. 1964. *Games People Play*. New York: Grove.

Bertalanffy, L. von. 1968. *General Systems Theory*. New York: Braziller.

Bion, W. R. 1974. *Experiences in Groups*. New York: Ballantine.

Birdwhistell, R. L. 1970. *Kinesics and Context*. Philadelphia: University of Pennsylvania Press.

Blau, P. 1964. *Exchange and Power in Social Life*. New York: Wiley.

Bleuler, E. 1966. *Das autistisch-undisziplinierte Denken in der Medizin und seine Ueberwindung*. Berlin: Springer.

Boring, E. G. 1946. Mind and mechanism. *American Journal of Psychology* 59: 173-192.

———. 1966. A history of introspection. *British Journal of Social and Clinical Psychology* 5: 95-102.

Borst, C. V., Ed. 1970. *The Mind/Brain Identity Theory*. London: Macmillan.

Bowlby, J. 1969. *Attachment and Loss*. Vol. 1. London: Hogarth.

Breggin, P. R. 1975. Psychiatry and psychotherapy as political processes. *American Journal of Psychotherapy* 29: 369-382.

Brenner, C. 1973. *An Elementary Textbook of Psychoanalysis*. Rev. ed. New York: International Universities Press.

Brunswik, E. 1937. Psychology as a science of objective relations. *Philosophy of Science* 4: 232-260.

———. 1952. *The Conceptual Framework of Psychology*. International Encyclopedia of Unified Science, vol. 1, no. 10. Chicago: University of Chicago Press.

Buck, R. C. 1956. On the logic of general systems theory. In *Foundations of Science and the Concepts of Psychology and Psychoanalysis*, ed. H. Feigl and M. Scriven, Vol. 11. pp. 223-238. Minnesota Studies in the Philosophy of Science, Minneapolis: University of Minnesota Press.

Buckley, W., ed. 1967. *Sociology and Modern Systems Theory*. Englewood Cliffs, N.J.: Prentice-Hall.

Buckley, W., ed. 1968. *Modern Systems Research for the Behavioral Scientist*. Chicago: Aldine.

Caine, T. M., and Smail, D. J. 1969. *The Treatment of Mental Illness*. London: University of London Press.

Cameron, N. 1947. *The Psychology of Behavior Disorders*. Boston: Houghton Mifflin.

Cameron, N., and Magaret, A. 1951. *Behavior Pathology*. Boston: Houghton Mifflin.

Cannon, W. B. 1929. *Bodily Changes in Pain, Hunger, Fear, and Rage*. 2nd ed. New York: Appleton-Century-Crofts.

Cantril, H. 1950. *The "Why" of Man's Experience*. New York: MacMillan.

Cantril, H.; Ames, A.; Hastorf, A. H.; and Ittelson, W. H. 1961. Psychology and scientific research. In *Explorations in Transactional Psychology*, ed. F. P. Kilpatrick, pp. 6-35. New York: New York University Press.

Carnap, R. 1938. Logical foundations of the unity of science. In *International Encyclopedia of Unified Science*, vol. 1, no. 1, ed. O. Nenrath, R. Carnap, and C. Morris, pp. 42-62.

———. 1956. The methodological character of theoretical concepts. In *Foundations of Science and the Concepts of Psychology and Psychoanalysis*, ed. H. Feigl and M. Scriven, pp. 38-76. Minnesota Studies in the Philosophy of Science, vol. 1. Minneapolis: University of Minnesota Press.

———. 1959a. Elimination of metaphysics through logical analysis of language. In *Logical Positivism*, ed. A. J. Ayer, pp. 60-81. New York: Free Press.

———. 1959b. Psychology in physical language. In *Logical Positivism*, ed. A. J. Ayer, pp. 165-198. New York: Free Press.

———. 1963a Autobiography. In *The Philosophy of R. Carnap*, ed. P. A. Schilpp, pp. 3-84. LaSalle, Ill.: Open Court.

———. 1963b. Reply: Herbert Feigl on physicalism. In *The Philosophy of R. Carnap*, ed. P. A. Schilpp, pp. 882-886. LaSalle, Ill.: Open Court.

———. 1963c. Reply: A. J. Ayer on other minds. In *The Philosophy of R. Carnap*, ed. P. A. Schilpp, pp. 886-889. LaSalle, Ill.: Open Court.

———. 1966. *Philosophical Foundations of Physics*. New York: Basic.

Carson, R. C. 1969. *Interaction Concepts of Personality*. Chicago: Aldine.

Casriel, D. 1963. *So Fair A House* (Synanon). Englewood Cliffs, N.J.: Prentice-Hall.

————. 1972. *A Scream Away From Happiness*. New York: Grosset and
    Dunlap.
Chomsky, N. 1959. Review of verbal behavior. *Language* 35 (Jan-Mar):
    26-28.
Crosson, F., and Sayre, K. M. 1967. *Philosophy and Cybernetics*. Notre
    Dame, Ind.: University of Notre Dame Press.
Cumming, J., and Cumming E. 1962. *Ego and Milieu: Theory and Practice
    of Environmental Therapy*. New York: Atherton.
Darwin, C. 1965. *The Expression of the Emotions in Man and Animals*. Chi-
    cago: University of Chicago Press.
Davidenkov. 1950. Nevrozy [Neuroses].– *Opyt sovetskoi mediciny v Velikoi
    Otechestvenoi Vojne*. Moskva: Medizdat.
Derbolowsky, G., and Derbolowsky, U. 1966. Bemaechtigungstherapie
    als psychotherapeutische Kategorie. *Praxis der Psychotherapie* 11:
    245-257.
Dollard, J., and Miller, N. E. 1950. *Personality and Psychotherapy*, New
    York: McGraw-Hill.
Dunlap, K. 1932. *Habits: Their making and unmaking*. New York: Liver-
    ight.
Edwards, P. 1969. Existentialism and death: a survey of some confusions
    and absurdities. In *Philosophy, Science and Methods* (Essays in Honor
    of Ernest Nagel), eds. Morgenbesser, Suppes, and White, pp. 473-
    505. New York: St. Martin's.
Eibl-Eibesfeldt, I. 1970. *Ethology: The Biology of Behavior*, New York:
    Holt, Rinehart and Winston.
Einstein, A. 1923. *Sidelights on Relativity*. New York: Dutton.
————. 1934. On the methods of theoretical physics. In *The World as I
    See It*, pp. 30-40. New York: Covici Friede.
Ellenberger, H. F. 1970. *The Discovery of the Unconscious*. New York,
    Basic.
Engels, F. 1942. Speech at the graveside of Karl Marx. In *Selected Works*
    1: 16. New York: International.
Erikson, E. H. 1950. *Childhood and Society*. New York: Norton.
Erickson, M. H.; Hershman, S.; and Secter, I. 1961. *The Practical Appli-
    cation of Medical and Dental Hypnosis*. New York: Julian.
Evans, R. I. 1968. *B. F. Skinner: The Man and His Ideas*. New York:
    Dutton.
Eysenck, H. J. 1952. The effects of psychotherapy: an evaluation. *Jour-
    nal of Consulting Psychology* 16: 319-324.
————. 1968. The contribution of clinical psychology to psychiatry. In

Modern Perspectives in World Psychiatry, ed. J. G. Howels, pp. 353-390. Edinburgh: Oliver and Boyd.

Ezriel, H. 1950. A psycho-analytic approach to group treatment. *British Journal of Medical Psychology* 23: 59-74.

———. 1952. Notes on psycho-analytic group therapy: interpretation and research. *Psychiatry* 15: 119-126.

Feigl, H. 1963. Physicalism, unity of science and the foundations of psychology. In *The Philosophy of R. Carnap*, ed. P. A. Schilpp, pp. 227-267. LaSalle, Ill.: Open Court.

———. 1967. *The "Mental" and the "Physical": The Essay and a Postscript.* Minneapolis: University of Minnesota Press.

———. 1970. "Mind-Body, *not* a pseudo-problem" In *The Mind/Body Identity Theory*, ed. C. V. Borst, pp. 33-41. London: MacMillan.

———. 1970b. The "orthodox" view of theories: remarks in defense as well as critique. In *Analyses of Theories and Methods in Physics and Psychology*, ed. M. Radner and S. Winokur, pp. 3-16. Minnesota Studies in the Philosophy of Science, vol. 4. Minneapolis: University of Minnesota Press.

Fenichel, O. 1945. *The Psychoanalytic Theory of Neuroses.* New York: Norton.

Ferreira, A. J. 1963. Family myth and homeostatis. *Archives of General Psychiatry* 9: 457-463.

Festinger, L. 1957. *A Theory of Cognitive Dissonance.* New York: Harper and Row.

Frank, J. D. 1966. Treatment of the focal symptom: an adaptational approach. *American Journal of Psychotherapy* 20: 564-575.

———. 1971. Therapeutic factors in psychotherapy. *American Journal of Psychotherapy* 25: 350-361.

———. 1973. *Persuasion and Healing.* Rev. ed. Baltimore: Johns Hopkins University Press.

Frank, L. 1910. *Die Psychonalyse.* Muenchen: Ernst Reinhadt.

Frank, P. 1932. *Das Kausalgesetz und seine Grenzen.* Vienna: Springer.

———. 1957. *Philosophy of Science.* New York: Prentice Hall.

Franks, C. M., ed. 1969. *Behavior Therapy: Appraisal and Status.* New York: McGraw-Hill.

Franks, C. M., and Wilson, G. T. 1974. The nature of behavior therapy: recurring problems and issues. In *Annual Review of Behavior Therapy: Theory and Practice*, vol. 2, pp. 1-9. New York: Brunner/Mazel.

Freud, S. 1912. The dynamics of transferance. *Standard Edition* 12: 97-108.

————. 1916-17. Introductory lectures on psycho-analysis. *Standard Edition* 15 and 16.

————. 1919. Lines of advance in psycho-analytic therapy. *Standard Edition* 17: 157-168.

————. 1920. Beyond the pleasure principle. *Standard Edition* 18: 3-66.

————. 1921. Group psychology and the analysis of the ego. *Standard Edition* 18: 67-145.

————. 1933. New introductory lectures on psycho-analysis. *Standard Edition* 22: 3-184.

————. 1940. An outline of psycho-analysis. *Standard Edition* 23: 141-208.

Fromm, Erich. 1962. *Beyond the Chains of Illusion: My Encounter with Marx and Freud*. New York: Simon and Schuster.

————. 1970. *The Crisis of Psychoanalysis*. New York: Holt, Rinehart and Winston.

Fromm, Erika, and Shor, R. E., eds. 1972. *Hypnosis: Research Developments and Perspectives*. Chicago: Aldine-Atherton.

Gergen, K. 196? *The Psychology of Behavior Exchange*. Topics in Social Psychology Series. Reading, Mass.: Addison-Wesley.

Greenson, R. P. 1967. *The Technique and Practice of Psychoanalysis*, vol. 1. New York: International University Press.

Grinker, R. R., and Spiegel, J. P. 1945. *Men Under Stress*. New York: Blakinston.

Grof, S. 1975. *Realms of the Human Unconscious* (Observations from LSD Research). New York: Viking.

Guntrip, H. 1961. *Personality Structure and Human Interaction*. New York: International University Press.

————. 1969. *Schizoid Phenomena, Object-Relations and The Self*. New York: International Universities Press.

————. 1973. Science, psychodynamic reality and autistic thinking. *Journal of the American Academy of Psychoanalysis* 1: 3-22.

Haley, J. 1963. *Strategies of Psychotherapy*. New York: Grune and Stratton.

————. 1973. *Uncommon Therapy*. New York: Ballantine.

————. 1975. Why a mental health clinic should avoid family therapy. *Journal of Marriage and Family Counseling* 1: 3-13.

Haley, J., and Hoffman, L. 1963. *Techniques of Family Therapy*. New York: Basic.

Hansen, J. C.; Warner, R. W.; and Smith, E. M. 1976. *Group Counseling: Theory & Process*. Chicago: Rand-McNally.

Harlow, H. F. 1971. *Learning to Love*. San Francisco: Albion.

————. 1975. Ethology. In *Comprehensive Textbook of Psychiatry*, vol. 1, ed. A. M. Freedman, H. I. Kaplan, B. J. Sadock, 2nd ed., 317-336. Baltimore: Williams and Wilkins.

Hartmann, H. 1958. *Ego Psychology and the Problem of Adaptation*. New York: International University Press.

————. 1964. *Essays on Ego Psychology*. New York: International University Press.

Hebb, D. O. 1972. *Textbook of Psychology*, 3rd Ed. Philadelphia: W. B. Saunders.

Heider, F. 1968. *The Psychology of Interpersonal Relations*. New York: Wiley.

Hempel, C. G. 1969. Reduction: ontological and linguistic facets. In *Philosophy, Science and Method*, eds. S. Morgenbesser, P. Suppes, and M. White, pp. 179-199. New York: St. Martin's.

Hess, E. H. 1970. Ethology and developmental psychology. In *Carmichael's Manual of Child Psychology*, vol. 1, ed. P. H. Mussen, 2nd ed., pp. 1-38. New York: Wiley.

Hilgard, E. R. 1973. A neodissociation interpretation of pain reduction in hypnosis. *Psychological Review* 80: 396-411.

Hill, D. 1970. On the contributions of psycho-analysis to psychiatry: mechanism and meaning. *British Journal of Psychiatry* 117: 609-615.

Hinde, R. A. 1970. *Animal Behavior*. 2nd Ed. New York: McGraw-Hill.

————. 1974. *Biological Basis of Human Social Behavior*, New York: McGraw-Hill.

Hoffman, M. L. 1970. Moral development. In *Carmichael's Manual of Child Psychology*, vol. 2, ed. P. H. Mussen, 3rd ed. pp. 261-359. New York: Wiley.

Holland, G. A. 1973. Transactional analysis. In *Current Psychotherapies*, ed. R. Corsini, pp. 353-399. Itasca, Ill.: F. E. Peacock.

Hollander, E. P. 1971. *Principles and Methods of Social Psychology*. New York: Oxford University Press.

Hollingshead, A. B., and Redlich, F. C. 1958. *Social Class and Mental Illness: A Community Study*. New York: Wiley.

Holt, R. R. 1967. Beyond vitalism and mechanism: Freud's concept of psychic energy. In *The Ego*, ed. J. H. Masserman, pp. 1-41. Science and Psychoanalysis, vol. 11. New York: Grune and Stratton.

————. 1972. Freud's mechanistic and humanistic images of man. In *Psychoanalysis and Contemporary Science*, vol. 1, ed. R. R. Holt and E. Peterfreund, pp. 3-24. New York: Macmillan.

Homans, G. C. 1950. *The Human Group*. New York: Harcourt Brace and World.

————. 1961. *Social Behavior: Its Elementary Forms*. New York: Harcourt Brace and World.

Horney, K. 1939. *New Ways in Psychoanalysis*. New York: Norton.

————. 1942. *Self-Analysis*. New York: Norton.

Hutt, S. J., and Hutt, C., ed. 1968. *Behavior Studies in Psychiatry*. Pergamon.

Hutt, S. J., and Hutt, C., ed. 1973. *Early Human Development*. New York: Oxford University Press.

Imboden, J. B. 1957. Brunswik's theory of perception. *A.M.A. Archives of Neurology and Psychiatry* 77: 187-192.

Jackson, D. D. 1954. Some factors influencing the Oedipus complex. *Psychoanalytic Quarterly* 23: 566-581.

————. 1957. The question of family homeostasis. *Psychiatric Quarterly Supplement* 31: 79-90.

Jacobson, E. 1970. *Modern Treatment of Tense Patients*. Springfield, Ill.: Charles C Thomas.

Janov, A. 1970. *The Primal Scream*. New York: Delta.

Jaspers, K. 1963. *General Psychopathology*. Chicago: University of Chicago Press.

Jennings, H. H. 1950. *Leadership and Isolation*. 2nd Ed. New York: Longmans, Green.

Jones, M. 1966. Progress in hospital community therapy. *Current Psychiatric Therapies* 6: 317-322.

————. 1968. *Social Psychiatry in Practice: The Idea of the Therapeutic Community*. Baltimore: Penguin.

Junova, H., and Knobloch, F., 1966. Psychogymnastik als ein Methode der Psychotherapie. *GFR Praxis der Psychotherapie* 11: 3-16.

Kadis, A.; Krasner, J. D.; Weiner, M. F.; Winick, C.; and Foulkes, S. H. 1963. *A Practicum of Group Psychotherapy*. New York: Harper and Row.

Kardiner, A.; Karush, A.; and Ovesey, L. 1959. A methodological study of Freudian theory I: basic concepts. *Journal of Nervous and Mental Disease* 129: 11-19.

Kelly, G. A. 1955. *The Psychology of Personal Constructs*. 2 vols. New York: Norton.

————. 1963. *The Theory of Personality*. New York: Norton.

Kernberg, O. F. 1975. A system approach to priority setting of interventions in groups. *International Journal of Group Psychotherapy* 25: 251-275.

Kilpatrick, F. P., and Cantril, H. 1961. The constancies in social perception. In *Explorations in Transactional Psychology*, ed. F. P. Kilpatrick, pp. 354-365. New York: New York University Press.

Klein, M. 1949. *The Psychoanalysis of Children*. 3rd ed. London: Hogarth.

Kline, P. 1972. *Fact and Fantasy in Freudian Theory*. London: Methuen.

Kneutgen, J. 1964. Beobachtungen ueber die Anpassung von Verhaltensweisen an gleichfoermige akustische Reize. *Zeitschrift fuer Tierpsychologie* 21: 763-779.

————. 1969. Musikalishe Formen im Gesang der Schamadrossel und ihre Funktionen. *Journal fuer Ornithologie* 110: 3245-3285.

Knobloch, F. 1941. O determinizmu a svobode vule [on determinism and freedom of will]. Prague: *Moderni stat*.

————. 1957. Le collectif de diagnostic et de traitment dans les névroses. *La Raison* 17: 35-58.

————. 1959. The Diagnostic and Therapeutic Community as Part of a Psychotherapeutic System. *Acta Psychotherapeutica, Psychosomatica et Orthopedagogica*, suppl. ad vol. 7: 195-204.

————. 1964. *Neuroses in Czechoslovakia and Their Characteristics* (in Czech). Published in mimeographed form by the Institute for Health Documentation, Prague.

————. 1965. Family psychotherapy. *Acta Psychotherapeutica Psychosomatica et Orthopaedagogica* 13: 155-163, suppl.

————. 1966. The rehabilitation centre for neurotics in Lobec, Czechoslovakia. *Journal of Psychiatric Nursing* 4: 385-390.

————. 1968a. The system of group-centred psychotherapy for neurotics in Czechoslovakia. *American Journal of Psychiatry* 124: 1227-1231.

————. 1968b. Toward a conceptual framework of a group-centered psychotherapy. In *New Directions in Mental Health*, ed. B. F. Ries, pp. 118-132. New York: Grune and Stratton.

————. 1971. La kinesiterapia como parte del sistema de la psicoterapia integrada en Checoslovaquia. *Revista Espanola de Psicoterapia Analítica* 4: 5-27.

————. 1974. Toward a theoretical integration of psychotherapies. In *Contemporary Psychoanalysis* 10: 209-218.

Knobloch, F.; Juna, M.; Junova, H.; and Koutsky, Z. 1968. On an interpersonal hypothesis in the semiotic of music. *Kybernetika* 4: 364-381.

Knobloch, F.; Junova, H.; Petrusova, M.; and Saposnikova, O. 1964. Psychogymnastika (in Czech). *Ceskoslovenska Psychologie*, 8:113-120.

Knobloch, F., and Knobloch, J. 1964. Psicoterapia en términos de la teoría de pequenos grupos sociales. *Revista Cubana de Medicina* 3: 78-91.

Knobloch, F., and Knobloch, J. 1971. From family therapy to integrated psychotherapy. *Proceedings of the V World Congress of Psychiatry*. Amsterdam: Excerpta Medica International Congress Series, No. 274.

Knobloch, F., and Knobloch, J. 1974. Psychogymnastik. In *Psychotherapie und Koerperdynamik*, ed. H. Petzold, pp. 203-216. Paderborn: Junfermann.

Knobloch, F.; Postolka, M.; and Srnec, J. 1964. Musical experience as interpersonal process. *Psychiatry: Journal of Interpersonal Processes* 27: 255-265.

Knobloch, F.; Reith, G.; and Miles, J. E. 1973. *The Therapeutic Community as a Treatment for Neurotics*. Presented at the Twenty-Third Annual Meeting of the Canadian Psychiatric Association, Vancouver.

Knobloch, F., and Sefrnova, M. 1954. A contribution to the technique of family psychotherapy in Czech). *Neurologie a Psychiatrie Ceskoslovenská* 17: 218-224.

Knobloch, J., and Knobloch, F. 1965. Family Psychotherapy, Aspects of Family Mental Health in Europe. *Public Health Paper No. 28*, pp. 64-89. Geneva: World Health Organization.

Knobloch, J., and Knobloch, F. 1970. Family therapy in Czechoslovakia: an aspect of group-centered psychotherapy. In *Family Therapy in Transition*, ed., N. W. Ackerman, pp. 55-80. Boston: Little, Brown.

Knobloch, J.; Knobloch, F.; Hausner, M.; Syristová, P.; and Tautermann, P. 1968. *Psychotherapy* (in Czech). Praha: Státní zdravotnické nakladatelstvi.

Koenig, O. 1971. *Das Paradies vor unserer Tuer*. Wien, Austria: F. Molden.

Kohut, H. 1971. *The Analysis of the Self: A Systematic Approach to the Psychoanalytic Treatment of Narcissistic Personality Disorders*. Monograph Series of the Psychoanalytic Study of the Child, No. 4. New York: International University Press.

Kramer, B. M. 1962. *Day Hospital*. New York: Grune and Stratton.

Kramer, S. 1968. Fixed motor patterns in ethological and psychoanalytic theory. In *Animal and Human*, ed. J. H. Masserman, pp. 124-155. Science and Psychoanalysis, vol. 12. New York: Grune and Stratton.

Kretschmer, E. 1952. *A Textbook of Medical Psychology*. London: Hogarth.

Kuhn, T. S. 1970. *The Structure of Scientific Revolutions*. The International Encyclopedia of Science, vol. 2, no. 2. Chicago: University of Chicago Press.

Langs, R. 1973. *The Technique of Psychoanalytic Psychotherapy*. 2 vols. New York: Jason Aronson.

Leuner, H. 1969. Guided affective imagery. *American Journal of Psychotherapy* 23: 4-21.

Leutz, G. 1974. *Psychodrama: Theorie und Praxis*. Berlin: Springer.

Lewin, K. ed. 1968. *Resolving Social Conflicts*. New York: Harper and Row.

Lorenz, K. 1965. *Evolution and Modification of Behavior*. Chicago: University of Chicago Press.

———. 1966. *On Aggression*. London: Methuen.

———. 1970-71. *Studies in Animal and Human Behavior*. 2 vols. Cambridge, Mass.: Harvard University Press.

———. 1971. Vorwort. In *Das Prinzip Handeln in der Psychotherapie*, ed. H. Schulze, pp. vii-ix. Stuttgart: F. Enke.

———. 1973. *Die Rueckseite des Spiegels*. Muenchen: R. Piper.

———. 1974. *Civilized Man's Eight Deadly Sins*. New York: Harcourt Brace Jovanovich.

Lorenz, K., and Leyhausen, F. 1973. *Motivation of Human and Animal Behavior: Ethological View*. New York: Van Nostrand Reinhold.

Lowen, A. 1975. *Bioenergetics*. New York: Coward, McCann and Geoghegan.

Lowry, T. P., ed. 1973. *Camping Therapy: Its Use in Psychiatry and Rehabilitation*. Springfield, Ill: Charles C Thomas.

Mahoney, J. 1974. *Cognition and Behavior Modification*. Cambridge, Mass.: Ballinger.

Mahoney, M. J., Kazdin, A. E. and Lesswing, N. J. 1974. Behavior modification: delusion or deliverance? In *Annual Review of Behavior Therapy: Theory and Practice*, Eds. C. M. Franks and G. T. Wilson, pp. 11-40. New York: Brunner/Mazel.

Malamud, D. I. 1976. Expanding awareness through self-confrontation methods. In *Emotional Flooding*, ed. P. Olsen, pp. 225-238. New York: Human Sciences.

Malamud, D. I., and Machover, S. 1965. *Towards Self Understanding*. Springfield, Ill.: Charles C Thomas.

Maslow, A. 1968. *Toward a Psychology of Being*. 2nd ed. New York: Van Nostrand Reinhold.

Maslow, A., and Abraham, H. 1970. *Motivation and Personality*. 2nd ed. New York: Harper and Row.

Marx, M. H. 1963. *Theories in Contemporary Psychology*. New York: Macmillan.

Masserman, J. H. 1943. *Behavior and Neurosis*. Chicago: University of Chicago Press.

———. 1946. *Principles of Dynamic Psychiatry*. Philadelphia: W. B. Saunders.

May, R., ed. 1969. *Existential Psychology*. New York: Random House.

Mead, G. H. 1964. Self. In *G. H. Mead on Social Psychology*, ed. A. Strauss. Chicago: University of Chicago Press.

Meehl, P. E. 1970. Psychological determinism and human rationality: a psychologist's reactions to Professor K. Popper's "Of Clouds and Clocks." In *Analyses of Theories and Methods of Physics and Psychology*, ed. M. Radner and S. Winokur, pp. 310-372. Minnesota Studies in the Philosophy of Science, vol. 4. Minneapolis: University of Minnesota Press.

Menninger, K. A., and Holzman, P. S. 1973. *Theory of Psychoanalytic Technique*. 2nd ed. New York: Basic.

Miller, G. A.; Galanter, E.; and Pribram, K. H. 1960. *Plans and the Structure of Behavior*. New York: Henry Hold.

Miller, N. E. 1975. Applications of learning and biofeedback to psychiatry and medicine. In *Comprehensive Textbook of Psychiatry*, vol. 2. eds. A. M. Freedman, H. I. Kaplan, and B. J. Sadock, 2nd ed., pp. 349-365. Baltimore: Williams and Wilkins.

Minuchin, S. 1974. *Families and Family Therapy*. Cambridge, Mass.: Harvard University Press.

Montagu, A., ed. 1962. *Culture and the Evolution of Man*. New York: Oxford University Press.

Moreno, J. L. 1934. *Who Shall Survive?* Washington, D.C.: Nervous and Mental Disease.

————. 1946. *Psychodrama*. New York: Beacon House.

Moreno, J. L., and Moreno, Z. T. 1959. *Psychodrama*. New York: Beacon House.

Moreno, Z. 1959. A survey of psychodramatic techniques. *Group Psychotherapy* 12: 5-14.

Morris, C. 1938. *Foundations of the Theory of Signs*. International Encyclopedia of Unified Science, vol. 1, no. 2. Chicago: University of Chicago Press.

————. 1946. *Signs, Language, and Behavior*. Englewood Cliffs, N.J.: Prentice-Hall.

————. 1964. *Signification and Significance*. Cambridge, Mass.: Massachusetts Institute of Technology Press.

Mowrer, O. H. 1948. Learning theory and the neurotic paradox. *American Journal of Orthopsychiatry* 18: 517-610.

Mowrer, O. H. 1964. *The New Group Therapy*. New York: Van Nostrand Reinhold.

Mullahy, P. 1968. Reply to critics. *International Journal of Psychiatry* 5: 72-81.

————. 1970. *Psychoanalysis and Interpersonal Psychiatry*. New York: Jason Aronson.

Nash, H. 1959. The Behavioral World. *Journal of Psychology* 47: 277-288.

Olsen, P. J., ed. 1976. *Emotional Flooding, Vol. 1: New Dimensions in Psychotherapy*. New York: Human Sciences.

Penfield, W., and Jasper, H. 1954. *Epilepsy and the Functional Anatomy of the Human Brain*. Boston: Little, Brown.

Perls, F. 1969. *Gestalt Therapy Verbatim*. Lafayette, Cal.: Real People Press.

Pesso, A. 1969. *Movement in Psychotherapy*. New York: New York University Press.

Petzold, H. 1974. Psychotherapie & Koerperdynamik, Paderborn: Junfermann.

Potter, S. 1951. *One-upmanship*. New York: Holt, Rinehart and Winston.

Powdemaker, F. B., and Frank, J. D. 1953. *Group Psychotherapy*. Cambridge, Mass.: Harvard University Press.

Pribram, K. H. 1971. *Languages of the Brain*. Engelwood, N.J.: Prentice-Hall.

Rapoport, R. 1960. *Community as Doctor*. Springfield, Ill.: Charles C Thomas.

Reich, W. 1949. *Character-Analysis*. 3rd ed. New York: Farrar, Straus and Giroux.

Reichenbach, H. 1959. The philosophical significance of the theory of relativity. In *A. Einstein: Philosopher-Scientist*, vol. 1, ed. P. A. Schillp, pp. 287-311. New York: Harper and Row.

————. 1968. *The Rise of Scientific Philosophy*. Berkeley: University of California Press.

Reith, G.; Knobloch, F.; and Miles, J. E. 1974. One and two year follow-up of psychiatric inpatients, day-care and therapeutic community treatment. Paper presented at the Twenty-fourth Annual Meeting of the Canadian Psychiatric Association, Ottawa.

Richter, H. E. 1971. *Eltern, Kind und Neurose*. Reinbek bei Hamburg: Rowohlt.

Rossi, J. J., and Filstead, W. J., eds. 1973. *The Therapeutic Community: a Sourcebook of Reading*. New York: Behavioral Publications.

Satir, V. 1964. *Conjoint Family Therapy*. Rev. Ed. Palo Alto, Cali.: Science and Behavior.

Saul, L. J. 1972. *Psychodynamically Based Psychotherapy*. New York: Jason Aronson.

Sayre, K. M. 1967. Philosophy and Cybernetics. In *Philosophy and Cybernetics*, eds. F. J. Crosson and K. M. Sayre, pp. 3-33. New York:

Simon and Schuster.

Schafer, R. 1968. *Aspects of Internalization*. New York: International Universities Press.

————. 1976. *A New Language for Psychoanalysis*. New Haven: Yale University Press.

Schechter, D. E. 1968. The Oedipus complex: considerations of ego development and parent interaction. *Contemporary Psychoanalysis* 4: 111-137.

Scheflen, A. E. 1960. Regressive One-to-One Relationships. *Psychiatric Quarterly* 23: 692-709.

————. 1965. Quasi-Courtship Behavior in Psychotherapy. *Psychiatry* 28: 245-257.

————. 1972. *Body Language and Social Order*. Englewood Cliffs, N.J.: Prentice-Hall.

————. 1974. *How Behavior Means*. New York: Anchor.

Schilder, P. 1950. *The Image and Appearance of the Human Body*. New York: Wiley.

Schlick, M. 1939. *Problems of Ethics*. New York: Dover.

————. 1974. *General Theory of Knowledge*. New York: Springer.

Schuetzenberger, A. A. 1970. *Précis de Psychodrame*. Paris: Editions Universitaires.

Schultz, J. H. 1966. *Das Autogene Training*. 12th Ed. Leipzig: G. Thieme.

Schultz, J. H., and Luthe, W. 1959a. *Autogenic Training*. New York: Grune and Stratton.

Schultz, J. H., and Luthe, W. 1959b. *A Psychophysiologic Approach in Psychotherapy*. New York: Grune and Stratton.

Schultz-Hencke, H. 1942. *Der Gehemmte Mensch*. Leipzig: G. Thieme.

Schutz, W. C. 1958. *FIRO: A Three Dimensional Theory of Interpersonal Behavior*. New York: Holt, Rinehart and Winston.

————. 1967. *Joy* (Expanding Human Awareness). New York: Grove Press.

Selye, H. 1956. *The Stress of Life*. New York: McGraw-Hill.

Sherif, M., and Sherif, C. 1969. *Social Psychology*. 3rd Ed. New York: Harper and Row.

Shibutani, T. 1955. Reference groups as perspectives. *American Journal of Sociology* 60: 562-570.

Shorr, J. E. 1972. *Psycho-Imagination Therapy*. New York: Intercontinental Medical Book.

Singer, J. L. 1974. *Imagery and Daydream Methods in Psychotherapy and Behavior Modification*. New York: Academic Press.

Skala, J. 1971. Rehabilitation of Alcoholics (in Czech). In *Rehabilitace v psychitrii*, ed. O. Skalickova. Prague: Avicenum.

Skinner, B. F. 1938. *Behavior of Organisms*. New York: Appleton-Century.

———. 1965. *Science and Human Behavior*. New York: Free Press.

———. 1971. *Beyond Freedom and Dignity*. New York: Knopf.

———. 1974. *About Behaviorism*. New York: Knopf.

Slater, E. 1972. Is psychiatry a science? Does it want to be? *World Medicine Annual Review* 1972 (Feb.): pp. 79-81.

Stanton, A. H., and Schwartz, M. S. 1954. *The Mental Hospital*. New York: Basic.

Sechenov, I. 1965. Reflexes of the brain. Mass.: The M.I.T. Press.

Stolze, H. 1959. Psychotherapeutische Aspekte einer Bewegungstherapie. In *Kritische Psychotherapie*, ed. E. Speer. Muenchen: J. F. Lehman.

Sullivan, H. S. 1953. *The Interpersonal Theory of Psychiatry*. New York: Norton.

———. 1964. *The Fusion of Psychiatry and Social Science*. New York: Norton.

Tart, C. T., ed. 1969. *Altered States of Consciousness*. New York: Wiley.

Thibaut, J. W., and Kelley, H. H. 1959. *The Social Psychology of Groups*. New York: Wiley.

Thoresen, C. E., and Mahoney, M. J. 1974. *Behavioral Self-Control*. New York: Holt, Rinehart and Winston.

Tinbergen, N. 1951. *The Study of Instinct*. London: Oxford University Press.

———. 1953. *Social Behavior in Animals with Special Reference to Vertebrates*. London: Methuen.

Tolman, E. C. 1966. *Behavior and Psychological Man*. Berkeley: University of California Press.

Usdin, G., ed. 1975. *Overview of the Psychotherapies*. New York: Brunner/Mazel.

Valins, S., and Nisbett, R. E. 1971. *Attribution Processes in the Development and Treatment of Emotional Disorders*. New York: General Learning Press.

Van Lawick-Goodall, J. 1971. *In the Shadow of Man*. London: Collins.

Watzlawick, P.; Beaven, J. H.; and Jackson, D. D. 1967. *Pragmatics of Human Communication*. New York: Norton.

Wiener, N. 1950. Maxims for biologists and psychologists. *Dialectica* 4: 186-191.

————. 1967. *The Human Use of Human Beings: Cybernetics and Society*. New York: Avon.

Wilson, E. O. 1975. *Sociobiology: The New Synthesis*. Cambridge, Mass.: Harvard University Press.

Wolberg, L. R. 1967. *The Technique of Psychotherapy, Parts I & II*. 2nd ed. New York: Grune and Stratton.

Wolberg, L. R., and Aronson, M. L. eds. 1974. *Group Therapy: 1974—An Overview*. New York: Stratton Intercontinental.

Wolpe, J. 1969. *The Practice of Behavior Therapy*. New York: Pergamon.

————. 1954. Reciprocal inhibition as the main basis of psychotherapeutic effects. *A.M.A. Archives of Neurology and Psychiatry* 72: 205-226.

Yablonsky, L. 1965. *The Tunnel Back: Synanon*. New York: MacMillan.

Yates, A. J. 1975. *Theory and Practice in Behavior Therapy*. New York: Wiley.

Zalesnik, A. 1965. Interpersonal Relations in Organizations. In *Handbook of Organizations*, ed. J. G. March, pp. 574-613. Chicago: Rand-McNally.

Zander, A. 1971. *Motives and Goals in Groups*. New York: Academic.

Zuk, G., and Boszormenyi-Nagy, I. 1967. *Family Therapy and Disturbed Families*. Palo Alto, California: Science and Behavior.

INDEX